# CREATING
# LEARNING
# COMMUNITIES

Creating a mural depicting social change in the 20th century. Commonfire Conference, Tucson, Arizona, February, 1999.

(Folk Education Association of America and North American Alliance for Popular and Adult Education. Photo by Chris Spicer.)

A *Project of The Coalition for Self Learning*

# CREATING LEARNING COMMUNITIES

## Models, Resources, and New Ways of Thinking About Teaching and Learning

*Edited by* **RON MILLER**

A *Solomon Press Book*

<F.E.R.> THE FOUNDATION FOR EDUCATIONAL RENEWAL, Inc.
Publishers

**CREATING LEARNING COMMUNITIES**:
Models, Resources, and New Ways of Thinking About Teaching and Learning
*edited by Ron Miller*

The Foundation for Educational Renewal, Inc.
P.O. Box 328
Brandon, VT 05733
phone: 800-639-4122
http://www.PathsOfLearning.net

This book was designed by Sidney Solomon and Raymond Solomon
and typeset by Eve Brant
in Century Schoolbook, Franklin Gothic, and Bernhard Modern fonts
Drawings by Lucie McAllister and Demian Schroeder

First printing July, 2000

ISBN: 1-885580-04-5

# Contents

ABOUT
THIS
BOOK

# A Coalition for Self Learning

THIS BOOK WAS written by an ad-hoc coalition for self-learning. Most of us have never met one another face to face. We met on the Internet on a listserve <CCL-LLCs@onelist.com>. Our common interests were the future of learning and the potential impact on society of the cooperative community life-long learning centers (CCL-LLCs) that are emerging and self-organizing from the rapidly growing homeschooling and other self-learning movements.

This social phenomenon is spontaneously self-organizing without leadership, without planning, without design, and without being noticed. It is a microcosm of the larger progressive, alternative, and transformational movements that are emerging worldwide, creating a transition from the dominator paradigm (to use Riane Eisler's term) to a "Gaian" Paradigm (to use Fritjof Capra's term). The transformation of the learning system is more than a related building block of the cultural transition. It is a fundamental foundation for a deep, holistic, cultural change.

Future citizens learn from birth the role they will play in society. Today's schools teach by the mode they use—hierarchy, self-interest, authoritarianism, patriarchy, competition, materialism, and survival of the fittest. Humanity cannot continue to exist with this value system. The Gaian social paradigm is based on the scientific revelation that everything is connected to everything else. We are interdependent entities, systems within systems, in a grand and mysterious holistic cosmos.

Our common experience tells us that all is not well with society. The family, community, values, economics, schooling, and other aspects of our culture need to change and are changing. All of the educators, home-schoolers, autodidacts, futurists, and others involved in this listserve are playing one role or another in transforming the learning system. After some discussion we decided that the importance of learning to the greater society was too important to be ignored by the progressive movement, the "cultural creatives" (those on the cutting edge of social transformation), and society at large.

*Creating Learning Communities* grew leaderless, unplanned, and undesigned, like cosmic evolution, like biological evolution, like social evolution, and like homeschooling itself. To use Newton's statement, "We stood on the shoulders of giants."

# Introduction

## From Schools to Learning Communities: A Historic Shift

*by Ron Miller*

THIS BOOK REFLECTS a new way of thinking about teaching and learning, about curricula and testing, indeed about the whole institution of schooling, that during the last few years has begun to make a great deal of sense to thousands of parents, educators, and a growing number of social critics and futurists.

Public education is struggling to adapt to an intellectual, social, and cultural transformation that has begun to emerge during the last thirty or forty years. New understandings on the frontiers of science, a growing awareness of the threats to planetary ecology, and a disruption of local communities and economies by the rise of globalization have made it necessary to rethink many of the basic assumptions that guided the development of modern industrial culture. It is increasingly evident that humanity faces the task of moving from an age of modernity into an uncharted post-industrial or post-modern future. By "modernity" I mean a cluster of ideas, beliefs, technologies, and institutions that emerged with factory production in the early nineteenth century and become solidly established during the early twentieth century. Modernity is a form of culture, a dominant worldview, that emphasizes rapid progress and growth over tradition and stability, material wealth over spiritual depth, individual success over communal solidarity, and technological mastery over organic process. Cultural historians like Lewis Mumford, Theodore Roszak, and Jeremy Rifkin have argued convincingly that modernity essentially views society as a great *machine* that needs to be managed by expert technicians, a machine whose purpose is to turn natural and human "resources" into commodities and profits.

Historians of education confirm that the designers of public schooling were motivated by an early version of this view of the world. Horace Mann, the leading promoter of state school systems in the 1830s, explicitly sought to promote the rise of corporate industry, and this meant training a then-agrarian and self-reliant population to accept the terms and conditions of work that factory owners offered them. Schooling was conceived as a form of social discipline that would enable the industrial state to harness the energies of the young generation to the demands of a competitive system of production. Industrialism became an increasingly powerful force in American culture after the Civil War, and its emphasis on expert management was deliberately applied to schooling by policymakers who sought "social efficiency." Historian David Tyack demonstrated in his classic study *The One Best System* that school leaders in the late nineteenth century believed that "obedience to bureaucratic norms" was essential to industrial development and social progress, and so "they tried to create new controls over pupils, teachers, principals, and other subordinate members of the school hierarchy." They succeeded.

Consequently, public education as it developed in the twentieth century became a mechanized process of inducting young people into the culture of modernity. By "mechanized" I mean carefully managed and controlled by a central authority, so that personal differences of style, desire, and aspiration were blurred by the need to conform to standards and preestablished roles. At the time, and still very much in our time, this definition of education has made sense; in a culture that values efficiency, competition, and the production and consumption of material goods above all else, what other purposes could schools serve? For the most part, modern people have not stopped to consider what a dramatic departure we have made from long-established understandings of what education is and what it is for. Our political, business, and educational leaders seek to train young people to fulfill their roles in a vast, impersonal social machine, but in traditional (that is, pre-mechanized) cultures, young people were welcomed into the adult culture through apprenticeship and deeply meaningful rites of passage. Modern education equips individuals to compete for success in a system that only caresabout their skills and credentials, while traditional cultures inducted (or shall we say conducted) young people into a social fabric where they had identities that gave their lives meaning.

This is not a nostalgic appeal for a romanticized past. Clearly the individualism of the modern age has liberated us from some oppressive, fixed identities. Apprenticeship was in many ways an exploitative and class-bound institution. Even so, we are beginning to realize that we have sacrificed upon the altar of modernity some crucially important dimensions of a whole, integrated human life. We are beginning to see the need to reinvent social and economic arrangements that nourish the soul and reconnect the individual to culture, to community, to the organic processes and cycles of the earth, and to avenues of spiritual fulfillment. Traditional forms of education were grounded in personal relationships and shared commitment to a craft or to communal purposes, while a mechanistic education is impersonal—it assigns children to grade levels and measures their success with objective symbols. Learning does not arise from the activity at hand, but is divided into subjects and packaged into textbooks and lesson plans. Teachers are not accredited for their mentoring skills, but for their training in methods of class management and curriculum delivery. Schools are not accountable directly to students and families, but to boards of education, state agencies, and mandates of the federal government. A mechanized system of education is not devoted primarily to learning, but to efficient management of human "capital."

During the past twenty-five years, education has become ever more standardized, ever more mechanical, as it serves a political and economic agenda of competition, production, and corporate profit. Young people in the present system are not perceived as growing, active human beings who seek meaning and connection to the world, but as units of production whose academic achievements contain primarily economic value. The age of modernity has reached its zenith, so that now even first graders—six-year-old children—are rigorously tested to ensure that they fit into the system, while those who resist mechanistic discipline are sedated with powerful drugs.

However, the human spirit rebels against mechanization, and this system is not sustainable. In the long evolution of civilization, the age of modernity is a brief span indeed. Human beings have lived close to the land, attuned to the rhythms of the days and of the seasons, in small bands or communities, for eight or ten thousand years; we have lived in a highly mechanized, centralized, industrial culture for about a hundred and twenty, give or take a few. We have been so dazzled and pampered by the sheer output of industrialism, from automobiles to antibiotics, from motion pictures to genetic engineering, that we have come to accept as common sense that modern technological culture is the pinnacle of human achievement. But in fact, it is far too soon, after only a hundred-odd years, to declare the modern experiment a success. On the contrary, an increasing number of observers—including scientists, philosophers, historians, artists, and spiritual seekers—are beginning to warn us that if modern trends continue, we are headed for an enormous cultural and ecological disaster. We are beginning to learn, they say, that human beings cannot survive in such a mechanized and systematized world. The moral, psychological, and spiritual costs, which are never figured into corporate balance-sheets or the Gross National Product, will prove to be painfully high.

Many of us are convinced that school systems, as they were purposely designed and as they currently function, are inhumanly mechanical, undemocratic, damaging to personal growth and community health, and, in a word, obsolete. We argue that they reflect a mechanistic view of the world that denies the noblest and best qualities of the human spirit. We are not the first generation to make these claims. From the very beginning of modern education, various rebels have questioned the values of mass schooling: In the 1840s, the transcendentalists (Emerson, Alcott, Thoreau, and their friends) objected to Horace Mann's efforts. Later in the nineteenth century thoughtful educators like Francis Parker and John Dewey began developing what would come to be known as progressive education—an attempt to engage young people's intelligence and creativity in meaningful rather than mechanical ways of learning. In the early twentieth century, the ideas of Maria Montessori, Rudolf Steiner, and Francisco Ferrer inspired radically new definitions of what "schools" and education could and ought to be. Most significantly, perhaps, in the 1960s a group of educators and social critics, including Paul Goodman, John Holt, A. S. Neill, Edgar Z. Friedenberg, George Dennison, Jonathan Kozol, Herbert Kohl, Neil Postman, Charles Weingartner, Ivan Illich, and others explicitly criticized the "technocratic" nature of schooling and called for a complete transformation in our understanding of education.

The writings of this last group, appearing against the background of the civil rights movement and massive student protest, were widely read and contributed to a brief period of substantive educational reform in the late 1960s and early 1970s. Out of this creative period came hundreds of free schools (most of which failed to survive long), public alternatives (which paved the way for magnet and charter schools), and the home-schooling movement. Although the "revolution" that many sought in the 1960s did not materialize, significant cracks did begin to appear in the system of public education. The voices of "romantics" and dissidents struck a responsive chord among parents, students, and educators who realized that something vital was missing from the schooling of modernity. Consequently, while the system has become even more rigid, hundreds of thousands of families have abandoned public schools to teach their children at home or to enroll them in numerous alternatives.

## Creating Learning Communities for Cultural Renewal

The model of "learning communities" that we present in this book follows from this dissenting tradition. As the contributors make clear, this model (in all its diverse forms) actually *works,* and offers a promising, exciting alternative to business as usual in education. The "collaborative community lifelong learning center" is not simply another educational fad or a modest type of school reform, but an attempt to rebuild society's educational system on a post-modern cultural foundation that is democratic and person-centered rather than mechanical, as well as ecological and life-centered rather than driven exclusively by economic forces. We offer this model as a seed for social and cultural renewal—a form of education that reclaims the organic qualities of learning from pre-mechanistic times for a post-modern culture in the making. Some of the writers in this book believe that community learning centers would *replace* schools as the primary educational agency in a truly democratic, collaborative, sustainable society.

More specifically, many of us believe that diverse expressions of open-ended, evolving, community-based education would replace fixed and hierarchical school *systems*. A post-industrial society may still find a need for various "schools" as we now know them—places where children go to be instructed by professional educators—but this society would no longer be obsessed with, or limited by, the mechanistic trappings of control and efficiency that for more than a century have made educational processes subservient to political and economic agendas. Places of learning would not be held hostage to narrow indicators of "accountability" such as grades, test scores, or graduation rates; learning would not be constrained by textbooks and curricula established by anonymous bureaucrats; teaching would not be made narrow and petty in the service of "standards" that elite commissions impose on all learners of all persuasions in all communities.

The contributors to this remarkable volume explore what teaching and learning could look like in such a society. They represent a wide variety of experiences and perspectives. Some are innovative educators who demonstrate that when we shed conventional assumptions, schools *can* become dynamic, exciting places of learning that are responsive to students, families, and communities. In this book's section on "school-based community learning centers," eight writers (many of them recognized leaders in the field of alternative education) explain different forms that some of these schools have taken. Other authors are homeschoolers—parents who have altogether removed their children from the institution of schooling and then sought other ways, more fluid and organic ways, to reconnect their children's learning to the larger community. One result is the model of the "homeschool resource center" so well described in the second section of the book. Still other contributors are scholars or activists who have explored learning in other community settings, or in the emerging "virtual" world of the Internet. Finally, the section on "philosophical roots" explains the ideas, the ways of thinking, that have moved the authors of this book, and so many other people in recent years, to seek alternatives to the modern system of schooling.

Some of these ideas are explicitly pedagogical. That is to say, many pioneers of the "learning community" concept are primarily concerned with how young people actually learn, and how we as adults can best help them learn. As John Holt argued so forcefully in several popular books

published between the 1960s and 1980s, *learning comes naturally to human beings*, especially to children, and the more we control it and parcel it out and measure it and push it, the *harder* it becomes. Give young people an interesting, encouraging, caring, and supportive environment, and they will learn, just as they will breathe and eat and grow taller. Mechanized schooling is not intrinsically interesting to most children. It is not encouraging, caring, or supportive, and so if we are truly dedicated to learning, say these authors, we must provide another kind of environment. A learning community is explicitly a place where caring, responsive people nourish each other's learning in the context of authentic relationships.

Other advocates of learning communities are more obviously concerned with the social and political implications of this new model of education. Aside from any pragmatic notion of what kinds of learning environments work better pedagogically, anyone who is committed to democratic values should be dismayed by the rigid system of thought control and behavior management that goes by the name of "public schooling."

While Jefferson (and even Horace Mann at times) argued that publicly supported common schools formed the backbone of a democratic society—an argument that liberals and progressives today continue to defend passionately—the historical record seems to suggest that massive institutions controlled by centralized bureaucracies do not—and perhaps cannot—serve the diverse interests of people in their intimate communities. In the late nineteenth and then the twentieth century, the successful effort by political and economic elites to construct "the one best system" obliterated cultural, intellectual, religious, and other forms of human diversity. Standardized education is an intellectual and spiritual monoculture that diminishes rather than encourages participation in the affairs of the community and state. Students are not taught that their voices matter, that they can collaboratively determine the conditions of their lives, but the opposite—that success comes only from playing by the established rules and competing against one's fellow citizens for scarce economic and social rewards. In contrast, the learning-community model deliberately involves participants in discussion, collaborative decision-making, and a sense of involvement in and responsibility toward the surrounding world.

We find still another perspective on the learning-center phenomenon in the writings of futurists and other observers who perceive that new scientific and cultural "paradigms" have emerged over the past thirty or so years. These writers believe that the worldview of modernity has entered a period of transition or transformation, and that some time in the future (whether in ten years or a hundred is hard to determine) humanity will in fact inhabit a global civilization as dramatically different from twentieth-century modernism as our present culture is from medieval times! (This emerging worldview is sometimes called "Gaian," after the ancient earth goddess Gaia who personified the organic unity of life on the planet.)

These observers claim that the global ecological crisis, new findings in science, the rapid pace of technological innovation, and other factors will force modernist culture to evolve to a more complex and dynamic—and ecologically aware—set of fundamental beliefs. As this transition proceeds, they say, it will become ever more evident that mechanistic systems of schooling are simply *obsolete*. Centralized, standardized forms of learning will increasingly be perceived as ineffective, stifling, and anachronistic, for they do not embody the more dynamic and holistic understanding of reality that the emerging paradigms represent. According to this view, the homeschooling movement is not merely a rebellion against public schools by a random lot of libertarians, but the first significant wave of a new educational culture in the making.

## Elements of a New Educational Vision

Despite the diversity of perspectives brought together in this volume, several themes appear consistently through the chapters. All of the authors are concerned with reclaiming a sense of authentic personhood from the roles we play in modern society—roles such as expert, teacher, student, consumer, employee. Each individual possesses (or simply *is*) a complex personality containing many dimensions of experience, knowledge, feeling, and purpose. According to the contributors to this volume, social institutions need to be made more responsive to this unfolding and dynamic complexity. Roles should not be frozen in place by the rules or the power structure of an institution—especially one devoted to learning!

Second, this emphasis on the uniqueness of each individual does not imply an atomistic society in which everyone simply looks out for his or her own interests. As we find throughout the "new paradigm" literature (systems theory, holism, etc.), there is a recognition of larger contexts within which individuality flourishes; we are all whole and our wholeness deserves to be recognized and respected, but at the same time we are part of larger wholes—family, community, society, culture, the biosphere of the planet, and some even larger dimension of cosmic purpose, which many people term the "spiritual" dimension. Not all the authors here are explicit about this holistic worldview, but any reader who is expecting a book so supportive of homeschooling to be a manifesto for rugged individualism or Adam Smith-style free-market solutions to social problems is in for a surprise.

The connection made between "learning" and "community" in this book is the very heart of its argument. Learning is a *relational* endeavor; it connects human beings to each other and to the world. Competition is one form of relationship, but a very limited one, and it is dangerous when elevated above all other forms. This book describes a vision of society in which mutual encouragement, support, and love take their rightful place above competition.

A third common theme might be termed "participation," as in participatory democracy. All the authors here suggest, if they do not say so outright, that individuals should be directly engaged in the affairs of their communities and, as much as possible, concerned with the health of the planet as a whole. If the age of modernity has given us rule by experts and CEOs (which we call *technocracy*), with the rest of us pacified by consumer goods, electronics, and sports, the post-modern society envisioned

by these educators is ruled locally and collaboratively by involved and concerned people. Face-to-face dialogues, supplemented perhaps by Internet contact with people elsewhere in the world, lead to creative, dynamic, and mutually beneficial solving of our common problems. When young people become involved in their communities in this way, they will no longer experience alienation to the point of murderous rage. When people of diverse racial, ethnic, and religious backgrounds can come together to learn from each other, rather than remain locked in competition for power and control over centralized institutions, then we have a chance to build what people in the civil-rights movement called "the beloved community"—a society truly devoted to peace and human fulfillment.

The authors of this volume do not prescribe exactly what schools or community learning centers should look like in the future. The diversity of models and ideas presented here demonstrates an openness to experimentation, innovation, and flexibility. There is not an ideological litmus test that parents or teachers must pass to qualify as genuine "postmodern" educators. If there are any defining hallmarks of the learning system of the future, they are precisely these qualities of openness and flexibility. I like the term *responsiveness,* suggesting that educational methods must not be practiced in an experiential vacuum, in the service of fixed ideals or standards, but should adapt to the needs of specific times, places, and personalities. The new educational vision presented in this book is not merely the "romantic," anti-intellectual, child-centered caricature that traditional educators have always projected onto alternative visions, nor is it tied to the leftist critique of education in capitalist society that many progressive scholars are discussing (primarily with each other) in journals and conferences.

The models and ideas presented in this book are fresh, authentic, spontaneous manifestations of a true grassroots movement in education. They arise from the experiences and insights that a growing number of parents, educators, and social critics have discovered in their search for more meaningful and fulfilling ways of learning and human development. We still have many challenges to work through—for example, making these ways of learning available across lines of class, race, culture, and socioeconomic status (what public education, in theory, was supposed to do)—but as this book documents so well, the work has begun. An educational revolution is underway, and it is gaining momentum. The future of learning *will* be different from the recent past.

## For Further Reading

Numerous books address the topics and questions raised in this introduction and throughout this volume. Editor Ron Miller recommends the following titles for beginning to explore these questions more thoroughly:

Stephen Arons, *Short Route to Chaos: Conscience, Community, and the Re-Constitution of American Schooling* (Amherst: University of Massachusetts Press, 1997). Arons, a Constitutional law scholar, examines how the standardization of public schooling has led to increased social conflict rather than democratic consensus during the last half century.

George Dennison, *The Lives of Children: The Story of the First Street School* (New York: Random House, 1969). This is one of the finest descriptions of the philosophy and practice of alternative education in the entire literature, still fresh and provocative after thirty years.

John Taylor Gatto, *Dumbing Us Down: The Hidden Curriculum of Compulsory Schooling* (Philadelphia: New Society Publishers, 1992). A boldly innovative public school teacher explains why he left the system. Mass schooling, he argues, does not support young people's learning or authentic development.

John Holt, *Freedom and Beyond* (1972, reprinted by Heinemann (Portsmouth, NH, 1995)), and *Instead of Education: Ways to Help People Do Things Better* (New York: Delta, 1976). These books encompass Holt's critique of modern schooling and his vision of a community-based alternative. Holt's other books are all worth reading, particularly *How Children Fail* (1964), *Teach Your Own* (1981), and *Learning All the Time* (1989).

Chris Mercogliano, *Making It Up as We Go Along: The Story of the Albany Free School* (Portsmouth, NH: Heinemann, 1998). This stirring book cuts through all the jargon and misconceptions surrounding modern schooling and reflects deeply on what we as adults need to do to nourish our children's hearts and minds.

Ron Miller, *What Are Schools For? Holistic Education in American Culture* (Brandon, VT: Holistic Education Press, 3$^{rd}$ edition, 1997). Describes the ideas underlying alternative education movements from Rousseau in the eighteenth century to the holistic education movement of the present, and contrasts these alternatives to the social and cultural purposes of the dominant system of schooling.

James Moffett, *The Universal Schoolhouse: Spiritual Awakening Through Education* (San Francisco: Jossey Bass, 1994). Moffett argues that standardization and obsessive testing run counter to what is truly important in education—the cultivation of every person's inner life. This book presents a compelling vision of a society that promotes authentic learning in many places and contexts.

Nel Noddings, *The Challenge to Care in Schools: An Alternative Approach to Education* (New York: Teachers College Press, 1992). Noddings, one of the wisest (and most readable) educational theorists of our time, reflects on the nature of education for a democratic society. She argues that we need to replace the emphasis on competition and academic achievement with values of caring and compassion.

Jeremy Rifkin, *Biosphere Politics: A Cultural Odyssey from the Middle Ages to the New Age* (New York: Crown, 1991). A panoramic view of the development of modernity, showing how science, politics, military power, and economics have turned all domains of the natural world into commodities for the benefit of powerful elites.

Theodore Roszak, *Person/Planet: The Creative Disintegration of Industrial Society* (Garden City, NY: Anchor Press/Doubleday, 1978). Roszak is perhaps the most astute observer of the emerging transition from modern to a more ecological post-modern civilization, and all his books are worth studying. This work presents his ideas concisely and contains a superb chapter on education.

Joel Spring, *Education and the Rise of the Corporate State* (Boston: Beacon Press, 1972). This is a fine historical study of the social and political forces that have shaped modern schooling. Spring is a radical scholar who, in other work, has written about libertarian alternatives to public schooling.

David Tyack, *The One Best System* (Cambridge: Harvard University Press, 1974). Acclaimed by other scholars as one of the finest studies of the emergence of modern schooling. Ironically, Tyack supports the concept of public education and would probably not like to see his work cited in this context.

# About the Author

*Ron Miller is an internationally known author, editor, speaker, and activist in holistic and alternative education. He was founding editor of the journal* Holistic Education Review *(now called* Encounter*) and recently launched the Foundation for Educational Renewal, the publisher of this book and of the magazine* Paths of Learning: Options for Families and Communities. *He holds a Ph.D. in American Studies from Boston University, specializing in the cultural history of education, and teaches at Goddard College. He co-founded and serves on the board of The Bellwether School near Burlington, Vermont.*

# Community Life-Long Learning Centers

*by William N. Ellis*

IN 1980 THERE WERE 12,000 homeschoolers.
In 1990 there were 300,000 homeschoolers.
In 1998 there were 1,500,000 homeschoolers.

At this rate of growth (20%) one quarter of all children will be home-schooled by the end of another decade. The phenomenon has developed without leaders, without planning, without design. It is an example of "spontaneous self-organization on the edge of chaos." It is also a phe-nomenon that will draw social and political attention. It also may provide models that can help us to understand the nation and the world in social organization beyond the narrow realm of the crisis in education and the crises of society.

## The Crisis in Education

An increasing number of educational critics, like New York teacher of the year John Taylor Gatto, have decried the schooling system.[1] They point out that early American schools were strict disciplinary centers in which students sat stiffly at their bolted-down desks in abject obedience, while stern teachers taught them the three 'R's by rote memory. The school's purpose, for well over a century, has been to prepare workers for an industrial culture. It worked well. Laborers in American mills and factories surpassed all others in bringing wealth to our nation.

Nevertheless, critics contend that the current mode of schooling is now teaching the wrong lessons. Conventional schools restrict the individual's natural curiosity and desire to learn. They exemplify our authoritarian, hierarchical, and patriarchal culture based on self-interest, competition, and survival of the fittest. They teach by how they teach, as well as by what they teach. They teach obedience to authority, the calendar, and the clock. The teacher, under controls set by the state and now the national government, determines what is to be learned. The clock and the calendar determine when and how long a child can learn in the disconnected elements of the school system.

Well before the current attacks on schooling and educating, John Dewey and other philosophers raised questions about this mode of education with their creeds of "learning by doing" and "child-centered education." Although the philosophy of education changed, the formalism didn't. Children are still gathered in rooms of twenty or so, each one trying to do his or her own thing. The result is that genuine teaching and learning are severely hindered. Many schoolrooms become chaotic. The educational system itself is now in an age of confusion at the edge of chaos. It is ripe for a radical transformation.

## The Paradigm Shift

Conventional schooling is in no way different from any other aspect of our dominant and domineering Euro-American culture. It is a hierarchical, patriarchal, and authoritarian system of control from the top down. It was molded by what Riane Eisler called the "dominator paradigm" that has been developing since the beginning of Western culture.[2] That paradigm was initiated by the Jewish creation myth, which was unique in its belief that the earth was made for the use of man. It was advanced by the Greek philosophical dictum that "man is the measure of all things." It was made "divine law" by the Medieval church, which held that the cosmos and the earth are parts of a chain-of-being in which man is a semi-god meant to dominate the earth, with only God and a few celestial beings higher than man. According to this theory, below man are all lesser forms—including women, children, animals, plants, and the earth's natural resources. And each rung is responsible to, and created to serve, the ones above. This paradigm was globalized by the sword (technology), the cross (Christianity), and the flag (nationalism) during the Age of Discovery. It was inherent in the first phase of democracy as conceived in 1776, which accepted many of the tenets of rule from above and the divine right of kings (and its transition to the supreme right of the nation-state). And it was finalized in Adam Smith's economic theories that placed self-interest and "the market" as the arbiter of all that is good. But this dominator paradigm, which has been the base for social organization for

5,000 years, is now being replaced. Complexity, chaos, and Gaian theories are revealing very different concepts of the cosmos and of evolution. They are revealing that the earth and its inhabitants have evolved as an interdependent network of systems within systems, known as Gaia. Each of us is a whole made up of smaller wholes and embedded in larger ones. Everything is dependent on everything else. This new scientific concept of the cosmos suggests a new worldview in which future society, including the future of learning, will be shaped. We call this new viewpoint the "Gaian paradigm."

Not only does the Gaian paradigm suggest that cosmic evolution— from the Big Bang, through the emergence of life forms, to social organization—is usually a leaderless, unplanned, undesigned, democratic, spontaneous self-organization, it also suggests that it is often nonlinear. That is, many phenomena do not follow a simple cause-to-effect straight line. Like the weather, a small change in initial conditions can have a large future effect. Brain research has shown that memories and concepts are nonlinear. They are not stored, immobile for all time in one place in the brain in linear chains of neurons, as was once believed. Instead they are distributed throughout the brain in neural networks. Each new idea becomes a network within the holistic interconnected neural networks intertwined and distributed throughout one unique brain. It is a nonlinear reinforcement that attaches onto all the ideas, memories, and concepts that already exist in that brain. The brain/mind is a whole in which each new entry is part, immersed in and harmonizing with what came before.

With this understanding of the brain each new piece of knowledge must adapt to the existing knowledge in each brain. Expecting twenty or more students in a class to learn the same chain of new knowledge at the same time in the same place in the same way is a hopeless illusion. The reality of nonlinear learning suggests that a more individualized learning system would be more efficient.

## Homeschooling

What we might call the Gaian transformation of education was initiated two decades ago when some families started taking corrective actions, one family at a time, by dropping out of the school system. This movement has come to be known as homeschooling, and it began to emerge in the early 1970s after Paul Goodman's urging that schools make more use of community facilities and services, Ivan Illich's concept of "deschooling society,"[3] and John Holt's analysis of how children learn.[4]

In the beginning, only a couple of decades ago, homeschools were autonomous family units, each one setting its own curriculum and providing its own supplies and services. In 1980 there were perhaps some 12,000 homeschoolers. From 1990 to 1998 homeschooling grew from 300,000 students to some 1.5 million. At this rate of growth, nearly 20% a year, the 1.5% of American children now homeschooled would grow to 24% in ten years. Since 1993 homeschooling has been legal in all fifty states, and participants have self-organized some 700 homeschooling associations in the United States. About fifty of these self-organized networks have a nationwide constituency.

A second phase of homeschooling evolved in the 1980s and 1990s as practitioners began networking to exchange information and to confront state laws that limited their rights. One aspect of this second phase of homeschooling was initiated when a few participants started providing special services for other homeschoolers. Most of the services provided to homeschoolers, like *Growing Without Schooling*, or Home Education Press, are primarily publications emphasizing exchanges among homeschoolers. Others organizations, like the Clonlara School Home-Based Education Center, provide a by-mail service with curricula, tests, and diplomas for homeschoolers. Still others are newsletters written and exchanged by homeschoolers themselves. A few, like Home Schoolers' Legal Defense Association, help homeschoolers with legal and legislative matters. One or two have books, equipment, and other material for loans to homeschoolers.

Closely associated with the homeschooling movement is a broad variety of alternative schools, free schools, community schools, and charter schools that are moving in the direction of child-centered education. In their *Handbook of Alternative Education*, Jerry Mintz, Raymond Solomon, and Sidney Solomon list 2,500 Montessori schools, a hundred Waldorf schools, and sixty Quaker schools, as well as the 700 homeschool associations.[5] In addition to these, there is a growing number of Folk Schools patterned after the Folk Schools of Denmark, "schools without walls," "open universities," and learning centers that do not fall within the province of being substitutes for the K-12 public schools. It is this group of learning centers and facilities with which we are most interested.

## Cooperative Community Life-Long Learning Centers

A third phase of homeschooling and self-learning has started to emerge in the last few years as local homeschooling networks and self-learners have started providing themselves with a new form of learning institution. They don't yet even have a universal name. To start examining them we could call them "cooperative community life-long learning centers" (CCL-LLCs). Every word in this label carries a different connotation from that of the dominator paradigm.

"Cooperative" implies that all the programs, supplies, and facilities are cooperatively owned and controlled by the member families they serve. The parents together buy and exchange equipment, provide services, and make decisions about what they will do together or do separately. Each cooperative makes its own rules, and sets its own standards.

"Community" has two connotations. One is what the learners get from the community. The other is what the learners give to the community.

Every aspect of the community is an integral part of the learning program. Libraries, museums, parks, health clubs, shops, banks, businesses, town offices, farms, factories, the streets, and the environment provide learning opportunities, facilities, and services for self-learners. At the same time, learning becomes a service to the community, as future citizens become involved in the local community taking part in any or all community activities.

Community, as we use it here, is not something imposed on us by the government or the place where we were born. It is a group of friends, a neighborhood, or any cooperative association for meeting common goals. It is an extended family providing the caring, belonging, and deep association that links family members with the world outside of it. It provides the diverse and varied human interactions that make life not only possible but enjoyable.

"Life-long learning" is the growing necessity of the information age. We no longer can learn knowledge and skills that will last a lifetime in the first eighteen years of our lives. Times change far too rapidly. "Graduation" is a concept of the past. Unlike schools, learning centers of the future cannot "graduate" their members in the sense of closing the doors to the facilities and services for learning. They must provide continuing learning opportunities throughout the life span of individuals.

Nor is "learning" something a superior authority causes to happen in a lesser one. "Teaching," "educating," and "schooling" imply that society, or the state, is acting on, controlling, indoctrinating, and forming some amorphous lesser beings. But in the new paradigm, learning is an act of self-volition. It is a self-actuated process of creating skills, discovering knowledge, and satisfying one's own natural curiosity. It is built on, and it teaches, the inherent right and responsibility of every individual to set her or his own standards. It honors the diversity of evolution.

Learning is becoming much more than being educated to play a role in the industrial society. Learning replaces the materialism and consumerism that is so much a part of today's society with a deeper love. It is a love of learning for the sake of learning—of gaining a sense of being rather than having—of valuing knowledge more than things.

"Centers" implies a library-like service center. Learning centers may provide counseling, mentoring, books, supplies, equipment, tests, facilities, workshops, laboratories, and classes. Each center is designed by, and to meet the needs of, the members of the participating families. For some it is little more than an Internet file to which member turn for mutual aid. For others it may be a data bank of learning opportunities in community, national, or global organizations. Still others may want a fully equipped building not too unlike the schools of today, but operating more like a library, providing services as called for.

Cooperative community life-long learning centers (CCL-LLCs) may be among the most seminal innovations of the past decade. They may be the seeds for a deep fundamental change in the education/learning system of the future. CCL-LLCs are to some extent an outgrowth of the rapidly growing homeschooling movement. But, as this book shows, models and resources for self-learning surround us on every side. As the body of this self-organized learning system grows, it is conceivable that CCL-LLCs could completely replace the state-controlled schools.

## The Basic Need for Belonging

The emergence of CCL-LLCs reflects much more than a change in educational practices. It is a transformation of the whole mindset of the value of knowledge, and the value of the person in society, in close harmony with the Gaian paradigm. The emerging view of learning respects the new understanding that each of us "belongs" equally to Gaia. "Belonging" in this sense is much more than merely "being a member of." Belonging is the scientific fact that we are all interdependent systems within systems. Belonging, then, implies not only being a whole within a larger whole, but being dependent on the well-being of the larger systems of which we are part. "Belonging" is a protoethical value inherent in the new science/social paradigm. It says that each individual is an integral part of and responsible for the health and well being of the family, the community, and the earth—that is, of Gaia. Inherent in this scientific concept of belonging is much of the perennial wisdom of the sages, which has recognized that humanity cannot continue to exist on earth without rules of conduct that emphasize our responsibility to and for one another and to our ecologies.

## Learning and Civil Society

This transition from "educating" to "learning" is being recognized by a wide variety of scholars. Management guru Peter Drucker in his *Post Capitalist Society* writes of a society based on knowledge, one in which all society is an open, life-long learning system in which every person can enter any level at any time.[6] From the other end of the spectrum, peace scholar Elise Boulding reports that a common feature of the many "World Without Weapons" workshops she has held with people of all walks of life and all ages is the vision of a "localist society" in which communities are self-reliant and "learning appears integrated into other community activities...everyone is a learner, and education is life-long."[7]

This theme of the "learning community" is fully integrated with the growth of civil society and all other aspects of the emerging Gaian cultures.[8] Around the world grassroots organizations (sometimes called nongovernmental organizations) are proliferating. People everywhere are solving local problems with local skills and resources. They are taking over where government and "the market" have failed. Within the industrial society, citizen-initiated social innovations are empowering people at the grassroots level and promoting local community self-reliance.

In our food system organic gardening, community-supported agriculture projects (CSAs), farmers' markets, and co-op food stores suggest that a new localized agriculture and food system is emerging. In hospitals, acupuncture, nutrition, mind-body healing, and a long list of alternative health concepts and practices are being accepted. In housing, intentional communities, CoHousing, ecovillages, solar building, and other technologies and techniques are gaining acceptance. In economics, local exchange and trading systems (LETS), socially responsible investing, local scrips, cooperatives, community land trusts, community-owned corporations, peer lending, and credit unions are among the ideas taking root. Transportation, communications, religion, and all other elements of society have similarly started creating a post-industrial world.

## Conclusion

The transition from the dominator paradigm to the Gaian paradigm is happening. It is hard to see how this social transition can come to full fruition as long as our future citizens are confined throughout their most formative years in the schools of the industrial age. The new millennium requires some reconstruction. We need to envision where society could go and how it might get there. Networks of cooperative community life-long learning centers could become the foundation for the global transformation. If our future is to be based on mutual aid, belonging, caring, cooperation, and community, our future citizens should start their lives belonging to caring, cooperative communities involved in mutual aid.

## Notes

1. John Taylor Gatto, *Dumbing Us Down*. Philadelphia: New Society Publishers, 1992.

2. Riane Eisler, *The Chalice and the Blade*. San Francisco: Harper & Row, 1988; *Tomorrow's Children*. Boulder, CO: Westview Press, 2000.

3. Ivan Illich, *Deschooling Society*. New York: Harper Colophon, 1970.

4. John Holt, *Instead of Education*. New York: Dell, 1976.

5. Jerry Mintz, Raymond Solomon, and Sidney Solomon, *The Handbook of Alternative Education*. New York: Macmillan, 1994.

6. Peter Drucker, *Post Capitalist Society*. New York: HarperCollins, 1993.

7. Elise Boulding, *Building A Global Civic Culture*. New York: Teachers College Press, 1988.

8. William N. Ellis, editorial, *TRANET* #92, January 1995.

# Pioneers in Community-Based Education

$S$EVERAL NAMES APPEAR again and again in the various chapters of this volume—John Holt, Paul Goodman, Ivan Illich, Paulo Freire, and John Taylor Gatto, in particular. Readers may not be familiar with some of these radical educational writers who have influenced the rise of alternative schools and homeschooling over the last thirty years, and so we introduce them here.

## Some Profiles

**John Holt** (1923-1985) taught in private progressive schools in Colorado and the Boston area in the 1950s and early 1960s. Gifted with an uncommon sensitivity to children's experiences and perspectives, Holt began to realize that conventional schooling routines hindered rather than promoted authentic learning. He published his careful observations in a landmark book, *How Children Fail*, in 1964, which established him as a leading educational critic just at the time when the civil rights movement and campus unrest were raising the public's awareness about the flaws of American institutions. Holt wrote numerous articles for popular publications, toured the country speaking to parents and students, and helped many people start "free schools" as alternatives to public schooling. Within the next several years he came out with additional books that presented his educational vision and social critique, including *How Children Learn, What Do I Do Monday?, The Underachieving School, Freedom* *and Beyond, Instead of Education, Teach Your Own, Escape from Childhood,* and *Learning All the Time.* By the early 1970s he concluded that school reform was an inadequate response to the problems of modern education, and began to support families who were educating their children at home, through his newsletter and mail-order resource catalog, *Growing Without Schooling.* Holt advocated for "unschooling"—allowing children to learn through their interactions with the adult world rather than through formal instruction. He strongly believed that learning is a natural, organic function of the human being that needs to be respected rather than managed. "I want to do away with the idea of compulsory learning, and the idea that learning is and should be separate from the rest of life."

**Paul Goodman** (1911-1972) was a poet, essayist, novelist, and scholar who was interested in a wide range of topics, from urban design to psychotherapy (he co-authored a classic text on gestalt therapy) to political theory to education. He was one of the leading American anarchist writers, describing an organic vision of society where "living functions" would be free from coercion and "abstract power." Although considered romantic and Utopian, Goodman traced his ideas to grassroots populism and John Dewey's thoughts on participatory democracy. In 1960, Goodman published a critique of corporate industrial society, *Growing Up Absurd,* that established him as one of the main intellectual influences on the New Left and youth counterculture. During the next few years his writings on the problems of mass schooling in modern society, particularly *Compulsory Mis-Education and The Community of Scholars,* made him (with John Holt) one of the major voices of the emerging free-school movement. "We can, I believe, educate the young entirely in terms of their free choice, with no processing whatever," he wrote. "It seems stupid to decide *a priori* what the young ought to know and then try to motivate them, instead of letting the initiative come from them and putting relevant information and equipment at their service...Free choice is not random but responsive to real situations; both youth and adults live in a nature of things, a polity, an ongoing society, and it is these, in fact, that attract interest and channel need."

**Ivan Illich** (1926- ) burst onto the educational scene with his book *Deschooling Society* in 1970. Illich had been a radical priest involved in popular education and social change through his Center for Intercultural Documentation in Cuernavaca, Mexico. After his book was published, CIDOC attracted various Americans, including John Holt, to courses and discussion groups focusing on the radical transformation of education through the abolition of schooling. Illich argued that the massive growth of institutions in modern corporate society had severely impaired individuals' and communities' opportunities to meet their own needs through their own initiatives. Schooling was key to this process, because people were trained at a young age to accept the authority of institutions over their own perceptions and judgments. In *Deschooling Society* and later books, such as *Celebration of Awareness, Tools for Conviviality* and *Shadow Work,* Illich analyzed the institutionalization of modern life and called for people to reclaim their autonomy and local collaboration. Illich wrote that "learning is the human activity which needs least manipulation by others. Most learning is not the result of instruction. It is rather the result of unhampered participation in a meaningful setting."

**Paulo Freire** (1921-1997) was exiled from his native Brazil in 1964 for teaching illiterate peasants to critically examine the conditions of their lives. Freire believed that education must serve the cause of social justice by empowering oppressed people and enabling all students to "read the world" critically. He rejected what he called the "banking" conception of education, which seeks to simply deposit knowledge in students' passive minds for safekeeping, and emphasized a more dynamic educational model involving dialogue and collaboration. Some of his best-known books include *Pedagogy of the Oppressed, Education for Critical Consciousness, Pedagogy of Hope,* and *We Make the Road by Walking,* a series of dialogues with Myles Horton, who practiced a similar form of liberatory education at the Highlander Center in Tennessee. Friere's passionate, radical thinking has inspired many educational writers including Jonathan Kozol, Ira Shor, Henry Giroux and Peter McLaren. According to Freire, education "is never neutral. When we try to be neutral, like Pilate, we support the dominant ideology. Not being neutral, education must be either liberating or domesticating... Students have the right to know what our political dream is. They are then free to accept it, reject it, or modify it. Our task is not to impose our dreams on them, but to challenge them to have their own dreams."

**John Taylor Gatto** (1935-  ) was named New York City Teacher of the Year three times, and then state Teacher of the Year in 1991. When he addressed the legislature upon receiving this award, he delivered a shocking indictment of public schooling and then left the system to write and lecture around the world. He has become the leading critic of public education in this generation. His book *Dumbing Us Down* (1992) is widely read among homeschoolers and alternative educators, and his finely crafted essays and speeches have inspired thousands of people who harbor doubts about the school system. Gatto argues, essentially, that public schooling was not designed to assist young people in their intellectual, moral and spiritual development, but to mold them into compliant citizens, employees, and consumers. He insists that genuine learning can only take place in intimate settings where caring adults engage young people in authentic, meaningful experiences (as he did, in resistance to the system, while a teacher in New York). "Was it possible I had been hired not to enlarge children's power, but to diminish it? That seemed crazy on the face of it, but slowly I began to realize that the bells and the confinement, the crazy sequences, the age-segregation, the lack of privacy, the constant surveillance, and all the rest of the national curriculum of schooling were designed exactly as if someone had set out to *prevent* children from learning how to think and act, to coax them into addiction and dependent behavior."

## Community Learning Centers from the Past

**The Peckham Centre** Created with state funding in 1935, the Peckham Centre in London, England, was designed by two biologists to explore health among working-class people, and the sorts of conditions and things people need to maintain their health. By creating a family club—swimming, cafeteria, gymnasium, plenty of rooms for a wide variety of meeting spaces—and providing annual medical check-ups for the families, the Peckham Centre allowed these scientists to view how adults and children chose to do or create important learning and health activities without professional management of their thoughts or movements. The authors of *The Peckham Experiment: A Study of the Living Structure of Society*, Innes H. Pearse and Lucy H. Crocker, concluded that "it is not wages that are lacking; nor leaders; nor capacity; certainly not goodwill; but quite simply—and one would suppose ordinary—personal, family, and social opportunities for knowledge and for action that should be the birthright of all; space for spontaneous exercise of young bodies, a local forum for sociability of young families, and current opportunity for picking up knowledge as the family goes along...Health is more, not less, infectious and contagious than sickness—given appropriate circumstances in society for contact." (*The Peckham Experiment*, by Pearse and Crocker, was published by Allen and Unwin, London, 1943; p. 274): For more about the Peckham Centre also see, *Being Me and Also Us*, by Alison Stallibrass (Scottish University Press).

**The Learning Exchange** In *Deschooling Society* (1970), Ivan Illich suggested that computers could be used to create "learning webs." Illich wrote, "What makes skills scarce on the present educational market is the institutional requirement that those who can demonstrate them may not do so unless they are given public trust, through a certificate. We insist that those who help others acquire a skill should also know how to diagnose learning difficulties and be able to motivate people to aspire to learn skills. In short, we demand that they be pedagogues. People who can demonstrate skills will be plentiful as soon as we learn to recognize them outside the teaching profession." (p. 90.) Illich suggested using computers to match up peers in every field of work or topic with people who wish to meet them as a way to avoid unwanted pedagoguery.
During the early 1970s, such learning webs were emerging around the US. John Holt described them in his book *Instead of Education: Ways to Help People Do Things Better* (1976). To give one example, he wrote about the Learning Exchange of Evanston, IL, that followed Illich's proposal

closely. The Learning Exchange was started in 1971 and ended some time in the mid-seventies. "The Exchange," Holt reported, "began its work in a borrowed office, with a borrowed phone, a small file box and some 3 x 5 cards, and $25 from Northwestern University. Six months and $27 later it had built up a file of two hundred and ninety topics. By the end of 1973 The Exchange had its own office, a staff or four, and the names of fifteen thousand persons interested in two thousand topics." Holt discussed numerous other learning resources and networks, distinguishing between "S-chools," institutions where education is compulsory, and "s-chools," diverse places where people willingly come to learn.

*Part One*

# SCHOOLS AS LEARNING COMMUNITIES

# Which Way:
# Top-Down or Bottom-Up?
### The Story of the Albany Free School

*by Mary M. Leue*

OUR SCHOOL, The Free School in downtown Albany, New York, like a lot of other schools that call themselves "free" or "alternative," is based on the rights of children—and is still going strong as it enters its thirty-second year! Every year more families are allowing their children to choose us. Every year we are approached by more people who want to learn more about us—or even to teach with us. We have more and more (self-chosen) learning options for kids to explore, like apprenticeships in all sorts of fascinating occupations and work/travel opportunities. The best thing about us, I believe, is our mix of kids from a wide variety of backgrounds. Most alternative schools, and many if not most public schools, are made up of fairly homogeneous groups—some because of financial limitations, others because of the socio-economic separation of the neighborhoods from which schools draw their students.

We bus in most of our middle-class kids. I find it heartening to see, consistently over the nearly three decades of the school's life, how many families there are and have been in our geographical area whose choice of a school has not eliminated our choice because of fear of "the ghetto," with all of its attendant statistical "undesirability" criteria! Kids are kids, and learning, kids'-style, is its own reward for everyone concerned—and flies in the face of fear and prejudice!

Some time during the early seventies we turned from a plain old "free" or "alternative" school into a school-community. And since we've got a school-community that has been and still is highly successful—both locally and globally—I am happy to tell the story of how it happened, why, and how other people might take heart in setting up learning centers of their own.

Timing is important, and ours was astoundingly tailored to the opportunities and failures of the time in which it began. The times of the new millennium are very different, although equally challenging, and present their own opportunities for people able and willing to violate or transcend the mores of "what everyone knows," as we did. So this is not a formula for success; it is rather an inspirational account of what we did, and an invitation to explore and venture on your own.

Before describing what we have learned ourselves in the Free School community, I need to offer you a model of human learning—whether that be learning by a child or by an adult—that differs radically from the practices of most educational systems, although not from the principles so eloquently advocated by educational philosophers like John Dewey, Maria Montessori, Waldorf founder Rudolf Steiner, anarchist founder of The Modern School movement Francisco Ferrer, A. S. Neill of Summerhill, and others. What I believe all these people have in common is a grasp of—and a devotion to—the *person*, whether large or small, about whom

one speaks when one looks at learning. It is the actual individual human being her- or himself who is paramount here, not some hypothetical or research-generated idea of who she or he is—and age is not a primary criterion. Grasping that fact as rock-bottom reality can be darned elusive to a person for whom twelve or more years of childhood were spent in attendance at an involuntary institution based on another model.

Most of what we "know" about education, alas, is based on tainted assumptions. The notions that learning should not be self-directed and that kids' learning should be segregated from that of adults have both been effectively negated by the success of the alternative and homeschooling movements. The belief that minority students have to be coerced into learning, or even that most of them are relatively ineducable has been shown to be false in several inner-city schools, like our Free School in Albany and the New Orleans Free School, and in schools dedicated to effective remediation based on humanistic principles, like the Community School in Camden, Maine. Thus, there is a great deal of successful educational experience on which to build an easily accessible, informally organized, community-based learning network to supplement the more traditional age-graded public schools. This suggestion for community learning centers is just taking the successes of the few alternative educational organizations already existing on to the next logical step.

In fact, it appears that this trend is already taking place with the success of resource centers for homeschoolers. An example is the Pathfinder Learning Center in Amherst, Massachusetts, under the guidance of Josh Hornick and Ken Danford. Additionally, there is the very interesting development and movement into wider communities of some of the older alternative schools that offer a variety of learning options for families, both local and online, such as Pat Montgomery's Clonlara School, with its homeschooling network and online Compuhigh. Increasing autonomy for both kids and families seems to be on the rise. Unfortunately, this encouraging trend is occurring mainly in the least needful areas of our country. Educators Jonathan Kozol and John Taylor Gatto both have stressed this inequality of opportunity for minority children. It may be that it is in this neglected aspect of alternative learning experiences that The Free School in Albany may be of use.

It has long been a shibboleth in American society that "a good education" is the keystone of a successful adult life, morally, culturally, intellectually, economically—even maritally. Common acceptance of the moral and intellectual inferiority of "the masses" in our ghettos is widely held. By contrast, John Taylor Gatto views children both as supremely themselves and as the adults of the future they will become. He sees the task of the school and the teacher as being to offer inspiration to children through the teacher's own passion and know-how, to support their individual genius or daemon, to provide as much space as possible for experimentation and practice with their future adult roles, and to support and protect children from the adults who have been assigned the job of indoctrinating them with the mores of the culture. For Gatto it is the personhood of the

September

I look out at the stars and I am thinking about my grandma's funeral today. The stars are glistening like cat eyes.

Elisha

At council meetings we talk out problems.

April

Poppy age 7

adults who shape children's primary environment that makes the crucial difference in the adults these fledglings will become. And this idea is far less simplistic than most "educators" and parents seem to think. "We teach who we are," as the saying goes—and we are who our children look to as their inspiration—whether positively or negatively!

Taking off from Gatto's model of human life, it follows that the learning experience is not something that can be fruitfully separated from ordinary life. Nor can it be limited to any one age group, to a building set apart for the purpose, to a specific curriculum, or even to a designated leader so chosen because he or she has taken university courses labeled "teacher preparation" and received a certificate verifying his or her qualifications for being the person given the task of "educating our children." Yes, of course we go to someone who has specific skills in some area we want to learn about—and yes, someone who can, for example, teach kids to read and write and figure is to be prized above rubies. But that person's "credentials" to teach children need to be personal, not simply symbolic or bureaucratic. They must be based on a passionate attitude toward the subject matter being taught, toward the process of teaching itself, and toward the kids being taught, as Gatto says.

The difference here is that learning is a process that only works well when it is basically self-chosen, which is why I pose the question, "Which Way: Top-Down or Bottom-Up?" as the title of this chapter. It is my profound conviction that we of The Free School have survived and thrived largely because we did very little in the way of prior planning for structure, but instead made it up as we went along. So you would have to say that we have lived by the law of "bottom-up." I doubt that we would have survived this long if we had pre-planned how things ought to go—because if we had, the second generation of people now coming into the community would have seen the school as already established, which would have left them no room for innovation or change.

This criterion of spontaneity goes for adults as well as for children. Engaging in the learning process on the basis of a voluntary choice for nearly thirty years has left me with no doubt whatsoever that this is the right way to go. And having worked with a socio-economically integrated group of children in the ghetto in an "unschool" (as you might call it) in which the designated teachers were also self-chosen for their roles—we have never hired a single teacher, nor fired one for lack of credentials, for "incompetence," or for any other reason—I can testify to the fact that it *works*! Our kids come to us by their own choice (not their parents'), and they leave us on the same basis when they want something else. So do our teachers. There are not two rules, one that applies only to children, another to adults, as there are in most learning centers. And we have always been open for visitation, because (unlike some free schools) our children love visitors! In fact, the children surround visitors, take them by the hands and lead them to wherever they want them to go! And bid them a fond goodbye when they leave.

I feel as though it is incumbent on me to describe how our school actually works, although that's really hard, perhaps impossible. I can tell you how we fund the school (with tuition that slides all the way to zero, plus the revenue from our eleven buildings, most of them three- or four-story row houses with multiple apartments, which we offer to tenant families on a voluntary basis in lieu of rent). I can tell you what hours of the day we keep, how many children and adults occupy the building on school days, and how the kids behave (they live their daily lives full-out, from the moment they enter in the morning until the moment they leave for the night!).

I can tell you what activities are available to kids and what kinds of things you would see if you paid us a visit. You might see groups of

children hovering over a table in a room engaged in some joint enterprise, or individuals bent over blocks of wood in the wood shop or lumps of clay in the crafts room—activities that might vary as widely as slogging away in math workbooks to drawing images for the school calendar. Or you might find kids excitedly creating costumes and dialogue for a play to be put on for the whole school, writing copy for the school newspaper on the computer, listening to someone reading out loud from a favorite storybook like *At the Back of the North Wind* or *The Hobbit*, excitedly planning a trip to a local apple orchard, creating a tiny village diorama with multi-colored modeling clay, or any one of a number of other activities, perhaps chosen jointly by students and a teacher, perhaps by a single student.

After lunch, you might see a couple of three-year-olds vying for the privilege of each taking a handle of the huge aluminum cooking pot, half filled with the scrapings from lunch, to lug down the stairs and out through the back yard to where the chickens cluck and strut, waiting for their daily treat. You might see others scurrying up the sidewalk to the neighborhood park to play baseball or swing on the swings, or to the museum in the state Mall, or scrambling into the school van for some trip they had all planned together. We are a busy, intense crowd, and time at school just flies. But how these things really work is impossible to stipulate, because every day is different from the previous one. Truly, we "make it up as we go along." And with luck, it will always be that way, because none of us ever wants it to be any different.

And when our kids finally leave us, they swing almost effortlessly into the routine of the new schools they are to be attending, because they have developed the habit of looking on school as sheer pleasure and stimulation. And the new routines and nightly preparations they now have to get used to seem to bother them not a whit, because school has not jaded their appetites for learning. They come back frequently to tell us how much they are learning in their new schools.

After having started as a school thirty-one years ago, we became a community learning center somewhere along the way. This happened because families who sent us their children came to realize that what we had—and were—was not just for children, but was for everyone! So, many families found houses to buy and fix up cooperatively in the same block as the school, and gradually we found ourselves living and working more and more with each other and with (and in) the school. We have never made sharp distinctions between any of the activities engaged in by adults and children, or between the school and the rest of the community. And there have always been personal incentives for adults to move closer to the immediate environs of the school to be in positions to take part in various school and community activities.

Because none of us ever had much money, we quite quickly saw the value of creating hedges against undue drains on the little we did have. And so we set up a whole series of support structures for affordable home ownership, health, financial security, access to group support for problem solving, further education, recreation, pregnancy support, skills learning, and, chief among them all, an on-going basis for developing a steadily increasing sense of personal and professional worth and expertise based on direct experience over time. This sort of result can happen only when and where there is a lifetime investment in community learning. The price is a deep commitment on the part of everyone in the community to making it happen. It's been a great way to live, for young and old alike.

## Postscript by Chris Mercogliano

I would like to conclude with a statement about our school, written by Chris Mercogliano as a proposed conclusion to the first version of his book about the Albany Free School, *Making it Up As We Go Along*. It is appropriate that "my" chapter in this book about community learning be at least partly written by someone other than myself. Our school has always been a shared enterprise, and no one person can really give its full flavor. Here's what Chris has had to say about us:

With the arrival of second-generation students and teachers, it appears certain that the Free School will be around for years to come. We will continue modeling true community-based education for an increasingly polarized and atomized nation; and we will go on providing safe haven to a handful of those children who are in danger of falling victim to the dark shadow of our compulsory education system, as well as fostering the growth of a certain number of children who would probably fare well in almost any setting. Given the steadily increasing number of calls, letters, and visits from people interested in discovering real alternatives to the standard version of school despite the waves of conservatism currently washing over American society, it seems we are answering a genuine need for us to keep making it up as we go along in our 130-year-old building on Elm Street.

Meanwhile, several questions remain in the air. First of all, does honoring the principles [we have described] require the pattern of organization called "school?" Hardly. Schools, as Ivan Illich and successors like John Holt and later John Taylor Gatto have pointed out, nearly always have and always will set themselves up in opposition to most or all of these principles. While some schools do a better job than others of avoiding what Illich calls "the corrosive effects of compulsory schooling," the fact remains that generations of state-enforced, centrally-managed education have quite literally schooled our modern minds, both individual and collective, out of the ability to picture things differently. In other words, the current generation of parents is almost entirely dependent on the notion of "schooling" as it now exists, having so thoroughly internalized the myths of school: that education is a scarce commodity of which a prescribed amount must "be gotten" before a person is declared to be a competent adult (Illich, Farenga), that children learn only in the company of professionally trained and licensed teachers (Holt), and that the system of public education in this country is a democratic institution, which with only a little more tinkering will one day soon begin delivering life, liberty, and the pursuit of happiness to its adherents (Gatto).

If all of this anti-school sentiment is on the mark, and I believe that it is, then the next question is, "So why the Free School?" The easy way out here, of course, would be to say that we are not really a school at all (we aren't free either, being tuition-based); but instead are a community. And while I stand by those assertions, we are nonetheless a school after all, imperfect at best and always struggling with the paradoxes and competing urges that underlie the whole business in the first place. Furthermore, some of our kids' parents would prefer that we were more of a school than we actually are, and all very much want and need us to contribute to the raising of their children to the extent that we do. In return we try very hard not to cause separation between them. Finally, instead of "giving kids an education," which implies some sort of passive exchange, or in some way "preparing them for the future," which is sure to instill a sense of ennui and futility, we try equally hard to unite the active principles of living and learning.

All of which leads to yet another unanswered question. If the Free School's approach to education is even half as efficacious as I have described in [*Making it Up as We Go Along*], then why don't we find parents lining up at our door to enroll their kids? The answer is a complex one, many of the component parts of which have already been addressed. What remains to be said is simply that not everyone wants their children to have fun in school, to construct their own problems to which they create their own solutions—and perhaps herein lies the crux of the matter—to be free to be themselves. (I lifted that well-worn phrase straight from the mission statement that the older students in the school recently wrote for a literary magazine they're starting up in order to raise money for a cross-country train trip.) Of course, the reason for this widespread reluctance to entrust children with the responsibility for their own growth leads us right back around the circle to Illich, Holt, and Gatto. So many of us have been so deeply conditioned to be cautious and fearful followers that the idea of setting our own kids free is perceived as some sort of ultimate threat. And according to what I hear from friends and associates whose kids are now doing their learning at home, the push and pull between the urge to control and shape their children and the willingness to let them go their own way is very much the same.

In any event, it behooves us all to remember that a schooled approach to learning, one that involves textbooks, lesson plans, and rote exercises, is at best an approximation of any true and lasting experience of the real world. In order to turn back the rising tide of artificiality, we have no choice but to become aware of the gap between ourselves and the true sources of learning, sustenance, and meaning in our and our children's lives—all of which our postmodern, consumption-driven economy is so hell-bent on luring us away from. Returning to Illich one final time, if the opportunities for learning amidst the everyday world were once again

abundant, then there would be no need for education as such. But returning to a romantic notion of the past is unlikely at best. On the national scene. all of the momentum remains in the direction of ever-greater standardization and centralization, all in the name of corporate efficiency, and in any event, there is mounting evidence that efforts to radically alter the educational system will always prove futile.

Meanwhile, real change is occurring wherever individuals and small groups are reclaiming responsibility for the raising of their children. Little, independent schools like ours are sprouting up all over the place once again, and the number of homeschoolers is growing exponentially. Furthermore, there is increasing collaboration between freeschoolers and homeschoolers as the two somewhat amorphous groups begin to recognize their abundant common ground. Thanks in large part to the homeschool movement, networks of apprenticeship opportunities are forming with the goal of once again enabling adolescents to enter the adult world success-fully without being forced to submit to state authority and control. Prestigious colleges and universities are discovering that free school and homeschool "graduates" make fine catches because they are often more worldly and mature—and better educated—than their conventionally schooled counterparts.

And there are signs of people's taking back control over the basic means of their lives in other areas as well. For example, increasing numbers of women are fighting for and winning the right to have their babies in the sanctity of their own homes. The term "community-supported agriculture," whereby produce is grown locally (and usually organically) on a subscription basis is coming into common parlance. A number of towns and villages currently are experimenting with various alternatives to money as the basis for the exchange of goods and services, thus taking the idea of bartering a step further than it was in the days of the 'sixties and 'seventies counterculture. At the same time, let us not forget that these are largely white, middle-class phenomena. As Jonathan Kozol has so starkly portrayed in his two most recent exposés, *Savage Inequities* and *Amazing Grace*, in many ways we remain two separate nations, one white and one not white, and the signs of hope in the increasingly segregated ghettoes of our major cities are few and far between.

In closing, it is becoming clear to me that there really are no grand conclusions to be had regarding the subject at hand. While what we choose to call "education" needs constant reexamination on a great many levels— sociopolitical, intellectual, emotional, and spiritual—it is not in and of itself the solution to any of the issues that I have raised in my book. If we look at our nation as being in the throes of a disease state, as Kozol and others would have us do, then suffice it to say that the domain of education and all of the problems associated with it are at the same time symptoms and causes of some greater illness. Or said another way, if the fundamental concern before us is the developmental well-being of our children, then to focus narrowly on the subject of schools, or even more broadly on "education," is to miss the mark entirely, and only serves to reinforce the myth that there exists a prescription for that well-being.

Thus I have told the Free School's story for one primary reason: to hold it up as just one example of how we can support the growth of healthy, sane children and truly endow them with the guarantees written into the Constitution by our forefathers. I will repeat one last time that there is no one right way to do it. To school or not to school is not the question. The question, which needs to be asked over and over again, is what is best for this child, or that child, or my child? In answering, let us remember two things: first, that the real answer lies largely within each and every child; and second, that the decisions that affect even one child, whether he or she be in Albany, New York, or Albany, Oregon, or Albany, Georgia, also affect children in the darkest and most sequestered slums of our major cities. In other words, just as there are no single answers, there are no simple ones either. The world always has been filled with injustice and paradox and confusion and danger, just as it has been filled with compassion and beauty and courae and hope. What saves humanity again and again is the miracle that within the spirit of every human child there exists a hardy seed of wonder and exuberance, one that freeschoolers and homeschoolers alike are determined to preserve for future generations. And that is why, together, we must continue making it up as we go along.

# The Community School
## Developing the Approach of "Relational Education"

*by Emanuel Pariser*

OVER THE PAST twenty-six years the staff and students at the Community School in Camden, Maine, have crafted an approach to teaching and learning that we call "Relational Education." This form of education places a primary focus on the development of trusting, supportive, and resilient relationships between all members of the learning community.

The Community School is our "laboratory" for the development of this approach. Until five years ago when we began our second program—"Passages," for teen parents—the form of the "Cschool" (as we most often refer to it) remained constant. Every six months we accept eight students from throughout Maine, and occasionally beyond, who are sixteen to twenty years old. Having chosen to leave conventional education for a wide variety of reasons, these young men and women decide that completing their educations is important. They come to us looking for a different kind of learning experience—one that makes sense to them and will help them achieve their goal of completion.

What the CSchool offers is unique and attractive—a six-month residence that combines work, community living, and academics, and results in a high-school diploma regardless of previous success or failure in traditional schooling. For students who have been told, as some of ours have, that they'll "never get out of ninth grade," this model offers a very different kind of learning opportunity.

For students who have attended the CSchool for two months or more, the results have been noteworthy: 80% have gotten their diplomas, 40% have continued on to post-secondary education, and 75% who were previously incarcerated or under some form of legal jurisdiction have remained free of serious legal difficulties. In five years of operation, twenty-three teen parents who had been forced to leave conventional school due to their pregnancies and the lack of resources available to them have graduated from Passages with high school diplomas.

## Why There is a Need for Relational Education

With all the discussion on a national level of educational "standards" and "accountability," of "outcome-based curricula" and maintaining a competitive economic edge, one would think that the primary problems facing educators and students in the United States today are ones of content mastery and assessment. The assumption seems to be that if we just hold our students and teachers to high cognitive standards, we will be able to develop a literate and effective work force.

What these discussions do not take into account, and what most conventional schooling has been extraordinarily slow to adapt to, are massive changes in the social landscape since the contemporary model of schooling was "perfected" in the early 1900s. First of all, and perhaps most importantly, since the 1960s the nuclear family has been disintegrating. More than 50% of the children in schools now have experienced the divorce of their parents. A large percentage of students have always lived with a single parent. Many students now live in blended or mixed families, where each member of the family can have a different last name, and no two children may have the same biological parents. The extended family has also weakened: in 1900, 96% of us lived within walking distance of a relative; in 1999, 4% of us do. There are few aunts, uncles, or grandparents to fill in when relationships at home get strained or stop working.

Economic and social forces have ripped traditional communities apart, so that most of us do not know our neighbors well. We commute to work, and live in families where both parents work full time (if we are lucky enough not to be the victims of massive layoffs in industry due to corporate downsizing and the shifting of work to cheaper labor forces in other countries). For many teenagers, informal time with adults is almost non-existent—in school, teenagers are in classes only with age mates, and teachers have no time. At home, both parents work, are tired or absent, and in the community most opportunities, like work, put students in a highly defined, unskilled role (hamburger flipper, cashier, etc.). Finally, with the full onset of a media-fashioned world spanning from TV to the Internet, students come to school, as one educator put it, "information rich and responsibility poor," when they used to come to school "information poor and responsibility rich."

At its most devastating, not changing our model of education to reflect critical changes can result in the Littleton, Colorado, scenario, where easy access to firearms and a huge impersonal school, combined with alienated, harassed, furious kids, led to trauma and loss of life. But disasters like Littleton are not the reason to change our ways. Solutions based on extreme cases are likely to be narrow and extreme themselves, ultimately resulting in more rather than less suffering. We need to look at how education is not working for the majority of students who, unsettled from a home life in flux, without serious responsibilities in any of their living environments (school, home, community), are drifting through life under a barrage of "identity creating" advertising that tells them that to be a real human being they have to own a fancy car and wear clothes with the right brand names on them, and to be truly known they have to be seen on TV.

## The Heart of the Relational Approach

As this is to be a rather brief article, I cannot go into depth on our model—but I would like to sketch the broad outlines.

First, as a disclaimer, let me say that schools, no matter how good they are, cannot remedy the cultural dysfunction we are currently experiencing. Education is generally a reflection of society rather than a force for changing it. On the other hand, by employing a relationally based approach we have the chance to have an enormous impact on the lives of the children we have in our care. They in turn may help our society move step-by-step toward more cohesive and nurturing communities where we can all experience our humanness more fully.

At our 1999 conference on relational education, "Terry," a graduate of the CSchool, commented that as a teenager she felt that her life had no meaning. Given that perception, what was the sense in trying to do anything? What could possibly come of it? Why not find pleasure whenever available, and avoid discomfort for as long as possible, before the whole miserable meaningless thing was ended anyhow? Fortunately, she also had a sense that there was something worth doing, and that perhaps if she finished school she would find it. As Terry reflected on her experience at the CSchool, she said that she began to take herself seriously because other people were listening to her. For the first time she experienced adults who took her seriously, who wanted to know what she thought and felt, and also expected her to manage a wide range of tasks and responsibilities. Her life began to have meaning to her because she saw that it had meaning to others.

• *Teachers as listeners.* So, one aspect of our approach is that teachers must become listeners. We actually call our faculty "teacher/counselors" because teaching has become so connected with information output, as opposed to receptivity and reflection, which we usually associate with counseling. To formalize this listening process, each student is assigned a "one to one," or advisor, whom he or she meets with regularly, on one level to go over his or her progress in the program, and on a more fundamental level to develop a trusting and supportive relationship in which the student can begin to experience his or her life as having meaning.

• *Time for interaction.* We have created spaces and times in our program to allow community members to go beyond our roles as teachers and students and experience each other as human beings. Teacher/counselors live-in at the Community School—most spend at least one night at the school, enabling them to be with students in a more full and natural context. Human interactions occur over a breakfast bowl of cereal, on a ride to work, in a late-night discussion in the living room, during "informal" times when our "official roles" in the community are not as sharply defined. It is here that we find out that we are more alike than different, that our experiences as human beings, despite the differences in our histories, ages, and experiences are remarkably similar—at our core we all wish to love and be loved, and to find meaning in what we do.

• *Trust.* Due to the cataclysmic betrayals and dysfunctions that our students have experienced—abuse, neglect, disinterest—they have good cause to be distrustful of adults. They have good cause to expect that the future will bring nothing worth working for, because "things never work out." At the most fundamental level for learning to occur, students must be able to trust their teachers as well as themselves. The key elements in the development of trust at the Cschool are: *choice*—students have chosen to come to us of their own free will, they have applied to the CSchool, gone through an extensive interview process, completed a set of "challenges" that take from one to two months to complete, and have chosen to stay after completing the two-and-a-half-week trial period at the beginning of the term; *sensible structure*—day-to-day life at the Cschool makes "sense"—students work at jobs in the community during the day, are responsible for daily household chores, and study at night; *academic engagement*—students are involved in the structuring of their own courses. Whenever possible, curricular subject matter is relevant to the student's interests and skill levels; and *democratic decision-making*—students are involved with faculty in making decisions regarding programmatic issues as well as codes and consequences for individual behaviors.

• *A sense of belonging.* As described above, contemporary culture lacks places for people to belong and has substituted material wealth for interpersonal richness. Because of its small scale (eight students, six faculty), residential nature, and focused goal, the CSchool creates a learning community that invites a sense of belonging from the participants. And the experience is short and intense—six months. The experience of belonging is enriched by the CSchool's Outreach program that works with graduates from seventeen to forty-five years old and their families to help them with their post-graduate lives. Students find that the CSchool has become very important to them, particularly after they have left: more than 600 times each year, former students contact the Cschool, looking for resources, connection, help with college applications, and to give or get advice. Former students also play a role with current students through volunteering as tutors, panelists, special class presenters, and working in the program.

• *Responsibilities and the "real world."* The relational approach understands that adolescents have been forced to "grow up absurd," to use the title of Paul Goodman's famous 1960 social critique. Our society has extended childhood by increasing the amount of time kids spend as recipients of our educational system, often without giving them meaningful roles in their families, communities, or economy. Students at the Cschool hold jobs in the community and owe room and board. They do not graduate if they are not paid up. They have to find and hold jobs in order to complete the program. This happens in the "real world" outside the four walls of our building. Similarly, students are held accountable by the community for their chores and their behaviors in the school. We are continually trying to break down barriers between the "real world" and the CSchool, because as one student put it so well, "What's the point of taking us out of the real world, if the idea of school is to prepare us for it?"

• *The co-creation of knowledge and resistance to authority.* In the relational model, teacher/counselors and students have reciprocal roles. The students teach how best they can be taught through discussion of their "learning autobiography"—oral histories of their schooling that address learning preferences, anxieties, strengths, and weaknesses. The teacher/counselors facilitate the students' progress towards completion of their competency exams and self-designed projects. As much as possible, the criteria for success in any academic endeavor are established together by the teacher/student dyad, and the hoped-for outcome is that, in tack-

ling academic problems together, teacher and student will co-create relevant, integrateable knowledge.

In her summary speech for our conference, Brenda Wentworth—a Cschool graduate from 1979 who is currently working as a Master of Social Work substance-abuse counselor with addicted, HIV+ clients—made it clear that she experienced her resistance to traditional school as deriving from the structural power that teachers seemed to have over her, and the weight this seemed to put on the teachers' "truth," as opposed to the students' "truth." She explained, "'Power over' is the nemesis of the traditional educational process. When a student feels 'less than' and a teacher feels 'more than,' there can be no real, helpful educational exchange. When a student realizes that a teacher's beliefs are just that—beliefs—the student often begins to challenge the teacher. The teacher, fearing exposure, often perceives this as a personal attack, and attempts to hide behind his armor of adult status and authority. The teacher then imposes punitive measures to shut down the student's assault. Students often retreat into despair, depression, and sometimes rage."

It is our job as relational educators to keep a vigilant eye on this dynamic, and always challenge ourselves to work from a co-creative rather than "power-over" position with our students.

## Passages—A New Program for Teen Parents

Inspired by Arnold Langberg, founder of the Jefferson County Open School in Colorado, and based on the Walkabout model of education, our Passages program for teen parents is non-residential. Teacher/counselors work with teen moms and dads in the comfort and chaos of their own homes. The program is founded upon the essential one-to-one relationship established between a teacher/counselor and a student. Although there are group requirements, most of the work is done through this dyad, and a primary goal of the program is to develop these young men and women as self-directed learners. Our task is to support and enrich the already responsibility-laden lives of these young parents by guiding them through a curriculum focused on their current life-situation as parents, and help them achieve a high-school diploma in the process. Since 1994 we have had twenty-three graduates.

## Conclusion

Relational Education works. Over 350 students have arrived at the Cschool since 1973. They have been demoralized, angry, resistant, yet hopeful and willing to give this new form of schooling a chance. As indicated at the beginning of this chapter, 80% of these students have completed high school, and a large number have gone beyond it. They have stayed out of legal trouble, and they keep in touch with the school after leaving it. And a majority of our graduates have created families that have been more successful than their families of origin. They have broken through cycles of despair, rage, and abuse to create meaningful lives in a culture that all-too-frequently values goods over goodness, and that all-too-frequently scapegoats our young people as the problem, instead of looking to them for their "truths" and their solutions.

To learn more about this form of education or its practice at the Community School, please contact me through the school or by e-mail at emanuel@cschool.acadia.net

# About the Author

Emanuel Pariser is the co-director and co-founder of the Community School. He has written many articles on alternative eduction since 1987, which have been published in journals such as SKOLE, Holistic Education, the National Dropout Prevention Network Newsletter, The Education Revolution, and other journals. He also envisioned and co-authored the book, Changing Lives: Voices From a School That Works in 1992. Emanuel has seved for many years on state-level task forces and commissions, and is the current chair of the Maine's Substance Abuse Commission, as well as being on the steering committee of Maine's Alternative Education Association.

For more information contact The Community School, Box 555, Camden, ME 04843, USA, phone: 207-763-3498 or 207-236-3000, fax: 207-236-2505, URL: http://www.thecommunityschool.org

# Community Learning Centers
## Tomorrow's Schools, Today

*by Wayne B. Jennings, Ph.D.*

SOME EXCITING SCHOOLS are taking shape in St. Paul, Minnesota, under the name Community Learning Centers. These can be considered models for reforming education—the "school" can become another center for family life. We believe schools and community agencies can collaborate to meet needs by pooling resources. In a sense, one plus one equals three. Schools, with their collections of computers, music rooms, gyms, and other facilities, need to serve the community many more hours than they do. Schools don't have to do it alone. We must move away from the isolationist position school people have taken in the past.

The model was developed by a New American Schools design team to accomplish top-to-bottom school reform. I was the leader of that team, and we called upon many experts and examined institutional change literature to create the Community Learning Centers design. I drew upon forty years of experience as a teacher, principal, and a central office administrator to reflect on school success issues.

I spent most of those years consciously as a change agent, seeking better approaches, reading about differently organized programs, examining literature from other fields, and testing new ideas in a variety of school settings. It was a great career life, but I concluded early on that schools had to be significantly different for tomorrow's world. Like others, I saw far too many students graduating from school weak in writing skills, math phobic, disliking science, and generally disengaged from the subjects they had studied under hard-working, dedicated teachers who used a carefully sequenced, comprehensive curriculum.

I came to understand that schools as we know them can't work for most of the students—at least not in the way the public expects. The current testing and standards movement aims at getting a little more mileage from the traditional model. It will not reform education. Schools need more than tinkering at the margins.

We have tested the Community Learning Centers model in a number of schools—urban, rural, reservation, and charter. Clearly, the degree of change has meant charter schools are better able to implement the model. In fact, our experience indicates that only charter schools set up as newly created schools using the Community Learning Centers design can make the necessary, significant changes. Existing schools could make the changes, but a morass of rules, traditions, old belief systems, contracts, and policies strangle change efforts, as they have so often in past reform efforts.

## *Two Foundational Questions*

The Community Learning Centers model rests on the answers to two foundation questions:

1. What is the purpose of schooling? Is it to learn subjects, or, as we believe, to prepare people for their major roles in life—citizenship, work, and self-development?

2. How do children and youth learn? This has lead us to progressive educational practices and brain-based learning. Certainly, schooling needs to be compatible with how the brain works. We know much about this topic. It means at a minimum that schools must be safe, mentally stimulating, active for learners, and provide personal feedback to the learner.

Four of our schools have adopted the Community Learning Centers framework in its entirety, though each of the schools is different. Their practices vary within the guidelines of the model. These schools are all in St. Paul, Minnesota: St. Paul Family Learning Center, Concordia Creative Learning Academy (both elementary), Learning Adventures Middle School, and Minnesota Technology High School. A number of other schools are also using the design.

The key features of the Community Learning Centers design and how they play out in practice are listed below:

1. "Transformational outcomes" determine learning experiences. The curriculum helps students reach these global outcomes—responsible citizens, productive workers, self-directed lifelong learners, creative and healthy individuals, and problem solvers. In practice, one sees few text-

books or worksheets in these schools. The outcomes are achieved through powerful learning experiences within and beyond the school walls. The curriculum tends toward thematic, interdisciplinary approaches using problems of interest to students and persistent life issues. Examples of themes or interdisciplinary approaches include time, power, immigration, and conservation. Such topics can be used at almost any grade level.

The strategy that makes this approach successful is to engage the students and use their questions and ideas. For example, students wondered what happened to a student who suddenly disappeared when he was arrested and sent to a detention center. This led to a study of juvenile delinquency with such topics as crime, the justice system, causes, etc. During the study students interviewed policemen, probation officers, and a judge, watched a courtroom trial, conducted a mock trial, surveyed parents and others, gathered statistical and other data, created charts and graphs, and made presentations.

2. Learning experiences feature modern learning principles and practices. The learning experiences are child-centered, life-centered and brain-based, that is, compatible with the power of the brain to assimilate and organize learning. Students have many burning questions, some of interest to all of their age group and some to just a few. To the degree that schools work with those interests in a safe, nurturing environment, students will work assiduously to get answers. The teacher who only uses textbooks misses the learning styles of many students—and even worse, limits the topic to a dry and compressed content. We must recognize that students have powerful brains eager to make sense of the world, and they possess personalities eager to establish and test their skills and knowledge in a variety of settings. Many approaches characterize this view: Foxfire, Expeditionary Learning, experiential learning, project-based learning, problem-based learning, active learning, learning by doing, etc. Too many schools persist in steady diet of separate subjects, formal rows of desks, teacher as presenter, and "correct" answers to questions. To be sure, there is a place for direct teaching and skill training, but it's not the whole diet. We find that our students learn enormously from community service, shadow experiences, helping senior citizens, internships, community research, and hundreds of active, real life activities.

3. We embed assessment into daily student work by observing projects unfold and seeing how well students handle themselves in many kinds of activities. Teachers continuously check for understanding as students work. They look for progress along a set of outcomes, from the broad-based transformational outcomes to specific skills and knowledge acquisition. The results of students' learning play out in real activities such as reports, presentations, action research, the kinds of questions raised, and the range of answers generated. Some outcomes can be checked against normed tests and community-established standards, though these have to be recognized as only a small part of the school's goals.

4. Each learner has a personal learning plan (PLP) for recording interests, strengths, goals, activities to progress toward goals and reach

them. We almost have an electronic version ready to make the process easier. Each learner has a personal advisor who meets periodically with the learner and the parent to review the PLP. Students are directly involved not only in the development of their learning plan, but also in decisions about the school program. Their ideas increase the pool of creative thinking for problem solving, and their school service responsibilities lighten the workload for staff. Students are a wonderful resource to the school.

5. Teachers as "facilitators of learning" are provided support staff to increase productivity. Our schools use the model of an educational assistant paired with a teacher. Both are facilitators of learning. Instructional staffs agree to three fundamental roles—teaching, advising, and participating in continuous improvement, both professional and school-wide. Each staff member has a professional development plan.

Staff development runs about twenty days a year based on individual professional growth plans. We spend about 3% of the budget on staff development, in contrast with a normal district expenditure of 1/4 of 1%. Each instructional staff member has a discretionary sum (currently $1,000) for attendance at workshops and conferences. Creating new schools requires a lot of heavy lifting and support mechanisms to sustain change, including an appropriate staff, staff stability, assurance of continued funding, site decision-making, feedback on progress for continuous improvement, and rewards and recognition. People make a program work!

6. Decision-making is decentralized. Stakeholders make key decisions about the program, staffing, and budget. Many districts tout their site-based decision-making program. But mostly these programs are a joke. The test of these school-based management plans is to ask if the school staff and parents control most of the program changes, staffing configuration, and the total budget. If little decentralization occurs, little accountability can be assigned.

In our programs, the facilitators of learning (instructional staff) make curriculum decisions, budget decisions, and hiring decisions, and are accountable for student learning outcomes. Decisions are databased and checked against outcomes and results. Parents are actively involved through participating in their child's conferences, sharing their skills and experiences, reinforcing learning at home, and participating on decision-making boards and committees.

7. We reallocate or redeploy resources. For example, far more is spent on instructional materials, instructional equipment, field trips, and community-based learning than in most schools. To accomplish this we spend less on staff. There are various ways to do this. We have differentiated the staff to a large degree and raised the student-to-teacher ratios, which, of course, is heresy in most quarters. Still, our student-to-adult ratio is low. We also consider a broader range of people as staff. These include parents, community resource people, and students themselves.

8. Maximum effective use of technology empowers learners and staff. All staff members have computers. All computers are hooked in a school-wide network and to a fast Internet line. Staff routinely uses word processing, e-mail, spreadsheets, Internet, desktop publishing, graphics, multimedia, and other programs. Part of the staff development time goes for technology training. The student-to-computer ratio is less than four to one. Large technology expenditures, such as buying computers or rewiring a building, are capitalized over time. Money is borrowed for major purchases and paid back over several years from the budget. We earmark about 8% of the budget for technology.

9. Partnerships with other units of government, public and private agencies, early childhood programs, and post-secondary education integrate use of community resources and reduce fragmented services and duplication. This is a difficult area, as schools tend to work alone by hiring their own experts. Today's students and families have more complicated needs than at any time in the past. Families have changed dramatically. Most parents work. The prevalence of controlled substances, medical problems, and family support-system needs can be better met by involving an "army" of private social-service agencies, governmental units, and contracted individuals available in most communities. We're making space available for dental chairs in one of our schools, an office for a community social-service person twice a week in another, and we open for parents to drop off their children before school and have programs for after school. Our schools run year-round (two hundred twenty days a year) with longer hours to better meet the needs of today's families. Our elementary schools hold regular "family nights" where children and parents join together for potluck dinners and fun activities.

The Community Learning Centers model is listed among the national models for districts to adopt. Our experience shows that it yields exciting schools, supportive communities, and better preparation of students for the rapidly changing world. Charter schools have been one way to avoid the gridlock and bureaucratic inertia that occur in many reform efforts. We believe any community can choose to change its schools, to make them true community learning centers for all.

## About the Author

Wayne Jennings is chairman of Designs for Learning and superintendent of six charter schools in St. Paul, MN.

# Experimenting with Futuristic Systems of Learning

## A "Snapshot" of The St. Paul Open School

*by Robert E. Skenes, Ph.D., with Carolyn I. Carlyle, Ph.D.*

THE CLASSES AND ACTIVITIES were only a part of my education at the Open School. Through the Open School experience, I've learned how to relate to many types of people from diverse ages, interests, and value levels. Another aspect of my Open School education is that I've learned to be more independent. The whole atmosphere at Open School facilitates this. You must choose your own classes and be responsible for getting there on time. No one is pushing you to do anything, so all the push comes from within. Which brings me to the most important part of my experiences at the Open School—the realization that learning is fun and enjoyable when the motivation comes from within rather than from external pressures. Now when I want to learn something, it is for me, not the teacher. This is most important to me because it will carry on through my whole life.     *—from an Open School senior's graduation essays*[1]

The seeds that eventually grew into the St. Paul Open School found soil in October, 1970, when the first North Country Festival was held. Put together by some Twin Cities free-school people, the program included speakers like Jonathan Kozol, Herb Kohl, and Don Glines, founder of a K-12 open school in Mankato, eighty miles south of the Cities. According to one observer, the speakers "ignited long-festering discontents and helped focus the dreams of those who wanted to build" an open school.[2] Soil for the grassroots effort that eventually followed was prepared by Glines' message that "no one will do these things for you; you will have to do them yourselves."[3]

After this conference, the Coalition for Better Schools set up a committee to study alternative schools. Interest in the idea of alternatives grew increasingly, and the committee evolved into a non-profit citizens group of parents, educators, and students from St. Paul called Alternatives, Inc. Starting from mutual feelings of dissatisfaction with traditional public schools, the group's goal soon became the establishment of an open school within the St. Paul public system. They wanted to create "a setting which enables children and teachers to learn in many directions, to develop talents and interests, to be excited about new things and people and ideas, to be in awe and wonder of the unknown—in short, to be enthusiastic, life-long learners."[4]

Alternatives, Inc. quickly gained momentum, growing to some 2,000 members. On February 16, 1971, they presented a resolution to the school board calling for creation of an open school within the system. To the surprise of many and through the cooperative energies of even more, the St. Paul Open School opened the following September.

This case study of the St. Paul Open School, based on interviews with the director and selected staff members, as well as cited documents, is like a snapshot. It presents a picture of the school at a moment in time five years after the school's creation (quotes not cited are from interviews conducted by the author). The first director and many of the original staff, parents and students were still with the school. This was twenty-four years ago, and the school is still going strong today![5]

The St. Paul Open School pioneered student-centered, community-based learning in the public school arena. With no bells, no grade levels, no course grades or credits, the Open School demonstrated that students could successfully learn through making choices and pursuing their interests with the help of supportive, facilitative adults both within the community of the school and in the broader community beyond the school's walls. At the time of this "snapshot," there were over 1,000 students on the waiting list to get into the school. There would have been more had people not gotten discouraged when they called to be added to the list and heard that there were a thousand ahead of them. Likewise, there was a waiting list of more than two hundred twenty-five teachers who wanted one of the nineteen formal teaching positions at the school. Something exciting and attractive must have been going on! (Today the school has four hundred fifty K-12 students and fifty-two staff members; however, the student waiting list fluctuates between twenty and sixty, depending on the time of year, and there are no teachers on a waiting list to join the staff.)

The success of the Open School has been validated in many ways over the years. A very visible one was by its selection (through a rigorous research and screening process) as an innovation worth replicating by the U.S. Department of Education's National Diffusion Network, which then funded teachers and administrators to come and study the school for replication in their communities.

Bill Ellis, the catalyst for this book, has written about Cooperative Community Life-Long Learning Centers as places where "learning is an act of self-volition" and where "learning appears integrated into other community activities." He notes that such centers are "cooperatively owned and controlled by the member families they serve" and that they provide counseling and mentoring as well as classes and workshops using "all aspects of the community for education." These are all key features of the St. Paul Open School, except that the Open School has found a way to do these things humanely *and* on a large scale (nearly five hundred diverse students aged six to eighteen), and with public education tax dollars and public accountability.

This study of the Open School during its early years, showing its structures and its humanity, is worth considering for inspiration about what is possible when people come together around core values with intensity, integrity, practicality, and commitment. Although the study was conducted nearly twenty-five years ago, the school continues to demonstrate these values in practice and offers a model for significantly changing conventional thinking about schools. However, the Open School faces challenges to its design and philosophy as an innovative public school because it is tax supported and must demonstrate results to the public at large. The Open School was an attempt to experiment as far as a public school could go within this constraint. It has proved that learning *does* take place in a much more open environment. The challenge today is for communities, parents, and policy makers to trust the open learning process and not regulate it to the point that its integrity and effectiveness are sacrificed.

## School Resources

Located in a remodeled warehouse in the St. Paul business district, St. Paul Open School[6] began as a public school with five hundred students in K-12 grades. A student-painted mural covered the wall along the sidewalk in front of the building, hinting at what awaited within. It was bright and gay and flowing. Mostly hidden behind the twenty-foot space between the wall and the building was a "sandbox" play area designed and built of old tires and railroad ties by younger students. Except for the wall mural and play area, the unremarkable rectangular building blended well with its neighbors in the commercial district—at least on the outside. Within, however, was a kaleidoscopic variety of "theaters of learning" demarcated by paint, carpeting, parachutes, cardboard, lofts, and other means.

Two examples of these theaters of learning were the shop area and the music/drama/dance area. "In the shop area, students work on projects of their choosing in wood, metal, plastics, electronics, printing, duplicating, motors, welding, crafts, etc. Students may be building bookcases, polishing stones, fiberglassing a canoe, or designing a school intercom."[7] The possibilities for projects, both individual and group, were almost endless.

The music/drama/dance area was just as rich. There was vocal and instrumental music (opera, popular, jazz, etc.) for individuals and ensembles large and small. Students who wanted to listen instead of perform had access to listening stations for music and dramatic readings. Available equipment included "tape recorders, video tape recorders, stereo, Moog synthesizers, and musical instruments." Students could also learn "classic, modern and folk dance or explore free or creative movement."[8]

The resource areas were small storehouses of information and equipment related to specific themes. Students went to them "to look things up, explore, delve into a topic, follow how-to-do-it materials and conduct research."[9] There were ten areas in all, each one supervised by a "liaison" person. They encompassed art, business, drama, early learning, foreign languages, home economics, industrial arts, math, music, physical education, reading media, and science.

Of course the building was only a fraction of the school's facility. Open School students also used out-of-school resources such as school district learning centers, local businesses, hospitals, museums, other city schools (for courses in chemistry, Latin, etc.), and the University of Minnesota and other colleges. Anywhere from half to two-thirds of the school's students could have been out of the building (sometimes out of the city or state) taking field trips, attending classes, interning, shadowing people who worked at jobs that interested them, or engaging in other learning activities. In addition, the school drew the city into itself through the involvement of volunteers (more than two hundred fifty a year) and invited guest experts in efforts to feed the interests of its students.

While many traditional schools might have been able to list a similar array of resources at the time, they were not likely to use them as the St. Paul Open School did. For at the Open School, one of the major premises of operation was that learning occurs through experiencing life.

## Paths and Means of Learning

Writing about the school in its first years of operation, then-Director Wayne Jennings noted some of the core values that guided its inception. "The school [is based] on some fundamental learning principles. These include that students learn most rapidly when they're interested in a subject, that students learn from concrete materials, from involvement, from participation."[10] These principles were reflected in the three basic paths of learning in operation at the time. The paths consisted of taking classes, participating in open labs and resource areas, and planning and accomplishing out-of-school experiences.

While students had a great deal of freedom in navigating these paths, they were also subject to the state and the local school district officials' views of what constituted an acceptable public alternative program. In order to graduate, students needed to demonstrate competence in six categories: career education, community involvement and current issues, consumer awareness, cultural awareness, information finding, and personal and interpersonal skills. The nature of the proof of competence varied from category to category. For career education, students documented their acquired skills in seeking jobs, developing plans for the future, and investigating career choices. They would also include "a brief description of post-high school plans."[11]

To fulfill requirements for competence in community involvement and current issues, they presented evidence from classes or projects to show that they had "the ability to actively participate in and learn from the community... and... to grapple with the complexities of current issues and events." To demonstrate consumer awareness, they showed competence in "comparison shopping, personal finance, or consumer protection." They also had to score at least 70% on the basic math competency test or "take the PSAT, SAT, ACT or other nationally normed math achievement test and score at the 50th percentile."

To demonstrate cultural awareness, students showed in some manner "an understanding of the differences in attitude, actions and experiences of one's own culture and at least two others, one of which must be Spanish-speaking American, Native American, or Black American." Competence in information finding could be indicated by proving their "ability to identify, use, and evaluate a variety of resources to gain information which is important and useful to the student."

Competence in personal and interpersonal skills required demonstrating an understanding of "(a) ...maintaining a healthy body through good habits, physical fitness and recreation skills; (b) ...interpersonal skills such as group process and decision making, conciliation, and how people react to each other; c) ...ability to write coherently, comprehend written information and communicate via other media (photography, painting, etc.)."[12] Students fulfilled these requirements through the various paths of learning.

With regard to one of the paths of learning—classes—the Open School offered a cornucopia of possibilities organized into three age groupings, each with specified locations in the school. The age groupings at the time were somewhat fluid, but in general the youngest one was for students five to ten years old, the intermediate one was for students ages nine to thirteen, and the older one was for ages fourteen to eighteen. Students weren't restricted to any one area and many classes were open to more than one age group.[13]

Students in each age grouping could choose from among classes that ranged from those resembling traditional academic subjects to more interest-based ones appropriate to their age level. For example, in addition to math and reading-related classes, five- to ten-year-olds might have selected "Suzuki Piano," "Guitar," "Bells and Xylophones," or "Beginning Band" from among the music classes. Or they might have signed up for "Growing Things," "Creative Writing," "What You Need to Know to Survive," or "Birth and Death." For chocolate lovers, "Brownies" might have been a personal favorite. What better way for a six- to nine-year-old to learn "reading, following directions, workmanship, making decisions, mathematics and some elementary principles of science!"[14]

A bridge class between the younger and middle-years students was "It's About Time." In the process of learning to tell time, students also learned "some of the ways of measuring it and its effect on our lives...[They] review...adding, subtracting, learn about the calendar, learn new vocabulary and spelling, etc." Students in the middle-years grouping might have selected "The Metric System," "Current Events," "Sports," or "Bronze Sculpture and Jewelry Casting." Or perhaps "Applied Music Theory," "Jazz Workshop," or "Improvisation" appealed to them. If they chose "Making a TV Show," they would not merely learn to use video equipment. Other skills needed and/or emphasized included "writing, talking, listening, using equipment, acting and organizing."

Older students might have been interested in "Shorthand," "Algebra," "Advanced Accounting," "Psychology," "Physics," or "Advanced French." Learners with an artistic bent would have been able to study "Watercolors," "Painting and Sculpture," or "Drawing and Printmaking." In preparation for life on their own, they could learn about "Grocery Shopping" or "Career Development." The latter course combined on-the-job training and a weekly conference with a coordinator. It was intended to help students learn about "making a career choice, record keeping, preparing a resume, interviewing, writing a letter of application, and filling in application blanks."[15]

Open labs, a second path of learning at the Open School in those early years, took place in the resource areas. "Trying Things," a class for ages five to nine, would have been typical. It entailed the use of "elementary school science units, which include puzzles, blocks, balancing, measuring and many other activities; a new set of activities every month." Since the course operated as a lab, students were encouraged to "Come when it fits into your schedule."[16] Students could also do lab work as self-directed learners for a course they were taking, use a resource area to do research related to a course, or take a hands-on course like "Baking Brownies" within a resource area.

Then-Director Wayne Jennings spoke in an interview about the advantage of size in making the resource areas a cost-effective path of learning at the Open School. "We thought that five hundred [students] was a minimum in order to have a somewhat comprehensive program...If you're going to have a functioning shop, when you spread it over fifty kids, the cost is so great that you can't have much of that sort of thing...I never thought very much of a model of education...where most of the program is conversation or discussion. I think kids like to *do* things, to work with materials...So I'm positive about a larger school."

While the open labs and resource areas at the Open School constituted an important part of the learning environment, so did the community at large. Numerous classes took students outside of the school for learning. If nine- and ten-year-olds signed up for "Finding Your Way Around the Cities," they would set off on "lots of field trips" and "learn how to find your way back to school from any place in the Twin Cities." Skills needed and/or learned included "map reading, question-asking, information getting."[17] Middle-years music students might have sallied forth on weekly field trips to "Meet the Entertainers" if they enrolled in the course by that name. Older students might have selected "Art Field Trips and Film" as one of their classes.

During one school year, students from the Open School took over three hundred thirteen field trips to a hundred and sixty-two places. Their destinations ranged from government offices (the Attorney General's office, the capitol, City Hall, the Better Business Bureau, a politician's campaign office) to cultural and nature centers (museums, the arboretum, the Children's Theater, a state park, the zoo) to business and industry (the airport, a recording studio, a department store, a fish hatchery, hospitals, a bank, the telephone company) to other schools and colleges.

On student-planned cross-country field trips, students might have learned how to get from St. Paul to Chicago, Pipestone, Minnesota, or maybe New York, and solve a host of travel-related problems. Author and Professor Joe Nathan, who was a full-time faculty member then, facilitated a number of those trips. He offered documentary evidence of their importance for young people learning to safely and competently find their way around their expanding worlds. "One year we did a study where we asked all the graduates what was the most important... learning experience they had here. Thirty-five to forty percent of them said it was one of those cross-country trips." That kind of learning experience, valued as it may have been, wasn't always painless. Nathan described the consequences of poor student planning on a trip to the Badlands:

> Students did not compile a checklist of equipment or practice pitching tents. After leaving some of the food and a tent at home, they discovered the value of such a checklist. Having to figure out at 10:30 p.m. how to put up a tent convinced them that they should have practiced before leaving St. Paul and begun putting it up earlier in that day. I had decided that students would not be seriously hurt by having opportunities to make these mistakes, and so I did not avoid their happening. The only thing I made sure of was that we had a first-aid kit along.[18]

In addition to going out of the building on field trips, students did internships and "shadow studies" as a way of learning about the worlds of work available to them. Some worked on museum exhibits; others spent time in child care centers or local hospitals and veterinary clinics. Some learned about areas as diverse as dance, food service, law, science, office work, and religion through interning. A student might have shadowed a taxidermist, an architect, a news broadcaster, or a stock salesman.[19]

Joe Nathan maintained that having students participate in out-of-school, experiential learning was vital for several reasons. It made learning more interesting. It exposed students to people at work in the community, thereby expanding their awareness of the diversity of jobs available. It taught them that people could have an impact. "We've found that even six-year-olds are fascinated by attempts to improve part of the world that's important to them (a park, TV show, etc.)"[20]

Students selected classes in consultation with their parents and their advisor. They could go to the first two sessions of a course to see whether they liked it. If not, they were free to drop out with no questions asked. After the first two sessions, however, they were expected to complete what they started. One staff member explained the policy in this way: "While there are no mandatory classes, we feel that once they choose, ... they have made a commitment and we expect them to be there. They may drop out, but only after having a conference with their advisor and with the teacher in that area to determine why they are dropping out."

During my visit to the St. Paul Open School in the spring of 1976,[21] I noted immediately that the school was not a place where students sat quietly at their desks to listen to teachers lecture. Instead, the emphasis was on learning by engaging and experiencing the world. The "Protect Your Rights and Money" course was a case in point. The headline of a brochure prepared by students in the class read, "Are you getting RIPPED OFF? If so write us and let us work with you. Consumer Action Service, St. Paul Open School." Intended to "help students learn about community organizations which are working to protect them," the class took an out-in-the-community, action approach.[22] Students visited and talked with people in consumer rights organizations, Small Claims Court, and other organizations to resolve problems presented to them by members of the St. Paul Open School Community or the community at large.

According to Joe Nathan, who was a facilitator for the course, students tackled a wide range of issues. Problems with the housing redevelopment authority, an insurance company that "ripped somebody off," and the sale of "a piano that doesn't work" are just a few complaints students addressed. Nathan reported that of the twenty-eight problems students had taken on to that point, they "solved twenty-two of them, with a couple of others pending."

The teenagers in the class liked "the way we get right to work on things instead of sitting on our duffs trying to figure out what to do." They liked the feeling of accomplishment from helping people resolve problems. They liked learning about their rights as consumers. One student made this comment: "I've learned that the majority of the problems are caused by misunderstanding. Being able to work effectively and look at both sides solves it faster. Usually everyone's first reaction is 'I'm getting ripped off by them,' but in many cases this isn't so and a compromise is what's needed. I've learned to think along these lines more after actually working on situations in class."[23]

The example of the "Protect Your Rights and Money" course illustrates three very important points about the St. Paul Open School at that time in its evolution. First, it was a learning community firmly integrated into the larger community. This was no accident but rather the result of the school's genesis and its charter. Second, students in the school were active learners posing questions about things that interested them and ferreting out the answers to those questions. Third, standard subjects were often organically blended instead of segregated into discrete units. Students might have been learning reading and math, for example, as they worked on a project to eliminate the odor and air pollution around their school or to build a canoe for a field trip. Such an approach carries some very specific attributes with respect to resources, paths of learning, and the roles of students, teachers/facilitators, and administrators.

## The Students of St. Paul Open School

The students of the Open School had some specific and optional responsibilities in those early years. As noted above, they were required to demonstrate an acceptable level of competence in certain areas in order to graduate. There were also behavioral norms, some of which are reminiscent of traditional schools (for example, Thou shalt not hit or bully younger, smaller students—or any students for that matter), and some of which were unique to the complex learning environment created by having so many students coming together in a new, large-scale experiment. Students could also take upon themselves the responsibility of teaching if they wished to share with others their own advanced skill or knowledge. In addition, some participated on school committees. The most important expectation held up for students at that time, however, was that they would take charge of their own learning.

Of the approximately five hundred students attending the St. Paul Open School in its early years, about 18% were black, Native American, Chicano, or Asian minorities. Students were selected from all neighborhoods in the city so that the student body reflected the social and economic diversity of the community. The student body mix was maintained by taking students from a waiting list of more than one thousand to "fill spaces" on the basis of age, sex, race, and neighborhood, rather than on a "first come, first serve" basis.

While at the St. Paul Open School, students learned how to function in a more open learning environment compared to traditional schools. Some were more effective than others in doing so. To provide structure for all students, but especially those unprepared for the lack of standard, traditional school routines, policy and decision-making groups made up of students, staff, parents, and community representatives identified student responsibilities. These included:

1. Checking in each day with one's advisor.
2. Meeting regularly with the advisor (usually once a week).
3. Serving the school some way from one to five hours a week.
4. Not infringing on the rights and activities of others.[24]

With respect to school service, students selected from a number of options, such as straightening and cleaning up in a resource area, assisting with classes, tutoring another student, helping a staff member, serving as a tour guide for visitors to the Open School, participating on one of the school's many committees, or teaching.

The chief decision-making groups at the St. Paul Open School were the Advisory Council, the Staff Steering Committee, and the Student Council. Students sat on two of the three bodies. Of the twenty-one members on the Advisory Council, ten were students. The Advisory Council was charged with making "recommendations on matters ranging from budget to staffing policy to visitors." It set up "forums for communication with the total school community ... and [was] also involved in the evaluation of the school's program." The Student Council attended to a wide range of issues, including communication among students, staff, and parents, and the creation of social events, workshops, and forums. It developed protocols for inter-school exchanges, conducted school polls and elections, and sponsored events to raise funds for student projects.[25]

As noted above, another way in which students could serve the school was through teaching, either informally or formally. Informal teaching occurred compliments of the school's use of cross-age grouping in classes, labs, and resource areas. Cross-age grouping was an intentional strategy for fostering diversity in learning. From his perspective as the school director, Wayne Jennings asserted that both younger and older students benefited. Older ones served as models for the younger ones so that the latter were introduced to "many ways to act, to be and to appreciate life."[26]

More formal teaching gave older students the satisfaction of sharing with others something they enjoyed. According to Jennings:

> One of the best categories of resource people are the students themselves. One teaches leatherwork, another has an extensive stamp collection, another is skilled and patient at helping young children read, another organizes a paper airplane club (along the lines of the *Scientific American* contest), another knows German... When students teach, they not only learn their subject more thoroughly, but also learn presentation, how to organize information, some psychology of learning, personal effectiveness, and how to be more articulate. They learn these things in one of the most efficient ways—by doing, by experience.[27]

Did cross-age grouping work in practice as well as in theory? One person observed early in the second year of the Open School that "many of the older students have just about run out of patience with the exasperating inquisitiveness of the younger boys and girls, and some of the latter sometimes seem overwhelmed by the presence of crowds of teenagers."[28] In contrast, an intern commenting at the end of the fourth year of operation was impressed by "how incredibly successful this place is at promoting relationships between kids of different ages... The way the big kids work with the little kids is just phenomenal."[29]

Although students taught and served as role models for one another at the Open School, their most notable responsibility was taking charge of their own education. To do this they defined goals and then, venturing forward on the paths of learning mentioned above, selected learning experiences that led to the achievement of their goals in pursuit of the competencies needed for graduation. How did this work in action? One staff member explained that students developed goals at the beginning of each trimester in consultation with their parents and advisors. At the end of the trimester, the students, parents, and advisors would meet to discuss the students' progress. Did the students meet their goals? If not, did they want to modify some of them? Out of that meeting came a new set of written goals for the next trimester.

When students neared graduation, they chose a graduation committee made of the program coordinator, the student's advisor, a counselor, and one other person. This committee "reviews the student's plans and provides support and ideas as needed.... [It] recommends the student for graduation. The recommendation must be made by at least three of the four members." Unfavorable decisions regarding readiness to graduate could be appealed to a committee of "the director, a parent and student selected by the Advisory Council from its members. At least 2/3 vote is necessary to overturn the Graduation Committee's recommendation."[30]

How did students cope with the freedom and responsibility of designing their own learning? It varied. During an interview, one mother related that during the first year of the school's operation her children did nothing until Christmas, when they got together with friends from the schools they had formerly attended. The comparison between what the friends had learned and what her two had failed to learn because of their own indifference shocked them into action. According to the mother, "They got down on their stomachs with their class schedules and decided they were going to keep up." She liked that. She liked "the fact that they were scared silly that they were getting behind and that they are becoming aware that this is their education."

Another student was a conventional school dropout. Nathan related how the boy "found his way to the Open School but spent most of his time away from the building. It turned out that he was busy organizing a center aimed at helping dropouts find jobs or encouraging them to return to school...He is now headed for college; he knows exactly what he wants to take; he is highly motivated—and his mother [initially at odds with the school for the freedom it allowed] realizes how good it's been."[31]

Many students fell somewhere in between the two extremes of "goofing off" or being highly motivated. Some exhibited the mindset that teachers were there to entertain them instead of finding the interest and passion within themselves for what they were learning.[32] Some chose to "get by" and forego the opportunities to be as enthusiastically productive as parents and teachers would have liked.[33] The responsibility for guiding all students—whether they were underachieving, highly motivated, or somewhere in between—through such a complex learning environment fell upon teachers, advisors, and the school's director.

## Teachers at St. Paul Open School

In the spring of 1976, the St. Paul Open School had nineteen certified teachers, ten educational assistants, and three aides. Unlike teachers at more traditional schools, those at the Open School acted as "learning facilitators," advisors and counselors, and resource-area developers. They also served on the school's various committees.

With regard to teachers as facilitators, then-staff-member Nathan referred to the work of psychologist Carl Rogers, specifically his ideas about learning. Rogers clarified the orientation of facilitators by contrasting them to non-facilitators. Non-facilitators, he surmised, might ask themselves, "What do I think would be good for the student to learn at his particular age and at his level of competence?" "What does the state require him to learn?" "How can I plan a proper curriculum which absorbs this curriculum?"

A facilitator begins with the students themselves instead of preconceived ideas or state-mandated requirements. "What do you want to learn?" the facilitator asks. "What things puzzle you?" "What are you curious about?" "What issues concern you?" "What problems do you wish you could solve?"[34]

For example, in a Nathan-facilitated class on shopping (for students seven to eleven years old), a student's question was, "What boots should I buy?" It was a good starting point. Once the class had a focus, Nathan noted, the role of the facilitator shifted to that of resource locator. "How can I find the resources—the people, the experiences, the programmed learning facilities, the books, the laboratories, the knowledge in myself—which would help my students learn in ways which would provide answers to the things that concern them?"[35]

In the boots example, the class started by listing questions: "How do the boots look and feel?" "How much do they cost?" "How long will they last?" These questions led to a discussion of how to find the answers, which led to visits to several stores, talks with sales people, relevant reading, and "a trip to a factory where boots are hand-made. The craftsmen are delighted that children have come to see them."[36]

At the end of the two-month project, the students synthesized what they had learned in a two-page paper. It described "'buys' for different factors (the longest-lasting boots if price isn't important and you won't get tired of them, places offering a variety of boots, styles the students liked, etc.)."[37] Nathan observed that "once teachers start consciously trying to build on interest, their ability increases tremendously. It's a matter of starting to think in a much expanded way."[38]

However, not all teachers want to be learning facilitators. In the beginning, staffing the Open School with people in agreement with its philosophy was difficult. Nonetheless, there was an emphasis on choosing staff based on "their attitudes about kids and education, their flexibility and willingness to innovate and change, their ability to work cooperatively and democratically with others, and their own personal life-style."[39] Because the Open School emphasized experiential learning, from its inception it sought people who, in the words of staff member Cynthia Gardner, had "done something other than go to school." In an interview, Gardner offered the example of one teacher who was a member of the

Peace Corps. Comfortable with immersing herself and students in another culture, she took groups to Mexico every year.

In addition to being learning facilitators, the Open School teachers and educational assistants served as advisors. Jennings described the crucial role of the advisor in the Open School structure:

> [The advisor is] the student's advocate, champion, expeditor and facilitator. The advisor acts as an "educational broker" by helping arrange learning experiences in and out of the school that achieve the student's goals.... The advisor helps students appraise their strengths and weaknesses to the end of becoming life-long designers of their own education.[40]

Students selected their advisors at the beginning of each school year. Should the relationship prove unsatisfactory, students could change advisors (although it was "not encouraged whimsically") if both the old and new advisors agreed.

Cynthia Gardner, an advisor for middle-years students, saw herself as a liaison between children, parents, and the school. It was up to her to balance the interests and needs of the children with the desires of the parents and the requirements of the school. To that end, she kept the records of her advisees, held conferences with the students and their parents, and wrote year-end evaluations. She also met weekly with the advisors of other middle-years students to discuss problems with children and learning goals and issues.

It wasn't always easy for the Open School staff to function as effective advisors. Nathan noted the sense of inadequacy staff sometimes experienced when, lacking training in counseling, they were nonetheless drawn into trying to help students with emotional problems that couldn't be ignored because they affected students' behavior and interfered with their learning. Consequently, advisors had to deal with emotional problems regardless of whether they felt qualified to do so.

Then there were the students who were being asked what interested them and they didn't know. One advisor related these examples. A high-schooler refused to discuss "goals" because "I don't know what I want to be yet." An eight-year-old had difficulty in developing a practical and feasible way of accomplishing the goal of "improving spelling" and had to be coaxed into picking a workable number of specific words to master each week.[41]

Faced with gaps in their own knowledge and skills, Open School staff showed a willingness to take action. At the end of the first year of operation, they identified a number of things that would improve their performance as advisors. These included interpersonal and counseling skills in working with both younger children and adolescents (observational skills, conflict resolution, gaining trust, and building rapport), increased knowledge about different cultures and ethnic groups, and goal-setting and organizational skills for themselves and their students. In addition, they identified "sources of grief" that had to do with organizational problems such as chaos, lack of communication, issues with staff accountability, and difficulty with record-keeping and follow-through.[42]

In the second year of operation, efforts were made to address these problems. To handle routine business more quickly and efficiently, the school created a Staff Steering Committee. Students were organized into the age groups described above, and staff support groups formed for advisors of each group. Staff and advisor manuals were created to offer guidelines and practical suggestions. Forms were developed. One helped advisors organize and maintain students' files. Others helped instructors report on student progress in classes. A list of items to be covered during advisor-parent-student conferences was created. Staff hammered out procedures for dealing with student behavior problems.

As part of their own growth and learning, staff participated in small group peer-evaluation sessions every two weeks. In addition, there was a more formal staff evaluation at mid-year when "all parents, students and staff write comments about each staff member. These comments... are reviewed by a parent-student-staff committee and discussed with the staff member. If consistent problems or complaints are raised, the committee can recommend a hearing to decide whether the staff member should be kept in the school."[43]

The Open School definition of a teacher as a learning facilitator, advisor, and resource-area developer carried unique challenges. Demands were great. Teachers had to be well organized indeed to keep track of their advisees, plan and facilitate classes, and contribute to the resource areas. And there was the disappointment of students who took advantage of the system to be less than they could be. Not surprisingly, the staff perpetually struggled with these challenges.

During interviews, one person observed, "We are constantly talking about dealing with children on an individual level. My goodness, this takes a lot of time... We give so much, and we find that we haven't been consistent. We do not follow through on things that we should follow through on." Another reflected that "we staff members still aren't as honest with each other as we ought to be. But I think we're moving towards that. There are all kinds of ways we ought to be working together, that we know we should be doing, but people are too tired to spend the time needed to do it, or they haven't figured out better ways for organization."

As if teaching and advising weren't enough of a load, staff also contributed to the day-to-day running of the school and helped develop policies and practices that kept it aligned with its charter. Four staff sat on the Advisory Council. (See "The Students of the St. Paul Open School," above, and "The Director of the St. Paul Open School," following.) Seven staff served on the Staff Steering Committee, described below.

Paradoxically, the very conditions that would sometimes challenge teachers to the limit were also the ones that unleashed the magic of learning. Teachers/facilitators/advisors had the pleasure of working in an innovative, interest-based learning community and seeing students "catch on" to being in charge of their own educations. They had the opportunity to know their advisees much better than most teachers know their students in traditional schools. They had the satisfaction of being part of a successful educational experiment that, according to Director Jennings, "should have fallen on its face."[44]

## The Role of the St. Paul Open School Director

In an interview, Wayne Jennings described his role as director of the Open School as if it were a combination of pioneer, liaison, networker, coordinator, and upholder.[45] How does a person become the director of an experimental undertaking like the St. Paul Open School? Jennings did it by accumulating more than twenty years of experience in teaching and in working with alternative and experimental programs. In college, he studied progressive education of the '30s and '40s. Later, he was involved in a "planning seminar that explored many educational ideas around the country." Before coming to the Open School, he worked with alienated youth and started a successful Career Studies Center in St. Paul. Jennings once described the Center as "a public school unit for the most turned-off secondary age kids that's built on progressive ideas."

Jennings liked the idea of alternative schools. "I see in [them] a possibility because you don't have to convert people. You can just operate independently and let the regular system continue on without feeling so molested or defensive about it." He viewed a large—and very important— part of his job as managing and maintaining good relations with the school board and the district administrators, a part made easier by the credibility he'd built up as a result of his years of experience in the St. Paul school system. He believed it was that credibility which kept the district administrators from "checking and double checking" everything going on when the school first opened.

For Jennings, the role of director was not so much executive decision-maker as it was coordinator of decision-making processes and executor of recommendations and decisions rising out of the community of Open School participants. As noted above, the three bodies primarily responsible for recommending and deciding were the Advisory Council, the Staff Steering Committee, and the Student Council. The Advisory Council was a large body of twenty-one members to which numerous subcommittees reported. The subcommittees dealt with topics such as evaluation, educational facilities laboratories, human relations, safety, volunteers, program, permanent records, physical plant use, graduation requirements, budget, enrollment, staffing, personnel problems, trip review, and interracial advising.

At one time, the Advisory Council tried to hold discussion on all school-related matters. However, that proved cumbersome. Hence, the Staff Steering Committee was created. Consisting of nine members including Jennings, its purpose was to make decisions regarding "routine business matters" so that operations didn't get bogged down by the need to take all affairs concerning the running of the school to the Advisory Council. The creation of the Steering Committee reflected one of the challenges of operating a school on democratic principles. Although a more representative body, the twenty-one member Advisory Council could not always address concerns and make decisions quickly enough to remain effective.

Jennings believed that willingness to entrust decision-making authority to the Steering Committee indicated two things. One was that people were worn down by trying to discuss the details of everything that needed attention. The other was that a certain level of trust had been achieved. "People said, 'I'm willing to trust the Steering Committee or trust Wayne to make some of these decisions.'" Reflecting on that time, he noted, "Maybe a school needs people who can work on trust-building too and deal with that—someone with some experience in group dynamics."

Although when I visited the school in 1976, the members of the school were still learning and growing with respect to crafting decision-making mechanisms that upheld their philosophy of democratic participation, it was remarkably successful. As Jennings stated, "The St. Paul Open School is not a flimsy, poorly conceived or half-baked idea. It is a bold and aggressive step melding many modern practices into a single project."[46]

> I know of no other school that's testing so many of the traditional assumptions about what schools are and should be, and testing them all at once. Not some little experiment in modular scheduling, but the whole concept of student-designed education. Not whether it's worthwhile to teach fifteen minutes more of math a day, but how you motivate kids to take math without ever forcing them to. And doing all these things with all-aged kids at once.[47]

To what, then, did Jennings attribute the school's success? One factor was the good fortune "to employ enough staff with this kind of vision (and I include myself) who seized on the opportunity, moved ahead, ... and no matter what the problems said, 'Let's try to solve it and stay on our original goal,' rather than changing goals every time we ran into an obstacle." He also cited the staff's "resourcefulness and political skills" in getting the school up and running without a lot of monitoring from the school district and central administrators.

Another factor was "the times." People were open to new ideas about education, thanks to books and TV coverage challenging the status quo. He believed that most important of all, however, were the parents who started the school. "The parents were farsighted... and progressive enough to set sort of general guidelines for the employment of staff and the thrust of the school. We've picked up on these and made the most of them."

Without doubt, parents played an important role in the St. Paul Open School since its inception, and their on-going participation was of prime importance in the learning community.

# The Role of Parents in the St. Paul Open School

Cynthia Gardner was in a unique position with regard to the St. Paul Open School. One of the parents involved in its formation, she was also a staff member. "All of us here agree that this is not a perfect institution," she said in an interview, "but it's a heck of a lot better than anything else we have. We look at the system and say, 'If this school fails, where do we send our kids? What do we do next?' We would rather continue to put in a lot of energy into this one to make it better than to just let it go and take our kids someplace else. There isn't any place else."

Gardner was not alone in her involvement with the school, nor in her disappointments and satisfactions with it. The findings of an external evaluation completed at the end of the Open School's second year of operation showed that about 20% of the parents (about two hundred ninety families had children in the school) "were rated as being highly involved with the school program. This is a higher proportion than would be found in most traditional schools."[48]

The foregoing descriptions of various aspects of the Open School supported these findings. Parents met at least four times a year with their children and the children's advisors to set goals and review learning. They participated on the Advisory Council and some of its various subcommittees. They served as volunteer teachers, helped organize resource areas, and did phoning. They communicated their opinions, feelings, and recommendations about school programs and staff via staff evaluations and questionnaires.

Parents pointed out where the school fell short and where it excelled. Regarding the need for improvement, some expressed concerns that the school could better meet the social and emotional needs of younger children and of addressing feelings of anonymity among some of the students. Some parents were not pleased about situations in which staff seemed reluctant to follow through on problems, set behavioral limits, and step in to prevent older children from bullying younger ones. Some parents wanted their children to know whom to approach to ask for help and to feel free to do it instead of holding back in reluctant confusion.[49]

> The same internal evaluation that highlighted problems also revealed strong satisfactions. Many parents report their children have made excellent adjustments to the informal structure and have progressed far beyond work done in traditional school. Parents like the flexibility of time and scheduling, the wide range of learning experiences, the opportunities to explore and experiment, and the individualization. They are pleased that their children can develop and learn according to their interests.[50]

And many parents reported satisfaction with seeing their children at ease with adults and with such a large, complex environment as the school. Many also believed the staff was warm, sympathetic, committed, aware of and concerned about the needs of children, accessible, willing, and helpful.

# Conclusion

Parents, students, staff—indeed, all involved with the Open School—knew in those early years that it was a work just barely begun. As Wayne Jennings wrote in his "Design, Rationale, and Implementation" paper:

> The program improves as perplexing problems are mastered. Progress is rapid but several years will be required to accomplish most elements of the design. Students and parents join with staff to seek solutions and to establish new norms of expectations and humanistic procedures. A common task builds strong bonds that sustain the school through its design shortcomings. In a sense, the building itself, the curriculum, the need for materials, becomes everyone's responsibility, everyone's problem, and everyone's pride as progress is achieved.[51]

Now, more than twenty-four years later, in January of 2000, the St. Paul Open School describes itself this way:

> We are a kindergarten through 12th grade community encouraging individual growth and self-directed learning from each other and the world around us. We believe that balancing independence and community responsibility is vital to learning and that takes place in the context of the entire community.[52]

Students still create learning plans with the help of their advisors and parents. They still demonstrate learning via portfolios rather than grades. Past graduates frequently come back and volunteer in the school, serving as validators for students' graduation competencies (which have now grown to eighteen in number). Current graduates reportedly do well when they go to college. Students still participate in school governance and decision-making on the Advisory Council and the Site-Base Council (where they are a majority). The school is in its fourth building since it began, and it has had ten, twenty, and twenty-five year reunions (and it's planning its thirtieth).[53]

And today, we find that Dr. Wayne Jennings is the founder of Designs for Learning,[54] which has developed a "Community Learning Centers" (CLC) model with a $5 million grant from New American Schools. Jennings' website (http://www.designlearn.com) states that "the project began with a year of research into the best in educational research and practice, followed by two years' work implementing the model on a pilot basis with nine schools in Minnesota. Designs for Learning now manages full implementation of the model in five charter schools." A great many of the basic elements and core structures of the St. Paul Open School form the heart of his CLC model. And a great many of what he calls the CLC "design specifications" sound like the kinds of things Bill Ellis describes so passionately in his CCL-LLC writings—things like "systemic or comprehensive" rather than piecemeal change, "transformational learning outcomes," "real world linkages" for learning through experience, "learning experiences... [that] are child-centered, life-centered and brain-based,"

"Personal Learning Plans," "elevating the position of teachers to 'facilitators of learning,'" "students... viewed as powerful resources" and participants in decision-making, "vigorously involved parents," partnerships with other entities in the community, CLCs as "headquarters for learning for the community," and programs based on needs that are "family centered and family supportive."

Dr. Joe Nathan has carried forward his learnings from the Open School as well. He directs the Center for School Change[55] at the University of Minnesota's Hubert H. Humphrey Institute of Public Affairs. He has consulted, researched, and written about parent and community involvement, strengthening rural communities to help increase student achievement, school choice, charter schools, and youth community service. He recently published *Charter Schools: Creating Hope and Opportunity for American Education*, and he writes an education focused newspaper column published in several Minnesota papers.

These are just two of the lives affecting other lives based on their St. Paul Open School experiences. One wonders what other seeds for growth, independence and democracy have grown in the more than one thousand graduates from the Open School since its founding.

## Notes

1. Concluding statement from a 1976 St. Paul Open School student's graduation portfolio.

2. Karen Branan, "The Sermon of St. Paul," *Learning*, November 1973, p. 20.

3. *ibid.*

4. *ibid.*, pp. 17-18.

5. As of January 2000, the St. Paul Open School is located at 90 Western Ave. S., St. Paul, MN 55102, USA; phone 651-293-8670.

6. The school is no longer at this location (see note 5 above).

7. "St. Paul Open School: It Works This Way for Some," in *Open School: A Research Demonstration Unit.* St. Paul: St. Paul Public Schools, pp. 43-44.

8. *ibid.*

9. *ibid.*

10. Wayne Jennings, "St. Paul Open School," *Trends in Elementary Education*, Fall 1972, p. 17.

11. From "Graduation Process," St. Paul Open School, 1976.

12. *ibid.*

13. The age-related locations were instituted in 1975 to give younger students the security of a home base in what might otherwise have been an overwhelmingly large space.

14. Teaching and Learning Research Corporation, "St. Paul Open School Year One Evaluation Report." Elmhurst, NY: Author, 1972, p. 3.

15. From the "Course List: St. Paul Open School," Spring 1976.

16. Teaching and Learning..., 1972, p. 3.

17. "Course List..." Spring 1976.

18. Joe Nathan, "What Does It Take to Teach in an Open School?" *K-eight*, May 1973, p. 25.

19. "St. Paul Open School Year Four Evaluation Report: 1974-75," St. Paul: St. Paul Public Schools Independent District #625, Publication #7576100, 1975, pp. A-26-28.

20. Joe Nathan, "What Does..." pp. 18, 20.

21. This field research was made possible with a grant from the Charles F. Kettering Foundation in Dayton, OH. The full report on the Open School is in Toward More Democratic School Systems: Case Studies of Three Schools, Final Report to the Charles F. Kettering Foundation, August 1977, pp. 245-378.

22. From course description in the class schedule.

23. From student self-evaluations shared by teacher, Joe Nathan.

24. Joe Nathan, "Report From an Open School," *K-eight*, January/February 1973, p. 20.

25. "St. Paul Open School Staff Manual," St. Paul: St. Paul Open School, pp. 1, 92.

26. In Karen Branan, "The Sermon of

St. Paul," *Learning*, November 1973, p. 20.

27. Wayne Jennings, "Design, Rational and Implementation: St. Paul Open School" (leaflet), pp. 4, 3.

28. Nancy Pirsig, "Bumpy Road to the Open School," *American Education*, October 1972, p. 19.

29. Minnesota Center for Sociological Research, "Evaluation of St. Paul Open School Developer/Demonstration Project," Minneapolis: Department of Sociology, University of Minnesota, 1975, p. 48.

30. From "Graduation Process."

31. Pirsig, "Bumpy Road..." p. 23.

32. *ibid.*, p. 21.

33. Minnesota Center..., p. 49; "St. Paul Open School Year Four...", p. 47.

34. Nathan, "What Does..." pp. 15, 16, 17, 25, 26.

35. Nathan, "Report From..." pp. 20.

36. *ibid.*

37. *ibid.*

38. Nathan, "What Does..." pp. 15, 16, 17, 25, 26.

39. Teaching and Learning..., p. 55.

40. Jennings, "Design, Rationale..." p. 2.

41. Pirsig, "Bumpy Road..." pp. 21-22.

42. Teaching and Learning..., 1972, p. 24.

43. Branan, "The Sermon..." p. 20.

44. Pirsig, "Bumpy Road..." p. 23.

45. The "St. Paul Open School Staff Manual" (p. 85) expands on the duties of the director, indicating that he or she "has the overall responsibility for the school" and for making sure that its activities are in keeping with its policies. To that end, he or she answers to the school board for decisions and actions taken in the school. The director is charged with managing the decision-making process and making sure those decisions are carried out. He or she must attempt to stay abreast of new ideas and activities within the school, and he or she "represents the school to other people who are trying to set up open schools." The director also reviews student problems that can't be solved by the advisors.

46. Jennings, "Design, Rationale..." p. 8.

47. Pirsig, "Bumpy Road..." p. 23.

48. Teaching and Learning..., 1973, p. 78.

49. "Internal Evaluation: Years Two and Three, St. Paul Open School," St. Paul: St. Paul Public Schools, Publication #480, July 1974, pp. 28, 29, 30, 32, 33.

50. *ibid.*, p. 28.

51. Jennings, "Design, Rationale..." p. 6.

52. http://twincities.citysearch.com/E/V/MINMN/0007/61/03/

53. Information from conversations with Open School principal Ruth Pechmann, program coordinator Jennifer Johnson, and group facilitator Lenni Augustine, February and March 2000.

54. Wayne Jennings can be reached at Designs for Learning, 1745 University Ave., Suite 310, St. Paul, MN 55104-3624, USA, phone: 612-645-0200, e-mail: wayne@designlearn.com

55. Joe Nathan can be reached at http://www.hhh.umn.edu/centers/schoolchange/, Center for School Change at the Hubert H. Humphrey Institute of Public Affairs, University of Minnesota, 301 19th Avenue South, Minneapolis, MN 55455, USA, phone: 612-625-3506, e-mail: jnathan@hhh.umn.edu

# About the Author

*Robert Skenes, Ph.D., teaches management and leadership in two alternative programs for working adults at National-Louis University's Virginia campus. He conducted a three-year grant project looking at ten different K-12 alternative schools and has taught in and helped run two other alternative college programs. He was a national Education Policy Fellow with the US Department of Education, and he is a past vice chair and active advisory board member of the National Coalition of Alternative Community Schools (NCACS).*

# A Resource Center for All
## Upattinas School and Resource Center

*by Sandy Hurst*

$S$ INCE 1971, TO THOSE WHO KNOW the name at all, Upattinas School has meant a place where children and young adults learn through play and experiences in a different and innovative way that used to be described as an alternative school. Upattinas was developed as a family cooperative in southeastern Pennsylvania near the town of Phoenixville. Before the word "holistic" became a way of describing what we do, the families in the program wanted for their children all that *holistic education* currently describes. During the 1980s, as people were becoming increasingly alarmed about their children's schooling and less and less able to afford private education, a number of families approached Upattinas in their frustration, asking for some kind of help with keeping their children at home. In response, the school welcomed people into its community, helping them to explore options for learning, and loaning books and materials to help that process.

At the time, Pennsylvania law was not uniform, so homeschooling permission could be granted only by the Superintendent of Schools of each locality. Now the law allows homeschooling, but it includes many requirements and does not assure that the student will be able to either use materials or graduate from their home school district. One of the important functions that is currently performed by the staff at Upattinas is to work with and stay friendly with the people in the public schools who have the power to give consent to our home education families.

Upattinas is an open community governed democratically by all of its participants. It welcomes all people who find its beliefs compatible and useful in their lives. Every member of the community is invited to join in the governing of the programs, either through becoming a member of its fifteen-person board of directors, or through joining committees or interest groups in any of its many component programs—full- and part-time day school, individual classes or workshops, sports teams, summer camp, home education support, and field-trip programs. Each age group within the ongoing day programs governs itself through its group meetings. Every two weeks there is an in-school meeting, which includes all the people at the center on a day-to-day basis. When an issue arises that will affect everyone at the center, this group of people, including students, staff, and parent helpers, holds discussions, makes proposals, and makes decisions based on either consensus or, occasionally, a vote that must represent a two-thirds majority in favor of the proposal. This meeting advises the board of directors, which has final responsibility for major decisions concerning money or over-all policies that might affect all the programs or the buildings and grounds. The board is elected from among all the constituents of Upattinas and represents students, staff, and parents, including home-educating members. It runs by consensus.

The campus includes seven-and-a-half acres of woods, fields, and a stream surrounding an old stone house and a large gymnasium/classroom building. On any day at Upattinas, you will find about eighty young people on the campus. They will be from about five to about eighteen years old, and they will be both working with and cared for by certificated teachers and qualified parent helpers who are there to facilitate activities already introduced by the children and to suggest other activities they think the children might like to pursue. This is not to say that the children are always being overseen by adults. They may be out in the woods together in small groups, making a fort in the trees, or creating a play in which they are the directors or designers. Although there are regular classes available at Upattinas, no person is ever required to go to them.

The yearly schedule is designed taking into account what the staff knows about the incoming students. It is revised several times at the beginning of the year until as many people as possible are satisfied. It will always include the usual basic subjects as well as many things that are alternative in nature, such as Transforming World Views or Native American Survival Skills. There is a fine line between not coercing people to learn or participate in something, and encouraging them to try new things and then to follow through the difficult parts of the learning. We find that, because of our trust in each other, our young people come to what is often thought of as conventional learning by themselves, when they are ready. We are not concerned about time lines or "rubrics." We offer many activities and people who are wonderful resources for learning and doing all kinds of interesting things. We also offer workshops designed to support parents, both of students in the school and people who are educating at home.

At Upattinas young people learn about the environment, not only through reading and talking, but also through actually doing farm work in a local CSA (Community Supported Agriculture) or helping to repair riparian zones damaged by housing developments in the area so that a pristine stream will not be destroyed. They work on community gardens in the city, join a local Waldorf program making gardens to be shared by mentally challenged people, and participate in meetings of local environmental groups.

Rather than trying to provide everything for its students, Upattinas encourages them to participate in their local community centers, libraries, helping agencies, and sports clubs, and in private lessons, dance classes, college classes, or real jobs. Our position is that children are learning all the time and everywhere they are, so we welcome their evaluations of that learning for credit toward graduation. They are limited only by their imaginations and energy.

On many Friday mornings students and teachers can be found having a discussion around coffee and cocoa at the café run by the Coatesville Cultural Society, a community theater in a nearby town where people of all races and ages come together to present a unique blend of traditional and improvisational performance, as well as to challenge each other in chess or to share their poetry. People from this organization also come to the center to teach African dance and drumming, which includes as many as twenty-five dancers from the youngest children to teachers and parent helpers, and as many as fifteen drummers and percussionists.

The staff of Upattinas School and Resource Center is always open to the contributions of family members and friends who volunteer to participate either in teaching or helping with projects. If enough students ask for a class in something not already available among our community members, the staff will search for a teacher who can come on a per-class basis.

Travel is an important part of this community school. Students and teachers may be found visiting other schools or sleeping on the floors of family friends so that they can have more time to explore the museums and neighborhoods of cities like Washington and New York. They take cross-country camping trips that may include adventures such as hiking, back-packing, rock climbing, or rafting, or they join the Appalachian Trail Hike for a month of intensive living and survival skills. And they can always be found at the Annual Spring Conference of the National Coalition of Alternative Community Schools.

Included in the programs of Upattinas is Nomugi Open Community School, an alternative school in Yokohama, Japan, which was designed to follow the principles of Upattinas. Each year students from this program come to school in the United States in an effort to help them grow and to develop their self confidence. This program grew out of the need of young people in Japan, who have chosen not to be in conventional schools, to have a satisfying and nurturing program. Students who come to us are placed with families so that they will learn English and be exposed to new ways of thinking about their education and their alternatives in making life decisions. Independent students from other countries are also welcome.

Although Upattinas provides a very open and free program on its campus and encourages people to consider an "un-schooling" approach in their home education, our families also include people who choose more structured schooling at home. Sometimes these families send their children for a day of play or to take a class in a foreign language or participate in a sports program. A lending library of textbooks and materials is available, as is the opportunity to work with staff in terms of their questions or concerns about legal issues or appropriate contexts for their children's learning. The staff includes people who concentrate on the Home Education Program, keeping up with resources available, keeping records for individual children, and doing counseling about jobs, college, or military service. High-school students who are studying at home may meet with their contact people every six to eight weeks, or consult with them either by phone or e-mail. Students who live too far away may be doing all their work at hoe and sending it to a contact teacher who updates records and makes suggestions or comments about the work submitted.

One of the unique services provided by this Home Education Program is that of reviewing and reinstating people who have, for various reasons, left school before they graduated. It is not unusual for a person who is in his or her twenties or thirties or even older to join the program in order to develop the credits needed to graduate from a licensed high school. We are very careful to advise people about the many other ways to "get an education" or get the credentials necessary to get on with their lives. But there are some places in which the lack of that high-school diploma is a limiting factor. My father-in-law was one of the most intelligent, well-educated men I've ever known. He was always frustrated and limited in his ability to climb the salary ladder in his field of work, simply because he did not have a high-school diploma. The GED would not have been enough. On the other hand, many students at Upattinas have used their college credits for high school completion, even as they continue on in college. They also often by-pass their last year and begin college early. It is not uncommon for a student to take a year off to either work or travel before finishing his or her high school experience. This, of course, also contributes to experiential learning and becomes part of the student's portfolio of credit. In essence, taking a year away from the school is not really taking a year off. It is creating another alternative experience.

Graduates from the Upattinas School and Resource Center programs can be found in all kinds of colleges and universities and working in many different kinds of jobs. They are Peace Corps volunteers, musicians, teachers, dancers, plumbers, builders, travelers, parents, environmentalists, forest rangers, movie-makers, home-makers, car mechanics, painters, photographers, computer technicians and programmers, business owners, and glass blowers.

Upattinas is funded largely by tuition, which is kept as low as possible while keeping the programs solidly funded and staffed. There are many scholarships and work trades available, and the children of teachers receive free tuition. The gymnasium is rented in the evenings and on weekends throughout the winter for basketball and indoor soccer. This also contributes to the funding. It is the policy of the center that every program must contribute the funding necessary for its own staff as well as contributing to the general fund. Community members may propose a new program to the board. Any new program must be philosophically compatible with the center and contribute to the life of the whole. There are, of course, many projects to be funded. When people really want something they may take it on as their special project. On the day before a recent holiday the children of the lower school program, with the help of their teachers and parent helpers, earned more than six hundred dollars toward the playground the are designing. There was honey from the bees in the back field, greeting cards from the drawing class, and candles, jewelry, ornaments, and wreaths made with the help of high-schoolers and parents. The children made the cookies and parents and high-school students brought a gourmet potluck lunch. And there was a wonderful, impromptu songfest led by a father who joined his daughter for the day.

This kind of ownership of projects, classes, and activities is the essence of a community based on creating from day to day a place of joyful learning. It is not without its problems and heartbreaks, but nothing that includes everyone, for better or worse, is without its own troubles. Community at Upattinas means sharing with and caring about everyone, no matter how small or large, young or old, who wants to join us in our journey.

## About the Author

*Sandy Hurst has been the director of Upattinas School and Resource Center since its founding in 1971. She has also been active in the National Coalition of Alternative Community Schools (NCACS), and is director of its Teacher Education Program.*

*For more information, contact Sandra M. Hurst, director, Upattinas School and Resource Center, 429 Greenridge Road, Glenmoore, PA 19343 USA, phone: 610-458-5138, e-mail: upatinas@chesco.com, URL: http://www.chesco.com/upattinas*

# Bayside Children's College

*by Karen Funk*

$B$AYSIDE CHILDREN'S COLLEGE is a purposely small learning center for fifty students ages five to eighteen, located downtown in the small community of Santa Cruz, California. It was founded in August of 1992 by Karen Funk, an experienced educator with, at that time, thirty-one years of service in private and public schools throughout California.

The director and fifteen-member staff of this sole proprietorship are dedicated to personalizing the learning experience for each student, as well as the mentoring experience for each adult. At Bayside it is believed that everyone learns best in a natural setting modeled after the family, with active community connection. Bayside offers a service-oriented learning center adapting to the needs, desires, and real-life schedules of our students, facilitators, and families. The young people and their families have direct access to the director and staff at all times, with no

77

bureaucratic red tape, and suggestions for changes are—if financially feasible, appropriate to the center's philosophy, and productive for the advancement of learning—able to be implemented without delay. Students are given daily emotional and social support to fulfill the promise they sign at enrollment—to respect and care for themselves, others, and things, and to make learning their responsibility and commitment.

Both full- and part-time participation are offered. Students may enroll for a daily program of classes and study (with no homework required unless they opt for it). Part-time students may schedule as much on-site time as they and/or their parents desire by combining homeschooling with selected classes or personal tutoring at the center to broaden homeschooling resources, or by setting up independent projects to fulfill graduation requirements at Bayside or elsewhere.

Bayside offers a full program of classes in languages, arts, sciences, and physical education (not, of course, competitive team sports, but personal fitness and health activities). The center contracts for some programs with agencies, businesses, gyms, and studios in the downtown area—all within walking distance of the center—and encourages use of local libraries, businesses, government centers, services, galleries, theaters, parks, and museums by students of all ages and interests during or outside of the school day.

The center is non-graded. Every student graduates every year to the next level of learning for that individual in a formal ceremony with personal feedback from the director, staff, students, and family, and with an award for the accomplishment she or he most cherished for that year. For graduation to college, Bayside's students matriculate based on readiness as assessed by a staff that knows them well, not based on the actual number of courses taken, attendance records, or grades. All of the student's work is saved, and the actual work and known learning patterns are evaluated by the staff in light of the student's plans for the next step into personal development, work, or institutions of higher learning. If required by the next educational institution that the student plans to attend, staff will translate the work done at Bayside into grades and credits in a special meeting with staff, parents, and the student, reviewing all the actual work on file. Every student is required to have an ongoing resume on a computer file, updated constantly, to develop a sense of capabilities and interests and for use in application for work or schooling.

Staff is chosen by the students. Each prospective staff member must spend voluntary time with the students to get to know their desires, needs, and personalities. Following this time with the students, the applicant must audition with at least two unpaid lessons or work sessions in the area of service she or he wishes to offer, and develop a following of at least six students who will approve the hiring. At this point the director determines budget possibilities and finalizes or puts on hold the employment of the applicant. Students interested in working with the applicant are allowed to try out the offering for at least two weeks before committing to stay in the class or keep working individually with the applicant.

Employment does not require a teaching credential. The director has never seen the possession of a credential as significant to the quality of learning facilitation. It is important for staff members to convey approachability, enthusiasm, and knowledgeability, from experience or education, in order to attract sufficient student interest to be hired.

Bayside has no entrance requirements at all, but reserves the right to ask the student who is unable or refuses to become a respectful and contributing member of the learning center community to leave. The center often serves as a transitional setting for students dissatisfied with traditional school, and as a setting for homeschoolers who feel the need to connect with other learners on a more personal and social basis. Personal choice is accommodated with as much flexibility as the center's basic philosophy will permit.

Karen Funk, the director, is ready and willing to act as consultant to anyone anywhere who would like to set up a similar learning center. She can guide an entrepreneur through the process step-by-step, from getting the word out to walking the walk, from humane considerations to legal red tape.

Call, write, or email to make arrangements for consultation. Contact her at Bayside Children's College, 1025 Center Street, Santa Cruz, CA 95060, phone: 831-454-0370, e-mail: karen@baysidechildrenscollege.com, URL: http://baysidechildrenscollege.com

# The International University, Japan

## A 25-Year Experiment
## in Restructuring University Education

*by Motoshi Suzuki*

FOUNDED IN 1975, the International University Learning Center (TIUJ) in Kyoto, Japan, is an attempt to implement at the university level, and to be in a position to promote at all levels, the ecologically oriented concept of community-based learning, as suggested and described in the writings of early 20th century visionary educators—particularly John Dewey, Lewis Mumford, Mahatma Gandhi, and in Japan, Tsunesaburo Makiguchi. Philosophically, the task of the TIUJ is perceived as that of helping the members of a society create a future based on democratic ideals and values. Practically, the TIUJ serves as a resource center designed to assist individual learners develop and pursue their own learning programs, through individual study and networking with other learners, with the help and guidance of experienced mentors.

I first heard about the International University Learning Center in Japan in 1990, fifteen years after it was established in Osaka (it later moved to Kyoto). Two years later, I enrolled to complete my university studies. The circumstances that brought me to that point, and the influence that decision has had on my life, illustrate the values and ideals that underlie the TIUJ. But before relating that story, let me provide some of the background that led to the establishment of the TIUJ in 1975.[1]

The International University Learning Center is the Japan branch of what is known as an holistic or alternative university. The main branch of the university is in Kansas City, in the United States. Actually, it is a miracle that the Japan TIUJ is still around after twenty-five years. When TIUJ was founded by Dayle and Miyoko Bethel and their co-workers,

alternative or holistic education was practically unheard of in Japan, except for a few special schools at the kindergarten and early elementary levels. such as Montessori and Waldorf schools. Alternative universities were non-existent. Japan was a *gaku-reki shakai* (education-dominated society), with all aspects of education firmly under the control of a Ministry of Education appointed by the central government. Japanese society was at that time approaching the peak of its "economic miracle," and its educational system, rather than being criticized, was almost universally lauded both at home and abroad as performing a key role in the creation of that miracle.

And so, there weren't many people interested in the idea that factory-type schools, from elementary school to university, which had developed after the Industrial Revolution, were unhealthy both for individuals and for societies. And particularly, there was very little interest in an "alternative university" during those first years of TIUJ's existence. One student enrolled in the year it was founded, and for the first fifteen years there were never more than two or three students in the university program. Many times there was not enough income to cover costs and the whole venture came close to ending, but when things became difficult, the staff kept telling themselves, "Let's try one more year." Fortunately, those early pioneers didn't give up or lose their vision. Today, TIUJ is playing an important role at the cutting edge of educational change and transformation, not only in Japan, but internationally as well.

This new university experiment was founded on the twin convictions that the worldview that has dominated Western civilization for 400 years, and which during the 20th century has come to dominate all the cultures of the earth, has serious flaws and limitations, and that a new vision is needed for human society, its values, and its relationship to the earth. For TIUJ, two major insights have helped to define and articulate the foundations of that vision. One pertains to the role of community in the human learning process, the other the proper role of a university in a society.

## Community-Based Learning

The initial inspiration for TIUJ's community-based approach to education came from a group of educator-philosophers, contemporaries during the first half of the 20th century, who, roughly at the same time and in widely differing cultures, formed a common vision of what constituted a good human life and a common conviction that the institutions of the industrial system originating in the West, then beginning to overrun their respective cultures, constituted a serious threat to the well being of people and planet. They were unanimous in predicting that the directions and policies of the industrialized and so-called democratic societies would lead to disaster for human civilization unless they could be redirected and transformed.

This, in essence, was the conclusion reached in the United States by Lewis Mumford and John Dewey, in India by Mahatma Gandhi, and in Japan by Tsunesaburo Makiguchi and other educators. Each of these eminent 20th century educators insisted that education, at all levels, must occur within the context of community and in intimate, direct relationship with the natural and social phenomena of the learner's environment. By the beginning of the 20th century, this relationship between learners and their natural and social environments had been lost as schools developed and students were secluded in school buildings. Makiguchi was especially critical of these developments. He believed that the indirect, second-hand educational system that had developed in his country was the height of folly. Primarily a product of implantation from Western cultures, that system of education, he charged, confined learners to classrooms and forced them to go through a meaningless routine of "memorizing and forgetting, memorizing, forgetting, and on and on."[2] Writing in the early decades of the 20th century, Makiguchi described the effects of the development of modern schools as follows:

In the days before there were schools, the prevailing method of
guiding young people to the proper roles in the general scheme of life
was an extended home life, whereby one apprenticed at the family
trade throughout one's formative years, with this training supplemented by things learned from the local community. Then came the
Meiji period (1868-1912) with its modern education and the spread of
schools...Everyone was taken by the hand and dragged off to schools,
and soon the other two schemes of learning fell into disuse. This was
the age of the school reigning unchallenged and omnipotent. Only in
recent years have we seen the grave error of our ways and tried to fill
in the gap with various kinds of adjunct education and youth groups
for extracurricular activity...From this point on, school education
must be aware of its own share of the educational role...It must
cooperate with the other two areas of education, the home and the
community, each with its own expertise...These three areas of education must link together in an orderly system of mutual complemen-
tarity.[3]

To accomplish this kind of community-based system of education,
Makiguchi proposed what he called a "half-day school" system, from
elementary schooling to the university, which would cut back on ill-
managed education that was wasting valuable work-learning time. If we
return to the other two areas of education much of their premodern
territory in overall life guidance, he claimed, only the remainder need be
taught in schools, and in a half day at that. This, he believed, would at
once prove more efficient, and would create an organic bond with the
other two areas. In a marvelous statement summing up the fundamental
purpose of half-day schooling, Makiguchi wrote that

> study is not seen as a preparation for living, but rather study takes
> place while living, and living takes place in the midst of study. Study
> and actual living are seen as more than parallels; they inform one
> another intercontextually, study-in-living and living-in-study,
> throughout one's whole life. In this sense, it is not the better eco-
> nomic budgeting of school programs but the instilling of joy and
> appreciation for work that becomes the main focus of the proposed
> changes.[4]

Half a century later, Jeremy Rifkin expressed a vision of education
very similar to that of Makiguchi and his contemporaries:

> The artificial separation between human culture and nature, charac-
> teristic of the Newtonian era, will give way to a new reunification of
> the two in the coming Solar Age. The concept of "man against nature"
> will be replaced by the concept of "people in nature." The educational
> process will reflect this basic change. In contrast to the current
> academic process, which separates students from the outside world
> for twelve to sixteen years in a hermetically sealed, artificial environ-
> ment, the educational experience in the entropic era will emphasize
> learning through day-to-day experiences in the world. Apprentice-
> ship will once again take on the importance it had in previous
> periods of history. At the same time, the large, centralized learning

complexes typical of the last stages of the age of nonrenewables will give way to the notion of "learning environments." In the Solar Age, going to school will mean going into the community to learn.[5]

## The Role of a University

The understanding of the role of a university that has influenced the development of the programs and policies of TIUJ has come primarily from two sources. One was Alfred North Whitehead's perception of the university. "The task of a university," Whitehead had written, "is the creation of the future, so far as rational thought and civilized modes of appreciation can affect the issue. The future is big with every possibility of achievement and of tragedy."[6]

It was obvious in the 1950s and 1960s in America that most universities were not contributing to the creation of a future based on democratic ideals and values. They were, rather, serving primarily to support and strengthen existing power structures and inequalities. George Barnett and Jack Otis, commenting on the implications of Whitehead's philosophy, concluded that the university had defaulted on its responsibility to help the members of society to envision and to create a positive future. The very disciplines that might be expected to develop the ideas that would help "keep man's corporate head on straight," they charged, had declined this responsibility. "Philosophy has gone analytic, claiming that it is no part of the philosophic office to declare moral ideals or to design the state of culture. Social science, in the name of objectivity, has confined its mission to describing the facts of life in society without evaluating them. Nowhere in the university is there a professional search for the knowledge that is most important to man. The university is no longer concerned in any significant way with ideals."[7]

As a result of this failure of the university to accept its rightful role in the society, and the intellectual vacuum resulting from it, the creation of the future had fallen to so-called "practical men"—politicians, businessmen, and militarists—who, deprived of the leadership and ideals that the university ought to have provided, were in a situation similar to seaman on the high seas without compass or rudder.

This analysis of the university made a deep impression on Dayle Bethel, who was engaged in graduate work and teaching during those years. He found two aspects of university education especially disturbing. One was the test-focused nature of instruction, which, he was convinced, totally perverted the nature of student learning. Universities, it appeared, had become little more than screening and credentialing agencies for corporations and government agencies. The other was that universities, in their eagerness to attract research funds, were coming increasingly under the influence and control of those very same corporations and government agencies.[8] It was these insights and concerns that triggered the vision of the structurally transformed university that he brought to Japan.

Thus, a vision of a university in which the quest for ideas and ideals, a university in which learning could be experienced as an exciting adventure in grasping insights and understandings in the company of other adventurers, was one of the key factors that influenced the development of the new university center. A cardinal principle of all learning sponsored within this restructured university system is that it is responsible—responsible to the future and future generations and to its mandate to help create a positive future, and responsible to the community of which the learner is a part. And at the university level, "community" means the immediate community, the surrounding natural bio-region, and the planet of which the bio-region is an integral part.[9]

## Study at The International University Japan Center

I am often asked the question, "TIUJ sounds great, but how does it work in actual practice?" Let me say first that each learner's program is designed individually, in accordance with his or her interests, needs, and situation. Following admittance by TIUJ to pursue a program of study, the successful applicant and a faculty program monitor arrange a meeting to create an initial plan of study, which will evolve and change by agreement of both parties. A typical program of study consists of core courses and elective courses, organized by the TIUJ or one of its partnering organizations, and learner-designed courses and projects created with the guidance of the monitor. While specific study procedures vary from learner to learner, they generally consist of a combination of:

• Personal study, research, writing, and projects—at home, at a TIUJ center, in libraries, resource centers, museums, and other learning resources available in the community.
• Meetings with one or more other persons—sometimes, but not always, other TIUJ learners—to discuss ideas, insights, and issues being studied, to make presentations and get feedback.
• Participation in study groups and seminars arranged by the learner and the faculty monitor.
• Learning encounters within the learner's community—as a participant observer, intern, or part-time worker in organizations, offices, shops, or farms; attending lectures, workshops, conferences, etc.
• Regional workshops, short courses, and conferences in which learners, mentors, monitors, and other resource persons and specialists in a given geographic area gather to share the outcomes of their individual studies and life journeys, and during which learners have the opportunity to make presentations, receive feedback, and try out new ideas.

It should be understood that it is the learner who is responsible for the learning that occurs. In the traditional, factory system of education, teachers are charged with the responsibility of transmitting a specific body of knowledge to students and then testing them to determine what proportion of the content transmitted can be given back on demand. In contrast, in our system the learner is responsible for his or her own learning, guided and encouraged by mentors who are specialists in the fields or areas in which understanding and skill are being sought.

The primary instrument for evaluating the learner's progress—both by the learner and by others concerned—is a portfolio, the content of which vary depending on each learner's program, interests, and goals. A portfolio may contain research papers, letters and articles to newspapers and magazines, progress reports, works of art or handicrafts related to the learner's studies, albums and notebooks, or journals describing feelings and analyses of progress or lack of progress, new insights, and ideas, problems, failures, successes, new beginnings.

At the undergraduate level, a learner may pursue a plan of study in almost any field, except medicine and law. At the graduate level, TIUJ offers programs in holistic and alternative education, institutional transformation and futures studies, community health education, environmental studies, community development, Third World studies, child development, anthropology, and social psychology.

The mentor (or mentors) for a given course or project may be one of TIUJ's six faculty members (three full-time, three part-time), or one of many cooperating mentors throughout the world. For example, a businessman in the United States, a professor in Japan, an organic farmer in Thailand, a community development worker in Nepal, a physicist in England, or a philosopher in India.

A sense of responsibility for one's community and the earth has been a central feature of the programs of students who enroll in TIUJ, as can be seen by a glance at the nature of their academic programs of study. Here I can mention only a few of them. The first student to receive the B.A. degree from The International University's Japan Center in December 1985, was Yoshiko Wakabayashi, whose graduation paper, "Warning from the Plants: Deforestation by the Production of *Waribashi*" (disposable wooden chopsticks), was one of the first research-based analyses in Japan of the role of *waribashi*, and the throw-away mentality that it symbolizes, in the deforestation of Third-World countries by Japanese companies. Another student, Kosuke Nishimura, is currently studying about and working with some of the alternative schools and organizations in his community. This includes helping to edit a book about alternative education. A second emphasis that has evolved in the course of his studies is the struggle of indigenous groups to preserve their languages and cultures, with special emphasis on the Sami people of Scandinavia and the Basque of southern Europe.

Two students currently pursuing doctoral programs in TIUJ's distance learning division, Michael Reber in Japan and Namrata Sharma in India, are extending and implementing concepts of community-based learning in their studies. Michael Reber is exploring means of supporting individualized student learning programs through the development of community learning centers (CLCs), particularly with reference to utilizing new developments in electronic media. He has become recognized internationally for his work and research in this area and is currently chair of an international, ad hoc committee composed of educational theorists and practitioners who are researching possibilities for human learning offered by CLCs. Namrata Sharma is engaged in a comparative study of the community-based learning ideas, proposals, and practical experimental projects of Mahatma Gandhi, John Dewey, and Tsunesaburo Makiguchi.

The opportunity to study and work at the TIUJ has opened up new worlds of experience and opportunity for me and many other persons who have participated in it during the past twenty-five years. Rajanyagam Sekaran, an Indian professor who spent a year at TIUJ in the mid-1980s, summed it up well: "The International University Japan Center is exceptional in its approach to learning: 'traditional' in imparting skills in orthodox disciplines, but 'non-traditional' in its ability to create a learning environment where learning is pursued for the joy and challenge involved in expanding intellectual frontiers rather than for passing tests. Perhaps the most important thing I can say about the TIUJ center is that it is a learning institution which produces not only 'scholars' but also 'persons.'"

As TIUJ prepares to enter its second quarter-century, the vision of its mission that I have outlined continues to inform and shape its policies and programs, but it is today being enriched and expanded by another source of insight and inspiration. In the year 2000, TIUJ will begin a new chapter in its history with the formation of a partnership with the Center for Communities of the Future (COTF) in Gastonia, North Carolina, in the United States. COTF is a virtual center that has developed an innovative approach to working with local communities to create experiments in various aspects of $21^{st}$-century community building. As far as we are aware, this will be the first time anywhere that two different types of "virtual organizations," our virtual university and COTF's virtual center, will be working in practical and symbolic collaboration utilizing $21^{st}$-century technology. In a key feature of the partnership, TIUJ will join forces with a team of specialists and "learning leaders" in each of the several "nodes" making up the COTF Center who are working to evolve a new framework of thinking for community transformation based on chaos/complexity theory. Through these cooperative efforts, a structured but flexible curriculum is being developed that will offer a unique approach for linking real-time learning with this new and evolving theory of community transformation.

## My Experience at TIUJ

As I indicated earlier, I transferred to TIUJ from a traditional university in Japan. I was born in Hamamatsu, Shizuoka Prefecture, and grew up there, attending public schools from kindergarten through high school. In those years the competitive, factory-like system of compulsory schooling was accepted by almost everyone without question and most students, including me, had to follow it obediently. But as many educational critics are now pointing out, this kind of education didn't allow me to have time to even think about what kind of learning was best for me or for human beings generally. We were treated just like empty buckets to be filled up. Learning was a matter of memorizing many facts transmitted to us by teachers. We were too busy memorizing a lot of meaningless, irrelevant facts to stop and ask ourselves what was really important or what the facts really meant. There was no place in that huge educational system for curiosity or a sense of wonder about the marvelous world we live in. No one cared about us as persons or about our individual interests and needs. Under these conditions, I was just like a robot. I didn't have to think about who I was or what the purpose of my life was. All I had to do was obediently accept what somebody decided should be transmitted to me.

I failed to pass any of the university entrance examinations, so I went to live with my uncle in Nagoya in order to go to a preparatory school. It was the first time that I was away from my hometown, which was all the world I knew. My uncle was really an aware person and we discussed many things every day. At that time, I tended to take everything for granted, and he severely criticized this attitude on my part. He encouraged me to think deeply about myself and about who I really was. Slowly, I began to discover myself. I began to see the world with new eyes. Even so, I was under heavy pressure from my parents to study and to pass the university entrance examination. Luckily, or perhaps unluckily, I was accepted by a university in Tokyo in 1990.

Before I began my university study I had thought, "Now I will really be able to study something important. Now I will have a chance to learn about the many new things I am seeing in the world around me." But I soon discovered that I was wrong. The university turned out to be little different from high school, and I found myself becoming apathetic, bored, and lazy like the other students around me.

During my second year, I thought about transferring to another university, so I visited several of the prestigious universities in the Tokyo area, which I hoped might be better for me. However, I concluded finally that all the universities were about the same. My uncle had told me about TIUJ when I was living with him in Nagoya, but my parents would not consider anything but a regular university at that time, so I didn't follow up on that possibility. Now, after two years of wasted time, I knew I did not want to spend two more years in a traditional university. So after inquiring about TIUJ, I transferred at the beginning of my third year.

Actually, my first term at TIUJ was very difficult for me. In all my previous school experience, somebody had always told me what to study, when to study, and where to study it. But at TIUJ no one told me to do anything. Since I was not forced to study, I found I could not do anything. For a while I was lost, but slowly I began to find things that I really wanted to learn more about. With the encouragement and guidance of concerned mentors, I began to experience the inner joy of gaining new insight and finding answers to questions that had puzzled me. I began to study, not to satisfy somebody else or to gain external rewards such as credits, grades, status, or prestige, but because I had become hungry for knowledge that I didn't have. It took me a long time, but slowly I made the shift from simply being a passive learner to being self-directed. Today, I believe this has been the most important discovery of my life. It has brought me a deep-down sense of joy and excitement and hope that I did not know was possible.

My studies at TIUJ have led to many interesting and exciting learning opportunities. The most recent is a youth exploration group that I am helping organize. We call it the "Life Discovery Project" or LDP for short. The LDP's purpose is to encourage young people to become aware of the world around them and some of the realities of that world. We are especially concerned about the fact that our future is being decided by a handful of business, financial, and government bureaucrats. We want to learn deeply about our society because we want to recover our right, as ordinary citizens, to participate in the decision-making process. We want to be able to affect the decisions that impact our future. The LDP is only a small group, but we hope that we can not only grow and learn ourselves, but also encourage and assist other young people to learn as well.

## Notes

1. The contents of this chapter are based on my experience as a TIUJ student and staff member and on interviews with Dayle and Miyoko Bethel, co-founders of TIUJ, with excerpts from articles and books written by Dr. Bethel in the fields of education and institutional transformation.

2. This observation about the effectiveness of student learning in Japanese schools was contained in Makiguchi's first major work, *Jinsei Chirigaku*, *(A Geography of Human Life)*. Seikyo Shimbunsha, Tokyo, Vol. 1, 39, first published in 1903. The passage is from a not-yet published English translation of the work by a team of translators working under Bethel's direction.

3. Dayle Bethel (ed.), *Education for Creative Living*. Ames, IA: Iowa State University Press, 1989, pp. 21, 168.

4. *Ibid.*, 156.

5. Jeremy Rifkin, *Entropy: A New World View*. New York: Bantam Books, 1981, p. 229.

6. George Barnett and Jack Otis, *Corporate Society and Education*. Ann Arbor: University of Michigan Press, 1961, pp. 259-260.

7. *Ibid.*

8. The extent to which universities have come under corporate control can be seen in the Bayh-Dole and related amendments in the late 1970s and early 1980s. Even Admiral Hyman Rickover, who set up the nuclear navy, called it the biggest give-away in American history. See "An Interview with David Noble," *Wild Duck Review*, Vol. IV, No. 2, 1998, 8. See also "What Corporate Welfare Costs You" in *Time* Magazine, issues for November 9, 16, and 23, 1998.

9. The influence of this community-based, future-oriented vision of education and society is today helping to challenge traditional, factory-style education in Vietnam, Italy, France, Brazil, and other countries, as a result of the translation into various languages of articles and books written and edited by TIUJ's staff and students.

## About the Author

*Motoshi Suzuki is a graduate student pursuing studies in holistic education and futures studies at The International University's Asia-Pacific Center in Kyoto, Japan.*

# Supported Open Learning and the Emergence of Learning Communities

## The Case of the Open University UK

*by Ray Ison* [1]

I HAVE HAD a longstanding interest in the social technologies that give rise to the universities we experience today, being particularly concerned with how differing conceptions of the university make possible effective learning. Over eighteen years I have had experience of three contrasting pedagogical models in university settings—a radical, student-centered approach to agricultural education theoretically based on experiential learning and systems thinking, a traditional Oxbridge-modeled faculty, highly didactic in style, and now, at the Open University (OU) UK, supported open learning. This paper is written to give you a sense of how the OU has contributed to a "national learning community," and how it, or similar models, might contribute internationally to building new learning communities. [2]

The OU has been described as the greatest innovation in UK higher education in the 20th century. [3] It has pioneered two significant new developments—open entry (entry with no prior academic qualification) and supported open learning (provision of personal tutor)—and it has created a unique learning experience that combines high quality with low unit cost. Moreover, it has demonstrated that open learning is popular with adults. The OU is the UK's largest university. Over 230,000 adults will study OU courses and not-for-credit study packs in 1999, and since 1971 it has taught over two and a half million people.

The OU has also been successful in recruiting students elsewhere in Europe, and is operating with partner institutions in a number of countries. The OU has also just established the Open University of the US Inc.

And policy makers in other countries have adopted and adapted the OU model to open up higher education to many more learners in new and flexible ways. More than fifty public open universities now exist around the world. The ten biggest have two million students between them.

Four key elements are claimed to have underpinned the OU (UK)'s success in delivering an integrated system of supported open learning. These are: high-quality, multi-media teaching materials, locally-based tutorial support, first-class research and scholarship, and highly professional logistics (e.g., large-scale processing of student inquiries, assignments and exams, and graduation details).

In this chapter I shall trace the history of the OU's development through three phases: 1) linear, one-way delivery; 2) feedback systems; and 3) self-organization and autonomous design. The first two phases have been realized; the third is a possibility. These phases are contextualized in the light of emerging global forces, which are likely to constrain or enhance the emergence of novel learning communities. I argue that when designing any contemporary education program there are advantages in considering the program as if it were a learning system. To be responsible, designers also need to consider this within a context of global, sustainable development.[4]

## The Linear, One-Way Delivery Phase (1969-1996)

When the OU was established, there was considerable skepticism about its ability to provide a learning experience for its students equal in quality to that enjoyed by full-time students in conventional institutions. Correspondence tuition, as it was then perceived, had a poor reputation. From the beginning, the OU has taken as one of its top priorities the development of instructional materials of the very highest quality. The OU has developed a team-based approach to course development, combining academics and other specialists, including in some instances academics from other institutions. The process of course development is monitored by an external assessor and, once in presentation, an external examiner.

The traditional multi-skilled approach to course development has led to the production of courses that use a wide range of media, with elements combined in various ways to achieve different learning objectives. At the heart of most courses is a series of specially produced textbooks or "course units" (which are also widely used in the rest of the higher education sector). They are closely integrated with a varying mix of set books, recommended reading, radio and television programs, audio and videotapes, home experiment kits, computer-based learning programs, and multimedia resources.

Students are allocated a tutor, called an associate lecturer (AL), who is responsible for supporting the student's learning as well as undertaking all of the continuous assessment marking. Contact between an AL and a student involves on-line (which is increasing), limited face-to-face, and telephone contact. Residential schools held at various places over a weekend or a week are also an integral part of many OU courses.

Research and scholarship are important in fulfilling the academic and educational objectives of the OU. Course materials must be authoritative, up to date, and written by authors who are fully conversant with the latest developments in the field. Because they are in the public domain in a way that other higher education teachers are not, they must be able to withstand rigorous external scrutiny. In addition, teaching strategies and educational technologies must be of proven effectiveness and appropriate for large-scale open learning. The environment and reputation of the OU must be such that it can attract staff and consultants of the very highest caliber.

The OU's administrative and operational processes provide the underpinning essential to ensure the quality and effectiveness of its materials and student support. Wherever students live, the courses they take have the same high-quality content and are taught to the same high standards. There is a sensitive balance between what is done in the OU's central headquarters at Milton Keynes and what is done regionally and locally.

Roughly three-quarters of the OU's 850 academic staff, most of its 900 administrative staff, and 1,500 clerical staff work at Milton Keynes. They plan, prepare, produce, and distribute the course materials using mass production and delivery systems. Some services (such as editing and design) are provided in-house; others (notably printing and publishing) are contracted out. The OU has a long-standing partnership with the BBC for the production and transmission of broadcast programs.

The rest of the OU staff is located in thirteen regional centers, three of which cover nation-regions (i.e., Scotland, Wales, and Northern Ireland). Regional centers deal with all matters that concern the way in which courses are presented to students. Academic staff in Regional Centers select, brief, train, and monitor tutorial and counseling staff, arrange tutorial timetables, deal with student inquiries and admissions, handle complaints and appeals, and attend to personal difficulties and special circumstances. A special cadre of staff called "staff tutors," each belonging to an academic faculty but regionally based, with the support of administrative staff allocate students to ALs, secure suitable study center sites and examination centers, and organize residential schools and graduation ceremonies within their regions. The whole operation is supported by data handling systems of enormous size and complexity.

The nature of students' learning at the OU is qualitatively different from that at other universities. Laurillard[5] discusses research that identifies five distinct ways in which university students describe what they mean by "learning." This research was replicated at many universities with the same result, except at the OU. Open University students see learning as a way of "changing as a person"—something that students at other universities did not identify. Open University students recognized that when you understand more about why things happen it changes the way you think about the world.

As a "learning system," responsibility for OU course and program development and its associated assessment has been centrally designed and delivered to students. This is what I mean by a linear, one-way delivery system. This does not mean that the learning materials are not designed to be student centered—they are. There are also organized surveys of student experience which feed back into design, albeit with lags and attenuation of the feedback process. However, as noted by Morris and Naughton,[6] while the printed learning resources use self-assessment questions and other structural devices to encourage active engagement of students with the material, the general nature of print and broadcast media have tended to reinforce the "information acquisition" model[7] that students often bring to their learning.

The OU, through its student's association and other alumni groups, has also triggered a substantial number of self-organizing learning communities that range from special interest groups to professional societies. I know of no detailed study of these "emergent" learning communities, but suspect their role in community-wide learning to have been more significant than is generally appreciated.

## The Two-Way Feedback Phase (1989 - ?)

The "digital revolution," with the advent of various forms of computer-mediated communication (CMC), has begun to offer new ways of providing and facilitating learning.[8] Some claim that "the Internet could destroy college as we know it—or, just possibly, save it."[9] From 1989, the OU has been making use of CMC to provide an additional channel of interaction with students. Morris and Naughton[10] discuss this phase in a case study based on their own experience of one of the first large-scale uses of CMC within the OU.

The case study is based on the OU technology foundation course, "Living with Technology" (OU code T102), with which Morris and Naughton were closely associated. The course represents about 480 hours of study time, and has had an annual registration of between 3,500 and 4,500 students. It is usually the first course taken by those intending to carry on to study subjects under the broad umbrella of "technology," including a substantial proportion interested specifically in computing and information technology.

From 1996 the course, using the FirstClass® conferencing software (SoftArc, Inc.) offered:

• E-mail, providing one-to-one and one-to-few text-based communication, including student-student, student-tutor, student-course team

• Conferencing, with asynchronous (i.e., separated in time) one-to-many communication, like tutor groups, discussions, seminars, chat, etc.

• Internet, one-to-online-resources

There were usually about 200 postings, from 100 active contributors out of the total population of over 3,000 on-line during any month. From their evaluation of this innovation, Morris and Naughton concluded that the "active engagement with the course material and with the course team was clearly a minority activity within the computer-mediated interaction" and "that the main use of the medium was to reinforce informal student-student interaction." The extent to which access to the new CMC facilitated the emergence of new learning communities among students is unknown, but worthy of appreciation given the growing collective experience of the Internet. Another outcome of this innovation was to recommend to the OU that electronic course conferences should not be optional, but fully integrated into the pedagogy of the course and thus compulsory (if relevant to meeting desired learning outcomes).

Naughton[10] has gone on to co-develop the OU's first high-population, totally web-based delivery course. The course, "You, Your Computer and the Net" (OU code T171), constitutes 30 points of study and was offered in a large-scale pilot to 790 students in 1999. In 2000 the student numbers have been pegged at 13,000 students on up to three presentation cycles per annum, mainly because of the lack of tutors to sustain the OU's supported open learning commitment beyond this number.

While the potential exists to break out of the linear model of course delivery via these new media, it is fair to say that this potential has yet to be realized at scale and via purposeful design. In the case of the new T171 course, this was quite deliberate. The course team decided early that Level 1 students (usually in their first year of OU study), new to the medium and new to study, couldn't be thrust into a highly hyper-linked environment and expected to develop sophisticated learning strategies.[11] In this course students are guided very explicitly as to what they should do over any two-week period (via e-mailed study guides) and the web site is essentially linear.

However, the assessment strategy in T171 does enable students to move beyond a purely linear model. Modules at the end of course are all assessed on web-based work, and it is clear that many students have gone far beyond the HTML (web authoring language) they are taught. For example, they produce very sophisticated web sites, accessing many resources of their own choosing in the process. In this sense the students are constructing their own learning experiences, with the course providing the meaningful context in which they can do so.

Innovations such as that for T102 and T171 are breaking down the one-way model. In doing so they challenge what it is to be an academic, and what a "course" might be. The structures and processes of the organization are challenged as these new technologies take hold, and as yet, their emergent outcomes are unclear. What seems important, to me, is to hold open two notions: 1) that learning emerges through participation in a network of conversation[12] or communities of practice,[13] and 2) that design for emergence and self-organization will become a central feature of *new* "academic practice."

Enacting these notions has the potential to enhance community-based participation and learning. But enacting them will be a struggle. As Weil[14] observes, "Disciplinary communities maintain their dynamic conservatism in the ways they patrol 'known' and familiar boundaries, through what can become self-reinforcing processes of knowledge generation and control. These involve writing and refereeing, external examining, and the formation of academic and disciplinary groupings that guard against dilution and interlopers." A central question is whether technology, possibly in the hands of others outside the traditional academy, will subvert attempts to maintain "the stable state" referred to by Schön.[15]

## Learning Systems as Self-Organizing

Self-organization can be observed when interactions between processes constantly evolve. When applied to human activity, other features of self-organization require attention—these include fostering enthusiasm and being aware of when consensus can be debilitating for action.[16] Self-organization can also be considered as the acquisition of variety by a "system" or the progressive emergence of novelty. An important notion in the concept of self-organization is that system and environment co-evolve, it is not a case of a system "adapting to" its environment.

Recent activities mediated via the Internet would seem to suggest that self-organizing, emergent learning systems will develop spontaneously. An interesting case in point is the development of the Linux software platform as part of the "open source movement."[17] The model of software development employed by Microsoft (and many other firms) has been described as the old "closed shop" model of commercial software producers. This is contrasted with the experience of altruistic programmers, working together across the Net on freely distributed code that's open for everyone's perusal and tinkering and that is regarded by some as more powerful and reliable software than Microsoft's. These altruistic programmers could also be regarded as enthusiasts. My own research, in other contexts, has been concerned with the fostering of enthusiasm for collaborative action.

A challenge facing the OU in the new millennium is to extend its commitment to openness through the design of enabling structures and processes for the emergence of novel learning systems in the context of sustainable development.

## Conclusions

I have identified two phases that the OU (UK) can be seen to have traversed since its inception in 1969. It is currently grappling with the implications of the second, a move away from an essentially linear delivery strategy, made possible by the "digital revolution." But at the same time it is being challenged by even more radical possibilities. The

OU has made a major contribution to life-long learning in the UK and beyond, and will continue to do so for some time. It has become in many ways a national icon. This is both problem and opportunity. The OU must avoid the reification associated with icons and to conserve that which has made it a learning system capable of changing people's lives for the better.

## Notes

1. The views expressed here are those of the author and do not necessarily represent the views of the institution.

2. While vitally important to any paper on this subject, I am leaving unproblematized what is meant by learning and what a learning community might be taken to be.

3. I have drawn on material from Open University (1998). *The Learning Age: a Renaissance for a New Britain: an Open University Response*. http://www.open.ac.uk/news.html; and Open University (1998) *OU Worldwide*. http://www.open.ac.uk/ouw/ for text relating to specific features of the OU as it is today.

4. R. L. Ison, "Supported Open Learning for Rural Development: Some Experiences from the Open University, UK," Proc. Seminar on "The Role of Distance Education and Open Learning for Rural Development in the Greater Mekong Sub-Region and South East Asia," 1998, Sukhothai Thammathirat Open University & UNESCO, Thailand.

5. D. Laurillard, Degree Ceremony Address by Pro-Vice Chancellor (TD), Preston, May 1996.

6. R. M. Morris and J. Naughton, "The Future's Digital, Isn't It? Some Experience and Forecasts Based on the Open University's Technology Foundation Course," *Systems Research and Behavioural Science*, 1999, p. 16.

7. M. S. Thorpe, Models of the Learning Process: Block 3 Document book T293 Communicating Technology. Open University, Milton Keynes, 1997.

8. R. D. Mason and A. Kaye, *Mindweave: Communication, Computers and Distance Education*. Pergamon Press, 1989.

9. Edmundson, *Crashing the Academy*. 1998.

10. John Naughton, "Cultural Responses to the Internet," *The Internet and the Global Political Economy*. University of Washington, Seattle, September 1999, pp. 22-24.

11. Martin Weller, personal communication, 1999.

12. D. Laurillard, *Rethinking University Teaching: A Framework for the Effective Use of Educational Technology*. Routledge: London, 1993.

13. J. Lave and E. Wenger, *Situated Learning. Legitimate Peripheral Participation*. Cambridge University Press: Cambridge, 1991; E. Wenger, *Communities of Practice. Learning, Meaning and Identity*. Cambridge University Press: Cambridge, 1998.

14. S. Weil, "Re-Creating Universities for 'Beyond the Stable State': From 'Dearingesque' Systematic Control to Post-Dearing Systemic Learning and Inquiry," *Systems Research and Behavioural Science*, 1999, p. 16.

15. D. Schön, *Beyond the Stable State*, Temple Smith: London, 1971; D. Schön, *The Reflective Practitioner. How Professionals Think in Action*. New York: Basic Books, 1983.

16. D. B. Russell and R. L. Ison, "Enthusiasm: Developing Critical Action for Second-Order R&D," in R. L. Ison and D. B. Russell (ed.s), *Agricultural Extension and Rural Development: Breaking out of Traditions*. Cambridge University Press: Cambridge, UK, 2000, pp. 136-160.

17. J. Naughton, 1998, London, *The Observer*. Accessible on the Internet at http://molly.open.ac.uk/personal-pages/pubs/981108.htm

## About the Author

*Ray Ison is professor of systems and director of the Environmental Decision Making Program in the Centre for Complexity and Change at the Open University. His research interests include the design of learning systems for sustainable development. He has just finished writing with his colleagues a new OU course entitled "Managing Complexity: A Systems Approach." Details are available at URL: http://www.tec.open.ac.uk/ccc/rayison/home.htm*

*Part Two*

# BEYOND SCHOOLING: LEARNING IN THE COMMUNITY

# When the School Doors Close

## A Midsummer Night's Dream

*by Linda Dobson*

SOCIETY FACES a controversy over the comparative merits of public schools and school choice. But this controversy is diverting important energy, time, and money of parents, educators, politicians, reporters, and policy makers from the real issue. The real issue is the difference between an educational free market and the monopoly system that currently exists.

To be truly realistic, we can't really compare educational choice to educational monopoly. The monopoly approach has had a long time in the spotlight. The monopoly approach has been subjected to a long train of adaptations that, judging by the results measured in myriad ways, are not working. But choice—true choice—is still a largely untried dream. True choice would provide us with a fresh start, one teeming with adaptive potential. So I think we have to start by expanding our thinking beyond the prevailing monopoly model that has shaped most of our ideas about education. We can really let our imaginations soar if we allow our thinking to move beyond the monopoly model toward a free-market model.

As a homeschooling mom, I've been fortunate to grow into the freedom and self-responsibility of true educational choice at a pace comfortable for me, but this wouldn't be the case if the doors suddenly closed on the forty-six million children whose parents are used to putting them on a bus in the morning. Parents who have been used to all-day childcare facilities would panic. I can picture neighborhood grandmas and grandpas pressed into service, and other grandmas and grandpas scurrying onto airplanes for an extended visit with the grandkids. Meanwhile, communities would have to respond with many and varied alternatives quickly and efficiently (the recruited grandparents would demand it). Mrs. Jones decides she would love to teach creative writing to about half a dozen neighborhood kids a couple of mornings each week. Mr. Barry would welcome the chance to share his eyewitness accounts of World War II. Mr. Madden sees an opportunity to supplement his Social Security check, so he dusts off his accounting books, brushes up a bit, and places a classified ad in the local newspaper. (Hey, what do you know? A few adults are interested, too. No problem—Mr. Madden will hold a class at night.)

Still other individuals recognize a business opportunity when they see one. A group of now unemployed teachers rents that empty storefront right downtown (how convenient!), and offers up the classic curriculum they would have loved to teach in government schools if only they had been able to decide what they could teach—well, now they can. Another entrepreneur, whose large factory building has been sitting empty since the door company left eleven years ago, decides to invest and hires local contractors to bring the building up to code, partition off rooms on two floors, smooth the third-story floor to a glassy finish, and sound-proof a large portion of the basement for a music studio soon to be the envy of the neighborhood. This entrepreneur doesn't want to get involved in administering his new learning center, so rather than creating a "school" based on the monopoly model, he instead recoups his investment by renting the rooms and studios to those who would like to offer learning opportunities there. He needs only to hire one full-time secretary to keep ads running, answer correspondence and the phone, and keep track of the master schedule.

Mr. Madden's accounting class has become so popular he rents a room at the learning center for two afternoons and two evenings each week. His class meets right next door to the senior citizen club's daily arts-and-crafts offerings, where children young and old gather to learn everything from how to make jam to quilting to basket-making. Across the hall from Mr. Madden is the classroom for the gardening group, but they spend most of their time outside getting hands-on experience in the ever-expanding garden they've created right behind the ex-factory. The carpentry class is building a potting shed, and the folks learning about solar energy will soon start work on a state-of-the-art greenhouse. If you look around your neighborhood, and think about the past and present learning your neighbors have under their belts, you'll realize that the possibilities here are endless.

Now we've got citizens scurrying all around town each day. Instead of allowing all those school busses to rot in the garage, a few local taxi companies decide to buy some of them. They hire drivers to drive back and forth through town all day long, shuttling learners to their locations of choice. Any learner who needs one, no matter what age, can purchase a reasonably priced monthly pass for the shuttle service. Meanwhile, the Chamber of Commerce hasn't been idle (members have kids who need learning opportunities, too). The Chamber calls an emergency meeting of all the local business owners and they debate and discuss how they can help. Some members bemoan this catastrophe and express fears about gangs of kids with nothing to do hanging around in front of their stores, scaring away customers. But other members realize that crisis, viewed with the proper perspective, creates opportunity, and they issue compelling arguments to establish a community-wide apprenticeship database. After all, some of the businesses are already hurting because a sizable number of employees, both male and female, have either quit or drastically cut back their hours to homeschool their children. Apprenticeships would not only help educate the children, they would provide useful, interesting things for the "hang arounds" to do. The Chamber of Commerce puts the database on the Internet, so it's accessible to families at home, and it convinces the local paper to start a new classified heading in the newspaper so all the townspeople can learn about new opportunities as soon as they open up. The Historical Society and the Nature Center just keep doing what they've always done. The only difference now is that more people start taking advantage of their offerings, and they have to put out a call for more volunteers to help. The requests are added to the Chamber of Commerce's database of apprenticeships.

Then there are all of our libraries, ready-made learning centers that would grow and prosper under the "no government school" educational model. People already come and go at will, whenever they find it necessary, all day long. They use computers to access information; they sit and read for a spell; they have meetings or classes or guest speakers; they pick up a videotape to watch that evening; they participate in or patronize art shows and craft sales, exhibits, and instruction. Libraries provide a guide to a new educational model because they just may be the last bastions of free inquiry we have left.

And what about all those new homeschoolers? Established local support groups are having weekly meetings to meet the demand (they rented a room one night a week at the learning center for this purpose), printing up recommended reading and resource lists, and generally knocking themselves out answering questions about phonics vs. whole language, Saxon math drills vs. new-new math, and how to turn your kitchen into a science laboratory. The questions are flying because these new homeschooling parents are getting an education themselves. Even though a child was getting As in school, Mom is appalled that her son's reading skills are at least a couple of grade levels behind what they should be. Dad, who graciously volunteered to take on the duty of teaching algebra to his high-school daughter at night, discovers that she doesn't have a firm grasp of the fundamentals necessary to approach the topic of algebra. He'll have to backtrack, and he realizes this is going to take more time than he originally thought.

Now that they're under pressure, more parents than ever before are realizing they already own one of the most powerful learning tools in existence—a personal computer sitting right there in the corner of the living room. I haven't tried it myself (I love books too much!), but I'm willing to bet that a family with a computer and Internet access could begin to homeschool for the cost of nothing more than the fee of an Internet server. Do an Internet search today, and you'll find everything from the text of the Constitution to a tour of the Louvre to NASA's home page to science experiments to a homeschool approach to obtain Scout badges to on-line writing courses to connection to a complete, ready-made curriculum. After a few months or a year of approaching education this way, families will begin to realize that lots of other "non-schooly" stuff on the Internet is just as educational as the classes offered in the neighborhood.

There are Usenet groups, e-mail groups, and chat pages devoted to every topic imaginable. When my son was having trouble creating his home page, he simply found a chat room where such things were discussed. He put his questions out into the electronic ether and knowledgeable folks gave him the tips he needed—within minutes. Does your son like to play chess more frequently than you can handle? There's a site where he can instantly find a challenger while the program keeps track of his win/loss record and ranks him along with the other players, too. Does your daughter want to discuss early American history with folks who share her passion? They're out there, discussing it every day.

To realize this dream, we need to examine and take better control of

the funds that support the status quo. What I'm trying to say is that before we put umpteen billions of tax payers' dollars into repairing the crumbling brick edifices known as schools believing that, as we've been told, this will somehow help "education," let's consider an important fact: Today—right now—*school buildings are obsolete!*

Our national education budget already contains, from all sources, an estimated $1 billion a day. Using this estimate, we can divvy that up between 365,000 learning centers operating on a $1 million per year budget. That works out to about one learning center for every 685 American men, women, and children. This may sound like chump change compared to the monopoly model budgets, but $1 million goes a long way where administration stays minimal, volunteers contribute, and materials are shared *a la* the interlibrary loan systems.

A cozier atmosphere could be created if we set our sights on 730,000 centers spending $0.5 million each year. With a more definitive community aura at this level, local businesses would find it in their best interest to donate human and financial resources, and offer apprenticeships to area residents. As things stand now, according to a 1990 survey of 200 major U.S. corporations, 22% teach reading, 41% teach writing, and 31% teach computation to their employees. An equivalent financial contribution to the neighborhood learning center wouldn't cost an additional dime, and would create an honest-to-goodness, win-win situation for all involved.

Now that we have an idea of what an educational free market can look like and accomplish, let's return to the change in thinking required to make it happen. It helps a lot to think about the true meaning of three little words—"free public education." Instead of viewing "education" as something we do to and/or for our youth, always with an eye on the nation's economic future instead of on the children's educational present, we can return to its original meaning, "to bring out that which is within." When this definition guides our thinking—if we begin from this starting point instead of the "pour knowledge into the kids, let them regurgitate it" starting point—our educational methods will truly change. We can't control that which is within individuals; we can only nurture it.

On to the term "free." Only one change necessary here; take the compulsion out of school attendance; "free" the kids. How can our children possibly find independence and decision-making comfortable or worthwhile if, from the age of five (and many times, younger), they are herded by legal and cultural force to endure conditions that, at least at the younger ages, go against their very natures, abilities, and capacities? If we start from the idea of "freedom to learn" instead of "compulsory attendance," those learners who guide their own journeys and choose the means by which they travel will recognize their vested interest in the outcome.

Last, we look at the word "public," which carries with it our current notion of public school as America's great equalizer, the opportunity for all to have a crack at the American Dream, usually expressed in increased ability to purchase things. The *American Heritage Dictionary of the English Language*, though, gives five definitions for public, all of which hold potential for a broader perspective on the term, and lead us to a different use of our one billion dollars per day:

- Of, concerning, or affecting the community or the people
- Maintained for or used by the people or community
- Participated in or attended by the people or community
- Connected with or acting on behalf of the people, community, or government, rather than private matters or interests
- Open to the knowledge or judgment of all

Why are "public" schools forced on everyone ages five to eighteen and denied to everyone else? If we truly understand the importance of education, if we truly want an educated populace, if we truly want children (and adults) to appreciate the joys and benefits of education, what we now call public schools should in fact be community learning centers, open to everyone who wants to partake of knowledge—or share it. And what a great way to get around the drive toward school-to-work, where your children are educated, not as the unique individuals they are, but to be compliant, faithful employees trained for narrow job descriptions, instead of for a lifetime of clear thinking. The current move toward creating huge databases filled with myriad pieces of information on your children—from their scores on school-administered "belief surveys" to attendance, grades, health, and juvenile justice records—would be thwarted with the free market approach, too. In fact, this may be "the people's" last effective way to protect the vestiges of a disappearing right to freedom and privacy that remain.

Believe it or not, families don't need schools or government to act as intermediary between parents and children. "We, the people," can take care of our own educational needs. All it takes is the willingness to expand our thinking, the knowledge that we can capably assume the responsibility we now unthinkingly turn over to others, and the will to make a dream of something better come true.

## About the Author

*Linda Dobson, homeschooling parent since 1985, is a nationally respected conference speaker and book and article author who has been* Home Education Magazine's *news editor and columnist since 1992. She coordinates the New York Home Educator's Network, is northeast regional contact for the National Home Education Network, local library board of trustees vice-president, and early years advisor for www.homeschool.com*

# Homeschool Support Groups and Resource Centers

*by Jerry Mintz*

MOST HOMESCHOOLERS eventually get involved with homeschool support groups. These groups often meet anywhere from once a month to once a week in informal get-togethers that give the parents support and give the kids a chance to meet other homeschoolers. But as the concentration of homeschoolers has grown in various areas, a new form of support program has emerged. In my travels around the country as director of a nonprofit that supports educational alternatives, including homeschooling, I've seen an interesting, new phenomenon developing as the homeschool movement grows—the homeschool resource center.

When I visited France in 1988, I saw what could be the forerunner of organized homeschool resource centers, the *Collectif Enfants-Parents* in a suburb of Paris. Their group met every day at a different house, and two parents at a time were always supervising and teaching—they only had to work for half a day each week, which enabled even working parents to participate. Every two weeks the group got together to make schedules for the next two weeks. One parent made lunch for the group each day at the house where they were meeting. They had been doing this for fifteen years, with great success. Day-to-day decisions and problems were dealt with in democratic meetings, and the students were quite skilled at this process. Their democratic and non-coercive approach reminded me of some effective alternative schools I had known in the United States. I asked one of the students what he liked about the school and he said what he liked best was that "it is not a school."

There is some danger that, in organizing homeschool resource groups, homeschoolers may re-create "schooling" and lose some of the learner-centered approach that they have been practicing as individual home-schooling families. On the other hand, isolated homeschool families and homeschool support groups that meet only occasionally, every week or two or less, may benefit by empowering the students in a group decision-making process. Some groups miss this opportunity by only having informal social meetings and decision-making by the adults.

In Providence, Rhode Island, Maria Sperduti organized the Educational Resource Center of Rhode Island (ERCRI). It served more than 30 homeschool families from a wide area. Various individuals offered classes, for which parents and students signed up. The center was generally open three and a half days a week, and gave homeschooled children a chance to get together and interact with each other and to choose from several classes that were offered by parents and other adults from the community. The group realized that there probably hadn't been enough input from students concerning what things they wanted to learn at the center. The emphasis had been upon what things the adults involved wanted to teach. True, the students and parents had a choice of classes, but the curriculum had not grown out of the students' interests. In addition, day-to-day decisions at the center did not have enough student input, and a mechanism for their involvement had not been created. So the people at the ERCRI decided to work on those problems, and make some changes in their approach.

To demonstrate a way in which curriculum could be developed for the center based on student interest, I showed them how to do something that I call "organic curriculum." As a tool for this, I did a "question class" for one of the younger groups. In just a few minutes, they came up with questions about all sorts of topics that interested them, which wound up constituting as broad a curriculum as an adult could have created for them—but in this case, they had created it for themselves. We then went back over the questions and determined the ones for which there was the most interest, and began discussing those questions. Obviously there was great involvement in those discussions, because the motivation for them had come directly from the students. Some of the questions concerned the war in Kuwait, which was just getting under way, but they also involved a broad range of other areas of interest. This center eventually evolved into Wellspring, a democratically-run community school.

In Lexington, Virginia, a group of people centered around Common Ground Community set up a homeschool resource center called Snakefoot. They met three days a week at the Common Ground Community, although most of the students come from the surrounding area. The home-school parents hired a resource person to work with their children, in addition to the parents. The students, who previously homeschooled without much regular contact with other students, all agreed that they enjoyed this new process very much. But, again, the group has discovered that they had to be careful not to have the group be too adult-dominated in its structure, and has moved toward more student involvement in decision-making processes. Snakefoot is breaking important ground in organizing homeschoolers.

Some independent schools that are set up primarily for homeschoolers include Mistwood in Eureka, California, Headwaters in Petigrew, Arkansas, and Clearwater School and Puget Sound Community School in Seattle, Washington.

Puget Sound Community School (PSCS) provides an example of an innovative approach in creating a homeschool resource center. Founded primarily for junior high-school through high-school students, it operates three days a week, meeting each time in a different, donated space around the city of Seattle. It has a democratic decision-making process that was originally inspired by Sudbury Valley School. On the fourth day the students participate in an internship program.

The director and founder is Andy Smallman and there are several other paid and volunteer staff members. Students may choose any classes they are interested in attending. PSCS does not have to worry about meeting any particular Washington State standards because it is technically not a school, although it has "school" in its title. But it is considered to be supplementary to the parents' home education. PSCS has made extensive use of the Internet throughout its history, and some of its students have become adept at its use. One of them was the webmaster for three years of our non-profit, the Alternative Education Resource Organization (AERO), starting when he was 14.

In Amherst, Massachusetts, the Pathfinder Learning Center has broken new ground in that state. It is set up as a homeschool resource center and is open five days a week for students whose families sign up for its programs on a yearly basis. They have about sixty students, two full-time staff members, and other volunteers.

There are scheduled classes and also the opportunity to just drop in and spend time at the center, visiting other students and staff members, using the computers and other equipment, etc. Although all of the students are homeschoolers, when the number of students at the center passed the thirty-student mark, parents of potential students began to contact Pathfinder and ask if their children could be enrolled in the "school." Pathfinder carefully pointed out that it was not a school, and was only for homeschooling families. The parents would then ask to be shown how to become homeschooling parents. Now the large majority of parents at Pathfinder were taught how to become homeschoolers by Pathfinder, a new phenomenon.

A homeschool resource center that started several years ago in Pensacola, Florida, demonstrates an important forerunner to another phenomenon around the country. This center started out as one of the thousands of tutoring centers, working after school and in the evenings with students who were having school problems. But the many homeschoolers in the area asked them to set up a program during the day for homeschoolers. Then they began to get students coming in who had been having serious school problems, but whose parents didn't know about homeschooling. Because it was not a school, like Pathfinder, the center then helped parents become homeschoolers, after which the students would return to public school or continue as independent homeschoolers, gradually being weaned away from the center, but using it as a resource. This new application of homeschooling could tremendously broaden its use for students whose needs are not met by the public school system.

One advantage of their approach was individualized attention, and smaller groups, but this kind of center will need to move away from curriculum based too much on the traditional approach.

I have seen some learner-centered alternative schools that are quite true to the unschooling ideas as described by pioneering education writer John Holt, although they are not called homeschool centers. One of these alternative schools is Grassroots Free School in Tallahassee, Florida. At Grassroots, all decisions are made by a "pow wow." There is no required class attendance, and much of what one sees around the school involves students getting together and organizing their own classes and activities. The students' relationship with the adults around the school is extremely positive, since there is no reason for the kids to fear the adults as they often do in traditional schools, and there is high motivation in any class because everyone in attendance wants to be there. The school is known for putting on excellent plays for the surrounding community.

Recently, a number of the older students left Grassroots to attend the public alternative high school called SAIL, in Tallahassee. Although they had virtually no experience in the public school system, and in some cases scored low on the initial achievement tests because they had never used a public school curriculum, within six weeks all of the students from

Grassroots were on the honor roll (except for one, who missed it by one point). One student I had known for a couple of years, through traveling to alternative school conferences, had hardly ever attended classes at Grassroots. Instead, he had worked on his own projects, like creating his own fantasy games. He is now a straight-A student at SAIL. This is not to say that alternative school or homeschool success should be measured by ultimate success in public school, but rather that these students are open to whatever learning they may need in life, and are therefore able to be successful wherever they go.

Pat Seery, the director of Grassroots, never had any doubts that students would do well. When the initial, low achievement test scores were reported to him by the director of SAIL, he said, "Good! These kids are going to make you look like a genius in a few weeks!" and he was right.

We did a consultation for a group of people in upstate New York in a town called Horseheads. They had also been running a diagnostic and tutorial program called the Achievement Center, which had been there for twenty years. They have developed wonderful and innovative techniques for students with various learning disabilities, and for others who simply want to excel academically. The parents of some of the students began to ask, almost demand, that the center become full-time.

That's when the owner and director, Laura Satterly-Austin, called upon AERO. We did two consultations with them, the first with Laura and her staff, the second with a group of parents and potential students. It seemed to us that establishing a homeschool resource center in conjunction with the tutorial programs would be the best way to go. The parents and students greeted these concepts with great enthusiasm. One parent said, "Originally I was thinking of this just for my child with learning problems. But I don't want my other children to miss out on this program!"

As a result, the homeschool resource center opened in September, 1999. The center helped parents write their Individual Home Instruction Program forms to their local school districts, to become homeschoolers. Using the same teachers they had been using in tutorial work, the center established groups in mixed grade levels. They take at least one field trip a month. "Students brainstormed and came up with our center rules and consequences. We voted on them and posted them," Laura said.

The feedback has been very positive, Laura says. "The children say they never want to go back to regular school. Reports from the parents are extremely favorable. We hear such comments as 'The other night we caught them reading,' and 'They are so relaxed and happy now, our whole family life in the evening has changed for the better!' "

The potential for this approach is amazing when you consider the thousands of tutorial centers that exist in practically every community throughout the country. For the most part they are not being used during the school day.

Some communities have been developed in which the educational program is an integral aspect. One such community in Texas evolved from being a private alternative school, and technically, it is still one. There are about fifty people in the community, and about twenty-five are children. All of the adults in the community are seen as resources for the students, and students make individual appointments with them to learn what they are interested in. But none of that is required, and the whole community is kind of a living, breathing school. The interaction between the adults and the students in that community is better than in any other place I've seen. There is virtually none of the fear of adults that you might see in other situations, with adults taking subtle or not-so-subtle control. In this community it isn't even necessary for the students to live with their own families, and in some cases they live with other families or have made their own structures to live in. They can even do their own cooking if they want to.

There are not clear lines and divisions between homeschooling, alternative schools, and homeschool resource centers. Alternative educations are not easily defined. In fact, South Street Centre near Santa Cruz, California, is a homeschool resource center that is part of a charter school in the public school system.

Some of the centers mentioned earlier in this essay are now not in operation or have changed form. But it is important to understand that it is not necessary to create an institution in order to create a center such as these we have described. Founders should not feel that they need to have the resources to create an institution. The most important thing is to create a form of education that meets the students' needs here and now.

The idea of the homeschool resource center will continue to grow as the population of homeschoolers grows. Since it is now at a beginning point, it is important to encourage these developing centers to incorporate the learner-centered approach and empowerment of the learner, which are so successful on an individual family basis and in alternative schools.

Leslie Hart, one of the foremost experts on brain research and its application to education, points out in his books that the brain is naturally aggressive, that it doesn't have to be taught to learn. Students don't have to be externally "motivated." Also, when students are forced to learn things that they are not interested in, this tends to extinguish that natural aggressiveness and desire for learning. Our most important job is to create a rich and resourceful educational environment, and then stay out of the way when we're not needed. So alternative schools and homeschoolers, particularly the "unschoolers" (who base their curriculum on the interest of the student), have been intuitively doing the right thing.

Structure and freedom are not mutually exclusive. The structure of these new homeschool resource centers must be one that has within it the ability to encourage the empowerment, confidence, and freedom of its learners.

# The Alternative Learning Center

## A Dream Come True

*by Katharine Houk*

*Imagine This!*

YOU ARE A PARENT in a rural area who, for a variety of reasons, has been considering homeschooling, but you are concerned about isolation and socialization for your children. You also have concerns about helping your children learn about subjects with which you are not familiar, or which would be better learned in groups—such as foreign languages or laboratory science. In looking for a local homeschooling support group, you discover that in your area homeschooling families get together twice a week at a learning center in a community building. Parents and children lead classes and workshops on a wide variety of topics. People from the community come in to teach, and field trips and opportunities in the community are also part of what the group offers. You decide to drop by to see what it is like.

On the day you arrive, outside in the sunshine on the wide steps of the building, five or six parents are discussing state testing requirements for homeschoolers while their children are busy indoors. In the lobby of the building you find more parents sitting and talking with one another while small children play nearby. These parents are planning an "astronomy night," when they will meet at one of their homes in the evening to explore the night sky with the older children. Upstairs you peek in on a French class and a class in which solar cars are being built. In the gym children are involved in cooperative games. Back in the lobby a woman shows you the bulletin board for announcements and items of interest. She also shows you the "mailboxes"—a container of file folders labeled with members' names, which people use to communicate with one another. She explains that the center is cooperatively run by parents and children. It all seems too good to be true, and you are eager to become involved.

Several things aren't obvious on your first visit: the slow and uneven process of the center's growth over the past nine years that brought it to where it is today, the ever-changing leadership, the different settings in which the center functioned and the evolving rules by which it was run over the years, the dedication, communication, and work it takes to keep it running well, and the growing pains the center is experiencing as more and more families are becoming involved.

## How It All Began

At the end of the year in 1990 I received a phone call from a woman who was looking for an educational alternative for her children. She had explored our rural area's public and private schools and had considered homeschooling, but was looking for something more. Because I ran a local homeschooling support group and had contacts in alternative education, we were able to call together a group of eight people to discuss educational philosophy. We agreed that a school was at that time more than the people involved could undertake. However, a learning center had the potential to grow into a school, and in the meantime could be used by people of all ages.

We each had a different vision of what the ideal learning center would be, and we dared to "dream big" as we started small. We approached the project slowly, and with careful listening and respect for one another's ideas and visions.

We put together a survey to ascertain the number of interested families, their geographical locations, and the types of programs and services that interested them. Based on this survey, we made plans, and at the beginning of September, 1991, The Alternative Learning Center (TALC) was incorporated as a non-profit organization and opened its doors for workshops three days a week at a community building.

During the first year, twenty families used the center, and eight families became members (membership was not a requirement for participation at that time, though it is today). It was eight months from the first meeting of parents to the day the learning center opened its doors. After a year at the community center, TALC moved into the homes of two of the members because rent and insurance costs had become prohibitive. After a semester in the members' homes, TALC moved to a local church that offered a nice space for $25 a month. A few years later, because of renovations at the church, TALC is back at the original community center, which it is now able to afford, having grown to serve over seventy children.

## Structure

TALC is set up as a parent cooperative. Its purposes, as expressed in its bylaws, are: "A) To provide a place for people of all ages to share educational resources and knowledge, and to organize and coordinate activities which further such sharing, and B) To operate a program of activities for children and youth, using the resources of the community, to encourage learning in its broadest sense."

TALC's governing board is called the Council, and any member who is interested can become a Council member. This Council adopts rules and regulations by consensus (and sometimes by voting), plans what will happen at the center, and holds an annual meeting as well as other meetings throughout the year. At planning meetings the upcoming semester's schedule is worked out based on information from workshop and field-trip proposal sheets submitted by each family. There is a rotating coordinator position, as well as a secretary and a treasurer. Sometimes two people share the coordinator position, and other positions are created as needed. All positions are volunteer. As the center has grown, there has been talk of hiring a coordinator because it has become such a time-consuming job.

Over the years the ways that the parents are involved and the scheduling of classes and events have changed according to the needs of the group. At the current time, each family is responsible for one workshop, event, class, series, or field-trip each semester. The families don't necessarily have to lead the class themselves, they can instead find someone from the community or arrange for a field trip or some other educational experience. Often what is offered is based on what the children have requested, and sometimes the children themselves lead the classes. Lately I've been hearing the complaint at the center that there is simply too much to choose from! What a wonderful "problem" to have!

Some of the offerings are very structured and "class-like," others are more free-flowing and experiential. The people involved try to strike a healthy balance among philosophies of learning. One of the mothers expressed to me that although she didn't always agree with the child-rearing and educational philosophies of some of the families at the center, she was glad that her child was being exposed to many different ways of being and doing, and saw the center's diversity as a strength. Diversity can also be a source of ambiguity and tension, but this tension can expand our vision and increase our tolerance, and the ability to live with ambiguity is not a bad thing to possess.

TALC is not a "drop-off" center. Parents stay and use the time for enrichment and support. If a parent cannot stay, he or she must find an adult present who is willing to be responsible for his or her children that day. Classes and events are multi-age, and there is no grading or compulsion. The center is open two days a week during school hours and field trips are on other days of the week, though sometimes TALC has had summer sessions. One of the beauties of homeschooling is its flexibility;

families need not follow a "school" schedule. Members don't always want to see TALC's fun end in May, and summer offers new possibilities for learning because of warmer weather.

Socialization for both parents and children is an important part of the center. Deep friendships among families have developed, and people often get together for extra outings and outside classes in the community as a result of the connections they've made at the center. The place is full of the noise of happy children who have chosen which classes to attend and who look forward to seeing their friends twice (or more) a week. At the end of each semester the center hosts Display Day, when the children bring in their projects from home and from classes at the center, and the drama group and chorus perform for relatives and friends. This festive event has become a TALC tradition.

During the first year of the center's operation, one of the workshop days chosen was Saturday because we wanted non-homeschoolers to be involved. We also tried having events late in the day so people could participate after school. For whatever reason, people beyond the home-schooling community did not take advantage of the offerings. Perhaps by the end of the day or week, kids had had enough of being busy with "learning" activities and were craving time of their own. Yet as time has gone on, every so often one or another parent has been known to take his or her child out of school for a day to attend something special at TALC.

The families themselves are responsible for meeting the state's legal homeschooling requirements. The learning center does not take care of the paperwork required by the state's homeschooling regulation. TALC's activities look great on the required reports, but the writing of the reports is up to the families.

## Money Matters

The amount charged per family has varied greatly over the years, based on rent and insurance costs and the number of families involved. At first, though we encouraged people to become members, even people who were not members could use the center (they paid for workshops that were free to members). There are two semesters—September through early December and February through April or May (it varies). Currently the membership fee for each semester is $35 per family with a $16 insurance surcharge per child for the year. Classes sometimes have extra fees if they require materials or are led by people who wish to be paid. Field trips to performances and museums also sometimes require extra fees. While the learning center seems like an amazing financial bargain to those people who might be able to consider a private school for their children, there are families in this area for whom the cost (which can range from about $85 to well over $300 per year) is a very large sum. For families needing financial assistance, the center offers scholarships (called TALCerships). In exchange for a reduction in membership fees, people devote extra energy and time to the running of the center beyond the basic that is required of each family.

Funds raised through membership fees are used to pay for rent, insurance, postage and printing, and sometimes for materials. The center operates in the black and has a nest egg for emergencies, and no one, to my knowledge, has ever been turned away for financial reasons.

## The Future

TALC's mushrooming membership, diversity in educational styles, and the variety of parental expectations of the center have produced growing pains that may lead to changes in structure, the search for a larger space, additional days when it will be open, more off-site classes and experiences, or possibly some spin-off groups or new learning alternatives. TALC's greatest challenge, but also its greatest strength, is its diversity. The learning center process can be very empowering to both parents and children, and some of TALC's programs are branching out into the wider community (a community chorus, for example). TALC is one successful way that people who might otherwise be isolated have joined together to create an educational alternative that meets local needs and is flexible and ever-evolving, and it could provide inspiration for similar efforts elsewhere. More information (including the philosophies underlying the center, copies of bylaws, sample registration materials, surveys, rules, and other forms) is available in the book *Creating a Cooperative Learning Center: An Idea-Book for Homeschooling Families*. Contact Katharine Houk, 29 Kinderhook Street, Chatham, NY 12037, USA, phone: 518-392-6900.

## About the Author

*Katharine Houk is co-founder of The Alternative Learning Center, a cooperative that offers classes, workshops, field trips, and other adventures for families involved in home education. Her own children, now grown, were home educated. Katharine is director of the Alliance for Parental Involvement in Education and author of the book,* Creating a Cooperative Learning Center: An Idea-Book for Homeschooling Families. *She lives in Chatham, New York, where she is involved in educational activism, art, writing, and interfaith work.*

# Homeschool Learning Clubs
## Model Grassroots Learning Organizations

*by Ann Lahrson Fisher*

L EARNING CLUBS ARE perhaps the best-kept secret of the homeschooling world! The prevailing homeschooling myth—smiling families poring over workbooks at the kitchen table—belies the complexity of homeschooling success. The kitchen-table image represents but one slice of the homeschooling pie; learning clubs represent another.

Understanding how these pioneering learning clubs function may help others develop models for successful cooperative community learning centers. Alternative and conventional educators may be able to apply the common elements of these richly varied clubs in other learning venues. This chapter explores the workings of learning clubs. Practical tips and suggestions for launching clubs, as well as descriptions of real clubs, are included.

## Why Learning Clubs?

Consider: most newcomers to homeschooling seek out a compatible support group. Families naturally get together to explore common interests, socialize, discuss, debate, and celebrate. These casual associations can be described as homeschool learning clubs. Because families begin to connect with each other so naturally and spontaneously and without fanfare, the importance of those connections is rarely appreciated or understood. Families often do not think of themselves as belonging to a club, nor do they consider that they are doing anything special. Like good food, plenty of sleep, fresh air and exercise, learning clubs are one more thing that good parents make available to their families.

The public invisibility of learning clubs is a sign of their enormous success. Clubs are often full to capacity with little or no advertising! It should be noted, however, that invisibility is *not* a requirement. More visible clubs, such as the ones offered through community centers, Boys and Girls Clubs, Parks and Recreation Districts, or libraries, enjoy the same successes as private, family-based clubs.

It is true that not all homeschooling families participate in learning clubs. For some families, the family and general community are sufficient resources. Each family must find a balance of family, club, community, and individual learning that works for them. For many families, though, learning clubs are a natural part of the homeschooling lifestyle.

## Commonalities of Typical Learning Clubs

1. Clubs are usually sponsored by one or more families who design the club to meet the unique needs of their families.

2. The desire to create clubs often arises from the children.

3. Parent-formed clubs are common; many young people have formed successful clubs as well.

4. Leadership is voluntary and unpaid.

5. Clubs tend to develop around interactive and participatory activities.

6. Clubs usually have no dues or cost requirements beyond actual expenses.

7. Attendance is optional. Clubs that are poorly managed or that do not meet the learning needs of the members either change or die from lack of interest.

8. Clubs may form among families who are already linked together in some way—a support group, an e-mail loop, a neighborhood, a church group, or a common interest. A newly formed club is usually announced through state or local support groups, newsletters, church, library, and community-center bulletin boards, or e-mail loops.

9. Clubs may limit membership. Sometimes a maximum number of students is set, or final enrollment date may be established. A Spanish club may want a larger group to defray the cost of paying a native-speaking teacher. A group planning to study microscopic pond life may be limited by the number of microscopes. Limits are sometimes set according to the size of people's living rooms. Theme type clubs seem to work best with about eight members. Clubs such as park days, swim days, and skating days are typically open to all.

10. Successful clubs usually admit participants based on interests, not age. Membership guidelines, when given, are broad categories: all, preschool, six to ten, teens, moms, boys, girls, etc.

11. Clubs may be very casual (occasionally visit a science center or do

a craft project together) or quite formal (study traditional school subjects from a traditional curriculum on a regular schedule).

12. Even the best clubs have a limited life. Less commonly, a group may continue to function despite the coming and going of students and even the organizers.

## Types of Learning Clubs

There are surely as many types of clubs as there are imaginative club leaders. Many fall in one or more of the following categories.

• *Theme or subject clubs* are a popular type of learning club. Math, books, writing, cooking, sewing, horses, computers, horses, space, dogs, collections, foreign language, magazine subscriptions, science, history, geography, sports, board and card games, community service. Just name a topic and there is probably a club.

• *Community service clubs.* These may be local or associated with national groups such as 4-H, Boy Scouts, Girl Scouts, Campfire and Youth Volunteer Corps.

• *Social clubs.* Sometimes it is fun to get together and hang out, or have a dance, go skating, or celebrate the events of our lives. Roller skating parties, swim parties, age-group clubs, girls clubs, Moms' (or Dads') night out, birthday clubs, dance clubs, and Advent groups are a few examples. Social clubs often spawn theme and service clubs.

## Real Life Clubs

Use these successful club ideas as grist for your own idea mill:

• *Roller-skating parties, homeschool swim days,* and *park days* are classic examples of homeschooling social clubs. Many learning clubs get launched at these events. Bi-monthly roller-skating parties have been scheduled in every skating rink in my city for more than six years, and homeschool swim days are becoming popular. This type of party is generally open to all homeschoolers. Exercise, meeting new friends, sharing information, and forming new groups are all part of the ambiance. Sessions are held during the week, perhaps on Monday morning or Friday afternoon, and are popular with pool and rink managers whose facilities are idle during the school day.

• *Chow and Chekhov.* For more than six years, families have gathered one Friday evening a month in one another's homes for a potluck meal. A theme for the food is picked each month by the hosting family—green food, dessert night, pizza toppings, foreign food, etc. After the meal, starting with the youngest child and moving by age to the oldest, everyone takes a turn to talk about his or her favorite book. Imagine a tiny child telling everyone—tots, teens, and adults—their two special sentences about *Hop on Pop!* as everyone in the room listens respectfully! When younger children finish, they drift off to play elsewhere while the rest of the group moves on to more complex literature. The founders of this popular event no longer attend, and the club has taken on a life of its own.

• *Little House on the Prairie.* This early group developed around the shared love of the Laura Ingalls Wilder books. The families read the books at home and meet for dramatic plays, field trips, and activities with pioneer themes. Soap and candle making, watching a farrier shoe a pony, historical field trips, dramatic play, and socializing are typical activities. Other literature themes that lend themselves to similar clubs include the King Arthur legends, the *Chronicles of Narnia, Anne of Green Gables,* Jane Austen's books, and the *Boxcar Children.*

• *Book clubs.* A straightforward type of club, book clubs abound in the homeschooling community. They are often patterned after adult book clubs. Groups may meet monthly to talk about books they have read. One group selects a genre (i.e., animal stories, mysteries) each month, then books from the genre are shared and discussed at the meeting. Afterwards, a related project or craft activity is offered to round out the meeting.

• *Latin club.* This club includes six families with students aged nine to seventeen. They meet twice a month. Each family purchases the same Latin textbook, as all group members were beginning students. One chapter is covered each meeting. Many fun and enriching activities are organized, such as a toga party, crossword puzzles, movies, preparing Roman food, reading myths, and so on. Parents and children learn together.

• *Destination Imagination* (DI). This international organization offers an annual, creative problem-solving competition. Teams of five to seven children select a problem in the fall and develop their solution for a presentation in March. Homeschooling groups have participated very successfully in DI competitions.

• *Youth Volunteer Corps* (YVC). Youth Volunteer Corps is a national program that is sponsored by Campfire. In our community, a YVC staff person first attended homeschool skating parties and recruited home-schooled teens who wanted to do volunteer work. Students ages twelve and up met once or twice a week. Projects, both staff and student generated, include working at a soup kitchen, cutting ivy in parks, building a worm bin, or visiting elderly people.

• *Teen activity loop.* More than twenty families participate in an e-mail loop that is used to announce various social activities for teens. Activities are scheduled at least monthly, with each family taking a turn. Typical activities include visiting a corn maze, game days, bowling, playing pool, going to the beach, and going to plays. Parents who drive often stay to visit each other and for support.

• *Historical costume design / writing club exchange.* Two moms spon-sor these clubs in order to share the sewing and design skills of one parent and the writing skills of the other. The group was formed by invitation. No fees were charged, and non-sponsoring parents had no obligations other than driving. The clubs include four or five teenagers in each of the two groups and meet one morning a week in the kitchen and family room of one of the families. The writing group designed its own format. It began as a combination peer writing group and teacher-directed instruction. As soon as students developed their own projects, teacher-directed instruction was dropped in favor of individual editing and coaching. The costume design group spends a good deal of time researching costumes of various eras and then sketching the designs they wish to create. They then design patterns for the costumes, shop together for inexpensive fabrics, and then sew their costumes under the skilled guidance of a knowledgeable parent.

• *Learning parties.* Five families plan a year's calendar of events. Each family picks a country and sponsors a monthly gathering with that country as a theme. They prepare food, games, activities, and crafts from the country. Guest speakers and fields may be scheduled. During the subsequent year, families may choose other topics, such as space or science.

• *Unit study co-op.* A group of families selects science or health topics, such as the eye or the ear, and parents take turns teaching each unit, bringing snacks, and babysitting younger siblings in a separate room. This more traditional school model works best with smaller groups of students of similar ages and interests.

• *Hire a teacher.* A group of parents hire a Spanish teacher, for example. The group meets weekly over a period of several years. This model is more effective when everyone, parents and students alike, is at the same level of learning and very interested in learning the subject, and when the age range is not too wide.

• *Homeschool gymnastics class offered by the City Parks and Recreation District.* While these classes are not really learning clubs, important elements of learning clubs are present: they are voluntary, interest based, and participatory; they involve small groups and have a limited life span. Spontaneous social time frequently follows each session.

## Advantages of Learning Clubs

1. Children who learn well in groups have an opportunity to shine.

2. Some activities are more enjoyable in a group setting; other activities require a group.

3. Clubs make a wider selection of expert knowledge available to more learners.

4. Parents share educational responsibility with others.

5. Learning clubs are affordable. Despite income disparity of group members, all members can participate on an equal footing.

6. Parents who work outside the home or who are single parents can participate without being overwhelmed.

7. Kids get to know a variety of interesting adults.

8. Clubs create equal access to learning resources.

9. Learning clubs provide opportunities for social learning.

10. Clubs increase social opportunities for parents and students alike.

11. Clubs create an opportunity for culminating learning activities, public speaking, projects, demonstration, performance, or simply celebration.

## Launching A Successful Learning Club

1. In the beginning, limit sessions to once a week. Student interest will remain high and parents will avoid burnout. Stand firm on this point! If some members want more frequent activities for their children, let someone else start a different club on another day.

2. First clubs should be of short duration—perhaps just a month or so—while you work out the logistics of planning and work. Figure the costs out ahead of time.

3. Keep your theme or subject-based learning club family-sized. Six to eight students is optimal. Twelve might work for very compatible groups. Larger clubs can easily become classes and prone to developing behavior management problems. Social clubs can be any size.

4. Expect to spend about half a day or more each time you meet. The time you spend together need not be all planned activities. Include some social time. Bring lunches to share, or potluck, or take turns providing snacks, or meet afterwards at a nearby park. Younger children need time to run off steam, older students need to huddle, and parents need to yak.

5. Remember that homeschool students aren't pre-programmed to change subjects every 45 minutes. They will focus on topics they enjoy for longer than you might think. Divide the time and schedule several activities that explore the subject in different ways. If you finish early, they can always play! If you complete just one activity, your plans are ready for next time. In the best clubs, the children rarely want to stop or go home. The line between joyous learning and pure play is wonderfully hazy.

6. Avoid the temptation to try to "do school." Clubs that are too school-ish fizzle out fast. One exception to this rule (there is always an exception!) is a group of older students who want to learn a subject together. Some students might even hate the subject, yet recognize that they need to learn it as a prerequisite to future studies. Studying with a group of peers may be preferable to struggling alone.

7. Remember that successful clubs are always voluntary. Be prepared to change the focus of the group to meet the changing needs of students, or to close the club and start a new one. Expect some students and families to move on to other activities as their interests change.

8. Be clear about the ground rules for the group. Answer these questions before you begin:

a. What is the maximum number of students that your group can handle?

b. Will parents drop students off, or be required to stay and participate?

c. What is the age range allowed?

d. Will younger siblings be allowed to attend, or will parents need to make other arrangements for them?

e. Where will you meet—your home only, rotate among members' homes, rent a facility?

f. Do you have a plan in place to help screen for compatible students and for helping mismatched members move on?

g. Do all parents fully understand that voluntary means voluntary, and that students really have the choice not to attend?

h. Finally, keep in mind the fact that not all students learn well in groups. If a student doesn't enjoy attending a learning club, don't despair. Try another group, let her start her own club, or try general community activities. Students give many clues about how to help them learn. Learn to follow those clues.

## Conclusion

Learning clubs can be thought of as cooperative, private learning centers, and are a sound model for developing cooperative community learning centers. Creating and participating in learning clubs is a natural step that parents take as part of their commitment to homeschooling. Greater access to clubs could make homeschooling a more viable option for many more families. Clubs are practical, efficient, and affordable. The bottom line? Learning clubs work.

## About the Author

*Ann is the proud mother of two independent learners, a veteran of 21 years as a homeschooling parent, and the founder of several homeschooling organizations. As the author of dozens of essays and three homeschooling books, including the forthcoming* Fundamentals of Homeschooling, *she envisions a future in which a multitude of educational options are available to every family. For more information write to P.O. Box 80214, Portland, OR 97280, USA, e-mail: ann@nettlepatch.net. Other writings by Lahrson Fisher can be found at http://nettlepatch.net/homeschool*

# Tuesday School
## A Model Mini-School / Expanded Homeschool Program

*by Ann Lahrson Fisher*

"**K**IDS, CAN YOU SAY *misnomer?*"

I absolutely did *not* want to call it "school." What we were doing was distinctly *not* school. In the end, though, the students prevailed. The name "Tuesday School" met their need for a group identity, enabling them to talk about "my school" to their friends. Yes, we did meet on Tuesdays. For me, Tuesday School has become a symbol of an incredible opportunity to expand to the community the good that homeschooling families have been creating among themselves for the past twenty years. The "mini-school" concept is springing up in communities throughout the country.

Students who attend a mini-school benefit from spending time with other adults. They may learn things that their parents can't teach them. They are exposed to rules and values that differ from their own. They meet other children. They learn to participate in a group. Parents enjoy several advantages when their children participate in a mini-school. They can avoid homeschool burnout and enjoy a change of pace. They may pursue personal interests. Some parents use that time for focused attention to another child.

Teacher/sponsors of mini-schools generate income. If their own children participate, the family benefits more. If the teacher has a passion for a field, he or she can share that passion with others. Teachers who thrive in the presence, noise, and activity of young children, or among angst-driven teens, can develop successful, general enrichment mini-schools. You might call these mini-schools a private-enterprise version of learning

Demian

clubs (as discussed in "Homeschool Learning Clubs" in this book). Except for the fact that the sponsor is paid, many of the benefits are identical. Yet key differences bear consideration.

## Representative Mini-Schools

I will describe two incarnations of a mini-school. The first is the general enrichment program that I ran. The second is a high-quality art program sponsored by an artist who has also homeschooled. Both are loosely duplicatable as long as the teacher/sponsor brings his or her own passions, talents, interests, resources, and commitment fully into the program.

## The Original Tuesday School

One way to express the mission statement of my Tuesday School would be: Within the boundaries of established house rules and my minimal requirements for order and structure, students enjoy an uncommon amount of freedom to discover and learn through social play, exploration, and directed activities. I set the age range at six through twelve, with a limit of nine students. We met during the nine months of the traditional school year. Fees were paid at the beginning of the month and covered most supplies and a snack.

Our days may have looked like those spent at an alternative or free school. Tuesday School met once a week, from 10 AM until 3:30 PM. Parents were free to stay or go. The core curriculum was the milieu of our home. Much of the house and resources were accessible to the students. In short, we were a homeschooling family with interests. The students came to sample our lives and to share their lives with us and each other. Our day began with sharing time, important for students who had not seen one another all week. Next we planned the daily schedule—all the nitty-gritty details of learning together. Art or craft activities, read-aloud time, and open-ended math and science explorations were typical. Free play and individual projects were always an option, and often chosen by the younger children. Some students scheduled and taught lessons of their own. Some study groups continued all year. The end of the day brought another group sharing time, problem solving, discussion, and planning for future activities. Parents often stayed to visit at the end of the day until our schedule squeezed them out the door.

## Dreamweaver Studio

This program offers weekly art lessons to homeschooling students on an ongoing basis throughout the usual school year. Sue Stauber, the founder. has a passion for and knowledge of art that is complemented by a desire to share her knowledge with youth. Sue understands the unique qualities of children who have not been schooled and tailors her program accordingly. She divides her time between developing her own art and teaching. The classes are held in her home studio, and are designed for students with an interest in art.

Classes are limited to six students. Family-sized classes maintain a homeschool type of environment and allow for greater individualization. Fees are paid monthly and cover instruction, a snack, and high-quality art materials. Younger students, age six to nine, meet for three hours once a week. Classes for younger artists focus more on imagination, creativity, and exploring a variety of media. Older beginners, age ten to teens, meet for four hours each week. These students begin each class with direct instruction, usually in drawing. Each day includes fine arts activities as well as crafts. Advanced students, age twelve to teens, meet for a full day from 10 AM till 3:30 PM. Fine arts are taught during structured lessons and directed projects in the mornings. Afternoons are devoted to crafts.

Sue's scheduling methods fly in the face of popular opinion. Home-schooled students are noted for having amazingly long attention spans in their areas of interest. Taking advantage of that ability to focus, Sue offers classes that range from three hours for younger students to five-and-a-half hours for a class of advanced teens. This model has proven resoundingly successful, as evidenced by full classes, a lack of behavior management problems, and a high rate of returning students each year. The end of the day is invariably met with groans of, "But I'm not finished yet!"

## Common Features of Mini-Schools

These and other mini-schools generally have the following in common. Mini-schools:

• May arise from the teacher's love of a subject or topic.
• May arise from the teacher's genuine love of and enjoyment of being with youth.
• Are most successful when the sponsor is well-grounded in unschooling or alternative education philosophies. Many traditional notions of schooling are detrimental to success. Dividing the day into forty-five minute periods for math, reading, or spelling, for example, squelches spontaneity, and in-depth exploration of topics is more difficult. Additionally, using second-hand resources such as textbooks and workbooks as a primary activity may spawn boredom and behavioral issues found in some traditional schools that use those methods. Involving students in hands-on activities optimizes involvement in the activity and minimizes side issues of boredom and behavior problems.
• Generally meet no more than three times each week. One or two

sessions a week may be optimal. Sponsors who need to generate more income should offer several different programs.

- Are typically located in the home of the sponsor—a spare room, the family room, a converted garage, or a private studio.
- Are paid for by fees.
- Have optional attendance.
- Are family-sized groups. Six to ten students is usually set as a maximum.
- Are offered to a broad age range.
- Are popular at all levels, and are especially in demand for teens.

## Conclusion

Mini-schools describe any learning arrangement where individuals are paid for offering learning experiences and activities to small groups of homeschooled students for one or two full or half days each week. Programs offer needed support for many parents. Sponsors may continue to homeschool their children while generating income. Although the name "mini-school" creates a desirable identity for students, the most successful models are quite different from traditional schools. Sponsors have the freedom to create the program they want out of their passion and commitment to the needs of homeschooling families. Like learning clubs, mini-schools can be developed in a multitude of directions.

I look forward to the day that unique mini-schools organized by passionate and knowledgeable individuals—not experts—offer every imaginable topic from alphabets to zeppelins, and can be found in every neighborhood.

# Pathfinder Center

*by Joshua Hornick*

K EN DANFORD AND I left school teaching to start
Pathfinder Center four years ago. Pathfinder is a community-based learning center in Amherst, Massachusetts, for teenagers who decide—with
their families—not to go to school anymore. We provide services to make
teen homeschooling a practical and successful avenue for any family.

Pathfinder has had a huge, positive impact on its membership and
staff. It has also had a substantial impact on many other people in the
greater community of which it is a part. Pathfinder's membership consists
of families with homeschooling teenagers. Most of the families did not
consider homeschooling a viable option before discovering Pathfinder.

Pathfinder provides two sorts of services: family support and teen
activities. Family support can be divided into start-up, planning, and
ongoing support. During the start-up phase, we discuss with members
what they believe is important and what their passions are. We brainstorm about possible activities (often new members don't think in terms of
starting their own businesses or 'zines, or they think they should have to
do things they hate and don't find important), and we help them craft a
plan. We help kids set up internships or other involvement in the adult

community. We also guide them through the legal process of homeschooling, which—although rarely a problem—is more complicated in Massachusetts than in most states.

On an ongoing basis, we meet with families to discuss how things are going. Over time, we have learned that this is extremely valuable to many families. There are a lot of wheels that don't need to be reinvented, and often a well-informed, caring third party can make a big problem much smaller or can suggest a great new approach or resource. It also gives us a way to get to know each family better. We call this work strategic planning.

Pathfinder's calendar of activities for teens includes two to six activities each day. Most activities meet once a week, unless there are rehearsals for a show. More than half of the activities are academic—writing groups, American history, chemical analysis, gender studies, mock trial, etc. Others are musical, artistic, or outdoors oriented. About half of the activities are run by Pathfinder staff. The rest are led by interested community members, parents, college kids, or members. Most activities have about ten young people in them, but sometimes they have only one (we do some personal tutoring) or two, or more than twenty. Our teen members can do as many or as few of our activities as they wish. Most members probably come to the center about three times a week to do three to five activities (total). They'll stay for half the day or all day, hanging out with other kids at Pathfinder or doing things in town.

Pathfinder is not a school. It has no requirements for its members, except to act civilly when on the premises. Members come and go as they choose. We have been likened to a YMCA. Significantly, we allow ourselves—the staff—very flexible schedules. Humane, gentle working conditions are an important aspect of the center.

## Pathfinder on a Busy Morning

Visiting Pathfinder on a busy morning, you might find something like this: You walk from the parking lot into a little yellow entryway. You then turn into the Big Room (15 x 30 feet). There you find me (Josh) at my desk, clipping articles from the *Science Times* and chatting with a couple of kids about racism. Ken's desk is empty. In the back of the room, a dozen kids are discussing the meaning of life or seeing how many can sit on one person's lap. Sarah Reid, our third staff member, works on the *Globe* crossword puzzle with two kids. There are old Macs on Ken's and my desks. There's a new computer running some academic software and an Internet link-up in the far corner.

There's a high-quality copy machine, a big bureau covered with literature, a big bulletin board with community events, opportunities, and messages. The walls are spotted with 8 x 10 inch black-and-white prints, processed in Pathfinder's little darkroom, which a fifteen-year-old set up last year.

In the classroom. there are eight kids ranging in age from thirteen to sixteen sitting or lying on a huge modern sectional, studying logic with Charlie, a community member who likes teaching logic. The little white board on an artist's easel is covered with incomprehensible symbols that you might find in a second- or third-term college logic sequence. They laugh a lot in this particular class.

The small art room has three kids in it. One is sketching with markers, and the others are cutting out decorations of some sort. In the meeting room/library, Ken is meeting with a mother and her fifteen-year-old son. It's a program planning meeting, and they are brainstorming activities that the mother and son might enjoy taking up together. The last room appears a bit disheveled. It is home to a little refrigerator, a microwave, and a toaster oven. The walls include some original art with quotes from Ani DiFranco and a Jimi Hendrix poster. At a fold-up table. five boys are playing Magic. Three other kids, two girls and one boy, are sitting in a big chair and a small couch. They chat together and with the Magic players.

Most Pathfinder members aren't at the center. They are at home. at the library, at an art studio, at a job or internship, reading a book on the town commons, hiking, perusing stores in town, at a community college class, or picking up a devil's-food cupcake at the bakery.

## Pathfinder People

Pathfinder is run by its founders, Kenneth Danford and myself, Joshua Hornick. We had both worked at the Amherst Regional Junior High School (a well-respected public school) before we left to start Pathfinder. Ken taught American history, and I taught general science. Both of us had six years of classroom teaching experience in a variety of schools. Together we commiserated about the plight of the junior-high teacher. Ken dwelled on the bad relationships between students and teachers. It's hard for students to be open and honest with adults when the adult's job is to make sure the kids have bathroom passes, to make them mind. and when it is the adult's duty to constantly judge them and punish them or reward them, grade them or discipline them accordingly. I tended to focus more on the death of motivation. Kid's love of learning gets squashed. No one wants that to happen or tries to make it happen. but the education system has developed to a point where it happens constantly—and I was part of that system.

Together we decided to find a better way for ourselves and the teens with whom we worked. We ruled out the alternative school route. We are passionate advocates for social justice, and we could not think of a way to make a viable school equally available to the poor and not become poor ourselves, which we ruled out. I had done my graduate research on homeschooled teenagers, and I had learned that parents don't have to work a lot to homeschool a teenager. Specifically, I learned that homeschooled teenagers rarely receive academic instruction from their parents. They mostly learn on their own. With this knowledge, Ken and I figured that we could set up an organization whose support would make teen homeschooling a practical alternative for any family. Any family could escape school and enter an exciting adventure in life and learning. We also thought that it would enable us to have honest and meaningful relationships with our students and to help inspire youth to love life and learning.

Our motto in those days was, Build it and they will come. Our dreams have largely been realized. We have meaningful, honest relationships with teens and their families, and we see their love of life and learning grow. We built it and people have come. But who has come? The one similarity of all Pathfinder families is that they all agree that this is a better approach to adolescence for their child or children than school. After that, they are a varied crew. Some, when they were in school, were high achievers. Others were low achievers. Some were always home-schooled. Some thought that school was okay. Others hated it. Most families are lower-middle class by income, but a few are middle to upper-middle, and a few are poor. There have only been a handful of kids of color. About half our members join us in September, making plans over the summer. The others join us throughout the rest of the year. Most are college bound. All of them are geniuses, but then so is every other kid.

## A Few Nuts and Bolts

When Ken and I started Pathfinder in August 1996, we hoped to be making the same salaries we got as public school teachers, about $30,000, after a few years. We're not quite there, but it's imminent. Our overhead comes to about $30,000 a year including $12,000 for rent. Other big expenses include health insurance for one family, maintenance and insurance on Pathfinder's station wagon, and postage and copying. The rest goes to salaries. We're aiming to push Sarah's salary up to $20,000. About $7,000 goes to the part-time staff and a few outside resources. We'd need a budget of about $115,000 to get the salaries we want. If Ken and I hadn't had savings, supportive families, and other financial resources, we never could have brought Pathfinder to where it is now.

Most of our income comes from membership fees. We charge $1,500 per member for a year, which includes unlimited consultations and all Pathfinder activities. A big bargain! Our membership is now about 50 kids. Families that can't afford our fee pay what they can and work to make up the difference in fund-raising activities, most of which Pathfinder sponsors. The biggest fundraiser is a Friends of Pathfinder campaign. Friends make contributions between $25 and $1,000 and receive our monthly, four-page journal, *Liberated Learners*, in which two families a month write autobiographical pieces. This raises about $9,000 a year. Other fundraisers bring in about $4,000 more. Much of our fundraising income goes to offset what families can't afford. We also make a few thousand dollars a year consulting (strategic planning) for non-members interested in teen homeschooling or setting up similar centers. We anticipate income of $80,000 this year. We hope that with membership growing to sixty-five or seventy, we will be able to reach our personal financial goals in the next year or two.

Pathfinder is a teacher/administrator-led model. It was created by and it is maintained by two former classroom teachers. Other teachers who are friends or acquaintances often ask us if we can hire them. Most teachers long for the kind of relationships that Ken and I have with our students. They would love to teach classes where all the students are there by choice. Untold numbers of great teachers get fed up and leave or consider leaving school every year. Instead, if they've got some resources, a little common business sense, and enough determination, they might consider creating a Pathfinder in their communities.

So far, Pathfinder has been a marked success, and we are near financial success as well. I hope that a Pathfinder opens in every community in the country.

*For more information contact Pathfinder, P.O. Box 804, Amherst, MA 01004, USA, 256 North Pleasant Street, Amherst, MA 01002, USA, phone: 413-253-9412, e-mail: plc@valinet.com, URL: www.pathfindercenter.org*

# North Star School
# and Homeschool Resource Center

*by Marcie O'Brien*

WHEN MY FAMILY AND I moved from Seattle to a rural area in South Kitsap County (approximately an hour away), we were disappointed to find no support networks such as those we had enjoyed in the city. We are "unschoolers," meaning we believe that learning occurs naturally for children and that rigid schedules and curricula hinder the process, and the only homeschool support organizations in this rural area were either religiously affiliated or products of the school district.

Quite accidentally, I stumbled upon a tiny ad for North Star School and Homeschool Resource Center. I phoned and had a long conversation with Kara Willowbrook, who shared our unschooling philosophy and was planning, along with Shari Weber, to open a homeschool resource center in the area. They would be holding a series of community information and planning meetings, and when I attended one of these meetings at the local community center, there was a lively discussion of all methods of homeschooling and the people in attendance debated many ideas.

A few weeks later, I toured the site Kara and Shari had found for North Star. The building had been a church. It had been neglected for a few years, but with a thorough cleaning and some sprucing up it would be a pleasant place for children and parents to spend time in. It is impressive in size and has a wonderful waterfront location with fabulous views. It has a large, open room with a high ceiling, an art center, play loft, library, office space, kitchen, dining area, bathrooms, and more. Outside it has a garden space, play area, and lawn.

During the spring and summer of 1999 we placed flyers around town, sent out press releases and held several more community information meetings. From the start the public was supportive. We cleaned the building and painted murals. A local paint store made a generous $1,500-donation of primer and paint. Kara's husband, Rick, dedicated weeks of his time patiently scraping and painting the building a cheerful yellow. This was an enormous job and a true labor of love. Shari and her husband designed our website. A fundraising rummage sale was held to raise much-needed capital. Lots of friends and families pitched in, and to see the combined effort was inspiring.

Our vision for North Star is to provide a democratically governed homeschool resource center where parents can cooperatively pool their talents and expertise while homeschooled children take advantage of "elective" type classes in the extras like music, drawing, theme unit study,

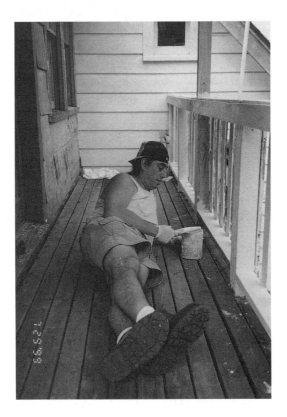

drama, newspaper, or participate in group activities. In addition, we provide a place for families to meet and share ideas. A food-buying co-op and a babysitting exchange were some of our early plans. Although we have an abundant supply of high-quality games, manipulatives, and art supplies, our belief is that the basics are best covered by the homeschool parents and their children individually. North Star is simply another "home" in which homeschooling families and children can learn and socialize.

North Star opened in September, 1999, with eighteen students grades K-6. Some had come from traditional school environments, some were lifelong homeschoolers, some had parents who hadn't considered homeschooling before but were looking for an alternative to public school for their children. In the early weeks we introduced the democratic self-government system and worked on theme projects such as apples and medieval history. It was clear to us right away that we were challenged by the ratio of kids to adults. We had deliberately not made any minimum time requirements on the parents who enrolled their children, figuring that it would exclude homeschooling single parents or families in which both parents work outside the home. This meant that there were some limitations on what we were able to do at North Star. With two or three adults and eighteen kids, we were well within our insurance policy's mandatory ratio, but unable to do all the wonderful things we would have liked. Still, we managed to take a field trip to press fresh apple cider and put on a medieval feast.

During the fall we experimented with the level of structure that best suits a wide range of ages, interests, and abilities. Our enrollment fluctuated slightly as families decided how this fit into their homeschooling program. We delved into theme unit studies on space, ancient Egypt, and horses. The children learned the democratic model of self-governance well. We began our food-buying co-op and the children were delighted when the eighteen-wheeler pulled up into our parking area with pallets of food to be unloaded. The kids were impressed to hear that the driver stopped at North Star to make our delivery before heading to large chain supermarkets. Experiences like this provide homeschooled kids a chance to see the food distribution system up-close and personal, and to practice real-life math. Dividing the bill and figuring totals was as much fun as measuring out pounds of flour and beans.

On December evenings we held both a craft night and a dessert party. North Star families had a great time at these events. After returning from holiday break in January we began a homeschool support group and a family board-game night, both of which meet monthly. In addition, we have started to bring in outside instructors to teach specific classes based on the children's interests. Currently a music class and a pirate theme unit are wildly popular. As many of the kids are young, our "elective" classes include things like papier mâché, nutrition, math games, newspaper, paper making, drawing, etc. We also offer chemistry, geology, theme unit study, writers' workshop, drama, and community-service projects that seem to appeal to older students. Kids also have time for individual studies or "down time" activities like baking a batch of cookies, having a tea party, etc.

North Star is evolving and changing as we go through this first year. We are learning what works and what doesn't. More parents each day are choosing to spend time here with their children and offering to teach classes or share ideas. We are hoping to foster babysitting co-ops and outside ways that North Star families can provide a network of support for each other as well as social contacts for the children. We are also working with a non-religiously affiliated homeschool support group based in nearby Bremerton to provide more services and information to home-schoolers living in the area.

North Star is a nonprofit organization. We receive no outside funding. Fortunately we were able to operate in the black financially from the beginning. Our tuition is based on the number of half days (three-hour blocks of time) each child attends. At this time it is uncertain whether our tuition scale will stay exactly the same next year. We are considering different ways to fund North Star, and are looking at many options including trades of services or instruction for evening and weekend use of the building and a plan to swap volunteer time for tuition.

*You are welcome to contact us at: North Star School and Homeschool Resource Center, 1880 Lawrence Avenue, Pt. Orchard, WA 98366, USA, phone: 360-876-7706.*

# Co-Creating Learning Communities in Mexico
### Preparing the Ground for Evolutionary Learning Community

*by Kathia C. Laszlo*

"**W**HAT OUR WORLD NEEDS...is...flexible and functional learning environments where people, young and old, can be exposed to concepts and ideas relevant to their present and to their future."
                                                                    —Ervin Laszlo

## Overview

This chapter presents experience gleaned from a project in Mexico that sought to promote learning communities as spaces for people to learn together in a self-organized and flexible manner. The project, "A Better World: Co-Creating Learning Communities in Mexico,"[1] took place in the city of Monterrey, where two learning communities were formed by people of middle-class socio-economic status. These individuals accepted the invitation and the challenge to get together once a week to learn and collaborate on issues—decided upon by themselves—that could enhance their quality of life and prepare them to participate in the improvement of their communities. One learning community, comprised solely of women, created a safe space for sharing life stories, and through conversation, strengthened self-esteem and the will to bring into the world the love, respect, and dignity that had been lacking in their life experiences. The other learning community, comprised of both men and women already engaged in community development activities, explored topics related to their roles in the improvement of their neighborhood and their roles as parents, which led them to make a commitment to form an on-going neighborhood learning community for parents. At the end of the project the participants felt that their involvement in this project had helped them to communicate their ideas more effectively, to think in a positive way, and to believe that they could achieve their goals when they were willing to work for them.

## The Project

The design of the project "A Better World: Co-Creating Learning Communities in Mexico" was based on the notion of learning communities as stepping stones toward an Evolutionary Learning Community (ELC).[2] In other words, the scope was limited to testing the idea of learning to learn in a different way and introducing some ideas relating to personal and community development—which are basic concepts necessary but not sufficient for the design of an ELC. The objective of the project was to create learning communities as a means to provide a learning opportunity to individuals in low-income social groups who did not have access to other forms of formal education in the northern industrial city of Monterrey, Mexico. The goals of the learning process were focused on topics relevant to quality-of-life enhancement and community development, at the discretion of the learners in the communities. Two learning communities were formed on a volunteer basis, and the experiences of their members (participants and facilitators) shed light on issues of the applicability of systems thinking and social systems design to community building efforts, and in particular to those that relate to the creation of learning communities.

The participants of this project were adults with an average of six years of formal education. The two coordinators of the project obtained a list of people in a middle-class neighborhood who had previously volunteered for participating in community development activities. In order to be involved in a learning community they had to have expressed an interest and willingness to learn and a commitment to their personal *and* community development. Potential participants were invited by telephone, and 85% of those who accepted were women. One of the challenges involved in the implementation of the project was to communicate concepts such as systems thinking and design in simple, applicable language.

For example, the participants learned about wholeness and interconnection through direct experience. They understood what a community is, what a learning community is, and how to co-create one, largely due to the fact that they were able to live the process of doing so. They also engaged in collective thinking about their roles in creating a better world—and more specifically, about improving the quality of living in their neighborhoods. In the final analysis, it was not necessary to make explicit the concepts behind their experiential learning, such as systems thinking and social systems design.

Another set of challenges was associated with the cultivation of partnership values that are implicit in each learning community (e.g., shared power to make decisions among the members of the community, openness to uncertainty and risk taking, synergy between individual and collective interests, and mutual supporting interdependencies), but which nevertheless are not intrinsic to Mexican culture, according to Geert Hofstede.[3] Through respectful, attentive, and minimally invasive facilitation, this challenge was met and the participants were able to form functional learning communities. In a similar way, cultural traits such as power differences based on socio-economic status and gender tend to be generalizable across major segments of the Mexican population. And yet the openness and interest to learn and to contribute to the improvement of their individual and collective lives allowed those who accepted the invitation to participate in this project to create learning spaces where participation and collaboration became the *modi operandi*. The facilitators and participants acted as equals, and everybody felt respected, honored, and esteemed. They were able to deal with the uncertainty and ambiguity involved in this extremely flexible and open learning process. The participants were able to understand that they were responsible for the direction of their learning. Neither of the learning communities experienced conflicts relating to incompatibility of individual and collective interests. On the contrary, both learning communities were safe spaces where individuals were able to express themselves freely, where they felt supported, and developed harmonious and caring relationships.

The project sought to facilitate the challenges intrinsic to the creative tension between difficult situations and hopeful possibilities. Many of the participants were already involved in activism, as advocates for improvements to make their neighborhoods safer places and to reduce the incidence of vandalism. Their approach had always been to complain to the local government authorities and to ask, for example, for more streetlights (some sections of the neighborhood were completely dark at night—and therefore dangerous). Through their engagement in the learning communities of this project, the participants realized that there was a lot they could do by themselves to complement the infrastructural support they were seeking—but rarely receiving—from the local government. They came to see that their roles as parents was one of the most important functions not only in their own individual lives, but also in the lives of their neighborhoods. Through future-oriented conversation, they were

able to perceive the connection between the education of their children and the quality of life in their neighborhood.

All the participants who accepted the invitation to get involved in the two learning communities of this project shared an optimistic outlook on life, even though many were immersed in situations in which other individuals may have resigned themselves in despair. For instance, the next-door neighbor of one of the participants was also invited to participate in the learning community, but rejected the invitation based on her belief that "things are the way they are and nothing can be done about it."

The learning-community approach was an excellent way of offering an educational opportunity to a sector of the Mexican society that generally does not have access to other forms of institutionalized education. In this experience, the learning-community format was appropriate for people with a diverse array of life experiences—from the housewife suffering psychological abuse and oppression by a dominating husband to the worn-out construction worker looking to see if he could do something more for his large family. The common thread that wove the participants into a community was their interest in learning, self-development, and improvement of their environments. One facilitator expressed her enthusiasm after her involvement, saying, "This project was really interesting. When I realized what it was possible to achieve, I thought, Wow! This is powerful! This is a new kind of education and it can be done with many people." What she saw as possible was the enabling of self-organized learning communities that can hold periodic gatherings in a community center or in the living room of one of the participants. By creating communities this way, always with the sharing of food and conversation, it became evident that the participants were able to empower themselves and to discover the joy of learning together for their common good.

The members of each learning community decided when and where to meet, they made adjustments when for some reason someone could not be there at the agreed-upon hour, and they decided on the focus of their conversations. Through their dialogues, the participants discovered power within themselves, since the project and all its possibilities were theirs to create and explore. In this case, the learning-community approach created the appropriate context—a safe and supportive "holding container"—for self-empowerment. One participant said, "I feel so happy. I experienced an unfolding of my interior. I feel inspired to tell you all that I feel really good, full of energy. I feel strong. I don't have negative thoughts, and I can deal with the problems I come to. Before I felt full of negative energy...I have learned to trust in myself." While it is evident that such a community-based learning process has similarities to traditional group-therapy processes, the key difference lies in their respective approaches to, and concern with, the future. The former is focused on "becoming" while the latter focuses only on "being." As mentioned earlier, these communities were stepping stones toward ELC. They were evolutionary in the sense that the interactions of their members are always future-oriented, with an eye to learning how they could cooperatively create a more healthy and authentic community given the dynamics of change in which they found themselves. It is the role of the facilitator in such a process to help create this orientation and to promote the visioning it entails. Group-therapy processes cannot be considered evolutionary in these ways, and they may or may not foster a readiness to learn how to learn, both collaboratively and contextually.

The particular focus and experience of these learning communities reflects the socio-cultural and psychological needs of their members. For instance, through reflection upon their lives and their relationships, the participants realized that a person cannot treat another person with dignity if they themselves are not treated with dignity. They were able to see the vicious cycle in which they were caught—repeating many of the mistakes and patterns of behavior of their parents. And this "being able to see" was a liberating experience, since now they know that through dialogue they can change such things.

Paulo Freire notes that "founding itself upon love, humility, and faith, dialogue becomes a horizontal relationship of which mutual trust between the dialoguers is the logical consequence."[4] This was clearly borne out by the project. He adds, "Dialogue cannot be carried on in a climate of hopelessness. If the dialoguers expect nothing to come of their efforts, their encounter will be empty and sterile, bureaucratic and tedious."[5] The optimism of all those involved in this project made it possible to for them to achieve rewarding and productive learning conversations.

The participants expressed the conviction that one of their main learnings was their improved ability to communicate with others; both with the other members of their learning community and with other people in their families and broader communities. It is interesting to take note of this emergent outcome since communication abilities were never made an explicit learning objective of either community. M. Scott Peck helps put this corollary in perspective, explaining that "the rules of communication are best taught and only learned through the practice of community-making. Fundamentally, the rules of communication are the rules of community-making, and the rules of community-making are the rules for peacemaking."[6]

Self esteem, a sense of community, and commitment to lifelong learning were the groundwork that enabled the participants of this project to engage in the collaborative design and development of their lives and of their communities. Maybe the most remarkable outcome of this project, particularly relevant for future work on ELCs, was the change in attitudes that resulted in the participants. From informal conversations and observations collected at both the beginning and the end of the project, the following emergent attitudes were expressed:

- Optimism and perseverance ("If I want to do it, I know I can do it!").
- Openness to learn from any experience, with every person, always.
- Strong desire to serve and to help other people in their communities; to learn and to improve.

• Sense of responsibility. Not remaining spectators but wanting to participate in the improvement of their communities.

• Sense of place, of self, and of shared identity; confidence in where they are going, both individually and collectively.

## Closing Reflection

This case testifies to the simple fact that when a group of human beings interested in learning and change get together to collaborate, wonderful things can happen. The participants in this project came away from it convinced that the future *can* be co-created—and that the possibilities for a better world depend in large part on our daily choices and our willingness to help each other bring them into being. Although major economic and political forces remained out of their control to influence, the participants in the two learning communities of this project realized what Margaret Mead expressed so powerfully: "Never doubt that a small group of thoughtful, committed citizens can change the world: Indeed it's the only thing that ever does."[7]

The experience of this project was empowering for both facilitators and participants, and it provides fertile ground for the design of Evolutionary Learning Communities. To move on to this next step in the genesis of a learning community, not only must consideration be given to issues of personal and community development, but to issues of environmental sustainability and inter-generational responsibility, as well.[8]

## Notes

1. This project was made possible thanks to the generous support of the Ryoichi Sasakawa Young Leaders Fellowship Fund. An executive report of this project, which describes its design, implementation, and other technical aspects in more detail, can be obtained through Syntony Quest, 1761 Vallejo Street, Suite #302, San Francisco, CA 94123-5029, USA, phone/fax: 415-346-1547, e-mail: info@syntonyquest.org, URL: http://www.syntonyquest.org

2. See "Learning to Become: Creating Evolutionary Learning Community through Evolutionary Systems Design" on page 231 in this volume for a more specific account of the concepts underlying this case study.

3. Geert Hofstede, "Motivation, Leadership, and Organization: Do American Theories Apply Abroad?" in *Organizational Dynamics*. American Management Associations, 1980, pp. 42-63.

4. Paulo Freire, *Pedagogy of the Oppressed*, 20th edition. New York: Continuum, 1997, p. 72.

5. *ibid.*, p. 73.

6. M. Scott Peck, *The Different Drum: Community Building and Peace*. New York: Simon & Schuster, 1987, p. 325.

7. Margaret Mead in Bela Banathy, (1999). "Guided Evolution of Society: A Systems View." Manuscript to be published by Plenum Publishers.

8. See "Learning to Become: Creating Evolutionary Learning Community through Evolutionary Systems Design" in this volume for the theoretical and methodological underpinnings of ELC.

# How to Maintain an Alternative Library

## The Civic Media Center Six Years On

*by James Schmidt*

Ⅰn 1993, A GROUP of independent publishers and supporters of alternative media came together in Gainesville, Florida, to launch an information insurgency. They decided to name their effort the Civic Media Center and Library, Inc. (usually shortened to Civic Media Center, or CMC). Originally conceived as a public archive and clearinghouse for independent, non-corporate print and recorded material, including a lending library, the CMC has grown in six years into a vital, progressive, community organizing and education space. These days the CMC provides the services of a library, meeting space, office space, music hall, youth center, arts center, and free school all rolled into one. It has been a fun but sometimes hectic and trying six years. There are some important lessons that folks interested in building and sustaining alternative libraries and community education centers can learn from the Gainesville community's experience with the Civic Media Center.

## The CMC Philosophy: Popular Political Education

The CMC's mission, as stated in the informational handouts we give to visitors and new members, is as follows: "To provide community access to information and points of view not carried or incompletely carried in the for-profit, corporate media. To provide a place for this information to be exchanged, in the form of books, papers and reports, talks, videotapes, audiotapes and periodicals. To provide support for projects that do this, particularly independent newspapers and magazines locally. To collect enough money from operations to be able to continue this mission." This mission statement was drafted by Jenny Brown, co-editor of *The Gainesville Iguana*, a progressive political news monthly that was one of the six independent publishers—five newspapers and one press—whose ·members founded the CMC.

The Gainesville Alternative Press (GAP) group, as they called themselves, took as a point of departure for their project the Left/populist critique of the mainstream media put forth by commentators like Noam Chomsky and Jim Hightower, who have been sounding the alarm with increasing urgency in recent years about the ways in which the establishment media serves the interests of the corporate world's economic elite at the expense of the public mind. The media, these critics say, dumb us down and distract us, in the service of the corporate bottom line, when they ought to be enlightening and informing us for the greater good, in the service of democracy. As Chomsky says in a quote often used in CMC literature, "Public relations—including the press—has become an industry spending a couple of billion dollars each year. They present the propaganda that insulates the centers of power from the anger of the people. Most of the people don't know what's being done by the corporations and don't even know they don't know."[1]

In this critical view, new communications technologies such as satellite television and the Internet, combined with the ever-increasing trend of corporate conglomeration, are hyper-accelerating this dimming and cluttering effect on the popular consciousness of the developed West, particularly in the US. It is a truism in both the popular and the critical/intellectual spheres these days that television and the Internet are swamping us with material that amounts to not much more than colorful, clever distraction at best, and vicious, hateful misinformation at its worst. In books, magazines, and newspaper editorials, in popular songs, and even on TV itself, the critics bemoan the "more TV, less content" phenomenon. Despite the vaunted "democratic" nature of the Internet and its demonstrable usefulness as an organizing tool in campaigns such as the protests against the World Trade Organization's Millennium Round in Seattle, many progressives and radicals remain wary of becoming too dependent on it. They are skeptical that a medium developed by the US military-industrial complex and currently overrun by advertising, misinformation, and faddish get-rich-quick schemes can ever be anything more than the kind of tool that other mainstream mass-media outlets have proven to be—sometimes useful, but usually suspect and subject to dangerous "backfires" when the democratic impulse runs up against the big-money bottom line. There is also, of course, the economic gap wherein high-tech access and expertise remain concentrated, despite some popularization, in the hands of upper- and middle-class elites.

Even public television and radio are increasingly beholden to corporate sponsorship for their very existence, and their programming reflects this change, with a shift away from progressive, populist educational and political programming, and towards more entertainment and business-oriented material. In recent years, public TV and radio are increasingly subject to the "creeping advertising" phenomenon, with more and longer slots devoted to plugging corporate sponsors and their products in between programs. On the domestic scene, government budget cuts and the threat of outright defunding of arts and education programs including public media, and blatant corporate invasions such as the infamous Channel One "TVs-in-schools" program, combine to further restrict any options for reasonable critical thought and dialogue in the public sector. On the international scene, corporate merger-mania and economic globalization, with their attendant increases in government/business collusion and all-out scrambles for markets and resources, are raising the stakes in the struggle for economic and political freedom and environmental preservation worldwide. In doing so they raise the stakes in the struggle for democratic communications as well.

In response to the increasingly dangerous and transparent role of both public and private media outlets as conduits for corporate propaganda, activists and thinkers on the Left are calling for a strengthening of what media critic Edward Herman has called the "civic sector," the independent, non-profit, grassroots-oriented media outlets such as alternative newspapers and magazines, cable access television, and community radio stations. In an article entitled "Democratic Media" written for *Z Papers*, an off-shoot of the Left journal *Z Magazine*, Herman asserts that "the very process of building a media civic sector is important in the learning process of democracy and as part of community mobilization."[2] It was in this spirit of expanding the opportunities for public political education and democratic participation at the grassroots level, in their own community, that the GAP group decided to open the Civic Media Center.

## History of the CMC

The CMC opened its doors on October 16, 1993. Two years earlier, during the escalation of the Persian Gulf War, the Middle East Peace Group had invited Noam Chomsky to come to Gainesville to speak on behalf of their efforts to organize local opposition to the war. Chomsky was so sought after at the time that the fall of 1993 was the earliest he could come. The GAP group organizers decided to use Chomsky's impending visit as an opportunity to highlight the opening of the CMC. Professor Chomsky was the guest of honor at the opening ceremony, and spoke later that evening to a standing-room-only crowd on the University of Florida campus. Civic Media Center activists passed volunteer recruitment sheets through the crowd that night, and many, myself included, enthusiastically signed up, thrilled to see that the incisive critical perspective Chomsky brought to his talk was going to be translated into hands-on direct action right here in our town.

The CMC was originally housed in a small suite of rooms on the second floor of a building directly across the street from the University of Florida. It was hoped that this physical location would help further the CMC's educational mission by making it easy to interface with students and faculty at that institution. However, with no storefront and a dark, steep flight of rickety old stairs between us and our public, we soon discovered that it was nearly impossible to get anyone other than activists who were already "in the loop" to come up to our space. In early 1994 we discovered an available store-front space only a few blocks away, right on the main drag between the university and downtown, within easy walking and biking distance from the school and surrounding neighborhoods. This new space was immediately attractive because it had a huge front window, right on the sidewalk. It had the added bonus of being about twice the size of the old space, for significantly less rent. This location has housed the CMC since May, 1994.

## The CMC as Community Education Space

The CMC's lending library, based conceptually on the example of the Alternative Reading Room in Asheville, North Carolina (no longer in existence), is still the anchor of the project. Thanks to generous donations of material from local radical publisher CRISES Press and many other organizations and individuals, the library has grown by leaps and bounds, and now includes more than two thousand books and hundreds of video and audio tapes. The collection also includes dozens of magazine titles as well; these are available for in-house use, with the *Alternative Press Index* as a research guide and photocopies available in the back room for five

cents each. One of the most unique parts of our collection is our 'Zine Library, which features a sampling of dozens of titles from the underground micro-publishing movement that has swept the world in the last decade. Books, videotapes, and audiotapes are available for checkout to our members, and all materials, including an Internet-equipped, public-access computer, are available to the general public for in-house use. Our collection is primarily political and is divided by subject into sections with titles such as "Women's Studies," "American Studies," "Ecology," "Middle Eastern Studies," and "Resistance and Revolution."

One of the most exciting features of our alternative library is the fact that our book collection is included in the electronic card catalogue of the local public library system. Through grants from Gainesville's Friends of the Library organization, we have been able to pay to have our books entered into the Alachua County Library District's computer database so that folks who do electronic searches of the county's system can be referred to the CMC for books that are often unavailable anywhere else in the area. This project is ongoing, and we believe it represents a unique and easily emulated cooperative effort by the public and "civic" sectors to better serve the people.

Civic Media Center memberships are available on a yearly basis for a sliding-scale donation of $10-20 and entitle our members to check out materials from the collection and receive our newsletters and other mailings. There is no "average" CMC member—our ranks include students and professors from local colleges, working people of all stripes, professionals such as doctors and lawyers, small-business owners, full-time community activists, retirees, artists, and homeless people. People use our collection for a variety of educational purposes. Sometimes professors interested in exposing their students to alternative points of view will assign whole classes to come down and do research in our library. Activists use our resources to gather information in support of their causes. Alternative journalists and local 'zinesters drop in to get the latest word from other independent writers and publishers. Very often folks just drop in to browse the collection, looking for some new source of information about issues they're interested in that runs counter to the deluge of entertainment-oriented, profit-driven corporate radio, television, and print matter that we are swamped with in our daily lives.

Many of the people that CMC volunteers interact with on a daily basis say they are refreshed and inspired to find a place where people who are concerned about truth, justice, and freedom can get together and share information to help build positive social change. Among volunteers and members alike there is a sense that what the CMC represents for the Gainesville community is something rare and precious, a chance for "we the people" to "do it ourselves," to teach each other and work with each other, without the corrupting influences of power and profit that are built into so many other institutions in our society, from the workplace to the university to the local newspaper. Civic Media Center member Stephen Roe had this to say: "The CMC gives the independent media of this country a palpable face; it gives access without the necessity of technology and spawns an information network throughout the community itself. It does not cure the ills of our society, but [it] makes the fuel available to help the group or individual in that task." Jason Tompkins, famous among our volunteers for having methodically listened to almost every audiotape in the Center's collection, says of his time at the CMC:

> Having been a member of, and currently a volunteer at, the Civic Media Center for four of the five-and-a-half months that I've lived in Gainesville, I can say that the variety of material offered there is extremely useful when wishing to delve deeper into the understanding of events than [what] is offered by our mainstream media outlets. Through my own experience I have grown quite fond of the CMC's audiotape collection, a collection covering topics from weapons trafficking and Latin American studies to U.S. foreign policies and the role of multinational corporations in them. Nowhere in all of my travels, both at home and abroad, have I come across anything as comprehensive and informative on issues of economics, labor studies, revolution, methods of nonviolence, and community organization.

Local activists appreciate and respect the effort that CMC workers put forth in building and expanding the CMC's role as a base of support for local progressive thought and action. "The women's liberation movement in Gainesville is strengthened and inspired constantly by the activism and solidarity of the Civic Media Center staff and volunteers," said past president of University of Florida/Santa Fe Community College Campus National Organization for Women and CMC member Candi Churchill.

People around the country and around the globe feel similarly about the need to promote "civic media," and are taking the same kind of direct action, creating similar "information insurgencies" in their own communities. From cooperative activist information spaces like Long Haul Infoshop in Berkeley and the Autonomous Zone in Chicago to collectively run booksellers such as Bound Together Books in San Francisco and the Wooden Shoe bookstore in Philadelphia, grassroots activists are getting together to make information for political action available in their towns. We at the CMC feel that we have been able to make a unique contribution to this movement, by showing that a grassroots-funded, progressive people's library can survive and grow to serve a truly "civic" role in the community. When San Francisco Food Not Bombs organizer Keith McHenry came to the CMC to do a workshop on vegetarian cooking and homeless people's rights as part of his 1996 tour of the continent, he told us that the Civic Media Center was one of the largest and most successful "infoshops" he had seen in North America.

These days, the Civic Media Center's various functions mean that we attract a very diverse mix of people to our facility. One of the strongest roles that the CMC has come to play in the last three or four years is that of cultural venue. Our music shows, poetry readings, and art openings appeal to Gainesville's large population of university and community-college students, high schoolers, and working-class youth. These events provide a creative outlet for artists, musicians, thespians, poets, and others, young and old alike, who are just getting started or cannot afford the costs associated with presenting their work at other venues. The longest-running arts series that the CMC hosts is a weekly open-mike poetry and performance happening, the Thursday Night Poetry Jam. The Jam has become one of the area's most well-known and productive grassroots-level arts events, providing a space for local spoken-word artists and musicians to get to know each other's work, and sowing the seeds for collaboration on other projects. The CMC's role as a music venue has similarly enriched the Gainesville scene, providing a smoke-free, "music first" listening room that many musicians see as a positive alternative to the cloudy, clamorous atmosphere of the bar circuit. We have hosted shows by a wide variety of local, regional, and even nationally known performers in a broad range of musical styles, from acoustic folk to rhythm and blues to punk rock.

Our political lectures, meetings, discussion groups, and presentations appeal to Gainesville's large progressive and radical activist community. Grassroots groups as diverse as Campus NOW, Food Not Bombs, Anti-Racist Action, and the Gainesville Committee for Democracy in Mexico use our space for their meetings and events. Many of the events that happen at the CMC are organized by staffers who reach out to people in the community who have ideas to share or causes to promote and ask them to consider holding a public informational event in our space. Others are organized by folks who come to us with a request for use of the space. Most events at the CMC are aimed at political education of one sort or another, but we also make time for events that are of a more general educational nature as well. We've hosted a wide variety of events, from slide shows of photographs from the HUBBLE space telescope presented by University of Florida astronomers, to lectures on the history of the US-supported genocide in East Timor given by local members of the East Timor Action Network, to videos on childbirth and midwifery presented by students and faculty from the Florida School of Traditional Midwifery, to a "Philosophy for the People" class led by a local poet, to workshops on holistic pet-care led by a local veterinarian. Other examples of events at the CMC include progressive-oriented forums for candidates in local elections, activist training workshops on how to handle various aspects of movement work, "community dinners" at which folks share food and political discussions facilitated by activists from local groups, "video nights" at which we show political movies from our collection and local independently-produced films and videos, consciousness-raising meetings on women's and workers' issues, and press conferences put on by activists with any number of grassroots causes, from Free Radio advocates to local government whistleblowers to a women's "top-free equality" activist who recently won her case in court.

One type of educational event that has been extremely successful at the CMC is the "Teach-In." Civic Media Center Teach-Ins are modeled on the grassroots political education actions that became popular in the

1960s. They are usually organized by local activists who wish to reach out to concerned citizens, and sometimes the media as well, with detailed historical perspectives on issues and current events that are being covered in an incomplete or problematic fashion in the news. Over the last couple of years Teach-Ins on the "low-intensity conflict" in the Mexican state of Chiapas, the Free Radio movement of radical unlicensed FM broadcast stations, and the effects of US bombings and United Nations sanctions on the people of Iraq have been particularly successful, drawing standing-room-only crowds of between fifty and a hundred people and encouraging a stepping-up of local action on those issues.

Another successful attempt at public political education is our "First-Hand History" series. We try to organize as many as four or five of these programs each year. First-Hand History talks focus on the personal experiences of individual activists, conveying their unique perspectives as participants in movements and activities that have made our history as a community and as a people. These talks are followed by question-and-answer sessions and discussions where audience members can expand their knowledge and understanding even further, by connecting the speaker's personal narrative with facts and ideas that they may otherwise have known only through print or broadcast media. A few of the folks who've shared their histories with us over the years are Bill Edwards, a retired steelworkers' union organizer, Harriet Ludwig, a career journalist and civil rights worker (and CMC co-founder) who continues to write and organize on local welfare and poverty issues, and Charles Chestnut, a Gainesville city commissioner and community leader who in his youth sat on the board that oversaw local school desegregation efforts.

## Gettin' By: Fundraising

Individuals and organizations do not pay set fees for use of the Civic Media Center's space. Instead, we ask for small donations at the door at performance-type events, and groups pass the hat to collect donations for the center at their meetings and political events. A varied calendar of events serves as an outreach and fundraising tool for the CMC itself, exposing new groups of people to the space and the resources it contains, and encouraging them to sign up as members and give concrete support for our activities in the form of their membership donations. We emphasize this aspect in our cultural programs as well, asking for sliding-scale donations at the door, passing the hat, and encouraging folks to sign up for memberships rather than charging set fees for poetry readings, art openings, and music shows. It is our policy never to turn anyone away simply because they cannot afford to donate the amount we request. As a non-profit organization we are bound to this philosophy legally; as a political organization we are committed to it ethically. It is our goal to make the CMC available and ffordable as a space to help empower students, working people, artists, and grassroots activists who might otherwise find it impossible to find a home for their activities. Some local grassroots organizations have even arranged to use small parts of the CMC for offices and storage space. Currently, Gainesville's Campus NOW chapter pays a small monthly donation to rent an office in one of the back rooms in the space, as does the Gainesville Women's Liberation group's "Health Care for All" project.

Funding has been the most consistent and most daunting problem that we at the Civic Media Center have struggled with. We are well aware that money is the bane of many a grassroots organization, no matter how visionary its goals, and we feel the pressure every month when the bills come in, when the rent is due, when it's time to pay the staff. In our small college town, the yearly economic cycle ebbs and flows in accordance with the schedule of the university that is the community's economic base. This is the case for our little non-profit project just as much as for the local merchants who are our neighbors. At certain times of the year the CMC is bustling with activities and money-wise we're fairly flush. At other points the people and the money are both scarce, and we have to be creative just to come up with the cash to pay the bills. The CMC has not yet risen above a hand-to-mouth mode of economic existence. Many of the people who've been involved in the Civic Media Center are relatively inexperienced organizers, and even the seasoned activists in our ranks have been more involved in shorter-term, less costly campaigns. The CMC is somewhat unique in Gainesville's progressive community in that it is place-based and (we hope) permanent, so strategizing on how to raise funds in a sustainable fashion is an on-going learning experience for all of us. For a long time now we have tried to maintain a low-key, locally focused approach to both our fundraising and our expenditures. It is only within the last year or two that we have begun to seriously consider going for more long-range, extensive fundraising projects, such as grants from national and international foundations.

It is important for folks considering a similar endeavor to understand that the Center was very lucky to enjoy an initial funding push that consisted of substantial out-of-pocket donations from individual local supporters, in particular CRISES Press publisher and CMC treasurer Charles Willett, who almost single-handedly paid the larger bills such as rent and utilities for the first year of the CMC's existence. This one-man bankrolling of the project was not what the organizers had planned. Mr. Willett decided to step in and donate as needed, at great personal expense, when the membership and community outreach fundraising programs that were initially set up did not bring in the revenues needed to keep the place open. It was only after changing locations that the Center really saw an increase in memberships and other income, as more people became aware of the space and got involved. For groups in communities where grassroots alternative education projects may not enjoy such generous support from individual donors, it is important to consider the option of going for large grants from outside sources to supply the initial start-up costs. However, we at the CMC have followed the advice of our comrades in other organizations, whose experience has taught them that too much reliance on fickle grant money can prove disastrous to a grassroots project. We've applied for and received a few small grants over the years, but have always concentrated our fundraising efforts in the local community. Our advice, based on our experience: build your roots up strong in the soil of your community! If you do your work well and provide services your community needs, the nourishment that flows in through those roots will sustain your organization and allow it to grow. From an initial budget of $20,000 per year we have grown to almost $25,000 per year.

From a critical perspective, experts who've done workshops on grassroots fundraising for CMC staffers have told us that we may be too cautious when it comes to taking risks and going for larger funding sources. They have recommended, and we are gearing up to pursue, a long-range strategy of grant-writing and other larger-scale fundraising programs to help us move beyond our current mode of just "getting by," and into a mode of growing and building our programs. It is our goal to do this in such a way that we remain consistent with our ideals of being grounded in and responsive to our community. I must admit that we are cautious, probably to a fault, in this endeavor, knowing all too well what happens to "grassroots" groups that lose touch with their home-base constituencies. Despite a move towards seeking outside funding sources, at this writing we are still concentrating on "keeping it local." Grant-writing and other fundraising schemes still take a backseat to our pursuit of individual donor/members and fundraising events in the local community.

The aspect of the original Civic Media Center design that has helped us the most in our efforts to build strong roots is the creation of our lending library as a kind of information cooperative, in which use of the collection is facilitated through paid memberships available for a yearly donation, as mentioned above. This membership program supplies us with a direct financial link between our project and the constituency that benefits from it. It has enabled the CMC to have a concrete record of its community base of support. By keeping detailed records of how much and how regularly folks are willing to pay for their memberships, we are also able to know whom we can reach out to for increased support over the years, and whom we can contact for emergency donations when funds are short. Some of our members pay more than the requested $10-20 for their memberships, and some pledge to make regular donations on a monthly or quarterly schedule. Others have made larger "spot" donations to help us through funding emergencies, such as repairs to equipment and facilities. From barely managing to scrape by our first year on the generosity of one big-money donor and a small pool of members we have built a membership base of over 700 individuals, approximately 350-400 of whom are paid-up current at a given time. This includes dozens of folks who generously give higher amounts ranging from $30 or $40 to $1,000 at a time in addition to their yearly membership donations.

Occasionally we organize special fundraising drives to pay for improvements to the space, such as fixing up the floor in our main room, or building a wheelchair-accessible addition to our building's back porch. We are working on writing grants for projects like these, but so far have been successful at raising the funds through donations from individuals in the community. Periodic membership renewal drives by phone and mail accomplish the same goal of stepping-up our level of fundraising in a more measured, sustainable fashion. Our membership database functions as an organizing tool as well. By sending out newsletters that include updates on the CMC's functioning and a list of planned events, we are able to bring people back again and again, to share information with them, and to get their input and participation in local political and cultural happenings that we help organize at the Center and at other sites around town.

Even when we decide to engage in a more large-scale (read: expensive) production, such as bringing a high-profile speaker to town or renting a local theater to show an important new documentary, we try to build on the well-established progressive community tradition of cooperative organizing. By co-sponsoring larger projects with other groups and engaging in cooperative exchanges of time, energy, and resources, we are able to be a part of a wide variety of projects in the community and get our name and our message out in different public arenas. We always try to construct projects like these in such a way that they are either self-funding or actually generate additional revenue for the CMC, even if it's as modest as being able to take donations for bumper-stickers and buttons at our table at the back of the room.

## The Freedom Crew: CMC Organizational Structure

Once the Civic Media Center got up and running and was beginning to be a self-sustaining project, the organizers turned their attention to internal structure and long-term planning beyond the basics of daily operations. Incorporation as an official 501(c)(3) non-profit organization was one of the first hurdles to clear. With a commitment to grassroots, not-for-profit economic practices established from the beginning, and a clearly educational mission, the CMC qualified easily for official non-profit status. The organizers secured pro-bono legal help with the necessary paperwork through the local legal-aid organization.

The precise configuration of the relationships among the board of directors required by law for incorporation, the paid staffers, and the volunteer staffers has been one of our longest-running confusions. We've intentionally kept our organizational structure flexible and inclusive in order to accommodate the varying degrees of commitment and availability among our corps of volunteers. This is usually an advantage for us, as it has allowed the CMC to change and grow in response to the needs and interests of the community. Sometimes it can be problematic though, when we find ourselves once again reshuffling responsibilities and trying to rethink the way we've been doing things so as to avoid reinventing the wheel or letting important work get lost in the shuffle. Non-profit corporate status gave the CMC's founders a basic idea of how to structure the group, but as Charles Willett states in his 1994 article "How to Start an Alternative Library," "Corporations need officers and a board of directors, but operations may be handled better as a collective."[3] Our experience at the CMC has proven that a collective model is the best basic structure to work from for a group of our size and with our goals and budget.

It was decided early on that for an operation as many-faceted and requiring such a large amount of fundraising, there should be at least one paid staff person. It was also decided that despite the on-paper hierarchy of board of directors and officers required by the state, decisions about policies and day-to-day operations at the CMC were best made as a group by those who did the work—the volunteers and paid staffers. Despite the reality of a high turnover rate among the mostly college-aged pool of volunteers, and an unfortunate tendency towards burnout among the usually solo paid staffers (there have been some periods in which two people have shared the paid position), this philosophy and practice of collective group process still governs CMC operations. We have experimented with various formats in terms of committees and officers, and have settled into a flexible collective structure that incorporates the varying levels of drive and availability among our volunteers by delegating responsibility to individual "mission chiefs" and a series of ad hoc committees.

Currently the paid staff-person keeps tabs on the various projects that the mission chiefs and committees are charged with, acting as a hub for CMC workers and their work, just as the CMC itself serves as a hub for local organizations and their work in the community at large. He or she also does a lot of the behind-the-scenes work that keeps day-to-day operations running smoothly, from training new volunteers to changing the message on our answering machine to include the new events for each week. Our board of directors meets several times a year and does community outreach and fundraising work, including organizing large fundraising events that raise significant amounts of money towards our yearly budget. We make collective decisions about day-to-day operations at weekly volunteer meetings, and policy-making and long-range planning decisions at a series of biannual retreats, which we jokingly refer to as "CMC Bootcamps." We use a decision-making process that is best described as "informal consensus," and have developed written policies detailing a group decision-making process of formal consensus, with a provision for voting if necessary, for handling more contentious issues.

We are working on developing a long-range fundraising and organizational readjustment strategy to help make the CMC more sustainable. Right now, with a shoestring budget and a constantly-changing corps of volunteers, most of the work of trying to maintain cohesion, coherence, and continuity for the project falls on the paid staffer(s) and a core group of dedicated volunteers who've maintained their commitment to the CMC over the years. It has been an interesting transition for those of us who've been around for the long haul to make the shift in consciousness from the kind of disempowered, reactive organizing mode that the Left too often finds itself stuck with in America, to the empowered, creative, proactive mode that a project like the CMC allows. One element of this transition is the realization of the pressing need for more people to be paid for this kind of work.

The CMC's paid staffer, usually referred to as "coordinator" or "office manager," was originally supposed to be paid a part-time stipend for part-time work. It quickly became evident, however, that the time and energy necessary to be our project's "brain" was closer to a full-time job. Much Left/progressive organizing that is done at the grassroots level is done by volunteers, as a labor of love, "for the cause." While fighting the good fight for freedom and justice can be one of the most fulfilling things that an individual can choose to do with his or her time, it can often entail a great deal of self-sacrifice. This is true even of the work that goes into relatively safe, staid "support" projects like the CMC. The Civic Media Center is a complex, challenging project, and can be very demanding on people's time and energy. There is a growing concern among the core group of CMC workers that our current structure, with only one paid staffer, whom we can afford to pay what amounts to only a part-time salary for full-time work, is clearly not sustainable in the long run. Both paid staff and long-term volunteers are vulnerable to a recurring cycle of over-commitment and burnout in this scenario. We are learning the hard way that if we are going to commit to having paid staff, we must look to the future and take steps now to build our fundraising and internal organizing up in such a way that more workers are paid, and paid well, for their labor at the CMC. When we see ourselves as part of a movement that is fighting for a just and sustainable society, in which all people have the freedom to live healthy, multi-faceted, fulfilling lives, we realize that we must do our best to provide those same conditions in the here and now for those who are willing to give themselves wholly to the work of trying to build that socety from the bottom up.

That said, it remains that for now and for the foreseeable future, volunteers are the lifeblood of the CMC. They staff the space and help members and guests during regular operating hours, set up and run events, maintain the membership, finance and collections records, assemble newsletters and other mailings, staff CMC tables at rallies, conferences and demonstrations in Gainesville and abroad, engage in fundraising phone drives, and perform many other tasks too numerous to list here, all of which are essential to making the CMC go. Most of our volunteers are students or college-aged young people, and many of them move on after a few months or a year, sometimes into career-type jobs or new educational endeavors, and sometimes into other kinds of volunteer political work. The CMC often acts as a catalyst in people's lives, opening their eyes to a whole world of information and experience that they never knew existed, and helping them to find their path in the world, as any good educational institution should. It is extremely rewarding to hear stories from folks who come back to visit us about how their time at the CMC inspired them to seek out similar grassroots projects in their new communities, or even helped launch them into careers in progressive political organizing and alternative media. All of us who've been with the CMC for a while can recall such stories. It makes our hard work seem all the more worthwhile when we learn the many ways in which this project that we've all worked so hard to build has borne such successful fruit. One such success story is that of local activist Sand Wrenn, who had this to say about her involvement with the Center:

> "I never saw myself as capable of contributing to political change. Then, after becoming interested in the indigenous people's struggle in Chiapas, Mexico, I learned that a Latin American solidarity group held meetings at the CMC. I got involved, and through time the mentors in the group helped me to hone my leadership skills and assume an important role. Later, as a Civic Media Center volunteer, I was encouraged to express creativity in developing and coordinating a CMC outreach project [on the University of Florida campus]. My future has been galvanized by my CMC experience; I am now an organizer with a human rights group at the University of Florida."

## People Get Together Now!

The Civic Media Center volunteers and staff have found fertile ground in which to plant the project's roots in the many layers of Gainesville's progressive community. It is these "people connections" that really make an operation like ours work. One of our greatest assets is the network of activists, union members, musicians, counterculture folks, professionals, and small-business people that CMC co-founder, former coordinator, and perpetual volunteer Joe Courter has cultivated in his twenty-plus years of living and working in the area. The struggle for freedom that drives projects like the CMC is really about people—their needs and desires, hopes and dreams—and Joe has taught many of us at the CMC by his example that almost anything is possible, even on a shoestring budget, when you keep the positive, productive connections between people at the forefront of all your work. Cynics often say of business and politics in our society, "It's not what you do, it's who you know." Looking back on the many powerful examples of organizing, education, and community-building that I have seen in six years of participation at the Civic Media Center, I have to say that the work of folks like Joe and the CMC volunteers continually reminds me that in grassroots community organizing, it's who you know *and* what you do.

The Civic Media Center is a heroic grassroots achievement. To the coalition of liberals, radicals, and counterculture folks who hold it together and keep it going, the CMC represents our little community's contribution to the next wave of popular resistance to corporate greed and government abuse of power—that is, organizing around access to information and the use of alternative information as a launching point for direct action on issues that affect the everyday lives of people in our community and around the world. Through the example of the CMC and the constellation of grassroots groups that have come to use it as a focal point for their activities, people see that the fulfillment of the promise of democracy resides first and foremost in the "civic sector," the autonomous people's organizations that work outside the locus of government and corporate control to meet the needs of the people, and to challenge both state and capital to answer their critique and match their forward strides. We hear it said time and again by folks who visit the CMC: "I wish my town had a Civic Media Center," or "Gosh, every town oughtta have a place like this." We agree.

Contact the Civic Media Center at 1021 West University Avenue, Gainesville, FL 32601, USA, phone: 352-373-0010, e-mail: cmc@gator.net, URL: http://www.gator.net/~cmc

## Notes

1. Harriet Ludwig, "Noam Chomsky: People Hungry for Real News," *F.A.C.T. Magazine*, November 1993, p. 15.

2. Edward Herman, "Democratic Media: Serving the People's Needs," *Z Papers* 1, #1, 1992, pp. 23-30.

3. Charles Willett, "Starting an Alternative Library," *Librarians at Liberty* 1, #2, January 1994, pp. 6-7.

*Part Three*

# LEARNING IN AN AGE OF INFORMATION: PERSPECTIVES ON TECHNOLOGY

# Haven
## A Collaborative Life–Long *Cyber*–Learning Community

*by Claudia L'Amoreaux*

## Beginnings

I BOUGHT MY FIRST 2,400-baud modem in 1985. Friends of mine were using these "lightning fast" communications devices to open a long-distance dialogue with people in the former Soviet Union in some of the first peace exchanges. I was intrigued. As a child of the '50s, raised with "iron curtains," a Soviet "enemy," and air-raid drills all through elementary and junior high school, this opportunity to create peace through direct action was a promise of planetary citizenship realized. EcoNet, later to join with PeaceNet in the IGC Network (Institute for Global Communications) blazed Internet trails in citizen diplomacy and helped launch me into cyberspace with their inspiring global activism.

When I connected the modem to my Macintosh Plus computer and logged onto the Internet for the first time, the Whole Earth 'Lectronic Link (the WELL) was my home base. Starting in the spring of 1969, a group of practical visionaries published the *Whole Earth Catalog*, offering "access to tools and ideas" that nurtured whole-systems thinking, right livelihood and sustainable business, and self-directed learning. The *Whole Earth Catalog* was a new paradigm tsunami, and long before GOPHER (an early system for locating documents on the Internet in specific subject areas) and the World Wide Web, I surfed its content-rich pages. The WELL grew out of the creativity of the *Whole Earth Catalog* community. One of the early computer conferencing networks, it was a result of the combined vision of catalog creator Stewart Brand and Larry Brilliant. Stewart and Larry were members of the EIES (Electronic Information Exchange System) network started by Murray Turoff at the New Jersey Institute of Technology in 1974. Murray developed EMISARY, the first computer conferencing system. He designed EIES to facilitate group decision-making based on collective intelligence. In 1985, Stewart and Larry turned their experience with EIES into the WELL. This pioneering electronic community is still thriving today.

The WELL took online conferencing to an entirely new level—people explored the ethics and responsibilities of "netizenship," with plenty of real sweat and tears shed along the sometimes arduous way. Thriving, long-term dialogues were carried on for years on an incredible range of topics from homeschooling to Generation X to the future. As a result, the WELL community has contributed a great deal of wisdom and guidelines for creating and sustaining online community. Howard Rheingold is one influential WELL veteran. He distilled his insights into a book, *The Virtual Community: Homesteading on the Electronic Frontier* (online at http://www.rheingold.com/vc/book/).

A few years later I joined Women's Wire, a San Francisco-based electronic bulletin board, or BBS, as they were known. It was the first online community for women, started by Nancy Rhine and Ellen Pack. Nancy had been a key staff member of the WELL community. These conferencing networks and BBSs—EcoNet and PeaceNet, the WELL, and Women's Wire—were the ancestors of today's online learning communities. They reflected and embodied two highly significant shifts—from teaching to learning, and from media consumption to invention and creation. These experimental communities encouraged participants in self-directed, life-long learning and in generating their own media. With EcoNet and PeaceNet, American citizens and then-Soviet citizens set out to learn their own truths about each other's culture through e-mail exchange, person to person, direct, not through their countries' textbooks and narrow, mainstream media. Environmental and peace activists could collaborate effectively on local and international projects, sharing information and organizing actions and responses.

Women's Wire offered women a place online to discuss their take on business, health, sexuality, parenting, and politics at a time when the Internet was still very much a man's world. Women coached each other in entrepreneurial skills. Editors gathered daily world news that focused on women's issues and created a women's "herstory" archive. The Women's Wire community became a networking hub for women preparing to attend the Beijing Women's Conference in 1995, and for those of us who could not attend in person, they helped us participate virtually. During a major staff turnover and conversion from BBS conferencing system to the World Wide Web, Women's Wire abandoned its community. That strategic decision left many women disappointed, but I know that all who were participants in their bold experiment are grateful to have ridden its wave.

# Paradigm Shifting: The Journey from Teaching to Learning, and from Media Consumption to Media Generation

> Ours was a house for children, rather than a real school. We had prepared a place for children where a diffused culture could be assimilated, without any need for direct instruction...Yet these children learned to read and write before they were five, and no one had given them any lessons. At that time it seemed miraculous that children of four and a half should be able to write, and that they should have learned without the feeling of having been taught.
>
> —Maria Montessori,
> about the first Children's Houses in the slums of Rome in 1907

I was fortunate to experience a shift in emphasis from teaching to learning early in my adult life. Drawn by a vision of ecstatic learning inspired by mentors like George Leonard, Ivan Illich, A.S. Neill and John Holt, I found my way to The New School, an unusual Montessori preschool and elementary "free school," as an intern. Along with visionaries like John Dewey, the Italian physician-turned-educator Maria Montessori was ahead of her time in leading the way towards self-directed learning. The New School's founders, Carol and Tom French-Corbett, translated Montessori's respect for self-directed learning into an extraordinary place. The New School was my first learning community. Parents and staff ran the school together, by consensus. (They weren't ready yet to extend the democratic vote to the children like Summerhill and the Albany Free School had, but attempting consensus government with staff and parents having equal votes was a big step in the right direction.) I left the teacher/student paradigm behind and crossed over fully to learning facilitator with the young people.

Several years later, as a founding member of an experimental media lab, I was able to take my explorations in learning community to the next level. The Cyberlab, later SynergyLabs, brought together a diverse group of artists, musicians, programmers, animators, "evolving systems" researchers, virtual-reality architects, video pioneers, men and women of all ages and races. Together we explored and practiced self-directed, cooperative life-long learning. In this experimental learning community, my teenage daughter and I were co-learners and collaborators. Extraordinary projects emerged, from live video performances with jazz musicians Ornette Coleman and Herbie Hancock to videoconferences like the first Summit in Cyberspace with then-Prime Minister Shimon Peres of Israel, then-President Nelson Mandela of South Africa, and former U.S. President Jimmy Carter.

My first introduction to media generation was also at the New School in 1973. We were using early black-and-white video cameras with "portapacks" to record the children and facilitators in the environment. We analyzed the video in slow motion for feedback on learning styles (facilitators' and children's) and the dynamics of interaction in an innovative process pioneered by Nancy Rambusch at Xavier University. It was life-changing to step behind the camera for the first time and "make TV." I never looked at television in quite the same way.

But my shift to full media empowerment came later. My work in the Cyberlab took me to the furthest reaches of media and technology. We played and experimented with some of the earliest videophones, connecting with new media explorers in other cities around the world (there was even an "electronic café" in China that had a videophone). Though these early videophones were black-and-white and transmitted only still images, they were extraordinary to use. Learning how to use them for creative collaborations was a significant advance in my journey from media consumer to media generator.

In 1992 I participated in one of the first demonstrations of a high-end videoconferencing system (PictureTel). I was in Monterey, California, at a new technologies and design conference, and I was videoconferencing with a man in New York City. His image filled the full screen of the monitor in front of me, in rich color, almost in real time—the video moved a little slower than we were moving, which actually heightened my senses. I was overcome by my feelings of intimacy in communicating with this stranger 2,500 miles away. It was a profound, life-changing encounter. I had a direct experience of the powerful potential videoconferencing had for learning in the future. I recognized that freedom from the need for geographical proximity opened up a world of co-learners and collaborators, enabling people to develop and sustain relationships across distance based on shared interest and commitment.

After that eye-opening experience, I began using software called CU-SeeMe, designed at Cornell University in 1993. It was the first Internet-based videoconferencing software that worked with a simple dial-up modem, and it was free. I was soon in touch with people all over the world using it for collaborative learning experiments. Today, from my home in Northern California, I can meet with a young person in Idaho who is apprenticing in deep ecology and new media journalism. Using the latest version of the CU-SeeMe software (White Pine's Classpoint), we can visit online articles and web sites about deep ecology and discuss them together "face to face." We can interview people working in deep ecology, and we can take each other on web tours, another feature of the software. It's an extraordinary communication medium.

Worlds Chat, the first networked, three-dimensional virtual world, debuted in the spring of 1994. It evolved from a project called Starbright, sponsored by Steven Spielberg's Starbright Foundation. Starbright World was a three-dimensional world that let seriously ill children use avatars (animated characters used for self-representation) to communicate with each other using computers on a closed-circuit network within the hospital. Worlds Chat was one of the first Internet-based, networked virtual worlds for the general public. Using the computer mouse, you navigated through a three-dimensional world much like you'd move through a video game, with the significant difference being that you could meet and interact with other people from all over the world who were in the virtual world at the same time as you. When you encountered other avatars, you could initiate conversations with their human counterparts by typing a message. Like my first experience videoconferencing, Worlds Chat gave me a preview of possible online learning communities in the future. These new learning environments would seamlessly incorporate multimedia and a three-dimensional visual and kinetic language to allow richer forms of cross-cultural communication. They would enable new kinds of learning—especially in mathematics and the new sciences of chaos theory and complexity, where text-based, two-dimensional approaches actually inhibit understanding. There was clearly a long way to go still, but I could imagine it.

Software like ActiveWorlds that followed in the path of Worlds Chat let people construct their own virtual worlds from the "ground up," offering a major turning point in the shift from media consumption to media generation. One young person who collaborated on a world using the ActiveWorlds software enthusiastically likened it to playing with Legos—it was second nature for him. He shared with me how stepping into the creator role had forever changed his relationship to more passive, consumer-style media like television and conventional video games. He was giving form to his own creative visions and gaining valuable skills of teamwork in the process. There was no going back—that is paradigm shifting.

Shortly after I discovered Worlds Chat, I had a *Eureka*! experience that changed my life. I saw the World Wide Web for the first time on an extremely fast computer (the SGI Indigo) connected to the Internet via an extremely high-speed line (called a T1 line, it is twenty to a hundred times faster than a dial-up modem). I was standing in an air-conditioned exhibition hall in downtown Los Angeles—it was 1994. I felt like I'd stepped into a time machine and was being transported several years into the future. Rather than seeing the Web where it was (most people were using much slower dial-up modems to access the Web at the time), I could see where it was going. I realized that these technologies—videoconferencing, three-dimensional virtual worlds, and the World Wide Web—would soon converge, enabling the emergence of an extraordinary new global learning environment. In that moment of awareness and insight, I made the decision to actively participate in creating that future, especially as it applied to the future of learning

I began to notice something significant. At the Cyberlab, we hosted many gatherings for our local community with a focus on learning. Over and over I heard people saying the same thing, whether parents, school principals or teachers—"I know education has to change, but I don't know what it could look like." I realized that from my unique experiences and my "future" vantage point, I did see how it could be. We were living one possible scenario at the lab, and it was an extraordinary experience appreciated by all the community members. I'd met and worked closely with many young people who were inhabiting a very different world, where self-directed learning was primary, apprenticeship was commonplace, and collaboration was key. Cyberspace and virtual worlds were a natural extension of their everyday world that opened entirely new possibilities for creativity and learning.

Time spent in dialogue and study with visionary social systems thinkers like Bela H. Banathy and Barbara Vogl helped me refine and evolve my visions of the possible. To differentiate this *self-directed life-long learning community/new media generative* paradigm from the standard teacher-directed/passive media-based education, I invented a new word—*edge-ucation*. It came from my own peak learning experiences, when I always found myself standing at an edge that offered an entirely new vista—I could see things I'd never seen before, and I could make extraordinary new connections. These were breakthroughs in my learning how to learn.

## Think Globally, Act Locally

In 1972, while he was advisor to the United Nations Conference on the Environment, René Dubos gave us the now-familiar phrase, "Think globally, act locally." He wanted people to realize that to make a difference in the global environment, we must begin by considering our local bioregion—essential wisdom that more and more communities are taking to heart. Peter Berg, one of the founders of the bioregional movement, states it succinctly:

> Bioregions are geographic areas having common characteristics of soil, watershed, climate, native plants and animals that exist within the whole planetary biosphere as unique and contributive parts. A bioregion refers both to geographical terrain and a terrain of consciousness—to a place and the ideas that have developed about how to live in that place...The bioregion is my window on the planetary biosphere and the means for participating in it.

Community learning centers are natural sites for "acting locally" and nurturing bioregional awareness and sensitivity. I see the spontaneous growth of community learning centers as one of the most exciting developments on the learning horizon today. One of the primary intentions of this book is to offer working examples of these community learning centers and simple guidelines for their creation to encourage their proliferation. Ideally, the community learning center supports self-directed, life-long learning in a non-hierarchical structure. Participation is voluntary. Forms of financial support vary from public funding to minimal membership fees to tuition. Learning facilitators assist participants in locating co-learners, mentors and learning resources, apprenticeships and internships, and in goal-setting and self assessment if requested, portfolio preparation, and sustainable livelihood coaching. A community may have several learning centers, serving the needs of a diverse population.

As the model evolves, facilitators and learning-community members will begin to network with other centers in their community to share resources, co-host bioregional events, collaborate on watershed restoration projects, share apprenticeship databases, etc. Computers with Internet connectivity will become an integral part of many of the centers. This will be especially valuable in offering access to young people and their families, and adults in the community who do not have personal computers and Internet access. Internationally, the community learning-center model is becoming a successful interim solution to the serious problem of universal computer and Internet access, often referred to as the "digital divide" (see *Access Issues* at the end of this chapter). I would strongly encourage anyone now at work on creating a community learning center to budget in at least one computer and Internet access. It's an important service you can offer community members—the Internet is a profound resource that we are only beginning to understand how to use.

With the explosive development of the Internet, particularly the World Wide Web, I think it is necessary now to reconsider René's statement. Perhaps today, more of us have a sense of what it means to act locally. But what does "think globally" mean in the twenty-first century? How do we begin? At the same time as we are evolving our sense of place ("reinhabiting our bioregions," as Peter Berg urges us to do), we are called upon to develop and evolve global thinking skills. I see this as one of the primary roles of online learning communities. They offer us an extraordinary and unprecedented context to practice global thinking by enabling international dialogue, exchange, and collaboration. This is not optimistic dreaming. Amazing global thinking experiments have been flowering for several years, supported by e-mail alone. EcoNet and PeaceNet, the WELL, and Women's Wire were among the first generation of online learning communities. They pointed the way by exploring how to create and sustain real communities in this strange new realm of electronically mediated communications.

Organizations like Thinkquest and the International Education and Resource Network (I*EARN) are examples of what I call second-generation learning communities. Thinkquest (http://www.thinkquest.org) was founded in 1996 by Advanced Network & Services, one of the early developers of the high-speed portions of the Internet used by universities and research institutions today. Thinkquest programs catalyzed the creation of the largest database in the world of educational websites created by young people for young people. Since 1996, almost 50,000 teens and educators from a hundred countries have participated in ThinkQuest, bringing together youth from widely divergent cultures and languages, levels of technology, and socio-economic backgrounds.

I attended the Thinkquest Conference in November of 1998 in Los Angeles, California, with the specific intention of meeting these teenagers who were collaborating across distance. I wanted to learn from these young cybernauts. Most of them were meeting face-to-face for the first time. They enthusiastically shared with me how their experiences had changed their lives. I was especially impressed with how the collaborations had given them incredible self-confidence and belief in their ability to master whatever it was they needed to learn to make their projects work. They had gained uncanny wisdom about encountering obstacles— language and time-zone barriers, expectations and disappointment, technological hurdles, conflict management and resolution. My conversations with these young people have encouraged and inspired me to trust where I am going in distance edge-ucation.

At the same Thinkquest conference, I met Ed Gragert, the director of I*EARN, and Adriana Vilela, a teacher from Argentina who was a participant in I*EARN's network. I*EARN (http://www.igc.apc.org/iearn/) was launched in 1988 to demonstrate that kids could work together to make a difference on the planet using low-cost telecommunication technologies, first between the U.S. and the Soviet Union. Today there are 50 countries involved. In an interview, Adriana told me how her work with I*EARN had been a force for positive change:

> It impacted not only the lives of the students and teachers, but also the lives of parents and the community. I'm one of the thousands of teachers in I*EARN whose teaching practice has been affected greatly, deeply by I*EARN. I live in a very isolated place, Patagonia, which is the southern region of Argentina. I've been working in a public secondary school with very underprivileged children. I've been there for twenty years now. I was a bit disappointed about teaching with very few resources that we teachers have in a developing country, especially in a very far-away place like the one where I live. Perhaps my anecdote as a teacher is that I was ready to quit, because I had given up. That's the truth. The year I was ready to quit the minister of education sent this proposal for the school to be one of the first five pilot schools in Argentina to work with this technology for telecommunications. Well, I was caught by this and I never left. I'm still a teacher in Argentina nearly eight years later because, working with this technology and I*EARN, I could see the difference that it makes for students and teachers and also the community where we live. It involves every pedagogical issue that we teachers are concerned about, like how to teach meaningfully, how to get the students more involved and in charge and take responsibility for their own learning, how to work collaboratively and take action in society. This is the first principle of democracy, really.

Supported by grants from corporations and family funds, Thinkquest and I*EARN leverage the potential of the Internet for educators and students around the world. These educators and students have been profoundly changed by their participation, naturally gravitating towards a new model of learning facilitators or coaches assisting collaborative learning teams. But these second-generation learning communities still have their foundations in a twentieth-century educational system. I see them as transitional, no doubt pioneers in their own right, evolving a twenty-first-century approach to learning out of the ashes of the old. Using new media technologies, they are enabling thousands of youth and adults all over the world to explore new models for learning—this is their unique strength and valuable contribution.

I'm especially interested in what I call third-generation online learning communities. These Internet-based collectives have their roots in the new paradigm of self-directed and collaborative community-based life-long learning (what I call edge-ucation). Their emergence parallels the evolution of the World Wide Web. They use discussion lists, websites, and three-dimensional worlds for their gathering spaces. They are guided by insights of visionary edge-ucators like Ivan Illich, John Holt, Bela H. Banathy, and Seymour Papert, and by the experiences of people living the new learning paradigm with their families and friends. They are deeply influenced and informed by the new sciences—complexity theory, systems thinking, second-order cybernetics. These learning communities can be accessed and participated in by teachers and young people in schools, but they are not tied to schools. They are philosophically partnered with the community learning-center movement. They are a recent phenomenon. Because of this, in their nature, they are experimental, evolving entirely new approaches to learning.

This book you are reading and its companion website are excellent examples of the efforts of a third-generation learning community. Thirty authors and about seventy other co-learners and contributors have come together on the "Learning Communities" discussion list over a period of a year in a remarkable "learning community about learning communities," completely online, in a challenging, text-only environment. Our moderator, Bill Ellis, is in Maine. The website host, Ib Bang, is in Denmark. I am in California. I've met only one list member face-to-face, and that was a brief encounter at an educational conference more than fifteen years ago.

When I discovered this network of kindred spirits, I was living in a cottage in a redwood forest, thirty minutes from the nearest small town. It was exhilarating to dive into a book collaboration with other community learning-center pioneers from all over the world with my computer and slow modem (phone lines in the woods were too old to support a high-speed modem) as the portal. I was suddenly immersed with people deeply committed to creating a new learning system. A Coalition for Self Learning, the name we gave ourselves, exhibits the characteristics of a third-generation learning community—it is self-organizing, collaborative, spontaneous, complex, emerging—qualities our catalyst and list moderator Bill Ellis is quick to emphasize to new community members.

So how do these two relate—local community learning centers and online learning communities? They complement each other. The online community can connect participants in local centers to people all over the world for exploration, co-learning, and collaboration. By contributing to and creating an online learning community, participants in the local centers become media generators. Helping to construct cyberspace changes our relationship to it dramatically. It is empowering. The local learning centers give online learning-community participants the place to put their feet on the ground and their hands in the soil. It's a haven in the physical world for sharing the joys and challenges of direct person-to-person contact and intimacy on the co-learning trail. Taking René's words to heart, the online learning community becomes the global counterpoint to the local community learning center, and the local learning center grounds the online learning community in an honest sense of place. It's a potent combination. Let's weave them together right from the start.

How might we begin the weaving? Some local centers will feel inspired to create their own online learning communities. Some may consider collaborating with one other or a few centers in other parts of the world to create a shared, online learning community. A Coalition for Self-Learning discussion list/community (see the Resources section) and the AERO (Alternative Education Resource Organization) discussion list and website (see Resources) will be helpful in facilitating these connections between local centers. Other centers may choose to participate in and contribute to existing online learning communities for which they feel an affinity. Haven is an online learning community that welcomes local centers to participate. The Edge-ucation Matrix of Haven supports community learning centers in creating their own online learning communities, and NEXUS, Haven's Learning Community Network, is a web directory for online learning communities to announce themselves.

## Haven

> There is no pregiven territory of which we can make a map—the
> map-making itself brings forth the features of the territory.
> —Fritjof Capra, *The Web of Life*

The best way I've discovered to learn about learning communities is to design, create, and participate in one. In the '70s and '80s, I catalyzed local community learning centers—one for unschooling families, and later one for teenagers. After my *Eureka!* experience in 1994, I began meditating on my ideal online learning environment—what would it be like?

Several years earlier, I had encountered the powerful ideas of Christopher Alexander, an iconoclastic architect. Studying hundreds of cities, towns, and buildings over a period of several years, he looked for underlying patterns that resonated what he calls "timeless qualities"—freedom, wholeness, completeness, comfort, harmony, habitability, durability, openness, resilience, variability, and adaptability. Christopher believes that patterns embodying these timeless qualities are what give structures their vitality. They touch the soul and vastly improve our daily lives. Nikos Salingaros, an architectural theorist, describes Alexander's work in these words: "There is an emphasis throughout on the potential of the individual, the importance of a spiritual connection to the built world; the need for cooperation among people; the empowerment of individuals or small groups of people to shape their environment." Christopher writes that "people can shape buildings for themselves, and have done it for centuries, by using languages which I call pattern languages...But in our time, the languages have broken down...To work our ways towards a shared and living language once again, we must first learn how to discover patterns which are deep, and capable of generating life." In his two-volume design guide, *A Pattern Language* and *The Timeless Way of Building*, he invites people to evolve and add to his 253 patterns, co-creating a common language for building everything from a sustainable community to a family dwelling, from cooperative workshop space to a children's bedroom or a garden path.

I began to apply his pattern language and design process to the architecture of online learning spaces. People in fields as diverse as organizational development and software design have appreciated Alexander's ideas and the parallels between the architecture of towns and buildings with information systems. The first "webmaster" I apprenticed with, Matisse Enzer, had also been deeply influenced by Alexander's work.

The faculty and staff at the University of Pittsburgh used a pattern language process to design the university information system. From the moment I saw the Web, I experienced the "space" of it. When I first began to imagine an online learning community, I was aware that I was experiencing and creating a space, not a website. Christopher Alexander's pattern language helped me to articulate the patterns and qualities I wanted Haven to express and evoke.

I started with one of the most basic patterns, "network of learning" (pattern 18 in *A Pattern Language*). Here is the essence of the pattern as I have evolved it: A network of learning facilitates a shift in emphasis from teaching to learning, helps decentralize the process of learning, and enriches it with contact with many places and people all over the local community (and extending the pattern to the Internet environment—all over the world). It supports voluntary participation in a diversity of learning opportunities by illuminating pathways of access. Skillful network guides help learners master navigation and assist them in finding their way to particular resources, peers, collaborators, mentors, and experts they are seeking. The learning network extends beyond the limited domain of credentialed teachers to recognize everyone as mentor and learner.

The network of learning is all-inclusive, valuing the experience and expertise of a fourteen-year-old computer programmer alongside the skills and insights of an earthworm specialist in Vietnam, a Shawnee native speaker, or a professor of linguistics. Responsibility for orchestrating learning is in the hands of the learner. Self-assessment replaces standardized testing.

## Haven's Patterns for an Online Learning Community

> We discovered that the process, the actual coming together, is as
> important as the original intent. Often, the thing hoped for is what
> brings the people together, but the coming together in a deep and
> passionate way is what makes the hoped-for thing happen, whether
> it happens on the first try or the eighty-first. The two are mutually
> reinforcing, and, for some, the community building aspect is fulfilling
> in itself.                                    —from "The Art of Community Building"
> *Orion Afield* magazine, summer, 1999, p. 9

Interconnection is the song at the heart of Haven. My particular
dream of a learning community came from wanting to share a space with
people who realize there is no separation between how we learn, how we
work, and how we live. The focal points are edge-ucation, right livelihood,
and deep ecology. It's a place to explore and restore the relationships
between these, and to reflect on and initiate transformation in how we
learn, and work, and solve the world's most pressing problems. Haven is
dedicated to young people to give them support to live interconnected
lives. It's a way-station for adults who aspire to create sustainability in
their personal lives, their communities, and on the planet. We aim to
nurture those aspirations. We're especially interested in exploring the far
reaches of learning how to learn.

On a very practical level, the Haven learning community encourages
self-directed design of ecstatic learning paths and supports individuals in
this endeavor, especially teenagers, through a combination of one-on-one
mentoring, collaborations, and apprenticeships in a distance-learning
environment. Recognizing that local learning centers and online learning
communities are significant new forms with incredible potential for transformation (societal and individual), we are dedicated to spreading the
news by studying and promoting the best of these experiments. The
Edge-ucation Matrix of Haven specifically intends to encourage the design and evolution of these new learning centers at both the global
(online) and local (community) levels. Informal study circles give community members the opportunity to explore existing resources for creating
community learning centers and online learning communities. Online
courses, called "Journeys," and the more in-depth Edge-ucator's Path
apprenticeships assist individuals and groups in practicing the skills
needed to participate in and significantly contribute to the creation of
collaborative life-long learning communities.

The "councils" and the "dialogues" are the basic processes at the center
of each of the three major zones in the Haven learning community—the
Edge-ucation Zone, the Right Livelihood Zone and the Deep Ecology Zone.
Councils and dialogues are the patterns unique to Haven to catalyze and
support a web-based network of learning. The councils present the ideas,
exemplary projects, and organizations of people who have given deep
consideration to the central Haven motifs of edge-ucation, right livelihood
and sustainable business, and deep ecology. The dialogues give partici-

pants the opportunity to explore ideas presented in the councils, as well as to initiate learning conversations about topics of interest. Until recently, participants used e-mail and discussion lists for the dialogues (known as asynchronous communication), but we are now experimenting with what we call "synchronous space" using the Haven Dialogue Zone, which lets a group of us meet together all at the same time using "chat" software. These dialogues can then be archived and read by others later.

We have identified eight essential skills to help us practice and develop our global thinking. They are storytelling, dialogue, collaboration, bioregional awareness, ecological/systems thinking, design literacy and competence, linguistic flexibility and inventiveness, and image-ination or visual thinking. Continually asking ourselves how we can nurture these skills helps shape all of Haven. The Journeys and apprenticeships explore these skills in depth.

Special projects and events let us bring festival and ceremony into cyberspace. Earth Day is a major holiday for us. Haven went live on the Web on Earth Day '95 amidst a face-to-face celebration with friends and contributors in San Francisco. It has become a Haven tradition to continue the celebration with a live online event every Earth Day. We send out an announcement to various e-mail lists and websites inviting people to participate in The Earth Stories Project, our Gaian Storytelling Festival. The Earth Stories Project encourages people to consider their interconnections in the web of life and share their experiences in story and art. We invite people to participate year-round, but on Earth Day a team of us stays online all day, posting the stories (words and/or images) in the Deep Ecology Zone as they come in from all over the world. It's always an exhilarating experience for everyone involved, and it introduces new people to Haven.

We welcome local learning centers to participate in the future. Children's contributions are especially appreciated. We celebrate both Earth Days, spring equinox and April 22$^{nd}$ of every year. Join us for one and get a feel for hosting your own online events. As singer/songwriter Patti Smith says, "Be a gathering." Our electronic newsletter, *Interconnect*, plays an important role in the life of our learning community. It lets community members know what's changed since their last visit. Haven's participants appreciate receiving e-mail updates informing them of new material, programs, and events. Every month in *Interconnect* we include reviews of other learning communities, favorite websites, insights from the dialogues, etc. And we use it to announce our Journeys and apprenticeships.

## The Structure of the Learning Community

Participants choose different levels of involvement in the learning community. Here's a glimpse of how it all works currently. The Edge-ucation, Right Livelihood, and Deep Ecology zones of the Haven web center (http://www.haven.net) present opportunities for self-directed learning and dialogue. We encourage participants to initiate their own learning conversations using asynchronous discussion and the synchronous chat software in the Dialogue Zone. Out of the wider community, some people step into roles as collaborators and contributors to the content in the web center, bringing a diverse range of stories and projects. Teens and adults who are especially drawn to the focus of the learning community and choose to get more involved enter The Edge-ucation Matrix. This is the core of the Haven global studies center. Here we offer short, introductory experiences called Journeys, and deep apprenticeships and mentoring, using a rich, multimedia mix of text, image, audio, and video communication (asynchronous and synchronous). Apprentices who complete three sessions in the Matrix can become interns and eventually may become facilitators, mentors, and resource guides in the learning community.

This same structure of collaborators, contributors, Journeys, mentoring, and apprenticeships is mirrored in the form of our local learning center, also called The Edge-ucation Matrix. Because there is quite a variety of programs in our community for younger children and their families, the Edge-ucation Matrix serves teenagers and adults. We support teens in creating alternate paths to higher learning through self-study (autodidactics), learning conversations, mentoring, and apprenticeships. We offer coaching in right livelihood and the creation of sustainable business, drawing on role models from the local community.

The Bayside Children's College (see Resources Section), a learning center in our local community, shares its space with us in the late afternoons and evenings. We are beginning to host informal salons on edge-ucation, right livelihood, and deep ecology. Our local learning center is just beginning to evolve. We are in the process now of building alliances with other organizations and learning centers like the Santa Cruz Live Oak Grange (our community center for sustainable agriculture), the Theater of Restoration (an organization facilitating the use of performance art for environment restoration in homeschool education), and the Order of Green Knights (a men's service group and lodge dedicated to helping men, especially teenagers, reconnect to the earth through rites of passage, restoration service projects, and earth literacy education).

For our first collaborative project, our four organizations are co-sponsoring a workshop on mapping our bioregion with Peter Berg. We anticipate that in the future, participants in the local Edge-ucation Matrix and these other organizations will become active shapers of the Haven online learning community.

Haven is also a *meta*-learning community focused on the design, creation, and networking of learning communities, particularly online learning communities. Since we perceive local learning centers and online learning communities as two of the most significant new forms capable of nurturing life-long learners and designers of sustainable democratic and ecological systems, we are committed to encourage and support the forms' flowering and proliferation. Through the Edge-ucation Matrix of Haven, we offer introductory courses on the online learning-community model and we mentor and/or consult with individuals and teams that are attempting to create local learning centers and online learning communities. The Edge-ucator's Path Apprenticeship is an in-depth design journey for people initiating online learning communities.

NEXUS is our online learning community directory and network. It serves the purpose of connecting online learning communities with each other to share resources and support. It also connects the online learning communities with individuals, families, edge-ucators, and local learning centers seeking to participate in creative learning communities. Descriptions of member online learning communities are provided with links to their websites.

The Haven facilitators continually review and feature the work of visionary learning communities in the Edge-ucation Zone of the Haven web center, the *Interconnect* e-newsletter, and the *PATTERNS* newsletter (the PATTERNS learning community is a founding member of NEXUS). Participants of online learning communities in the network are invited to share their stories, image-inations, and projects in the different zones of Haven. Members are welcome to use the Haven Dialogue Zone for their conversations and study circles. To help support NEXUS, learning communities in the network pay an annual membership fee.

Our ongoing work as distance learning consultants and course designers/coaches creates a foundation for us to build upon. We have chosen not to seek advertisers to date. Consulting work and membership fees from NEXUS and monthly fees from the Journeys, formal mentoring relationships, and apprenticeships are beginning to help sustain Haven. In the Greentrade area of the Right Livelihood Zone, we have a business directory. We plan to actively seek more businesses for this section in the future, and will charge an annual membership fee for the listings. In addition, we are writing grant proposals to expand some of our projects.

Haven is on the more elaborate end of the spectrum of online learning communities. Keep in mind that it is six years old. It started small and has grown organically. Effective and engaging learning communities can be as simple as an e-mail list with homepages on the Web for participants. Explore a wide range of learning communities and check out their models for sustainability. This will spark ideas. Brainstorm with your community. You'll undoubtedly invent your own unique combination of strategies.

## The Future

Our local community has several home-centered-learning charter schools in the area and we are exploring ways to work together. I'm coaching facilitators, parents, and young people on using the Internet creatively in a charter program that is focused on watershed ecology.

Long-range, I am working towards a collaboration where the homeschool programs and charter schools can subcontract with Haven for distance learning services. This will make our Journeys, apprenticeships, and mentoring alliances available to area young people free of charge. We are also seeking sponsorships from local businesses so that more educators in our community can participate in Journeys and the Edge-ucator's Path apprenticeship. We are connecting with our local university's field studies programs to set up education and environmental studies internships in the Haven online learning community.

It will be a while before the Web is navigable in networked three-dimensional worlds. But for some, it's a reality now, especially for people under twenty five. A generation of young people who have grown up with legos, logo, html, vrml, Java, Adobe Photoshop and Premiere, Sonic the hedgehog, Laura Cross, Ultima Online, Asheron's Call, and personal avatars, are architecting the cyberspace of the future today. What vision-ary educator Seymour Papert calls *megachange* is on its way:

> The decision to make is not whether we will continue with school or change it. It will collapse. Our question is whether we'll wait until we're driven to the wall and the system is collapsed from within from its own internal contradictions before we decide that we're going to create conditions that will allow a new system where there'll be diversity of learning paths, diversity of teaching methods, diversity of subjects to be learned.

How can we best prepare ourselves to flow with megachange as it sweeps us up? One very direct way is to practice image-ination or visual thinking. Over 31,000 years ago, our ancestors were painting the most extraordi-nary images of animals in the Chauvet-Pont-d'Arc cave in the Ardèche region of Southern France. The skill of these artists working with ocher, charcoal, and hematite contradicts previous theories of a slow and steady maturing of art through various ages from primitive to more sophisticated style. The Chauvet artists have stunned us with their use of proportion, perspective and depth. The French Ministry of Culture writes that these cave paintings, rediscovered in 1994, "have revolutionized hitherto ac-cepted concepts on the appearance of art and its development, and prove that *Homo sapiens* learned to draw at a very early stage." It seems that image-ination is a defining characteristic of *Homo sapiens*, central to our nature.

Today, we're still working with ocher, charcoal, and hematite but we've added supercomputers, graphics workstations, and elaborate three-dimensional software to paint the DNA spiral and reoviruses (known to kill cancer cells), and to model tornado vortices and the ozone hole. These visualization tools are quite literally global thinking tools—they let us see our planet in ways never before seen, and in ways absolutely necessary to reverse environmental degradation and create sustainable development.

My daughter started studying photography when she was fourteen. A disenchantment with the toxicity of darkroom chemicals drew her into the digital world, and she apprenticed with a master of digital photography. She has grown up using a videocamera for her journal. Recently a friend gave her a video conferencing camera for her birthday. I have one, too. We were excited about connecting with them since we live in two different cities. Software called NetMeeting let us connect via the Internet. She suggested we try the "shared whiteboard," which I had never used. We could each draw and see what the other was drawing. We could even draw together. Then she uploaded a photo of a lizard she'd shot in the desert on her recent camping trip. It came up on the "whiteboard." I was awestruck. I quickly uploaded some images I had been collecting, and we were in another world together. A visual world. I can't come up with the words easily to describe to you what a shift in communication this was. And what fun!

We both realize that with these tools, one day we'll be working and creating with friends on the other side of the world. If my Portuguese is weak, and my Brazilian collaborator's English is rusty, our image-inations can help us bridge the gaps. We can share photos, video, even animations to illustrate our thoughts and ideas. I will never forget the moment I opened a photo attached to an email sent by my Brazilian collaborator Saulo Petean. We had not yet met in person. Together with another Brazilian, Alexandre Lage, we were assisting a Mebengokré Indian community in creating a website. Saulo sent photos taken with a digital camera of himself and a child in the village. Those digital images transported me from my desk in San Francisco to the Amazon rainforest.

Some people will question why I put so much emphasis on this. We're experiencing a profound shift in how we communicate. For those of us raised on penmanship and text-based book-learning, this can be a hard one to see coming. The future online is very *visual*, and it is three-dimensional (if not four-dimensional). Words won't go away, but multimedia is more than jargon. Visual thinking is powerful, transformative, life changing. It can help bridge language barriers. It is essential to understanding and working with the mathematics of complexity, chaos theory, systems modeling.

Ralph Abraham is a mathematician and a pioneer in the field of dynamical systems theory. In a 1996 interview with Haven facilitator and *PATTERNS* editor Barbara Vogl, Ralph remarked, "The more complex the system, such as the one we live in, the more chaotic its behavior. Chaos theory provides us with a better understanding of such processes. And if we don't understand chaotic behavior, then we can't understand the complex system we live in well enough to give it guidance and play a part in the creation of our future."

## If You're Ready to Begin...

Here are a few suggestions. Talk to kids about how they are using the Web. Involve young people as equals at the visioning, planning, design, and content levels of the learning community.

My "imagician" daughter Zohara designed some of my favorite graphics on the site. Young people are key consultants in the evolution of the Haven learning community. I think it is no accident that many of my friends' webmasters are their children. Given the opportunity, kids learn how to construct cyberspace really quickly. At a local learning center in my community, a teenager does the coaching in Internet skills, Photoshop and other software. Haven's intern, Lisa Felten, alias Blue Rose, came to us through an announcement in a local homeschooling newsletter. She has designed some beautiful pages for the Deep Ecology Zone.

Consider creating an online learning-community team at your local learning center. Try a cluster design for the learning community so that small interest groups can create and evolve their own independent but connected zones. Trust the kids to lead the way and to be tremendously capable of managing the complexity of the ongoing maintenance of a web learning community.

Find collaborators. Share tasks. Pool equipment. Seek interns. Be patient. It can be slow going, with unbelievable techno-hurdles presenting themselves every step of the way. Enjoy the surprises. As your community grows, encourage members to contribute. Your strength will come from their unique contributions. Seek diversity—young, old, multiracial. Reach out through cyberspace to people in the opposite hemisphere. Share stories with each other. Aim for international. Record your experiences along the way and make them available to others. Spread the wisdom gained. Value your sense of humor above all. And don't forget to get your hands in the dirt. Plant seeds.

# Bibliography

Christopher Alexander, *A Pattern Language*. New York: Oxford University Press, 1977.

Christopher Alexander, *The Timeless Way of Building*. New York: Oxford University Press, 1979.

Peter Berg, *Reinhabiting a Separate Country: A Bioregional Anthology of Northern California*. Planet Drum Foundation, 1978.

Marion Boyars and Ivan Illich, *Deschooling Society: Social Questions*. Marion Boyars Publishers, 1999.

John Holt, *Learning All the Time*. New York: Perseus Press, 1990.

Seymour Papert, *Mindstorms: Children, Computers and Powerful Ideas*. New York: Basic Books, 1980.

Seymour Papert, *The Connected Family: Bridging the Digital Generation Gap*. Atlanta, Georgia: Longstreet Press, 1996.

Seymour Papert, *The Children's Machine: Rethinking School in the Age of the Computer*. New York: Basic Books, 1993.

Howard Rheingold, *The Millennium Whole Earth Catalog: Access to Tools & Ideas for the Twenty-First Century*. New York: HarperCollins Publishers, 1994.

# Webliography

| The Haven Learning Community | Other Websites Mentioned |
|---|---|
| Haven<br>http://www.haven.net | Institute for Global Communications<br>(PeaceNet and EcoNet)<br>http://www.igc.apc.org |
| The Edge-ucation Matrix<br>http://www.haven.net/edge/matrix.htm | The Well<br>http://www.well.com |
| NEXUS<br>http://www.haven.net/edge/nexus | Order of Green Knights<br>http://www.haven.net/edge/council/<br>paddon.htm |
| PATTERNS newsletter—http://<br>www.haven.net/patterns | Santa Cruz Live Oak Grange<br>http://www.greengrange.org |
| The Earth Stories Project<br>http://www.haven.net/deep/greentms/<br>project.htm | Some notes on Christopher Alexander by<br>Dr. Nikos A. Salingaros<br>http://www.math.utsa.edu/sphere/salingar/<br>Chris.text.html |
| Interconnect e-newsletter<br>http://www.haven.net/interconnect | Theater of Restoration<br>http://members.cruzio.com/~hearth/<br>index.html |
| Greentrade Business Directory<br>http://www.haven.net/greentrade | The Chauvet-Pont-d'Arc Cave<br>http://www.culture.fr/culture/arcnat/<br>chauvet/en/gvpda-d.htm |
| | Bayside Children's College<br>http://www.baysidechildrenscollege.com |

# About the Author

*Claudia L'Amoreaux (cl@haven.net) is a distance learning consultant and life-long learning facilitator. She especially enjoys supporting teenagers who want to create their own learning paths. She hosts the Edge-ucation Dialogues, a video series of conversations with visionaries at the edge of learning how to learn. Visit http://www.edge-ucation.com for more information about her work. The Haven online learning community is on the Web at http://www.haven.net*

# Access Issues: Technology in the Service of Community

*Remember when you visit and participate in online learning communities today, this is early in their development. Access is still a tremendous issue. Only a fraction of voices are represented. Make access issues a focal point of inquiry and action in your local learning center and online learning community. With increased awareness of international access issues, we can work to insure that no one is left behind. Local learning centers can make a significant contribution here by functioning as community access centers. The unique possibility that online learning communities offer is global participation. Our children will grow up taking this for granted. It is up to us to help shape the quality of that participation and the diversity of voices represented.*

*For your own research into access issues, here are a few places to begin. Art McGee of the Institute for Global Communications (www.igc.org/ amcgee/e-race.html) maintains an excellent page of links. The Benton Foundation, in cooperation with The National Urban League, hosts the Digital Divide Network website (www. DigitalDivideNetwork.org) and the DIGITALDIVIDE mailing list. The list serves as a public forum for Digital Divide issues with a special emphasis on finding practical solutions. To subscribe, send email to digitaldivide-request@list.benton.org and put "subscribe DIGITALDIVIDE yourname" in the first line of the message body. For additional resources on access issues, be sure to read the extended, hyperlinked version of this chapter on the Creating Learning Centers website. Publish your insights. Write about exemplary models you find. In the words of E.M. Forster, "Only connect!"*

# NetSchool of Maine
## A Resource Model for Local and Regional Home Education Groups

*by Frank J. Heller, MPA*

WELCOME TO THE WORLD of cyberlearning and Web (Internet) accessed educational resources. These Internet resources include nearly everything a professional educator, parent's group, or community-learning-center-based teacher who is interested in developing an information-transaction-facilitated independent-studies program would need to create his or her own individualized resource web.

These resources include fundamental training (i.e., web design and course conversion technology for web delivery and management). Also available is a wide range of curricula from tried-and-true (i.e., Beka and Ed Hirsch) to unique (like Vermont-based "Stars Stories," which uses astronomy) and progressive (like California's UN-endorsed Laurel Springs School, and the homeschooling favorite, the Willoway School). Also included are the "nuts and bolts" of such a resource center—lists of mentors and distance-learning-enabled teachers, web-enabled tests and assessment programs, teaching resource data warehouses organized by subject, and even sources of teachers, students, and financial aid. Vocational, career, public sector, technical, and even military oriented schools are included.

All the community learning group has to do is organize these resources into a coherent body of knowledge usable by students and parents alike, based on the needs of their learners and instructors. This essay establishes a "skeleton" one can follow that is both user-friendly and allows one the opportunity of easily adding in components as part of the site maintenance. Interactive community chats can also be incorporated, as well as resource libraries that can be downloaded, and shopping baskets for creating learning communities that sell instructional materials, courses, and other educational items to members.

## What is Distance Learning and Why Is It Such a Revolutionary Trend in Education?

Recent improvements in the reliability and accessibility of the Internet have made possible the delivery of educational and instructional content over vast distances. The average desktop computer in a mid-coast, Maine, household can now receive and originate interactive video conferencing over the Internet using phones, radio, and the new, two-way, satellite dishes.

Thousands of colleges, universities, corporations, training centers, public and private schools, and other educational centers have made their instructional programs available on the Internet. There are now tens of thousands of educational offerings for nearly every age learner. Geographic and age barriers have been shattered in the process, as hundreds of colleges and universities have "packaged" college and secondary classes for delivery to independent learners around the world.

Younger students may even take college classes for dual credit, enabling them to leave high school at the 10th or 11th grade, and enter college. The college course credits are applied towards both the high-school diploma and the college degree. Middle-school students have successively petitioned their school boards in Maine to give high-school algebra and have the credits applied to their diplomas. Stanford University, widely acclaimed as the world's best science and engineering school, has created a "virtual student" and offers the first four-year degree available over the Internet. A bright student in rural Mascoma, New Hampshire, school district can now take AP calculus from Johns Hopkins University and earn herself a chance at entering their pre-med program. A student in Bethel, Maine, who missed her AP history classes because of her competitive snowboarding regime can make them up in the summer through a distance learning program. A student at a public high school in New Hampshire can take a class through Clonora's (a well-known home-schooling resource) new cyber high school, with the credits accepted by her public high school.

Gould Academy has joined with Maine's first charter school, the Maine School of Science and Mathematics, and Telstar High School (in Bethel, Maine) in creating a cyber school whose first classes will be available soon, along with the Virtual High School Consortium and other public and private cyber schools. Brigham Young University now markets a complete program to the independent learner of high-school age or younger, including scholarship opportunities.

Many other colleges are following in their footsteps in Iowa, Nebraska,

California. and other progressive states. So far Maine has been lagging behind, being rooted in an earlier age with educational television networks linking the University of Maine system with the public schools. Now satellite dishes have been replaced by the fiber-based ATM (a large packet method of transmitting IP information) system, but still linking classroom to classroom, not desktop to desktop. Some rural districts however, like Lubec public schools will be using both systems—a global classroom on the Internet and an ATM link to other high schools in Maine.

Along with the revolution in computer-based CD-ROM interactive multimedia educational software and the Internet, homeschooling has never been easier or more in demand. Early reports from large states like Wisconsin and Texas indicate that hundreds of thousands of children will soon be homeschooled in a variety of ways. The Internet can provide tutors, mentors, teachers for individual subjects, lessons and lesson plans, approved courses from well-credentialed schools that range from the best prep and progressive schools to technical, craft, and trade schools.

The best in educational software from companies such as Jostens Learning, which previously was only available to public schools, is now available to homeschoolers. Usually the curriculum is incorporated into a delivery shell and the "package" is called instructional software. For example, the American Educational Corporation has a K-12 curriculum that includes authoring modules so teachers can add their own lessons, an assessment module that measures the degree of attainment of educational objectives and then recommends lessons based on the level of mastery, content tests for each lesson sequence, and a way of linking both web resources and third-party software into the lesson sequence. Some school districts and Canadian provincial departments of education are now putting their curriculum on a web site and making it available to all. This is one of the more exciting aspects of working with web-based resources— the equivalent of a library of the best textbooks to choose from. The software is for sale, some can be rented, and yet more, like the Horizon's curriculum, is available only by logging into a central web server. Universities and individual teachers will put bits and pieces up for free. A curriculum specialist can quickly integrate these courses and lesson sequences into a coherent, individualized learning plan for a student.

Parents who travel find distance-learning courses provide them the freedom and flexibility to take off and sail for a year. Area marinas are familiar with cruising families who homeschool—only now they use cell phones, radio telephones, and satellite dishes to stay in touch with home schooling resource groups and learning centers.

Perhaps the greatest benefit to students who master distance learning over the Internet is that corporate America and many government institutions such as the Army and the VA use web-based distance learning to train their employees. Lubec Schools are considering links with Norwegian and Chilean fisheries for their vocational students. Maine's small colleges now realize that distant corporate recruiters may pass them up because of the time and cost considerations, but will schedule videoconference interviews for qualified prospects. Students shopping for colleges can do so over the Internet, right down to virtual tours and interviews; saving their parents much time and money. A student who can't decide where to enroll may take distance-learning courses at different schools to see which is best.

Distance Learning over the Internet is revolutionizing educational opportunities at all levels, from kindergarten to senior learning centers.

## What Makes It Possible for Local Learning Groups to Set Up Their Own "NetSchool" for Use by Community Members?

Setting up and maintaining high-quality Internet web sites is now far more inexpensive than organized mailings to members. Plus, they offer the prospect of direct interactivity and instant communication. You can even set up organizational meetings over the Internet using "chat" programs and, eventually, full videoconferencing. The introduction of Office 2000 and improvements to ICQ Chat and Real Audio and Video, as well as modems that support telephony (digital phone calls) are going to make real-time audio and video just a mouse-button click away. Computers are now designed to facilitate multi-tasking involving applications and on-line video conferencing.

Best of all, competition has driven costs down appreciably. I am now working with Great Works Internet to "bundle" a homeschooling computer system with their Internet service. They in turn will provide a "home" for a community-based learning center that wants to have its own learning resource site. Hardware vendors have been working with Internet providers to "bundle" in a free computer with several years of Internet service. Web design and maintenance is no longer the arcane science it once was. Many inexpensive programs offer web-page authoring as a feature, while Office 2000 features assume one can easily access something on the web all the time.

## Organizing the Web Site

As something of a visionary and entrepreneur, I just designed my own site using Front Page 98. I knew what I wanted and am very well organized, so the site was able to accommodate the various categories of information I wanted on it, and I could expand and contract it as necessary. I also profited by joining a two-day charette (poster session) that developed the judging criteria for evaluating the first national contest for best school web site.

There are many "traps" out there for the first-time web-site developers. The worst are the "free" sites. They are really not so free, since your members will be collected for advertisers and marketing companies, or you will suddenly find bills for special services appearing. Nearly as bad are the sites delegated to a fifteen-year-old web programmer who doesn't have a clue as to what you want but only wants to show off for his friends. Your needs are sacrificed to his agenda.

What I suggest is that you hold your own charette of interested members. Be sure to include those who may be barely computer literate, but have a strong knowledge of homeschooling. Here are the key areas to focus on:

• *What are the priorities of your members for resource information?*

What do they call or write to you for now? What do you have to put into letters and brochures and handouts? Whose books are you constantly referring to?

• *Who likes to chat with whom now?*

What kinds of interests are shared among members now? How can you include these interest areas into a chat window or chat area on your site? For example, some people will want to buy and sell educational materials—create a used book room for them. Some will want teacher training—so organize a training library and on-line workshops for them. The kids will want to chat with each other—create a chat service for them.

Chat services can be rich and complex or fairly simple. For young kids, Microsoft COMIC chat is interesting. It offers comic strips with cartoon characters that participants "adopt," balloons for the words, and even moods for each character. For adults, adopting ICQ™ or even a public, yet secure chat service is preferred to get things started. Secure commercial chat services offer the greatest protection for activities like association board meetings in the winter. If you'd like more information on ICQ chats, go to www.icq.com.

Eventually it will be commonplace to have videophone chats using the new H.323 telecommunication standards developed by Intel, Microsoft, and other major computer companies. I have them now and have reasonably good video transfers and audio. The problem is, when more than two people are involved, then a commercial multiplexing service or a secure server must be used to relay the calls back and forth. There are now small, underutilized servers available for small groups, and Microsoft has software that enables an association with a bit of computer savvy to dedicate a computer as a videoconferencing server.

For more information on videoconferencing go to PACBELL at www.kn.pacbell/wired/vidconf, or read the Video Conferencing "cookbook" at sunsite.utk.edu/video_cookbook/

• *Are members looking for tutors? Mentors? Study Groups? Certified Teachers?*

Great, because there are now cyber mentors and teachers looking for jobs over the Internet. You can develop a "yellow pages" for ones close to home or who have unique teaching experience for the state you live in. You can also screen other services available nationally and recommend them to your members. People love expert opinion, but because there is so much available over the Internet your guidance is even more appreciated. No one wants to search for something and find two million answers!

You will need to set up standards and criteria, however, to screen people who are listed. Your ability to discriminate among all the people who will show up will be greatly appreciated.

• *What about your version of the state's homeschool certification process, requirements, etc.?*

Here is a great source of interest from those many fence-sitting families who have a lot of questions about the government's many interests in regulating home schools. Most states have a .pdf or .doc version of the application form and the guidelines to filling it out on-line. What you can do is have several sample versions of a filled-in form, and then link in explanations to puzzling portions. Parents will write to you with their questions, and you can also have an interactive chat linked to this resource.

• *Do you want to post lessons or curriculum on the site for parents to use?*

This poses many questions and elevates your site to higher levels of complexity. First are the legal and licensing issues behind distributing lesson plans. Some are clearly in the public domain, and others originate from who knows where. Ditto for other instructional materials and resources. For example, I am familiar with one math lesson-plan author who'd like to link into your site, but she is reluctant to have your site "offer" her lessons. This is the common problem—they want you to come to "their house," but not the other way around.

Putting software up also means compatibility problems with the authors' HTML program, JAVA scripts, and other elements of professional web pages. It may mean specialized programming for downloading the latest version of viewers, and commercials for doing so, e.g., Real Audio and Video, Adobe, etc. People are getting the latest "bells and whistles" and automatically expect your site to have the same. Often the materials you would want to post were developed with software that incorporates these cutting-edge features. Streaming audio and video, interactive chat, and special programmed scripts linked to data warehouses are all common features on large sites.

If you do plan on posting lessons and other resource materials for your group members, you may want to set some minimal standards on size, virus protection, and potential copyright violations.

• *Paying for your site.*

There is a strong temptation to put advertising frames and banners on your site. Internet marketers make these deals very attractive, especially with free server space. The downside is they control the content, look and feel, and other aspects of your site, including the all-important headers. Their intent is to use your site to make them money via advertising money and session logins, which identify the caller to them. Search terms are what bring people to the site and free servers frequently reserve the right to change them. If you are an association, your members who use the "free" site may find themselves the targets of advertisers, and their email addresses sold to the highest bidders.

But then there are the costs: site design, web-site "gardening" or maintenance, server space costs, and software upgrades. I would suggest that you include in your site a small "shopping mall" or area that features the goods and services of members for a small fee of $25 per year. Twenty such advertisements will probably cover a year's worth of expenses for a conventional site. Another possibility is to offer one-time "specials" by the larger home-education advertisers. Conferences, workshops, sales, etc., can be relegated to a visible place on your homepage and promoted. You should receive revenue for them. The hardest part is asking for money. All of these enterprises advertise, and you might as well get a small portion.

Other sources of income are:

∗ Commissions on referrals to distance-learning correspondence schools.

∗ Commissions on referrals to tutors, mentors, and teachers.

∗ Sales of homeschooling magazines and books.

∗ Banners for the businesses of members.

## Summary

Getting started and converting from a conventional library or computer word-processing files into a web site is a daunting undertaking for even an experienced computer user. The hardest part is designing the site, because unless it meets your specific needs, taking it apart is very difficult. A simple design facilitates the perpetual task of weeding and gardening—a tedious task since it involves everything in the site and the links between them that form the "web." Agreement on organization and a common understanding of the elements and components of this organization among all members of your creative learning community is more important than buying HTML books and application generators.

Think of it as an organic growth process, starting with how you want the site to function, and then adding the skeleton, face, and other elements. Don't get carried away with the features in commercial and professional sites—those were done by professionals using software and utilities that can cost tens of thousands of dollars. If you want a slick piece of programming, i.e., a market basket and a credit referral, define it and contract for it with one of the thousands of web design shops that have sprung up. What is most important is how the site functions for the learners in your community, not whether it has a shimmering water JAVA applet to impress visitors.

*Frank J. Heller, MPA, NetSchool of Maine, 12 Belmont Street, Brunswick, ME 04011, USA, e-mail: global@gwi.net, URL: www.netschoolofmaine.com*

# Learning Communities
# and "Virtual" Realities

*by Ron Miller*

ﾠ A S WE DISCUSSED the ideas that gave rise to this book, and again later, as I edited the chapters that were submitted, it was evident that many of the people who are working to redefine our ways of teaching and learning are extremely enthusiastic about the educational possibilities of "cyberspace"—the Internet, distance learning, educational software, and the like. There is no question that the computer, with all its technological extensions and applications, is a powerful tool, that it is welcomed and eagerly used by millions of people in nearly all parts of the world, and that it is here to stay. Without a doubt, cyberspace opens up many new possibilities for teaching and learning beyond the traditional classroom. Claudia L'Amoreaux's account in this volume of the ways in which new technologies dramatically expanded her world reveals exciting possibilities. This book itself arose from an Internet discussion group.

Nevertheless, I want to make the point that the educational transformation we are advocating in this book, based on principles such as self-directed life-long learning, community-focused education, and more authentic, holistic, experiential, and relevant forms of learning, is not *necessarily* tied to technological innovation. These are moral and philosophical principles, not simply byproducts of electronic gimmickry. Even further, I would claim that if we truly take these principles seriously, we will approach the use of electronic tools and cyberspace cautiously and critically.

Computer technologies are useful because they provide access to a tremendous range of *information*. For many reasons and purposes, this is worthwhile in itself. Information is vitally important for making decisions, for enhancing the quality of life, for mastering fields of knowledge, and for understanding other people's experiences, as well as our own. But if we begin to assume that information is *all* we need for these purposes, we enter dangerous territory: We start to reduce the wholeness of human experience into two-dimensional images. Human beings do not live in a "virtual" reality that can be logically constructed from bits of information—we live in an actual reality that is enormously complex. Our experience is rooted in numerous contexts that give it multiple meanings: We are biological creatures living in an ecological context, social beings living in cultural, economic, and political contexts, and spiritual beings expressing a wondrous diversity of psychological, archetypal, and mysterious evolutionary forces. To call all these contexts "information" is to lose their texture, their essential meaning. The sense of awe we feel gazing at the Milky Way, or our appreciation of form, depth, and beauty in a great work of art, is not merely information. A person's commitment to social justice or to relieving human suffering is not inspired by information, but by other dimensions of the soul.

As Theodore Roszak eloquently argued in his 1986 book *The Cult of Information*, it is not information but *experience* that enables human beings to find moral, life-enriching meanings in this complex reality, and the difference between the two is precisely what distinguishes holistic

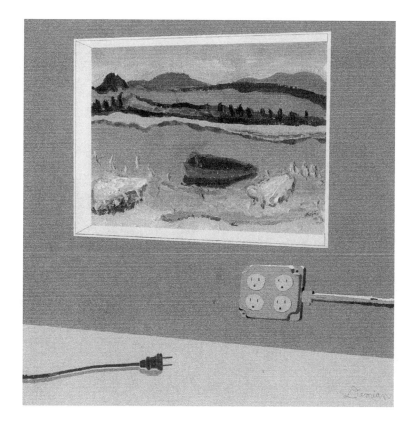

(experiential) forms of education from the dry, lifeless, academic exercises that make up the bulk of conventional schooling. The kind of knowing that gives rise to wisdom is rooted in historical, geographical, and biological contexts—it is not neutral information that can be gathered at will from a computer screen. Such wisdom, Roszak suggested, comes from *ideas*— "integrating patterns which satisfy the mind when it asks the question: What does this mean? What is this all about?" These patterns arise from imagination in response to experience—flesh-and-blood engagement with the realities of the world. Ideas connect us to larger contexts. They are not limited to the information at hand, no matter how much is available.

What takes place when two people meet over a meal to talk about their lives? Picture two longtime friends, or business associates, or young lovers on a date. The meaning of their communication involves facial expressions, body language, inflection of voice, and other situational factors—it is nonsense to claim that they are merely exchanging "information" contained in the words they speak. The quality of their engagement is affected by their emotional state at the moment, by the environment in which they are sitting (is it noisy? elegant? romantic? too cold?), even by the food they are eating. All of this is absent from "messages" they could send each other via e-mail. If we understand education as communication between human beings, as meaningful engagement in a learning process, then the same conditions apply. In fact, these conditions are even more essential, for education at its best goes beyond personal communication and connects us to the ecological, cultural, economic, political, and evolutionary forces around us. A great deal of information can be shared through impersonal channels, but it lacks several dimensions of experience that make it fully meaningful and alive.

As we think about new learning systems, then, we should ask ourselves: Are we embracing new technologies that merely advance established assumptions about the nature of knowledge, learning, and human development? Or do we envision education as a process of cultural transformation that raises fundamental questions about our social institutions and ways of living together? In other words, what assumptions are embedded in our educational vision and in the language we use to describe it? I would like to reflect on Frank Heller's chapter, "Netschool of Maine," with these questions in mind. Heller provides a detailed introduction to the exploding use of computer technologies in learning, and suggests how this is already revolutionizing our understanding of schooling. Still, I wonder about the assumptions embedded in the language of the computer revolution. Heller observes, for example, that "hundreds of colleges and universities have 'packaged' college and secondary classes for delivery to independent learners around the world." If we view education as the "delivery" of information, then this is a good thing—the more efficient the packaging, the better. The words that Heller uses to describe distance learning—programs being "marketed," employees being "trained," and students "shopping" for colleges—reflect an implicit acceptance of existing social and economic institutions. Similarly, using educational software and computer equipment involves competition, advertising, and "deals." Education is seen as an appropriate arena for entrepreneurs.

This is still the dominant understanding of education in our culture. Quite possibly, the development of distance learning programs and "netschools" is the next natural step in the evolution toward new learning systems. If they liberate us from the constraints of standardized learning, state-approved textbooks, and police-guarded school buildings, they are welcome innovations indeed. Still, we might go further. If we challenge the modern industrial world with a more holistic worldview, a worldview concerned with wholeness, meaning, interdependence, sustainability, and spirituality, then we come up with an understanding of education that Kathia and Alexander Laszlo describe in their chapter on Evolutionary Systems Design: "Learning is a complex activity that involves the whole human being and implies interactions with other human beings and with the natural and sociocultural environment." Computer-mediated interaction is better than none, but the information it supplies to us does not substitute for the sensuous, emotional, meaning-seeking encounter that is only possible in a live engagement with other human beings and the multifaceted world we share.

Our challenge is to use technologies to serve higher, more holistic purposes, without being utterly seduced by the power to manipulate information that these technologies offer. As many wise thinkers are telling us these days (Wendell Berry, Parker Palmer, Charlene Spretnak, Bill McKibben, C.A. Bowers, and Jerry Mander come to mind, among many others), human existence is meaningful and fulfilling only when we are ecologically rooted in a sense of place, when our hunger for power is tempered by restraint and a sense of proportion, when we recognize moral and spiritual dimensions of reality that transcend our information-based knowledge. Cyberworlds and virtual realities too easily cause us to forget these boundaries to our egoistic striving. It would be ironic, and deeply troubling, if the idea of community-based learning, which essentially seeks to situate the individual within a moral and ecological sense of place, becomes corrupted by the Siren call of information technology.

# The Importance of Computers in Education Does Not Compute

*by Patrick Farenga*

ECHNOLOGY IS NEVER neutral. It affects change, one way or another, and therefore we need to be far more critical of technology than we are in awe of it. The issue, I've come to believe, is really one of proportionality, not one of whether or not we should use computers. What is an appropriate use of a machine that has insinuated itself into nearly every economic transaction we make in our lives? The real fight, I usually discover, is a personal one: How much self-discipline will I exhibit in my use of this technology? How do we discipline ourselves as a society in our use of this technology? So far, it seems that anything goes. Advertising encourages more and more computer consumption and use, and quite possibly dependence. By de-emphasizing the glamour of technology I hope to encourage better uses of it, not its eradication.

When it comes to education, however, I am puzzled and concerned about our zeal to educate children by making sure they spend lots of time with computers. It does not compute that, because we put millions-of-dollars worth of computers into our schools, we will therefore get computer-literate students. We have had more than a hundred years' worth of education theory and practice, and millions of dollars spent, and we still can't help all children read and write, despite the ready availability of books and pens. There must be something more to learning than just having access to the latest technology.

It does not compute that using a computer to communicate with other humans is better than other means. Computers, in and of themselves, will not make us better writers or more sociable beings. How we use computers, and how our communications are limited by computers, determines the effectiveness of our communications. The telephone, slide projector, motion pictures, television—all were considered to hold great promise for revolutionizing education. None have really done so. As these tools and media have become a part of our lives, so have computers. And like these other media, computers are having a similar effect on children's ability to learn in school—very little. What does really affect children's ability to learn in school is other people—children and adults—and how they relate to one another towards individual and common goals. It does not compute that a computer will be a good substitute for human relations.

It does not compute that we need years of compulsory schooling to learn to use computers. We don't need trigonometry, calculus, specialized programming languages, or months of computer literacy courses in order to effectively use a computer. These may be desirable for those who are curious about how computers operate, and for those who wish to create their own programs, but the vast majority of us will continue make do with "user-friendly" programs and interfaces that don't require years of schooling to understand.

It does not compute that being able to communicate with hundreds of people from all over the world is a great thing. The benefit of sending text rather quickly across continents to hundreds of people is offset, to me, by the potential feedback of hundreds of people across continents. The benefit of corresponding with many people at once is offset by the lack of personalization. Since there is no proportionality to my message any-more—anyone with e-mail can broadcast to thousands of people at once—it will be as meaningless, or at best of equal value, as the many other messages we receive via email each day.

Further, the noise of this medium frequently overwhelms the data; the quantity does affect my perception of its quality. I confess, I don't read every message that gets forwarded to me by my listserves or that strangers send to my personal e-mail.

It does not compute that having access to greater amounts of information through computers makes one a better-informed or smarter person. There is as much misinformation or outdated information on the Internet as there is useful information. Governments and research foundations can and do misinterpret, misrepresent, or overlook important information about projects, and they did so before computer information deluged us. Therefore, the possibilities for errors increase as the amount of information increases. Further, the alleged downing of Flight 800 by missiles and the "documentary evidence" of *The Blair Witch Project* are but two recent examples of how misinformation is given legitimacy simply by being promulgated on the Internet.

Some worship at the altar of information technologies; I fear this is a false god that we are indoctrinating our children to follow. Having mentors and docents who can show children how they use research and evaluate information is far more important than giving children personal computers and Internet access.

It does not compute that computers expand our world. They also shrink it and homogenize it; they standardize it and parse it into manageable computer pieces. Computers reduce our possibilities as humans as much as they expand them. Suddenly the world is at our fingertips—and in English, if we choose the correct settings in our Internet browser. This might seem like a good idea to some, but to me it is a nightmare of global standardization. This is not the real world, but an edited virtual world, a Disneyland of world cultures. Making children learn that the world and its people are easily explored through computer use is simplistic and dangerous because it must, to have mass appeal and be accessible to school children, be marketable. This often means downplaying or ignoring sharp cultural, religious, and historical differences among people.

Computers are big reducers. They further reduce our most precious and complex feelings into emoticons, data, and texts, our social well being and people into numbers and statistics, physical hugs into inspirational verses. Not that these are bad things, but they are different things. They are not the same, and we delude ourselves by thinking that technology is neutral and doesn't affect our humanity.

It does not compute that using computers will necessarily make our children learn better or improve our quality of life. Our chosen means contain the seeds of the end we desire, and community-centered life-long learning centers based primarily on computer technology can become a Trojan horse for technological consumerism, under the guise of "education," to enter our lives in even more areas than it does now. Let us beware.

# Computer Caution

*by Ann Lahrson Fisher*

MY COMPUTER IS a fantastic tool with myriad fascinating and useful applications. And yes, the Internet is the greatest research tool on the planet. And yes, the networking, communications, educational, and commercial capabilities are astounding. Yes, yes, yes, the computer is transforming our lives. This glamorous tool fuels our idealistic hopes and dreams for a better future.

Still, a full array of disadvantages and dangers lurks behind the potential for misuse and abuse of computers. The disadvantages and risks are readily glossed over by the zealous promotion of computer believers. Parents and teachers must find a balance of caution and common sense when using computer technology to educate their children.

I offer one curmudgeonly voice for caution. I suggest that we review several trends and assumptions about computer use with young children, and take seriously the potential disadvantages and abuses.

***Popular trend***: A mad race is on to get very young children started using computers. Parents of children as young as one year old are targeted, and parents scramble to obtain these products. Promoters use clever marketing drives to empty parents' wallets for their children's sake.

***Danger***: Excessive computer use flies in the face of what we know about how young children learn. Developmentally sound educational practice and good parenting is abandoned in the effort to have the first computer-literate baby on the block. No matter how lovely and interactive the software or Internet site, learning at the computer pales when compared to the sensory vividness of hands-on immersion-type activities. Interactivity claims ring hollow when compared to the richness of learning through actual life experiences.

Wouldn't we scream in outrage if untested medications were being injected into infants to build a better baby? Yet computer use by young children is untested and the impact will not be known for many years. Information and training put into children's minds through their eyes and ears may not have immediate danger, but who can guess if there is a potential of harm over the child's lifetime?

Computer use wastes precious childhood. Computers consume an enormous amount of time. Given the knowledge that the current generation of computers will be obsolete many times over by the time today's children reach maturity, do children really need to proficiently use today's computers in order to be computer literate as adults? Instead of promoting computer use, parents and educators should use computers and the Internet selectively and balance that use with a variety of other methods and media that offer first-hand experiences as a priority.

***Popular trend***: Traditional workbook-type curricula have become widely available on the Internet at an affordable price. Promoters of online or software-based curricula suggest that all you need is a computer to get an excellent education with their materials.

***Danger***: Traditional workbook-type curricula on computers are inaccurately promoted as interactive. Don't believe for one minute that a workbook with clickable answers is more interactive than fill-in-the-blank answers in paper workbooks! Traditional workbook curricula have essentially the same advantages and disadvantages whether on computer or in paper format. At least with a paper workbook, a kid can take it under the table, in the car, or up a tree, and if she's really lucky, she'll lose the darn thing!

For some children, the pre-chewed and spewed content of workbooks, whether paper or computerized, is mind numbing. Instead of providing an efficient learning opportunity, the carefully sieved content backfires, turning the child away from his interests and dulling his natural desire to learn.

For children who learn easily from a traditional workbook-type of curriculum, the computer does offer a nifty choice of paper or electronic formatting, and of course children will enjoy having a choice. Still, for the majority of children, computer-based workbooks are best used as occasional reinforcement rather than as a primary instructional tool.

***Popular trend***: Theorists suggest that computers-as-teaching-machines, high-quality computer-based learning simulations, are the ultimate in educational practice, and that it is only a matter of time before simulations can take over many of the functions of teacher, parent, or educational facilitator.

***Danger***: Enthusiasts who project that simulations are a panacea to all teaching and learning problems misunderstand the nature of learning. A key problem is that much of what we learn is "how we learn" not "what we learn." With that in mind, we can see that simulations may indeed have a dark side. For example, fascination with sharp-shooting skill is a common and unintended result of popular educational computer programs. Do we really mean to teach young children to shoot? Other concerns: Do competitive simulations develop a drive to win without regard to human sensibilities or life itself? Does the loss of contact with actual humans during the early years harm healthy human relationships and understanding?

Curriculum developers should bear in mind that children are superbly adept at learning. The best sites and software allow many options for children to create their own learning experiences.

***Popular trend***: The computer and its many peripherals are believed to save enormous amounts of time.

***Disadvantage***: In reality, computer use is a massive consumer of time. While my computer saves a great amount of time with tasks such as bookkeeping and word processing, that is not the only way I choose to use it. I am addicted! I suspect that I have inadvertently developed some lazy mental habits, such as substituting the ease of computer use for rigorous thinking and planning. Mental habits will certainly change, for better or worse, as individuals spend more of their days at the computer.

***Popular trend***: Hive-mindedness. I can see it all now—each family member curled up in his or her own cell—I mean room—with his or her own computer, sharing e-mail messages and friendships with people he or she has never met, even with mom and pop, at their computers in the next room. Playing games, getting the news, working, shopping, and studying, all from the comfort of our screens.

***Disadvantage***: Are we prepared to deal with the loss of humanity that accompanies hive-like behavior? Shouldn't we concern ourselves with potential dangers as we continually separate ourselves from real people and real experience? We can pooh-pooh these concerns today, but what might the impact be on society in thirty or fifty or one hundred years?

***Popular trend***: Many daily activities can take place at the computer.
***Danger***: Am I the only one whose eyes, back, and neck ache, whose

optometrist, chiropractor, and physical therapist have been enriched by my computer use? Am I the only one whose pocketbook is emptied again and again into ergonomic keyboards, new and improved mice, chairs, workstations, lighting, bigger and better monitors, etc.? Am I the only one who doesn't get quite enough exercise to compensate for the physical inactivity of computer use? Am I the only one who is concerned about a generation of young people developing computer-aggravated health problems caused by excessive computer use during the early years?

Now, with all these dangers and disadvantages, should parents completely forego computer use for children, especially in the early years? I don't believe that is the best answer. Instead, I would suggest finding a balanced way to use this powerful educational tool. Use computer curriculum for reinforcement, not primary instruction. Select sites and software carefully. Pay attention to how a child responds to particular software and adapt as needed. Perhaps the most important thing parents can do is restrict the amount of time (some would say as little as twenty to thirty minutes daily per child) spent at the computer, especially for young children. The benefits of the computer can then be enjoyed without worrying about risks.

If parents and educators maintain a cautious approach, resist being swayed by marketing hyperbole, and instead demand that computer products be developed to suit their own standards, they can squeeze the most out of this very useful tool with minimum risk.

*Part Three*

# PHILOSOPHICAL ROOTS

# Philosophies
# of Learning Communities

*by Ron Miller*

W E TURN NOW from describing the methods and practices found in diverse community-learning models to examining more closely the underlying philosophies that have given rise to these programs. Philosoph*ies*, not philosophy, because the community-learning approach is rooted in the belief that there are many legitimate ways to learn, and many useful ways to support learning. Rather than fighting to establish one "correct" approach to teaching and learning, the community-learning model recognizes that each educational philosophy is appropriate for particular needs and specific situations. Growing children differ in their styles and rates of learning, and in their temperaments and interests; families differ in their values and aspirations; communities differ in their social and economic characteristics; and, quite simply, times change. By understanding the range of educational options, communities and families can deliberately choose modes of learning that address their most important needs.

Paradoxically, perhaps, this attitude of openness to different ways of learning itself reflects a particular philosophical position. Educators and parents who choose community-based learning are quite deliberately saying "No!" to the dominant worldview of the modern age, which values standardization, materialism, efficiency, profit, and power. Instead they affirm an alternative or "postmodern" worldview that recognizes diverse human needs and the moral, cultural, and ecological contexts within which these needs arise. The recognition of diverse ways of learning reflects a belief that education and other social institutions need to be *responsive* to people's experience and understanding; the systems we set up to guide our lives need to be *flexible* and *organic* and *relational*. In their chapter, "Learning to Become," Kathia and Alexander Laszlo call this an "evolutionary systems" perspective. While not every contributor to this book would use the same terminology, I think most would agree that rigid, authoritarian educational systems represent a flawed conception of human development and a narrow understanding of the living systems within which we exist. The chapters in this section explain why the mechanistic, competitive, and increasingly standardized system of schooling given to us by the industrial age is no longer adequate (if it ever was) in an emerging post-industrial era.

In order to provide an overview for the chapters that follow, it is useful to compare community-based learning approaches to other theories of education that are more familiar to educators, parents, and citizens in the modern age. Following (and expanding) upon the work of Canadian educator John P. Miller,[1] I would like to present a brief outline of four basic educational orientations. This is not an exhaustive description of all possible ways of teaching and learning, but it does help us classify our choices according to several broad purposes. Miller identifies three orientations, which he calls "transmission," "transaction," and "transformation." I would add a fourth, which we might call "self-direction."

A *transmission* approach asserts that the primary purpose of education is to induct young people into the established values, beliefs, and accepted knowledge of the existing society or community. Teaching transmits information to students, who are expected to absorb, memorize, or otherwise master the material they are taught. Learning is seen as a receptive activity—the taking in of external data. Knowledge is seen as being stable and for the most part predetermined. There is an emphasis on "basics"—those pieces of knowledge that are widely considered essential. E.D. Hirsch's popular series of books defining lists of facts and concepts that children should know at each grade level, and William Bennett's popular books on moral education, reflect a transmission orientation. Families or communities with strongly held religious or cultural beliefs who want to ensure that their children adopt these beliefs also tend to favor transmission approaches. Indeed, any educator or parent may find certain situations in which the transmission of specific knowledge is an appropriate strategy, and some children do appear to learn better from direct, carefully planned instruction. But most schooling in the modern age is heavily influenced by this understanding of education, to the point where it has become authoritarian and rigid. Today, government officials, along with leaders of corporations, foundations, universities, and other institutions, determine what all students "need" to know, and this becomes educational policy, expressed in standards, state-mandated textbooks, high-stakes testing, and relentless control over teaching and learning.

A *transaction* orientation, according to John Miller, is more sensitive than the transmission position to the social context of learning. Knowledge is not an objective entity that students compete to acquire for themselves, but is generated in relationships between people, through conversation and dialogue, and in relationships between the learner and the larger world through meaningful activities, experimentation, and adventure. Knowledge is not completely fixed in advance (that is, it does not consist merely of information or facts), but is "constructed" as the learner makes sense of his or her experience. Thus, there is more room for individual differences, more respect for diverse understandings and points of view. Transaction education is not trying to mold young people into the shape of the existing society, but allowing them to develop a more thoughtful and critical attitude toward their society. This approach is generally concerned with strengthening democracy in education and society because only a democratic community encourages such dialogue and experimentation. Although the teacher is not treated as the authority figure she or he would be in a transmission approach, she or he plays an important role in students' learning by engaging in dialogue, questioning, and being a thoughtful and caring mentor. This understanding of learning was promoted by John Dewey and the progressive education movement, and also by the psychologist Jean Piaget and "developmental" educators. Some versions of it have been called "humanistic" education.

Education for *transformation* is somewhat more difficult to describe, because it represents a more radical, even a countercultural, philosophy. Both John Miller and I call it "holistic" education. Essentially, this approach sees human development within social and cultural, as well as ecological and spiritual, contexts. To educate a human being is not merely to make her or him a knowledgeable, productive members of society (transmission), or an active, engaged citizen (transaction), but also to help each person discover the deeper meaning of his or her life. Who are we? Why are we on earth? What is our relationship to other living beings, and to the evolution of the cosmos itself? Holistic educators do not supply answers to these questions (that would be transmission), but they believe that every person is at heart a spiritual being who thirsts for insight and wisdom about such questions. To ignore the questions is to diminish our education as well as our humanness. "Transformation" occurs when people are able to see through their own cultural conditioning and limited ego identities, and realize their connections to the unfolding universe itself (however this might be experienced or described). Education should be practiced in such a way as to encourage young people to pursue this understanding. Essentially, this starts with teaching a reverence for life. Rudolf Steiner, Maria Montessori, Krishnamurti, and Joseph Chilton Pearce are probably the best-known advocates of such an approach, but while it is countercultural, it also has roots in the ideas of respected philosophers such as Emerson and Whitehead.

There is, I think, a fourth general educational orientation that John Miller does not address—which I will call "self-direction." We find it well expressed in the writings of John Holt and A. S. Neill, and in the various democratic, anarchist, and "free" schools that have been established in this century. It seems to be the primary basis, as well, for the "unschooling" portion of the homeschooling movement—where parents follow their children's interests, rather than imposing *any* of the trappings of school upon them. This approach is grounded in a basic trust in human nature. It holds that we are naturally learners, and if social institutions would stop cluttering our paths with various prejudices, agendas, and limitations, young people would spontaneously and efficiently learn all that is necessary to live meaningful and productive lives. According to this view, a teacher is certainly not an authority, not even a mentor unless a learner requests it, and only in rare cases should be concerned with anyone else's spiritual development. The initiative for learning comes from the learner, and teachers are resources for the learner, whom he or she freely seeks out and selects. Most or all of the structures of schooling—grades, lesson plans, age groupings, teaching strategies, and so forth—are, in this view, pretty much irrelevant to genuine, self-directed learning, and are usually a hindrance. This orientation is qualitatively different from the first three (and was probably left out of Miller's list) because it is concerned with *learning* and has little or no interest in *education* as a specific profession.

As we see in diverse ways in this book, the idea of community learning centers springs primarily from this last educational orientation. Advocates of self-direction—led by homeschoolers, for the most part—want to replace schools (and all their trappings) with resource centers that learners freely use according to their individual needs. This is an important revolution in educational thinking, because our culture has organized schools with an extremely unbalanced and unhealthy emphasis on a transmission style of education. But the beauty of the community learning center is that it is not merely an individualistic reaction against oppressive education; rather, it opens possibilities for the balanced, flexible, and appropriate practice of all educational orientations. Families and individuals can, to be sure, use community learning centers in spontaneous, unstructured ways, but other kinds of learning can take place alongside purely self-directed learning—discussion groups or seminars, more highly structured courses (or tutoring) focusing on specific skills, and opportunities for mentorship and apprenticeship that could serve various purposes—from learning a craft to exploring the meaning of life. I envision peoples' learning from each other's different choices, expanding their own perspectives by seeing how others work. A parent who comes in assuming that "basics" must be drilled into children might discover that some people learn them quite well in a freer atmosphere. A family committed to unschooling might find that some children do enjoy and benefit from direct instruction in some cases. A seeker of holism, like myself, might be surprised to discover how often children can find answers to life's big questions without explicit guidance, or how often, when young people find themselves in an environment where adults take such questions seriously, the children feel encouraged to explore them.

The important result of this openness to diversity would be the relaxing of our prejudices and defensiveness. Our society is becoming more fragmented, competitive, and divisive as various groups seek to defend their beliefs and their turfs from the cultural and political forces of standardization. If we could come together in places where our views were respected and allowed, where we could dialogue freely with those who hold different views and see how their views make sense, we would make a giant step toward building a genuine, participatory democracy. We have been told that local public schools are essential to democratic community life, but it is more and more clear that cultural and political conflict over education divides our communities bitterly.[2] The contributors to this book envision a society in which communities provide dynamic, open-ended learning centers and welcome all citizens into them. We see these centers as truly public spaces in which people of all ages and persuasions can come together to learn and practice democracy. But this can only happen when all educational orientations are granted a legitimate place, and none of them, including self-direction, is privileged over the others.

The following chapters explain the beliefs, ideals, and values that support the model of community-based learning. These are diverse writings from a diverse group of authors, yet they speak to a common theme—a society that forces young people into mechanistic systems of learning diminishes both their individual potentials for growth and the health of their communities; authoritarian education is not *sustainable* because it violates inherent human needs for meaning, relationship, an authentic sense of self and a sense of place. The industrial age model of schooling is obsolete and damaging, and it needs to be replaced.

## Notes

1. See John P. Miller, *The Holistic Curriculum*. Toronto: Ontario Institute for Studies in Education Press (revised edition), 1996.

2. Stephen Arons discusses the divisiveness of public schooling in *Short Route to Chaos: Conscience, Community, and the Re-constitution of American Schooling*. Amherst: University of Massachusetts Press, 1997.

# What Is Holistic Education?

## by Ron Miller

T HROUGHOUT THE two hundred year history of public schooling, a widely scattered group of critics have pointed out that the education of young human beings should involve much more than simply molding them into future workers or citizens. The Swiss humanitarian Johann Pestalozzi, the American transcendentalists Thoreau, Emerson, and Alcott, many of those in the "progressive" education movement, and pioneers such as Maria Montessori and Rudolf Steiner, among others, all insisted that education should be understood as the art of cultivating the moral, emotional, physical, psychological, artistic, and spiritual—as well as intellectual—dimensions of the developing child. During the 1970s, an emerging body of literature in science, philosophy, and cultural history provided an overarching concept to describe this way of understanding education—a perspective often termed "holism." A holistic way of thinking seeks to encompass and integrate multiple layers of meaning and experience rather than defining human possibilities narrowly. Every child is more than a future employee; every person's intelligence and abilities are far more complex than his or her scores on standardized tests.

Holistic education is based on the premise that each person finds identity, meaning, and purpose in life through connections to the community, to the natural world, and to spiritual values such as compassion and peace. Holistic education aims to call forth from young people an intrinsic reverence for life and a passionate love of learning. This is done not through an academic "curriculum" that condenses the world into instructional packages, but through direct engagement with the environment. Holistic education nurtures a sense of wonder. Montessori, for example, spoke of "cosmic" education—help the young person feel a part of the wholeness of the universe, and learning will naturally be enchanted and inviting. There is no one best way to accomplish this goal, there are many paths of learning and the holistic educator values them all; what is appropriate for some children, in some situations, in some historical and social contexts, may not be best for others. The art of holistic education lies in its responsiveness to the diverse learning styles and needs of evolving human beings.

This attitude toward teaching and learning inspires many home-schooling families as well as educators in public and alternative schools. While few public schools are entirely committed to holistic principles, many teachers try hard to put many of these ideas into practice. By fostering collaboration rather than competition in classrooms, teachers help young people feel connected. By using real-life experiences, current events, the dramatic arts and other lively sources of knowledge in place of textbook information, teachers can kindle the love of learning. By encouraging reflection and questioning rather than passive memorization of "facts," teachers keep alive the "flame of intelligence" that is so much more than abstract problem-solving skill. By accommodating differences and refusing to label children as "learning disabled" or "hyperactive," teachers bring out the unique gifts contained within each child's spirit.

The community learning center model is not necessarily bound to a fully developed "holistic" philosophy of education—any given community could decide to set up a resource center with an emphasis on helping people acquire job skills, for example. Even so, any transition from a hierarchically managed system of mass schooling to local, participant-controlled places of learning is likely to foster more experiential, more cooperative, more personal forms of learning, and would thereby produce a more holistic educational system, in the broad sense of the term.

## For Further Reading

For further reading on holistic education, see:

Krishnamurti, *Education and the Significance of Life* (orig. 1953; San Francisco: Harper San Francisco, 1981).

David Marshak, *The Common Vision: Parenting and Educating for Wholeness* (New York: Peter Lang, 1997).

Jane Roland Martin, *The Schoolhome: Rethinking Schools for Changing Families* (Cambridge, MA: Harvard University Press, 1992).

John P. Miller, *The Holistic Curriculum* (2nd edition; Toronto: Ontario Institute for Studies in Education Press, 1996) and *Education and the Soul: Towards a Spiritual Curriculum* (Albany, NY: State University of New York Press, 1999).

Ron Miller, *What Are Schools For? Holistic Education in American Culture* (3rd edition; Brandon, VT: Holistic Education Press, 1997).

James Moffett, *The Universal Schoolhouse: Spiritual Awakening Through Education* (San Francisco: Jossey Bass, 1994).

Parker Palmer, *To Know as We are Known: Education as a Spiritual Journey* (orig. 1983; San Francisco: Harper San Francisco, 1993).

Holistic Education Press carries additional books and publishes the journal *Encounter: Education for Meaning and Social Justice*, the primary periodical in holistic education. Contact them at P.O. Box 328, Brandon, VT 05733 USA, phone: 800-639-4122, URL: www.great-ideas.org

# The Seasons of Education
## Shifting Our Cultural Metaphors in Education

*by Robin Martin*

*C*ATERPILLAR *to Butterfly: "How do you become a butterfly?"*
*Butterfly: "You have to be willing to die."*
*Caterpillar: "Die?"*
*Butterfly: "Well, it feels like you're dying. But it really turns out to be*
*a transformation to something better."*

As we examine our schools today and our culture in general, the topic of transformation is a recurring one. At a deep level, what does it mean to transform? Is it really necessary to our joyous survival on this planet? As I examine the writings and patterns of social and educational change, I am convinced that transformation is necessary. I'm also convinced that relatively few educators or parents understand the deeper meanings of transformation in a broader context of cultural shifts, and how we as individuals can attend to this change by becoming more aware of our own cultural assumptions and how to shift them.

We may not have to be willing to die, as the butterfly suggests to the caterpillar, but we must be willing to see the world from fresh perspectives. Another metaphor that shines light on the problems of education is one that portrays transformation as being akin to the seasonal changes of nature. Just as when we move from winter to spring, so too must we step outdoors to feel the new spring breezes upon our faces.

A growing number of educators (like Parker Palmer, Ron Miller, Don Glines, and Edmund O'Sullivan, to name a few) and futurists (like Duane Elgin and Riane Eisler) have written about the necessity for transformation in schools and beyond. As I attempt to begin synthesizing the many writings that strike my heart most deeply around this topic, I wish to create a framework that will allow me and perhaps others to understand more clearly two contrasting modes of thought between which we often stumble.

## Two Contrasting Modes of Thought

There are dozens, perhaps hundreds, of ways in which one can examine the patterns of culture and why societies choose, consciously or unconsciously, the directions that they do. To simplify some of the pivotal issues of social transformation, I shall examine two modes of thought for viewing life that greatly impact how we live our lives and the growth of institutions such as education that support our lifestyles. The first and dominant mode of thought is often labeled "materialism." The other mode of thought goes by many names as it is still in the process of being defined. For the purposes of this paper, this evolving mode of thought shall be called "holism."

Materialism is powered by rational thought and normal science encompassing research firmly based upon past scientific achievements. Rooted in an objective (or object-oriented) reality, materialism underlies a set of cultural practices that leads to the continual and unquestioned acquisition of more and more material objects by individuals as well as by groups. Due to the history behind materialism, it is primarily associated with Western development and capitalism. The society that evolves from materialism is what cultural researcher and author Riane Eisler calls a "dominator model," where half of society outranks the other half, and persecution and violence are considered a "normal" part of human nature.[1]

When our views of reality are determined primarily by objects and scientific facts that are outside of ourselves, this leads to a scarcity for meeting human needs because those needs are also perceived to be outside of ourselves. In the material world, there are always limits on what or how much each community member can have, which leads to a "dominator model" in which certain groups of people attempt to control the scarce resources to their own benefit. In the material world of achievement, power is based on what you have, what you know, or what you can do; it is not an inherent part of who you are. As such, power can be abused as society breaks down into the "haves" and the "have nots."

In contrast, holism is powered by rational as well as non-rational thought encompassing science *and* reflective practices that integrate personal meaning with external observations. While rational thought allows the use of logic to deduce or induce conclusions based on facts and evidence in the external world, the use of non-rational thought taps into the internal world, and thereby gives greater viability to intuitions, dreams, values, emotions, and all that which may not have a strictly logical foundation. Holism allows people to conceptualize the world beyond a materialistic focus on mind and body. It values the internal world of spirit where meaning is not derived from the logic around the scarcity of objects in the world, but from one's personal interpretation of the world. Holism directly relates to spirituality, though it is not tied to any one religion but has roots within all religions and goes beyond religion to include the inspirations of individuals, families, and communities. In some religious practices such as Buddhism, the related concept of valuing the internal as well as the external is often called "contemplative experience." In early Christianity, it was called "gnosticism." In normal science, some scientists might label it "subjectivity." The type of society that derives from this mode of thought is what Riane Eisler calls a "partnership model" of society. When a society places its primary values on internal processes rather than external objects, then the need to dominate scarce resources is eliminated and people can work in partnership toward common goals such as community peace and well-being.

In an intense dialogue between a Western philosopher (Jean-Francois Revel) and a scientist-turned-Tibetan-monk (Matthieu Ricard), this father and son duo try to find the historic and intellectual roots of their two very different paths in life. This engaging dialogue highlights the critical differences between rationalism and spirituality, which in many ways reflect the materialism/holism dichotomy as well. In one part of their book, *The Monk and the Philosopher: A Father and Son Discuss the Meaning of Life*, Ricard wonders why more and more people are turning to advice outside of science. He says, "Why is there such renewed interest in these collections of advice based on practical wisdom? Perhaps it's to compensate for the fact that our educational systems these days hardly deal at all with becoming a better human being. Modern education, more secular than ever, is primarily designed to develop the intellect and accumulate knowledge."[2]

Unfortunately, the lens with which we see the world from one set of thoughts can often not see the world of the other. So, while alternative educators can talk about "holism" and "transformation," if traditional educators are firmly rooted in an "achievement" orientation and are using the materialist lens wherein becoming a better human being is not part of what education is supposed to do, then how can they exchange any shared meanings for true communication? It would be like the butterfly trying to talk to the caterpillar when neither creature believes in its heart that the caterpillar will ever be anything other than a caterpillar. Dialogue between holistic educators and traditionalists is only rhetoric until experience leads both parents and educators to see beyond their boxes and to realize where their modes of thought, thinking, and being intersect in the world. Until the caterpillar is ready to transform itself into the cocoon stage, it does not even need to believe in the world of butterflies.

## Materialism and the Winter of Education

According to Duane Elgin, "Just as we humans evolve through major stages of development, so, too, do civilizations. Like the inexorable passing of seasons, civilizations also pass through their seasons of growth and decline. In my judgement, a number of industrial civilizations have already passed through their spring and summer of growth and have entered their autumn and winter of decline. Unless creative actions are taken soon to move beyond the industrial era, we will move deep into a harsh winter of civilizational breakdown."[3]

In his book, *Voluntary Simplicity*, Duane Elgin goes into some detail about why most industrialized countries are currently in the winter of their growth, a stage of systems breakdown. Emphasizing the critical time in which we live, he writes that "if we continue along our present course, children alive today will inhabit a warming world whose climate is so destabilized that it disrupts food production and results in massive waves of starvation; a planet with easily accessible supplies of petroleum depleted; with widespread deforestation; with the goodwill of the human family ravaged as nations fight over access to remaining resources."[4] To deny that such suffering exists and is escalating is to willfully ignore the facts.

For Elgin, the answer to a smooth transition from the winter ("breakdown") era of despair to the spring ("high growth") era of faith appears multifaceted—cutting across many dimensions of ourselves and our society. He writes about the importance of moving toward a greater awareness of possibilities for recreating meaning in our lives and finding a common social purpose toward revitalizing civilization.

In the winter of education, materialists have felt that the child's mind is barren and needs clothing to survive as an individual in today's cold, harsh world. The clothing comes in the form of knowledge of facts and intellectual tools for problem solving. Materialists view each individual as separate from the whole. There is an "I" that can be talked about, analyzed, and nurtured, and it is the central focus of most institutions. For example, from a student's perspective, schools are built around the idea that "I need improvement. I need more knowledge and skills. I need to prepare for the future." The target of education is the individual separate from others, rather than the human being as part of the community. We talk about wanting to instill in our youth social values, and indeed we create programs for more "group interactions" and "collaborative learning." Yet it is the individual who gets the grade and the individual who gets the credential.

Within such a framework, the mind is considered, for the most part, the primary instrument that we are developing within school. The mind is viewed as something we each have—separate from everyone else's and often separate from our own humanity. If humanity is viewed as that which connects our souls to all other humans, how can we be fully connected to our humanity within structures that consistently emphasize our separateness over our relatedness? Or, if being connected with humanity is viewed as the process of becoming a better human being, how can we do that in schools when this individuality myth leads us to create curricula designed primarily for developing our minds and skills alone?

The snowflakes of winter are all wonderfully unique, clearly distinct and observable too. Students, like snowflakes, can be categorized, counted, and measured. Just as we measure the feet of snow on the ground, we can know the number of students from any given school who go on to college, specialize in trades, or become unemployed. When preparing the sand, labor, and snowplows for the next storm, reliable predictors are important for efficiency.

Equipped with the tools of individuality, students and teachers are fully prepared to face an "objective" world. Objectivity allows us to presume that reality is a fixed thing composed of separate objects. Steven Glazer explains this phenomenon beautifully: "In our schools, we learn to approach the world as an assortment of separate objects, rather than as an interconnected whole. We learn to see things at face value; as fixed; as in and of themselves. We learn and share in a cultural mythology that the world is made up of matter, and that matter is free to be owned, manipulated, and consumed. Plants, animals, and elements are all considered merely 'substance,' with no spirit, no feelings—and certainly no inherent rights or liberties."[5]

If the world is made up only of objects, then one of the necessary tasks of education must be to help us learn how to manipulate those objects. In such a world, we do not become more deeply connected to the earth, as it is not a living, breathing entity like we are. We learn to make distant, rational decisions based on cost/benefit analysis. As we do this, it is only another short step from disconnecting from our emotions altogether as we begin to treat people as objects also. Just as factory managers become more efficient at moving products through an assembly line, educators are trained in methods for moving students through the system so that they are prepared for functional roles in the future.

In the recent Littleton massacre at Columbine High School, it was easy to blame the media or the parents of the killers, or the young killers themselves. Yet, what is it within a school culture that could allow students to feel so much like objects of the social or educational system that they could possibly treat other human beings with such ultimate disrespect, unable to feel the pain of others? In "The Teachings of Tragedy," Chris Mercogliano explores a number of interrelated dynamics that question the "sacred cows" of education. Among other issues, he notices relationships at the alternative school just a few miles from Columbine where he was visiting on the day of the murders in contrast to Columbine:

> One last, very important detail: every student at Jefferson County Open has a mentor, so that no one goes unnoticed. Each child is valued for his or her personhood. Contrast all of this with what John Taylor Gatto recently reported to me. Author of *Dumbing Us Down* and outspoken critic of the tyranny of compulsory education, he received several phone calls from Littleton residents in the aftermath of the tragedy. More than once he was told that students escaping the blood bath at Columbine were heard to have said when they reached safety, "We're only products there; that's all they care about." Funny, I don't remember reading that in *Time* magazine.[6]

Mercogliano does not believe the murders were the school's fault, any more than they were fault of any one person or any single institution, but that the tragedy is a symptom of faulty assumptions within schools that need to be more closely examined and called into question.

A growing body of evidence points to the importance of interconnecting with people and the power of emotions and social skills in helping people to learn more effectively.[7] Still, the underlying intention is to learn more effectively. That's what schools are for after all—to learn. To learn what? To learn the arts and sciences that lie behind production and consumption in the material world through physics, math, English, psychology, and now interpersonal and social skills for managing the other learning—all categorical ways of manipulating and studying the objects of the world.

## Rights and Responsibilities of Elders and Youth

In the deep cold of winter, any individual has the right to go outside without a coat on, but it is the responsibility of the wise one to explain, in a fashion that the younger one is able to hear, that a coat might be a good decision. For a community member to allow another community member of less wisdom to suffer due to a lack of knowledge would be cruel and inhumane. Within our objective and material reality, we have a twist of personal freedom with individual rights and responsibilities. What makes this a part of the materialist mode of thought? Couldn't it be part of the spring, rather than winter, in our cultural and educational metaphor? Civil rights and personal freedoms are progressive indeed, but they do not necessarily fall outside the bounds of materialist reasoning and logic that are often progressive and certainly caring of the individuals. If I am separate from you, then our rights and freedoms as individuals are an important political issue for maintaining efficient systems. Efficiency is an important ingredient to rational thought.

However, personal freedom does become more complicated when we ponder the rights of students in an authoritarian system where there is an objective reality (and standards) that the elders feel are important to teach. Whether we're talking about teaching 2 + 2, or teaching social values, this issue of personal freedom within education is a bit slippery. For example, when is the right time to teach math? If we believe that developmental theories can give us the answers, we can study "natural development" and deduce the best time within a range for learning basic math. Yet what if the exact time within that range is important, and what if teaching all children math at the same time might damage their internal motivation? Should students have the right to learn only when they are ready enough to ask the question? And even then, do we give them the freedom to learn on their own, or do we take the responsibility to teach to them? Within a material reality, all these questions can be answered by careful studies of what works best most of the time. So we simply hire educational specialists to figure out answers to optimize efficiency with as many students as possible. For the students who fall between the cracks, we design alternative programs to catch as many as possible. In this way, we can be responsible, and within that responsibility, still give students the amount of freedom or structure that seems optimal.

## Authorities for Monitoring the Winter Weather

In the wintertime, we don't know when the spring will come, and it is natural to ask those who have more experience. Rather than calling on the wise ones or the animals who seem to have an inner knowing, our tendency in the age of materialism is to listen to the authorities with credentials—the meteorologists whose authority comes from training and years of experience. In keeping with the idea that we can be certain about truth in the physical world comes the related metaphor that there is someone who knows the truth—an authority who can convey it to us in words and facts. Some authorities are more trusted and more knowing than others, but all authorities have access to more skills and knowledge than those without training. And certainly, it is easier and more time-efficient to ask the authority than to do the research ourselves.

Last week in the comparative education course that I'm taking, a graduate student asked the professor, "What do you think about...?" (It was an opinion question that could be answered as much from one's own experiences and observations as from any particular readings.) The professor obligingly poured forth a great essay of ideas in response to the question. Meanwhile, I sat contemplating. Why did she ask the professor rather than the whole class? And would the professor *know* more than the collective wisdom of the class? This scene is likely repeated in thousands of classrooms around the world every day. Even though we know how important it is to engage the students in reflective dialogue, both students and teachers have this ongoing tendency to defer to "authority" for the answers to questions.

We view the truth as something that we can "get" from someone so that we can come to clearer ideas on what the truth really is. Even though most teachers and indeed most students understand intuitively that there are many topics for which there is no one "right answer," they continue to probe authorities to look for greater external certainties.

## Mending the Roof: The "Fix It" Mentality

During the winter, if the roof caves in from too much snow, the most logical solution is to build stronger supports underneath. There is certainly no need for a new house. Unless conditions change drastically, the framework is not in question, merely the support system. In this age of materialism, school and community problems are all something that can be fixed with similar amends to the basic structure. It is just a matter of coming up with the right tool or idea to create the needed support.

Within this "what needs fixing" mentality, there is no need to reframe our perspectives or try to see things from a new light. Rather, it is a matter of adding on to what we already know. If $x$ doesn't work, we can try $y$, and then $z$. If schools are too violent, then we can add more monitoring and violence-prevention programs. There are always more possible solutions. And even if the systems crash (which in the computer world, they do frequently) as long as we have our wits about us, we can still fix them. Techies, for example, don't worry about the Internet's crashing because they know that even if it were to happen, it could be fixed—it's just a technical problem. We don't need to meditate or change our culture to figure out the answers; the answers are there if we only look long enough and with the right programming lens for tackling the problem.

## The Power of Money

Money relates to the trend of materialism in so much as the materialist perspective has greatly influenced many aspects of our commercial culture. Not all materialists are concerned with the acquisition of material belongings, yet this theme of consumerism continues often to distract us from broader concerns of systemic change in education. In the cold days of winter, he who pays the fire-maker gets the biggest and warmest fires. Whenever I begin speaking about creative school alternatives, one question inevitably arises: Who is paying for it? At a national level, we see the power of money in dialogues about the national budgets and how much goes to education versus military spending. Teachers who don't feel they're getting enough go on strike or constantly make underhanded comments about how little they make and how much more they deserve (and rightly so).

Money is power, and it is such a pervasive and underlying metaphor for how we think about power that little else can be added. From within the materialist's framework, there is no route to power, success, and happiness without money. We may talk a good yarn about love, time, joy, and other important values, but in the end, money also plays a decisive role in our decisions, often keeping us in our place or allowing us to soar.

So says the winter of materialism.

## Holism and the Spring of Education

Parker Palmer writes, "We all know that what will transform education is not another theory, another book, or another formula, but educators who are willing to seek a transformed way of being in the world. In the midst of the familiar trappings of education—competition, intellectual combat, obsession with a narrow range of facts, credits, and credentials—what we seek is a way of working illuminated by spirit and infused with soul."[8]

From within the field of education, I find that explaining holistic, respectful, community-based learning environments to those who grew up in the industrialized public schools is often like trying to explain the springtime to someone who has only known winter. It seems too ideal and outlandish to be real, yet there is a dream-like longing for it at the same time. In reading the following notes about the metaphors of the spring-time in education, some educators may be tempted to think, "Oh, yeah, we do this at our school." But I would challenge all readers to question the degree to which the mode of thought being described is fully embraced in their day-to-day practices. The learning environments being described in this section of the essay are fundamentally different from most schools. For traditional schools to believe that they are in the spring of education is like the caterpillar that believes it has experienced the sky. Even many holistic schools are only halfway out of their cocoons.

## Authentic Life Experiences As the Foundation of Education

One critical aspect of holism is an internal faith that nature (God, or some higher power) will provide what we need in life. The lessons that we are ready to learn are found naturally in response to our own actions. One of the most noticeable strategies of holistic educators is that they don't smother students in curriculum, tests, or extra "busy work." Like planting a tree in fertile soil, ample sunshine and rain are plenty for allowing the tree to grow. In fact, too much water or foreign agents in the soil is the surest way to cause the tree to wither and die.

Humanistic psychologist Carl Rogers was an avid advocate of this concept, which he and many others have called "experiential learning." In his book *Freedom to Learn*, he explained:

Let me define a bit more precisely the elements which are involved in such significant or experiential learning. *It has a quality of personal involvement*—the whole person in both his feeling and cognitive aspects being in the learning event. *It is self-initiated.* Even when the impetus or stimulus comes from the outside, the sense of discovery, or reaching out, of grasping and comprehending, comes from within. *It is pervasive.* It makes a difference in the behavior, the attitudes, perhaps even the personality of the learner. *It is evaluated by the learner.* He knows whether it is meeting his need, whether it leads toward what he *wants* to know, whether it illuminates the dark area of ignorance he is experiencing. The locus of evaluation, we might say, resides definitely in the learner. *Its essence is meaning.* When such learning takes place, the element of meaning to the learner is built into the whole experience.[9]

For many people, what Rogers describes is a bold step that requires teachers and parents to gradually let go of their own egos and much of their own sense of what children "should know" and "should study." It does not mean letting go of one's values or a belief in what should be taught and learned at a broader level of human virtues. However, it does mean releasing the idea that the systematic accumulation of knowledge is more important than a person's natural (freely chosen) growth and experiences of the world. This further requires a belief that given choices and natural consequences, over the long run, human beings will choose growth and goodness. There is ample evidence in humanistic psychology and holistic education to support this belief. Before people can really "hear" the evidence, however, they must be brave enough to release their fears that people are naturally bad and must be controlled. One can find evidence to support either point of view; it all depends on whether you choose to live in the winter of discontent or the springtime of hope.

Using experiential learning, the teacher's role becomes that of helping students interpret and make sense of the world within a much broader framework of possibilities, rather than telling students or even guiding them to what facts they should pay attention to. Here, the uniqueness of students as noted through their individual choices is no longer seen as separate from the world, but as an integral part of the world. The learning that each student experiences is interwoven with personal choices, so that what, how, and why a student studies becomes a unique statement and process of that student's living in the world, rather than merely preparing for it.

Many successful learning environments are rooted in this kind of "experiential learning" that allows students to learn from the wisdom of elders by engaging in authentic life experiences. In progressive home-schooling families, for example, as David Guterson describes, "Many are dedicated to the proposition that real learning takes place in the world beyond institutions and that no 'instructional delivery system' can begin to approach the instruction delivered by life itself. They see the content of education—the knowledge and skills an education develops—as emerging out of experience in the world and not out of classrooms and workbooks."[10]

Beyond homeschooling, there are also alternative schools where students are given a level of freedom for experiencing life that is not unlike the experienced-based learning of many homeschoolers. Some present and historical examples include:

- Jefferson County Open School (a public alternative school)
- Albany Free School
- Puget Sound Community School
- Sudbury Valley School
- Miquon Upper School
- Liberty School
- Wilson Campus School
- First Street School[11]

In visiting with students, staff, and parents from holistic schools and homeschooling families and reading widely in this field, I'm most struck by the students' deep enthusiasm and connection with life and learning that I've rarely seen in traditional schools. I have been equally fascinated by the diversity of forms in which this foundation for "experiential learning" can be created in both private and public schools, as well as home learning and other programs outside of schools.

In the holistic mode of thinking, teachers are partners with parents. Their job is not to make sure that Johnny learns $x$, $y$, and $z$ by the end of the year. Their job is to help ensure that Johnny becomes the kind of human being at all levels of interaction and learning that best fit Johnny's developmental capabilities and personal passions within the context and values of the school culture and the larger community. In holistic learning environments, teachers and parents begin this task by first respecting each student's uniqueness and natural wisdom[12] and not expecting him or her to complete a "canned curriculum" in the same way that every other student does. As teachers and parents learn to respect and honor the innate wisdom of students, they can provide opportunities for cooperative learning in safe and integrated ways, far beyond the "curriculum-based" structures of traditional education. And from this deep respect that is modeled by the teachers, parents, and other adult mentors, students learn to respect and honor each other in similar ways.

## Essential Relationships for Growth and Survival

In the winter of education, knowledge was the key to survival; in the springtime, it is relationships. The cold days of winter are gone, and it is time to come out of hibernation and meet, face-to-face, the people in our communities. When crisis strikes, knowing how to survive a hurricane or tornado is less important than having a reason for survival. Whether it is one's relationship with nature, with family, with God, or with friends, how we define ourselves in relationship to our world and other people serves as the core for how (and whether) we will survive on this planet. This theme of relationships comes up repeatedly in research about cultural shifts as well as in research on humanistic schools.[13]

Whether little Jackie learns to read when she is six or nine is of much less importance than that she can get along with her neighbors and find friendship and meaning across the generations of wisdom. Learning comes naturally and with great vigor once students have developed deep and meaningful relationships with those whom they have chosen as teachers or mentors. When academic requirements are removed, students often surpass expectations with flying colors (or at least they get by well enough and with personal satisfaction to do what they wish in life). For example, at Sudbury Valley School (www.sudval.org), students are not required to learn to read. However, when students decide they want to learn to read (and they all do eventually), most of them learn very quickly and with relative ease. So it is also in arithmetic. When a group of students (all different ages) at Sudbury Valley approached a teacher about learning math, they covered six years of elementary curriculum in twenty weeks (twenty contact hours), and they learned it well. Sudbury Valley also offers solid documentation showing how its alumni have not just survived after graduating, but they have gone on to engage in a rich diversity of successful career and family lives.[14]

Once a community has shifted from materialism to holism as its primary mode of thinking, learning comes more naturally for students. By giving students and teachers more freedom to think and act in ways most natural to them, they can relate to each other as fully functioning human beings and negotiate new and fresh relationships each day. What forms and methods this takes in each learning environment vary widely. Some students and teachers agree to written contracts, others use verbal agreements. Some projects involve many students, others only one. Some students choose many subjects, others focus only on special interests. Some schools get many community volunteers involved at the school, others take the school into the community. In all cases, holistic learning environments are concerned about the level and depth of interactions between students and other community members. They are not usually concerned about measuring it, but about seeing students blossom in unique ways that show positive and healthy reltionships between them and the world.

## Shared Responsibility Within Community

The issue of how much freedom to allow students is a point of contention between more radical and less radical holistic educators.[15] There are schools and teachers that effectively demonstrate several avenues. Some "free" schools give students total freedom to choose what, when, where, and how they will learn (examples: Sudbury Valley, Summerhill, Albany Free School). These schools also use a democratic process whereby they can trust that students will not get out of hand because the students are governing themselves (with adults having an equal vote as well), and indeed, this seems to work for them. (Of course, the school staff also has a higher tolerance for more chaotic behavior, believing that it is an important part of the learning process.) In terms of responsibility, adults in these schools believe that their responsibility to give children the freedom needed to learn most optimally from their own self-chosen life experiences.

Other schools offer a great deal of freedom within a specific framework for learning (examples: School Around Us, Liberty School, Venice Hill School, Puget Sound Community School). Members of these schools tend to believe that the adults have a responsibility to guide the overall direction of the types of experiences students encounter and to help students interpret those experiences in healthy ways. In addition, there are yet other schools based on the ideas of such philosophers as Rudolf Steiner, Krishnamurti, Sri Aurobindo, or Pestalozzi, in which the founders believe deeply that freedom is an internal condition and schools must be structured so that both the students and adults can continually question their assumptions about life as they work on their own self knowledge and grow together as communities and individuals. Within homeschooling as well, one finds this wide array of differences between families who have taken steps to consciously consider the issues of freedom, responsibility, and the ultimat purpose of education, and each comes to its own personal conclusions.

In whichever form freedom is manifested, holistic educators find that responsibility is learned naturally because students are (and should be) at least equally responsible for their own education. In all cases, what makes each learning environment successful in its own terms is perhaps less related to the specific forms or levels of freedom and more related to the conscious and critical reflection of the individuals allowed to take responsibility for themselves. Not only are they allowed to take more responsibility for themselves, but in the process they also learn to take more responsibility for the whole community. In a student-centered school, the teaching, learning, and parenting roles are expanded so that everyone is more fully responsible for themselves in relation to everyone else, and their understanding of that responsibility and relationship to others changes as they grow and change. Those who are ready to take on more responsibility take it. Students teach classes when they have something to share Parents volunteer when they see a need or have a skill to offer. Teachers with specific types of knowledge and skills design classes to best meet the needs of the students who choose to take their classes. It's not about who has the authority. It's about sharing authority and co-creating classes and experiences together so that everyone can share his or her wisdom and learn from the wisdom of each other.

Communication structures are designed, such as all-school meetings (or family meetings within homeschool environments), where open and honest sharing can happen, where people learn to really listen, and all participants feels their voices are heard. As each person figures out what is best for him or her by observing the effective and ineffective communication patterns of others, he or she finds how to best contribute to the learning environment. Everyone takes ownership. If students are bored, they are responsible for their boredom and so is the teacher. No one blames anyone (or they learn not to blame as they are nurtured in that direction); instead, they look for creative solutions that satisfy everyone.

As this happens, another remarkable thing happens. Members of the learning community begin to get more interested in the global community. As they feel the surge of responsibility and power for controlling their own learning environment, they become better prepared to take on what the Dalai Lama calls "universal responsibilities" too. They have seen that their feelings, thoughts, voices, and actions can truly make a difference.

For this level of responsibility to unfold, the communities must be flexible enough to change when community members express a concern about how things are working (or not working). They must be open enough to take a six-year-old's criticism seriously. They must be wise enough to listen to the elders and those with more experience. They must be patient enough to hear beyond logic and listen with their hearts.

## Learning Together for Meaning and Justice

In the object-reality of the materialist, the "what" that is being taught is more important than the "who" that is teaching (or learning). In contrast, for holistic educators the two are not separate, as who they are is manifested directly by what and how they teach. While they may teach math or world religions, what they really teach is not any given topic, but the wholeness of their personal realities. Students may learn about math or world religions, but at a deeper level, they learn ways of being in the world, the physical world of objects, the natural world of our planet, and the human/spiritual world of people. The math teacher is as responsible for this teaching as the psychology teacher and as the parents. As Ricard explained, "The principal quality of a true teacher is that he's a living illustration of the perfection he teaches. That perfection can't just be the coherence of a system of ideas; it should be transparently manifested in all the person's different sides."[16]

In school and home-learning environments that I have visited, the most effective teachers (and parents) are the ones who not only know their subjects, but who have a definite and sure sense of themselves in relation to the world. They are not spouting off knowledge to anyone; they are sharing ideas in a way that allows for the fullness of both the students and the teachers to unfold. It is an art of teaching (along with the flexibility of a system that allows for such teaching) that involves letting go of "knowing it all" and becoming co-learners with the students. The students and the teacher may not be learning the same thing or at the same level, but they are all learning. This way of teaching allows for more spontaneity, more laughter, more deep dialoguing, and more questioning, so that together teachers and students can begin to catch glimpses of the deeper truth of what they are studying in relation to who they are. While this level of teaching happens in many classrooms all around the world, in holistic schools it happens because of the system, not despite it.

Within this holistic mode of thinking, methods and procedures are used, but they are not the focus. Lynn Stoddard, a thirty-year public-school veteran and holistic education author, emphasizes the importance of adopting effective *attitudes* rather than getting caught up in refining teaching methods. For Stoddard, these attitudes are concerned with *identity* (an attitude of respect and self-worth), *spirituality* (an attitude of humility and love), *inquiry* (an attitude of curiosity and contemplation), *autonomy* (an attitude of integrity and responsibility), *interaction* (an attitude of community and cooperation), and *unity* (an attitude of charity and creativity).[17]

## The Power of People and the Weakness of Money

Finally, holism as a mode of thinking is also tied to simplicity, a growing movement in the West and an ongoing set of cultural practices in the East, in which personal meaning and community, rather than the accumulation of material abundance, are the guiding priorities by which people make decisions. In contrast to the East, in the West simplicity is not a way of life that happens by the default of history or economics, but rather it is a conscious choice away from the alternative of materialism.[18] The schools that have transitioned to the springtime of education are most often not the ones with the big corporate sponsors, the large government grants, or the wealthiest parents. They are the schools whose founders and current members have shifted their own ways of thinking and committed themselves to a new way of learning. They are managed by the people who understand that it *is* people, not money or things, who have the power to change how we construct our world and certainly how we treat our children and design our schools.

As my friend, an experienced, eighty-two-year-old simple-living advocate from Seattle, Arnie Anfinson, recently wrote to me in an e-mail, "I keep reminding myself that the fact that something has never been done before doesn't mean that it cannot be done! The lack of acceptance of this fact is probably one of the major stumbling blocks of our present educational system. This tends to keep us fixated on trying to change things by using methods of the past. Einstein said something to this effect—that science has created problems that cannot be fixed by repeating methods of the past...It is *so hard* to get people to grasp that *money* is not necessarily the answer to our problems. In a capitalist, free market, corporation-led economy, it is *so hard* to move people past this fixation." It is not that we are not mindful of money's influence in the springtime, but as the Dalai

Lama has explained, "Material comfort alone is not sufficient. We are more than our material identity, and other values—human and spiritual values—are very important as well...The questions we must ask are how to promote these other human values. How to teach the development of a good heart?"[19]

## Moving from Winter to Spring

This essay was written for all those caterpillars afraid of what lies ahead, as you begin to spin your cocoons or break free of your cocoons, to let you know of the beauty in the blue skies. Another essay would be needed to discuss the clouds of springtime and the hurdles of holistic education, but they are decidedly less violent than the storms of winter.

As we see ourselves in the context of our culture, let us try to understand how our own thoughts and the stories we tell about our reality impact the learning environments we create. And the learning environments, in turn, impact the stories that we tell. We are at a crossroads in time wherein we could go deeper into the harshness of winter or choose to realize the seasons and become aware of the springtime for warmer, more humanizing, less rigid structures for learning and living.

In summarizing Toynbee's "law of progressive simplicity," Elgin writes, "This law asserts itself that as evolution proceeds, a civilization will transfer increasing increments of energy and attention from the material to the nonmaterial side of life and that this will be expressed through developing culture (music, art, drama, literature) and a growing capacity for compassion, caring community, and self-governance. A progressively simpler way of living, then, is not only essential for responding to the ecological crisis (maintaining ourselves), it is also a vital expression of an evolving civilization (surpassing ourselves)."[20]

Here we are at the beginning of a new millennium, at a crossroads potentially between the material winter and a non-material spring, where learning more holistically becomes as important as living more simply. It is a crossroads for all the institutions of humanity—education, science, government, media, and perhaps especially family. Although many people are still engulfed in conventional and materialist modes of thought, others are moving toward something different and striking at the lost meanings within our spirits.

> *Caterpillar to Butterfly: How do you create more healthy learning environments?*
> *Butterfly: You have to be willing to change your metaphors and cultural myths.*
> *Caterpillar: But our metaphors have served us well through the winter of cultural chaos.*
> *Butterfly: Well, it may feel like a leap of faith, but really, it turns out to transform your systems into something more human, and thus helps to call forth the springtime of civilization.*

## Notes

1. Riane Eisler, *The Chalice and The Blade*. New York: HarperCollins Publishers, 1987.

2. Jean-Francois Revel and Mattieu Ricard, *The Monk and The Philosopher: A Father and Son Discuss the Meaning of Life*. New York: Schocken Books, 1998, p. 165.

3. Duane Elgin, *Voluntary Simplicity: Toward a Way of Life That Is Outwardly Simple, Inwardly Rich* (Revised Edition). William Morrow, 1993, p. 163.

4. *Ibid.*, p. 171.

5. Steven Glazer (ed.), *The Heart of Learning: Spirituality in Education*. New York: Jeremy P. Tarcher/Putnam (Penguin Putnam Inc.), 1999, p. 9.

6. Chris Mercogliano, WWW document, 1999, *The Teachings of Tragedy*. URL: http://www.edrev.org/crisis.htm

7. Daniel Goleman, *Emotional Intelligence: Why It Can Matter More Than IQ*. New York: Bantum Books, 1995.

8. Parker J. Palmer, "The Grace of Great Things: Reclaiming the Sacred in Knowing, Teaching and Learning" in Glazer, *The Heart of Learning*, p. 15.

9. Carl Rogers, *Freedom to Learn*. Columbus, OH: Charles E. Merrill Publishing, 1969, p. 5.

10. David Guterson, "Family Matters: Why Homeschooling Makes Sense" in Matt Hern (ed.), *Deschooling Our Lives*. Gabriola Island, BC, Canada: New Society Publishers, 1996, p. 78.

11. Descriptions of some of these schools are found in Mercogliano, *Making it Up as We Go Along: The Story of the Albany Free School*. Portsmouth, NH: Heinemann, 1998; George Dennison, *The Lives of Children*. New York: Vintage Books, 1969; Claudia Berman, *School Around Us: 25 Years*. Kennebunkport, ME: School Around Us Press, 1994; Don Glines, *Creating Educational Futures: Continuous Mankato Wilson Alternatives*. Saline, MI: McNaughton & Gunn, Inc., 1995; Arnold Greenberg, *Adventures on Arnold's Island and Other Essays on Education*. Blue Hill, ME: The Left Bank Press, 1994; Daniel Greenberg, *Free at Last: The Sudbury Valley School*. Framingham, MA: Sudbury Valley School Press, 1987; Jefferson County Open School students and staff, NCACS Annual Conference Presentation: Passages Program. Evergreen, CO (April 22-24, 1999), see also http://www.ncacs.org, http://www.webwrks.com/public_html/jcos.html; Robin Martin, *PSCS: A School Where Learning is Rooted in Joy, Supported by Growth, and Nurtured by Community*. URL: http://www.inspiredinside.com/learning/pscs-01.html

12. For an extensive discussion of "natural wisdom" from a holistic perspective, see Josette Luvmour and Sambhava Luvmour, *Natural Learning Rhythms: Discovering How and When Your Child Learns*. Berkeley, CA: Celestial Arts, 1994.

13. Eisler, *The Chalice and the Blade*; Robert Skenes, *Free Forming: Greater Personal Fulfillment Through Living Democracy*. Colonial Beach, VA: DaySpring Productions, 1978.

14. Greenberg, *Free at Last*, p. 17; Daniel Greenberg and Mimsy Sadofsky, *Legacy of Trust: Life After the Sudbury Valley School Experience*. Framingham, MA: Sudbury Valley School Press, 1992.

15. Scott Forbes, *Holistic Education: An Analysis of Its Intellectual Precedents and Nature*. Doctoral dissertation, University of Oxford, England, Green College, 1999 (to be published by Foundation for Educational Renewal Fall, 2000).

16. Revel and Ricard, *The Monk and the Philosopher*, p. 192.

17. Lynn Stoddard, *Growing Greatness: Six Amazing Attitudes of Extraordinary Teachers and Parents*. Tucson, AZ: Zephyr Press, 1995.

18. Cecile Andrews, *The Circle of Simplicity*. New York: HarperCollins Publishers, 1997; Duane Elgin, *Voluntary Simplicity*.

19. His Holiness the Dalai Lama, "Education and the Human Heart," in Glazer, *The Heart of Learning*, p. 87.

20. Duane Elgin, *Voluntary Simplicity*, pp. 195-6.

# Alternatives for Everybody, All the Time

*by Roland Meighan*

WHEN TWENTY EDUCATORS MET at the University of Nottingham, UK, for two one-day seminars late in 1997, all agreed at the outset that the climate of uncertainty due to continuous change was not going to go away. "Continuous adaptation" was here to stay. The educators were from a wide variety of backgrounds ranging from home-based educators to head teachers to university teachers to parents, and they had agreed to be involved in an exchange of ideas on the theme of Education in the Year 2020.

Some common ideas emerged from the discussions in small groups and also in report-back sessions about education in the year 2020. Nobody present saw mass, compulsory, coercive schooling as the way forward. All over the world, it has proved to be a system that is expensive, increasingly obsolete, and counter-productive in producing anachronistic intellectual, social, political, emotional, and economic habits.

## Features of the Next Learning System

The common ideas that emerged at the Nottingham conference for education in 2020 included the following:

1. Learning will be undertaken in much more flexible institutions than at present. Not least among the reasons is the escalating effect of modern computer and communications technology, which free us from

any specific location for learning. "Everywhere and anywhere" learning will become a reality, and flexi-time learning commonplace.

2. Open learning centers will replace present-day schools. Some saw these as being open from 8:00 in the morning until 8:00 at night, and open every day of the year. Others even thought there might be learning centers open 24-hours. Such centers would support a non-ageist provision without excluding opportunities for some age- or gender-based activity. Thus early childhood centers with a focus on young children and their families would be available. The general model will be that of the public library, not the custodial model of our present schools.

3. The central concern of such open learning centers will be learning, not teaching, although some formal teaching would be available on request. Such centers would help create a culture of learning that would include everyone and build learners' confidence and self-esteem

4. The role of the teacher will change to that of learning coach, learning consultant, or learning "travel agent." The teacher as access-agent to scarce information is already obsolete, and the logic of this will become irresistible. Present teacher training is, therefore, largely a preparation for obsolescence.

5. Interactive learning systems such as CD-ROM programs, opportunities for purposive conversation, self-programming groups, and tele-conferencing will replace a great deal of classroom teaching. The danger of excessive individualization would be offset by opportunities to learn in democratic groups and develop "team-player" co-operative skills.

6. Life-long learning expectations will place a premium on the development of computer skills in adults. Voice-driven computers would become generally important here as well as for some specific needs such as dyslexic adults and children.

7. Courses to develop experts will still be needed, but the Open University model would have dislodged the obsolete "three-year course for young adults" model of current universities, which is based on a preceding, and also obsolete, "Grand National Race" concept of schooling. Young people are required to fall at each hurdle, losing self-esteem in the process and often being turned off of learning, so that "winners" can be identified.

8. Financing will become much more diversified. Some funding out of taxation would be used to support particular requirements for experts, or particular innovative social concerns such as parenting skills, democratic skills, personal health skills, and even "green" living if environmental survival (the "doomsday" scenario) continues to grow as an issue. Industry would support activities particular to the needs of commerce. Individuals and families would provide some finance. Local Exchange Trading Schemes (LETS) or Time Dollar schemes would provide another element for paying for personal learning exchanges. There would also be some voluntary learning exchange elements. The net result would be better results for less money than at present. (Home-based educators have already shown that their route to university level can cost half as much as a conventional school route.) The current technology of swipe cards can

incorporate all these elements of finance, and record and monitor them.

9. Democratic control and democratic value-systems will replace present authoritarian control and value-systems. The open learning centers will be run by elected representatives of the partners in learning—learners (parents and children), staff (paid and voluntary), and other interested parties such as local industry and local community. Real choice according to the needs of learners will be a key feature of the next learning system. This freedom will be subject to the democratic values of human rights and responsibilities.

10. One group's summary was that 1) "time-lock" learning ideas such as key stages will disappear in favor of the flexible, irregular patterns of personal learning plans, 2) "school" will give way to flexible learning arrangements, 3) "prescribed curriculum" will give way to a catalogue curriculum with learner-driven elements, state-targeted elements, and industry-targeted elements, 4) the precedence of a "content" of shallow, subject-based learning will give way to the precedence of the deep learning of a questions-based, problem-solving approach. The home-based educators at the conference proposed that their practice already involved many of the above features, so they were something of a test bed for the success of these approaches.

11. The fear of diversity, which is based on an expectation of disorder, will give way to an awareness that all solutions are temporary in a constantly changing environment. Thus adaptability, creativity, flexibility, and re-learning are key skills.

12. The multiple purposes of education will be recognized, in contrast to the one-right-way tendencies of present times, e.g., education for "saving" the country's economy.

13. The movement away from nationalistic concern to European and global ones will lead to the replacement of the calls for learning competitive attitudes with calls for co-operative behavior.

14. A new language will develop to define the next learning system, e.g., open learning centers instead of schools, the catalogue curriculum international instead of the national curriculum, personal learning plans instead of teaching schemes and key stages.

## The Time Switches of Change

There are a number of influences at work in modern society that are operating as the time switches of change. They include the following:

1. *The arrival of the information-rich society.* When mass schooling was established, people lived in an information-poor environment. Assembling large numbers of children together in one place called a school, with teachers who had been exposed to the scarce information made a kind of sense. Since then, radio, television, the explosion of specialty magazines, computers, videos, and the like have all provided the means of making

most of the products of the knowledge explosion readily available to anyone who wants it. This is just one of the reasons that home-based education is so successful, and its practitioners outperform schools with relative ease.

2. *We now know much more about how the brain actually works.* New technologies allow us to watch a living brain at work. As a result, most of the assumptions of behavioral and cognitive psychology are in question. As John Abbott explains in *Education 2000 News* (June 1996), "Studies in neurology challenge the common metaphor that the brain is like a linear computer, waiting to be programmed... the metaphors of choice are increasingly biological—that is, the brain as a flexible, self-adjusting organism that grows and reshapes itself in response to challenge, with elements that wither away through lack of use."

3. *We now know of at least seven types of intelligence.* Howard Gardner in his book *The Unschooled Mind* (1994) reports his work on multiple intelligences. Seven types of intelligence (analytical, pattern, musical, physical, practical, intra-personal, and inter-personal) are identifiable. Only the first is given serious attention in most schools. Yet, we now know that so-called "ordinary" people are capable of feats of intellectual or creative activity in rich, challenging, non-threatening, co-operative learning environments. And the narrow, competitive tests currently in use to achieve "the raising of standards," just prevent this from happening.

4. *We now know of thirty different learning styles in humans.* It follows that any uniform approach is intellectual death to some, and often most, of the learners, and is therefore suspect. These learning differences fall into three broad categories, cognitive, affective, and physiological. Some learners have a style that is typically deductive, in contrast to those whose style is usually inductive. Others learn best from material that is predominantly visual as opposed to others who respond best to auditory experiences. There are contrasts between impulsive learners and reflective learners. Some learn better with background noise, others in conditions of quiet, and so on.

5. *It is now clear that in a complex, modern society, all three behavior patterns or forms of discipline—authoritarian, autonomous, and democratic—are needed.* Effectively educated people need the flexibility to turn to each of the three major forms of behavior and discipline (as analyzed in my 1971 book, *A Sociology of Educating*), as and when it is appropriate. So, we need to be autonomous when driving a car and take responsibility for any outcomes, behave in an aircraft according to the rules of that authoritarian situation, and if we go on to help crew a boat, behave co-operatively in a team. People schooled in only one form of behavior are handicapped in the modern world. As I indicated in *Flexischooling* (1988), rigid forms of schooling produce rigid people; flexible forms are needed to produce flexible people. Rigid university experiences build on this foundation. As John Abbott points out in *Education 2000 News* (June 1996), "We continue to get graduates who think narrowly, are teacher-dependent, and have too little ability to tackle challenges or embrace change. The

situation makes us wonder whether the traditional classroom is right for the task—the need may be less for 'reform' than for fundamental redesign of the system."

6. *Adaptability has priority in a rapidly changing society.* There is now widespread recognition that with rapidly changing technologies, economies, and life-styles, there is a chronic need for adaptability and flexibility in learning and in behavior. A system based on uniformity is, therefore, counter-productive.

7. *The recognition of the need for life-long learning.* The idea that essential learning is best concentrated between the ages of five and sixteen, and for some up to twenty-one, has increasingly given way to the necessity for life-long learning.

8. *Democratic schooling has become an international concern.* After the demise of state communism in the former USSR and Eastern Europe, new governments look to schools in the USA, the UK, and elsewhere hoping to find democratic models of schooling in operation. They find, to their surprise, the familiar model of authoritarian schools, which are not just non-democratic, but anti-democratic—perhaps less in a few countries such as Denmark than elsewhere. A key feature of democracy is the principle that those who are affected by a decision have the right to take part in the decision-making. This is expressed in slogans such as "No taxation without representation!" If we apply this to schools, we get, "No learning and therefore no curriculum without the learners having a say in the decision-making." In the authoritarian approach to schooling, however, there is a chronic fear of trusting students and sharing power with them, and a general fear of opting for the discipline of democracy.

9. *Home-based educators are trailblazers.* In the UK and the USA and in various other countries, an unusual, quiet revolution has been taking place in the form of educating children at home. At the same time that fierce debates about mainstream education have been taking place concerning a national curriculum, testing, "back to the basics," etc., some families have just quietly been getting on with a "do-it-yourself" approach to education. In the USA over a million families are now "homeschoolers." In the UK more than 10,000 families are estimated to be operating home-based education.

This phenomenon is more accurately described as home-based education because the majority of families use the home as a springboard into a range of community-based activities and investigations, rather than trying to copy the "day prison" model operated by the majority of schools. People find this quite hard to grasp, and this is shown in the asking of questions about whether such children become socially inept. After a little thought, it is clear that learning activities out and about in the community give children more social contacts, and more varied encounters, as well as reducing the peer-dependency feature of adolescent experience, than the restricted social life offered in the majority of schools.

People often try to generate generalizations and stereotypes about families educating the home-based way. The only ones that the evidence supports are 1) that they display considerable diversity in motive, methods, and aims, and 2) that they are remarkably successful in achieving their chosen aims.

Schools often take up the posture that if home-based education is to be tolerable, the families should learn how to do it from the "professionals." The evidence is different and demonstrates that schools often have more to learn from the flexibility of practice of many families, than vice versa.

Home-based educators are not the only trailblazers. Those developing all-year-round community learning centers, charter learning centers, community arts projects, learning clubs, and co-operatives and other non-coercive learning opportunities are also blazing a trail.

10. *Communications information technology is a catalyst for change.* We are all fated to live all our lives in ignorance of most of what is around us because the world of knowledge is now so vast and it is changing all the time. Without the research skills and some personal confidence derived from practicing them, we cannot even make sense of what is necessary to our immediate well being, and are forced to rely fatalistically on "experts" who often fail to agree among themselves. Computers, the Internet, CD-ROMs and new developments in the pipeline that link mobile telephones to talking databases, give us the tools to be constant and effective researchers for ourselves.

## Conclusion

In summary, the new synthesis means a new learning system with more flexible patterns. The new situation demands *alternatives for everybody, all the time.* People trying to persist with the domination of the inflexible authoritarian approach of mass schooling are consigning our children to the obsolescence of the rigid mind-set.

The future of learning is exciting, but we will need to scrap or recycle most of the current system to build one that is more humane, flexible, personalized, democratic, and educational. One person's learning career is likely to be varied, with spells of home-based education—sometimes full-time, sometimes part-time—short experiences of residential learning centers, local and international periods of learning, regular use of all-year round and all-age learning centers, periods in small charter learning centers, or any combination of these and other "learning sites" in society. The aim is to make learning just too good to miss out on, rather than something needing compulsion and coercion.

## About the Author

Roland Meighan is founder of the not-for-profit Educational Heretics Press, which exists "to question the dogmas of schooling in particular and education in general." Details are on http://www.gn.apc.org/edheretics

# Learning to Become
## Creating Evolutionary Learning Community through Evolutionary Systems Design

*by Kathia C. Laszlo and Alexander Laszlo*

*From There to Here*

WHEN WE THINK of the kind of world we wish to bequeath to future generations, we imagine one in which we finally have found ways to live in harmony with each other and the other inhabitants of this planet, and are consciously and ethically engaged in the most fascinating explorations of our human potential. This is our vision of a "sustainable and evolutionary future." By sustainability we mean the capacity to maintain the viability of the biosphere, since without it, neither healthy life nor healthy societies are possible. Evolution, as we are using the term, implies the conscious capacity to unfold into new ways of self-organization that allow for a fuller expression of the creative potential of the universe of which we are part. In this sense, sustainability is a necessary but not sufficient condition for an evolutionary future. But combined, these two features provide a powerful attractor[1] for the ethical co-creation of desirable futures.

We have a lot to learn to bring about a sustainable and evolutionary future. But unless we learn to learn in new ways, we will not be able to transcend the interrelated set of global problems facing us today. By recognizing that we cannot create a new society with the same ways of thinking that got us here, the authors have focused their work on envisioning a new form of education dedicated to the development of the competencies and sensitivities for individuals and groups to purposefully design experiences of community that are learning-oriented, self-empowering, environmentally sustainable, and evolutionary. We call this new form Evolutionary Learning Community (ELC). In our search for disciplined, creative, and participatory forms of learning, research, design, and action that facilitate the emergence of ELC, we have also developed an approach that we call Evolutionary Systems Design (ESD).

In contrast to other social change approaches that project the present into the future, ESD seeks to transcend current realities by engaging in the creation of an ideal image of education—ELC—by which to guide collective self-development efforts. That is why, rather than exploring ways of going "from here to there," ESD explores ways of getting "from there to here."

## Evolutionary Learning Community

Evolutionary Learning Community (ELC) is an ideal image of a future educational system. The three interrelated concepts that comprise the ELC construct (evolution, learning, and community) make explicit the key assumptions and aspirations underlying this image of education:

• It is a *community*-based educational system. Rather than functioning on the assumption that we need to go to school to learn, to go to work to be productive, and to go "away" to enjoy ourselves and have fun, ELC suggests the integration of work, learning, and enjoyment throughout life (i.e., intergenerational learning) in all our communities (e.g., family, neighborhood, organizations).

• It is a *learning*-oriented education, rather than a teaching-based one. Its focus is life-long learning and the development of human potential.

• It promotes self-directed, flexible, ongoing collaborative learning through *learning community*. This is not simply collective individual learning, but synergistic collaborative learning—learning content issues together, while at the same time learning process issues about *how to be* community.

• It seeks alignment with the *evolutionary* processes of which we are a part and empowers people to participate in conscious evolution.

## Evolution

Evolution, both as a scientific theory and as a universal myth—or a myth about the way in which the universe came to be—is a powerful story for the transformation of consciousness and society[2]—a story of the leaps and bounds of systems[3] of all kinds from simpler to more complex forms of organization. The evolutionary process manifests a dynamic pattern of differentiation and integration, which is starting to be comprehended through the "new sciences," also known as the sciences of complexity.[4] The appreciation of the general evolutionary process allows us to see the evolutionary history of our species in a broader context, and thereby to better understand our role in it. The astrophysicist Eric Chaisson believes that "an appreciation and understanding of evolution...can provide a map for the future of humanity,"[5] and the psychologist Mihaly Csikszentmihalyi concurs, noting that "in order to make choices that will lead to a better future, it helps to be aware of the forces at work in evolution."[6]

The development of the sciences of complexity has produced "the beginnings of a general theory of evolution that covers everything from molecules to humankind."[7] From this perspective, evolution is conceived as irreversible change that moves a system further and further from the inert state of thermodynamic and chemical equilibrium.[8] The process involves periods of dynamic stability (homeostasis), and when this stability can no longer be maintained, the system enters a period of turbulence—signaling a bifurcation[9]—when it transcends (self-organizes) into a larger whole with a higher level of organization, structural complexity, dynamism, and autonomy. In this way, open systems become more complex and dynamic, more self-directed and able to influence their environments, as they move further and further from thermodynamic and chemical equilibrium.[10] This conception of evolution describes an order-producing universe, and according to the systems scientist Sally Goerner,

> has dramatic implications for human beings because, like the Copernican revolution, it creates a radical change of perspective... It denies classical science's image of a sterile mechanical universe of directionless colliding particles and accidental life. The Copernican revolution showed that we were not at the center of the universe. The nonlinear revolution shows that we are embedded in a deep, creative, and directed process that is the physical universe. We are part of something much larger, more coherent and more miraculous than just ourselves.[11]

Perspectives such as this are shedding light on the ways in which a deeper understanding of evolutionary dynamics can inform the conscious creation of sustainable futures. Unfortunately, given the restricted access to learning opportunities inherent in our current educational paradigm, popular misconceptions about nature of evolution abound. Even mainstream scientific considerations of evolution remain biological and strongly Darwinian—dominated by conceptions of competition and survival of the fittest—just as the dominant Western worldview is still rooted in a mechanistic and reductionistic way of thinking. It is through learning, and access to learning opportunities, that these outdated conceptions can be updated, transformed, and shared more broadly.

## Learning

In the past few decades, the human species has put at risk not only its own future, but also that of life on earth.[12] Our contemporary ways of living are ecologically unsound, our social systems are breaking down, our societies are not at peace. Current limits to human will and to human understanding obstruct paths toward a better future. Albert Einstein and Bertrand Russell considered that "we have to learn to think in a new way"[13] in order to apply our knowledge and provide creative and ethical solutions to our problems. To learn to think in a new way may depend on our ability to learn to learn in a new way.

Learning is a transformative process that holds the potential for being "the greatest source of change in social systems."[14] However, "learning" means different things in different contexts. Sometimes learning is confused with or taken as a synonym for teaching. Sometimes learning cannot be separated from what happens in a formal educational institution, or is constrained to a process for children and youth. Sometimes learning is limited to cognitive, rational, and verbal processes that only deal with data and knowledge, but not understanding and wisdom. But learning can be much more than all of these. For instance, physicist Fritjof Capra considers that to learn is to be alive.[15] Clearly, learning is a complex activity that involves the whole human being and implies interactions with other human beings and with the natural and socio-cultural environment. It is a process of change that can have many results, including, for example, the acquisition and generation of knowledge, the development of skill, the appreciation of sentiment, and the reformulation of value and perspective.

Educators, psychologists, organizational consultants, and philosophers, among others, have theorized about different kinds of learning. Yet, one kind of learning is particularly relevant for the change of mindset called for by Einstein and Russell, as well as for ELC—evolutionary learning. Evolutionary learning enables the learner to cope with uncertainty and change, renew perspectives, and creatively design new forms of social systems.[16] Evolutionary learning encompasses a continuum of enabling and empowering processes that go from inner development (characterized by the expansion of consciousness) to outer transformation (involving the co-creation of evolutionary social systems). In other words, by catalyzing the transformation of the learner's values and perspectives so that they are aligned with broader evolutionary processes, evolutionary learning enables the transformation of communities and society so that they are consonant with the dynamics of their larger environment. Evolutionary learning is a journey that enables the evolution of consciousness through conscious evolution.

## Community

In its most fundamental conception, community can be considered "a group of two or more individuals with a shared identity and a common purpose committed to the joint creation of meaning."[17] M. Scott Peck suggests that a community is "a way of being together with both individual authenticity and interpersonal harmony so that people become able to function with a collective energy even greater than the sum of their individual energies."[18] Authentic communities are able to enhance their own development, while at the same time enhancing that of each individual in the community, thereby promoting both freedom of personal choice and a sense of responsibility for the whole. In such communities, the operating principle is that of unity in diversity.

There are different types of communities, and attention to their distinct characteristics helps clarify the particular orientation of ELC. Four types of communities are relevant for this consideration: Traditional Community, Surrogate Community, (simple) Learning Community, and Evolutionary Learning Community.[19]

• **Traditional Community**: A closed, stable system where the individual's identity is determined by a collective identity rooted in transmitted myths, values, norms, rituals, and beliefs. That is, an individual born within this kind of community is socialized into the local culture. Many indigenous communities are good examples of traditional communities. They are natural rather than designed communities. In many cases, change within this type of community is slow and gradual unless it is caused by a violent imposition of values from an external dominating group. Traditional communities *have* been the primary social manifestation of human evolution since the formation of tribal hunter and gatherer groups. Within them, humans developed relationships of mutual support in exchange for a sense of belonging, security, and well being. But this kind of fealty did not bind others outside their community. In our current interconnected world, such orientations tend to be limiting. As creativity scholar Ruth Richards astutely points out, "Our survival has become strongly dependent upon our commonalties as human beings, not on the differences between each other as individuals and as members of narrow reference groups."[20]

• **Surrogate Community**: A closed, unstable system artificially created to attract and satisfy disenfranchised individuals yearning for community through imposed norms and values. Modern industrial societies have fragmented the traditional experiences of community for which human beings yearn. Surrogate communities are identified as artificially designed means to satisfy the need for shared identity and a sense of belonging among individuals who would otherwise not have access to authentic forms of community. Surrogate communities are not authentic in the sense that individuals who join them must accept pre-established values, beliefs, and rules—as defined by others—under which the community operates. For instance, there exists an organization ostensibly dedicated to encouraging community in the US and abroad. To do so, it sells community workshops—two-day encounters for individuals interested in having a cathartic experience leading toward feelings of empathy and connectedness among each other. After the workshop is over, participants must continue to pay a substantial fee in order to "experience community" again, or else they will "lose community" and life will continue for them much as it did before the workshop. Gangs, cults, and some political parties are also examples of surrogate communities.

• *Learning Community*: An open, dynamic system in which individuals collectively learn to adapt *to* their environment. The "learning organization," the idea that organizations can integrate the function of learning as a means to change and improve performance, is a case in point. In both organizational and educational contexts, the notion of Learning Community has become a focus of attention in recent years.[21] Individuals in learning communities have an explicit common purpose: to learn together. However, in some cases there is no difference between a learning community and a community of individual learners. Even when a learning community demonstrates creative and fluid processes of collaboration and synergy by which to adapt to its environment, it tends to do so in a reactive mode. Such simple learning communities are often excellent means for learning about "doing things right," that is, increasing efficiency and efficacy in a rapidly changing world. And as such, they are ideal spaces for exploring new ways of working, learning, and enjoying life in an integrated way. But they rarely incorporate an ethical-futures perspective, such as required for "doing the right things." Such an ethical-futures concern marks the quest for sustainability and for the sort of evolutionary possibilities explicitly espoused by ELC. In this sense, simple learning communities can be stepping stones toward Evolutionary Learning Community.

• *Evolutionary Learning Community* (ELC): An emergent (self-designing) learning system demonstrating dynamic stability by adapting *with* its environment and generating developmental pathways that are sustainable in the context of broader evolutionary flows. ELC is a human activity system that strives toward sustainable pathways for evolutionary development in synergistic interaction with its milieu. It does so through individual and collective processes of empowerment and learning how to learn[22] and through an ongoing commitment to evolutionary learning. "ELCs do not adapt their environment to their needs, nor do they simply adapt to their environment. Rather, they adapt with their environment in a dynamic of mutually sustaining evolutionary co-creation."[23] Just as the concept "system" is more a pattern than a thing, ELC is best conceived as an ideal image of community that can serve as a beacon for the design of new social systems appropriate for a new evolutionary era.

## *Evolutionary Systems Design*

Evolutionary Systems Design (ESD) is an approach for learning about evolution and acting accordingly. As a species, our actions and interventions on this planet have been largely driven by chance and, at best, "20/20 hindsight." However, as Margaret Mead noted, we are at a point where, for the first time in human history, we are able to explain what is

happening while it is happening.[24] ESD builds on this relatively new
meta-reflective competence by serving as an instrument for the evolution
of consciousness and for conscious evolution. It suggests that with the new
understanding of evolutionary dynamics and effective approaches to the
participatory design of social systems, our species can stop drifting upon
the currents of change and begin to adjust its sails in view of sustainable
evolutionary futures.

ESD draws on Social Systems Design,[25] General Evolution Theory,[26]
and lifelong transformative learning orientations.[27] Those engaged in
ESD must select and design appropriate approaches for addressing their
particular purposes rather than following a generic approach designed by
someone else. Communities that face practical challenges for socio-
ecological survival must learn to move "toward what will work to provide
answers where no reliable guides exist."[28] This does not mean that ESD is
methodologically eclectic, or that it disregards the need for a coherent
body of theory to inform its practice. Rather, it suggests that ESD will
look different when adapted to the design and development of concrete
evolutionary learning communities. By empowering evolutionary change
agents neither as activists nor as theorists, but as a synthesis of the two,
ESD offers a way—an integral path—for human becoming in partnership
with earth.

## Evolutionary Learning

Evolutionary learning is a core aspect of ESD. We have developed an
operational learning framework for the stages through which individuals
and groups pass as they become evolutionary systems designers
(ESDoers). The four stages and their corresponding objectives are:

• Evolutionary consciousness: To create an awareness of the evolutionary history, of the changing conditions of change, and of the challenges
that sustainable human co-habitation with life on earth entails.
• Evolutionary literacy: To develop a basic scientific understanding
and an empathic appreciation of the challenges facing humanity that are
both personally significant and societally attuned.
• Evolutionary competence: To gain a sense of responsibility that is
coupled with the change management competence (i.e., the learned ability
to manage processes of change in social systems) of respons*ability* so that
we can affect purposeful, positive, evolutionary change in the communities within which we work, play, and learn.
• Evolutionary praxis: To learn how to become catalysts for change by
learning what modes, methods, and means are best for clearly articulating
and effectively communicating to others the need for change.

The four stages along the ESD path of life-long evolutionary learning
can best be illustrated as follows:

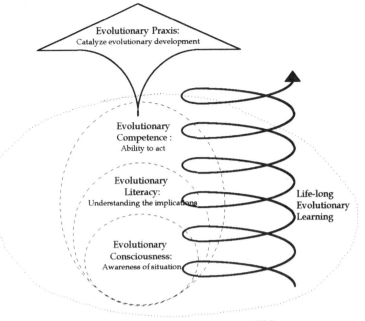

The evolutionary learning framework of ESD.

The ESD orientation to future creation is essentially possibilistic. It assumes that human beings have the choice consciously to participate in the co-creation of the future. And yet it seeks neither to predict nor to "socially engineer" the future. Rather, it seeks to create the conditions for the emergence of evolutionary futures:

> In systems such as contemporary society, evolution is always a promise and devolution always a threat. No system comes with a guarantee of ongoing evolution. The challenge is real. To ignore it is to play dice with all we have. To accept it is not to play God—it is to become an instrument of whatever divine purpose infuses the universe.[29]

## *Conclusion*

Evolutionary Learning Community can serve as an attractor and guide for the design of new learning systems. Evolutionary Systems Design is an approach for realizing the vision of a sustainable and evolutionary *learning* society—a *paidea*, as the ancient Greeks called a society where the promotion of life-long learning and the achievement of the human potential in the broadest sense was a central priority.[30] ESD involves learning to learn together about our values, and to use the resulting understanding to co-create pathways for socio-ecologically sustainable futures. The challenge is to find practical ways of living in harmony with nature; to learn to live lightly, meaningfully, and simply in and with earth, and to realize an extended sense of identity that moves us from anthropocentric to ecological and evolutionary ways of being and becoming with the world. The design of ELC through ESD seeks to do just this. By expanding our sense of self to include the natural and physical environment and creating conditions that foster conscious evolution—in ourselves and in others—we embark on a path by which to realize the evolutionary opportunities ahead of us.

## *Notes*

1. The notion of an "attractor" as used here derives from the study of non-linear dynamical systems (as through chaos theory). It indicates "a pattern of behavior that a system moves toward over time...[whose] output never repeats but no point [of which] falls outside a limiting shape.... attractors show how a complex system may have endlessly unique behavior that is nevertheless clearly ordered. The long-term behavior of the system is non-repeating yet attracted to a clear form." (Sally Goerner, 1994. *Chaos and the Evolving Ecological Universe.* Langhorne: Gordon and Breach, p. 212).

2. David Feinstein and Stanley Krippner, *Personal Mythology: The Psychology of Your Evolving Self.* New York: Jeremy Tarcher, 1988. pp. 212-213.

3. A system is an interconnected whole that is structurally divisible but functionally indivisible. In other words, it cannot be separated into its component parts without destroying the essential properties of the system. For instance, the molecules of hydrogen and oxygen in water, when separated, loose the property of "wetness" present only when $H_2O$ is a system. Systems are more patterns than things. Molecules, organisms, societies, and the solar system are all examples of systems.

4. The sciences of complexity deal with chaos, self-organization, and new understandings of evolution. Among them are: general system theory, cybernetics, nonequilibrium thermodynamics, autopoietic systems theory, chaos theory, and dynamical systems theory.

5. Eric Chaisson, *The Life Era: Cosmic Selection and Conscious Evolution.* New York: W. W. Norton, 1987, p. 200.

6. Mihaly Csikszentmihalyi, *The Evolving Self: A Psychology for the Third Millennium.* New York: Harper Collins, 1993, p. 4.

7. *Op. cit.,* Goerner, 1994, p. 20.

8. There are three thermodynamic and chemical systems states: at equilibrium, near equilibrium, and far from equilibrium. The first is an inert state, for example, a closed boxed with equally distributed gas from which no energy can be generated. The second is the state of things that tend to run down (as per Newton's second law of thermodynamics), like a car that needs constant maintenance and gasoline to continue to function. The third state is characteristic of systems that work against the second law: rather than running down, they complexify, like living systems that grow and evolve.

9. A bifurcation is a period of indeterminacy in the evolutionary trajectory of a system characterized by turbulence and organizational instability when, because of changes in either its internal or external environment, it transcends its current functional structure and self-organizes at a new level of organization (a new dynamic regime) that is re-establish a new state of dynamic equilibrium or flowing balance. Inability to do so—that is, to reach a new dynamic regime—implies devolution and possibly extinction.

10. Ervin Laszlo, *Evolution: The General Theory.* New Jersey: Hampton Press, 1996, p. 12.

11. *Op. cit.,* Goerner, 1994, p. 21.

12. Ervin Laszlo, *The Choice: Evolution or Extinction?* New York: Tarcher/Putman, 1994, p. 1.

13. A. Einstein and B. Russell, "The Pugwash Manifesto." Proceedings of the First World Conference on Science and World Affairs. Pugwash, Nova Scotia, 1957.

14. Bela H. Banathy, *Designing Social Systems in a Changing World.* New York: Plenum, 1996, p. 318.

15. Fritjof Capra, *The Web of Life: A New Scientific Understanding of Living Systems.* New York: Anchor books, 1996.

16. *Op. cit.,* Banathy, 1996, pp. 318-319.

17. Kathia C. Laszlo, and Alexander Laszlo, "Partners in Life—Syntony at Work." Proceedings of the Ninth Interna-

tional Conversation on the Comprehensive Design of Social Systems. Pacific Grove, CA: ISI, 1997, p. 6.

18. M. Scott Peck, *The Different Drum: Community Building and Peace.* New York: Simon and Schuster, 1987, p. 239.

19. S. McCormick, C. François, A. Laszlo, K. Laszlo, B. and Nanay, "Designing Sustainable Evolutionary Learning Communities." Proceedings of the Ninth Fuschl Conversation. Austria: Austrian Society for Cybernetic Studies, 1998.

20. Ruth Richards, "Seeing Beyond: Issues of Creative Awareness and Social Responsibility." *Creativity Research Journal*, 6 (1&2), 1993, p. 168.

21. See Peter M. Senge, *The Fifth Discipline: The Art and Practice of the Learning Organization.* New York: Doubleday Currency, 1990; P. M. Senge, A. Kleiner, C. Roberts, R. Ross, G. Roth, and B. Smith, *The Dance of Change—The Challenge to Sustaining Momentum in a Learning Organization.* New York: Currency/Doubleday, 1999; Renate Caine and Geoffrey Caine, *Education on the Edge of Possibility.* Alexandria, VA: ASCD, 1997.

22. Kathia C. Laszlo, and Alexander Laszlo, "Building a Design Culture Through Evolutionary Leaning Communities." Proceedings of the Seventh International Conversation on the Comprehensive Design of Social Systems. Pacific Grove, CA: ISI, 1995.

23. Alexander Laszlo, and Stanley Krippner, "Systems Theories: Their Origins, Foundations, and Development," in J. S. Jordan (ed.), *System Theories and A Priori Aspects of Perception.* Amsterdam: Elsevier, 1998.

24. Alfonso Montuori, *Evolutionary Competence: Creating the Future.* Amsterdam: J.C. Gieben, 1989, p. 27.

25. *Op. cit.,* B. H. Banathy, 1996.

26. *Op. cit.,* E. Laszlo, 1996.

27. Dean Elias, "It's Time to Change Our Mind: An Introduction to Tranformative Learning," *ReVision,* 20 (1), 1998.

28. Marcia Salner, "A New Framework for Human Science," *Saybrook Perspectives.* San Francisco: Saybrook Institute, 1996, p. 8.

29. *Op. Cit.,* E. Laszlo, 1996, p. 139.

30. Lester W. Milbrath, *Envisioning a Sustainable Society: Learning Our Way Out.* New York: State University of New York, 1989, p. 94.

# About the Authors

Kathia C. Laszlo, Ph.D., is co-founder and executive vice-president of Syntony Quest and a Fulbright Scholar from Mexico. She is now working on her second book, and has published in the areas of values in education, future trends in education, technology and learning, and systems thinking. Her doctoral research in the field of human science at the Saybrook Graduate School focused on social and institutional change. She is holder of a Masters degree in education with specialization in cognitive development, and of a B.A. in marketing.

Alexander Laszlo, Ph.D., is co-founder and president of Syntony Quest and former dean of the doctoral program in management at the Graduate School of Business Administration and Leadership (ITESM) in Mexico. Currently full professor of learning and human development at the California Institute of Integral Studies, he teaches in the learning and change in human systems doctoral program. He is on the editorial boards of Systems Research & Behavioral Science and Latin American Business Review, recipient of the Sir Geoffrey Vickers Memorial Award, active member of several systems science societies, and author of over thirty journal, book, and encyclopedia publications.

Syntony Quest is an evolutionary learning organization dedicated to helping people learn to cope with change and uncertainty in ways that foster community and sustainability by tapping the creative potential of individuals and groups and facilitating the emergence of Evolutionary Learning Community through conversation, design, and action. Syntony Quest is a 501(c)(3) tax-exempt educational organization.

For more information, contact Syntony Quest, 1761 Vallejo Street, Suite 302, San Francisco, CA 94123-5029, USA, phone/fax: 415-346-1547, e-mail: info@syntonyquest.org, URL: http://www.SyntonyQuest.org

# The Education Emperor Has No Clothes

### Ideas for Nurturing A Culture of Learning

*by Patrick Farenga*

IN THE EIGHTEENTH CENTURY it was not common to suggest that slavery was a sin against fellow human beings. In the nineteenth century it was not common to suggest that women deserved the same privileges of citizenship as men. In the twentieth century it is not common to suggest that children can learn without attending schools. All three are examples of how the cultural attitudes of a population influence not only their views of reality, but also create social structures that reinforce and perpetuate those views. Science, medicine, and law were used to keep slaves and women in their place until cultural attitudes towards these people changed. Likewise, we are in the midst of a gradual change in our perception of children. At the start of the twenty-first century some people are realizing that children are people—not little adults or cute kids, but real people. Yes, children are often inexperienced, innocent, and have various needs that caring adults should address, but they are people nonetheless. As they are recognized as people, children, like slaves and women, will also be treated with respect and allowed more autonomy in their lives.

This is not a polemic for children's rights, but simply a statement that some parents and other concerned adults are working with children in ways that make them view children as people, rather than generic students in need of standardized education. By viewing children as people, as individuals, it becomes harder to classify them as we do in school: A student, B student, and so on down the line. It also becomes harder to teach them subject matter without regard to their emotions and interest in learning it. People usually don't like having their interests dictated to them by others, their time conscripted by outsiders, and their performance in areas they are forced into being judged in public. The cooperative community life-long learning centers (CCL-LLCs) that this book proposes are one direction we can take to help humanize education and grant a degree of respect and autonomy to children in one part of their lives—what they choose to study, to think about. Such centers can probably only come into being on a wide scale with some sort of major funding and legislative approval. However, as the growth of homeschooling and alternative schools demonstrates, one need not wait for the rest of the world to catch up before one can attempt to make the world a better place. The larger-scale CCL-LLC concept is based on existing grassroots models that I will draw upon in this chapter.

The models and analysis I present are meant to be guidelines for people in and out of school to consider, though my examples are primarily from my experience as a homeschooling father for thirteen years and a homeschooling activist for nineteen years. In any case, by starting from the premise of respect for children, and the expectation of getting respect back from children, the cultural attitudes and institutions one discovers for helping children learn and grow into responsible adults are radically different from those developed when starting from the premise of educational need. As I participate in the CCL-LLC project I am making a conscious effort not to hijack the concept of community-centered learning into serving as a vehicle for other agendas I feel are important—children's rights, environmentalism, spirituality, gender equity, and so on. What I've learned from my years as a homeschooling activist is that we should be more concerned with growing the general movement, rather than managing the specifics of how each family or school implements the freedom such a movement gives them.

Homeschooling has grown to over a million children,[1] not because it only appeals to cultural and religious conservatives, or only to cultural creatives and communards, but because it is broad enough to encompass a wide variety of rationales and approaches. John Holt envisioned the difficulties of such diverse groups working together, but also helped lay the path for their cooperation in 1977 when he published the second issue of *Growing Without Schooling* (*GWS*) magazine and wrote, "What is important is not that all readers of *GWS* should agree on [the reasons for a family to homeschool], but that we should respect our differences while we work for what we agree on, our right and the right of all people to take their children out of schools, and help, plan, or direct their learning in the ways they think best."[2] I hope the CCL-LLC concept will grow according to this same broad principle.

I wish to provoke the reader to reconsider the role our culture at large has in helping people learn, to provide a broad outline of conventional education assumptions that are challenged by existing alternative models, and to provide concrete examples that community-centered life-long learning centers can emulate and expand upon. Most parents who home-school do so only to help their children learn best; they are rarely homeschooling to start a social movement or prove the effectiveness of a new educational approach. Nonetheless, simply by homeschooling these parents are demonstrating that there are many other places, people, and schedules to help children learn and grow besides school.

# Reclaiming Independent Learning from the Education Economy

Education has become big business in modern times. Personal expenditures by citizens on education, plus federal, state, and local tax expenditures total many billions of dollars every year. I use the phrase "education economy" to denote expenditures of money we make in schools, as well as our contribution of personal time to participate in these institutions as part of the education economy. But the education economy does more than make us pay for educational opportunities; it attempts to determine what learning is valuable and worthy of funding and what is worthless. By turning education into a commodity that is purchased and sold publicly and privately and in need of regulation by the government, we have all but dismissed the value of the learning we do of our own volition. The education economy disembeds learning as an integral part of our personal experience, and embeds learning in the larger social context of market forces. It has become incredibly difficult to critique the expansion of school into areas that used to be the responsibility of family, church, and community because we need something to fill the gaps these institutions are leaving. However, are these institutions withering on their own, or are they being pushed into disuse by the growing education economy? It is hard to say absolutely, but as any parent who wishes to teach his or her own children has discovered, it is obvious that the grasp of school is far stronger on family life than we think.

John MacKnight has pointed out that our institutions have seriously crossed the boundary from being in the service of individuals to being in the service of the economy:

> We say love is a need. Care is a need. Service is a need. Services meet needs. People are collections of needs. Society has needs. The econ-

omy should be organized to meet needs. In a modernized society where the major business is service, the political reality is that the central need is an adequate income for professional services and the economic growth they portend. The masks of love and care obscure this reality so that the public cannot recognize the professionalized interests that manufacture needs in order to rationalize a service economy. Medicare, Educare, Judicare, Psychocare are portrayed as systems to meet needs rather than programs to meet the needs of services and the economies they support. Removing the mask of love shows us the face of services who need income, and an economic system that needs growth.[3]

One of the steps community-centered learning must take, in my mind, is one Ivan Illich has urged for decades: to study how the institution of education has disembedded learning from living, and to explore what proportion of institutional services to human activity is truly appropriate for people and communities to thrive. Aaron Falbel shows how Illich's thinking about education is inextricably linked to modern economics:

Illich...links education with the notion of scarcity. He defines education as learning under the assumption of scarcity...By scarcity, Illich does not mean a temporary lack or shortage but a generalized condition or perception that things are of value in proportion to their rarity. Money is the most obvious scarce commodity. If money were abundant and freely available, it would cease to have economic value—it would become just paper. The same is true for abundant human activities that are rendered scarce: they become commodities. Learning, dwelling, working, walking, and healing become education, housing, jobs, transportation, and health care. Verbs are turned into nouns. These latter nouns are scarce and must be obtained or purchased from someone else...Thus education only appears when we feel a need to make sure that certain scarce knowledge is imparted. Knowledge that is abundant in the world is readily learnable and therefore needs no special arrangements.[4]

The economics of education dictate that since knowledge is scarce, there must be winners and losers, high test-scorers and low test-scorers, and school is the mechanism for sorting them into their economic destinies. As Falbel notes, people are hungry in the U.S. today—not because there is a shortage of food (we discard billions of pounds of edible food annually), but because some people don't have the scarce money or jobs necessary to purchase it. Likewise, the economics of schooling attempts to determine who will reap the rewards of scarce knowledge and prevent uncredentialed but otherwise qualified people from gaining access to similar rewards. For instance, in New York City one cannot be a sanitation worker without a high-school degree. In some retail stores, one cannot be considered for a job without having a two- or four-year college degree. Jobs that only in the past twenty-five years did not require any college degree—secretarial work, air-traffic controllers, graphic design— now increasingly demand them. Community-centered learning centers that view learning in human, rather than economic terms, can avoid this educational doctrine of survival of fittest. After all, it isn't credentials that ultimately matter in the workforce, but demonstrable competence.

This does not mean that people using community-centered learning will be non-participants in local, national, and international economies. All it means is that no one will be disqualified from access to these economies based on their educational credentials. Instead, performance tests, resumes, portfolios, work experience and recommendations, proof of completing specific courses needed for specific tasks, life experience credits, perhaps even assessment of computer simulations for certain tasks and functions, can be used in lieu of diplomas and standardized test scores. This is exactly how homeschooled children, and graduates of little-known alternative schools, gain entrance to college or work without traditional diplomas and degrees.[5] One of the key differences between community-centered learning and our current school system will be economics.

## Being Different

Many parents choose alternative schooling because they hope their children will turn out differently by being treated and taught differently. For them, having children who march to the beat of a different drummer is desirable. However, many other parents who enroll their children in alternative education settings are concerned that they are depriving their children of future opportunities because the children won't learn certain things in certain ways. There is little evidence to support these fears. Homeschoolers and alternative school graduates find work worth doing and get into selective colleges without special difficulty, as research and case histories have shown for decades. Further, evidence demonstrates that gaining high marks and honors in school is no guarantee of high income and honors in adult life after school. What we, as parents and teachers, need to remember is that while we are important and have influence, we are not the sole determinants of how our children will grow. Children may grow to "be different" despite our efforts to make them conventional! How many radicals have children who grow up to be capitalists, and vice-versa? How many college professors have children who become carpenters, and vice-versa? There are no guarantees that schooling children in any particular way will make them turn into the adults we think they should be. What we can do as concerned adults is nurture and bond with our children as much as possible so that when they do grow in directions we don't expect they will take our admonishments, or encouragements, seriously, and love us as we love them through thick and thin.

Homeschoolers and alternative educators try to raise children in ways that are consistent with their shared beliefs, but that also put their beliefs into action. Homeschooling and community-centered learning allow families to live and share their activism each day, not just after school and on weekends. A homeschooler from Vermont puts it this way:

> Letting lawmakers and school officials know that we're not satisfied with current educational systems and opportunities is important, but it's also nice to be able to supply living proof of a better way. In activism expressed by lifestyle, we have begun to question the disproportionate amount of power our nation consumes by taking steps to supply our own. We have one solar panel so far...Our family certainly isn't unique in this form of activism. I often read about homeschoolers who run home businesses, do home births and grow their own food. I also read a lot about modern-day homesteaders who also homeschool. Our country was most innovative during the era when its citizens were most independent. I'll be eager to see what happens with this next generation of independent activists![6]

One need not move to a rural area to live an activist lifestyle, nor must one hold any activist beliefs to homeschool successfully. It is quite common to homeschool conventionally too. A public schoolteacher I met, also from Vermont, is a very traditional teacher who wanted his children to learn the public school curriculum, but at home. He does not use or believe in portfolio evaluations or other alternative education techniques. He simply had all three of his children use standard textbooks that he purchased, and the children paced themselves through each text with Mom and Dad's help. His son earned a National Merit Scholarship using this method. Further, his kids completed their textbook assignments with plenty of time left in each day for independent study, group activities, and community service. The children did not become textbook grinds.

There is a great degree of latitude and possibility in homeschooling that community-centered learning can build upon, but it will take courage to do it simply because it flies in the face of conventional school practice. For instance, though there is no biological clock that determines when one should learn to read, administrative directive, disguised as learning theory, dictates that children in public schools should read by age seven solely because they will otherwise fall behind the school schedule and be ridiculed by teachers and students. However, late reading is a common occurrence in homeschooling and alternative schools, particularly Waldorf schools. A researcher at the University of London Institute of Education studied one hundred homeschooling families and found that "learning to read 'late' is a feature of home education, at least for those children who have never been to school...As long as children have the necessary pre-reading information processing skills, and these are crucial, we should not be too concerned about when they start reading. The trouble is that this does not fit in with school organization requirements."[7]

Neil Postman notes how the concept of school-managed child development was created not by studying children developing in their communal surroundings, but by the preferences of schoolmasters. The stages of childhood—what we expect children to learn and at what ages—was determined and organized by how schoolmasters sequenced the curriculum for use in school. The point, Postman writes, "is that the mastery of the alphabet and the mastery of all the skills and knowledge that were arranged to follow constituted not merely a curriculum but a definition of child development. By creating a concept of a hierarchy of knowledge and skills, adults invented the structure of child development."[8]

Homeschoolers who do not use this structure of child development discover that children learn at widely varying rates. Some children who are labeled "learning disabled" in school lose that behavior when they learn outside of conventional school, indicating that, for some, the learning environment may be more toxic to learning than the child's genes.[9] Like some homeschooling families, not all community-centered life-long learning centers will adapt to the learner's schedule. Conventional school schedules about what and when people should know things still appeal to many. Some learning centers will probably resemble existing schools, in the sense of having regularly scheduled classes and curricula, and many parents will continue to use them as they always have. Other parents and children will want formal school structure for some subjects, but not for all subjects. Some learning centers will resemble crafts shops, and others will be like living rooms with lively discussions going on, or counseling centers with private rooms, or playgrounds for young children. The idea is to allow as much institutional flexibility for learning to occur as we can provide. This is happening already on a small scale in the homeschooling community. All the examples above can readily be discovered in most cities with homeschoolers.

Those who defend conventional schooling to the exclusion of other alternatives often ask, "How can society risk such flexibility in education? How do we know the children will turn out okay?" First, universal compulsory schooling is a modern experiment in the West; it only began about two hundred years ago in Prussia. In Eastern countries, China and India in particular, I have been told that compulsory schooling goes back at least a thousand years and was used to assure that each social caste kept its place in society. However, in the West, families and communities have long raised and taught children in the milieu of work, ritual, and play, creating schools for limited times and purposes, not to mold and shape all children throughout their youth by force of law. Periclean Greece, Elizabethan England, and Colonial America are but three of many societies that did not force all children to attend school throughout their youth. Yet the ad hoc and brief nature of their schooling in no way diminished the considerable cultural and intellectual achievements of these cultures. The question should really be, how can we continue to risk having an education system that is so inflexible?

Second, contrary to popular wisdom, school attendance is not vital to making money, living a good life, or becoming an intellectual. The list of well-known millionaires who never attended college includes Andrew Carnegie, Richard Branson (Virgin Atlantic Airways), Horace Greeley (founder, *New York Tribune*), Soichiro Honda (Honda automobiles), H. L. Hunt (oil tycoon), Ray Kroc (McDonald's), Dave Thomas (Wendy's),

Adolph Ochs (Founder, *New York Times*) Bill Gates (Microsoft), and Steve Jobs (Apple Computer). Famous people who rarely or never attended school or college include Bertrand Russell, Germaine Greer, Florence Nightingale, Sean O'Casey, Teddy and Franklin D. Roosevelt, Woodrow Wilson, Woody Allen, Burt Lancaster, Jane Goodall, Jack London, Bobby Fisher, Alexander Graham Bell, Thomas Edison, Ansel Adams, and Isadora Duncan.[10] Finally, studies of homeschooled children who are now adults in the United Kingdom and the United States show that they are well-adjusted citizens. Roland Meighan notes that one study of fifty-three adults who were homeschooled found that three quarters of the sample had felt that being educated at home "had actually helped them interact with people from different levels of society... When asked if they would want to be educated at home if they had their lives over again, 96% replied Yes... Not one of the sample was unemployed or on welfare... and two thirds were married—the norm for the age group."[11]

Many stories published in a variety of homeschooling publications over the past twenty years have described what teens and young adults are doing after leaving their homeschool. *Growing Without Schooling* magazine contains a directory of "grown homeschoolers" willing to talk about their experiences, such as how some got into college—including Ivy League colleges—and how others found work they like without going to college.

## *Alternatives to School that Help People Learn*

Educators Raymond and Dorothy Moore began researching and proposing many types of cooperative arrangements between homes and school starting in the late 1950s. For instance, they created a flexible work-education program that encouraged schools to assign each child a number of hours during which he or she had to perform some helpful service in the home.[12] Based on their research, particularly in reading, the Moores openly questioned the wisdom of sending children to school at earlier ages and for longer periods of time, and they argued for delaying formal schooling. In 1976 Dr. Moore wrote:

> If the parents will provide warm, consistent, responsive care for the child under eight or ten, the child will usually receive a far better educational background than if he had gone to school at four, five, six, or seven. This is even more true for boys than for girls. ...[These children] become independent in the right sense. They are stable, highly motivated, and ready for school.[13]

The Moores' argument at that time focused on children's going to public or private school at later ages, but in the past twenty years they have become some of homeschooling's most ardent and articulate support-ers. I mention their work as an example of how schools and families can mutually benefit by doing things differently. But sadly, to suggest to a school that delaying entrance until age eight or ten, or to consider chores around the home educational, is to court a reputation of being "odd." If the Moores' ideas of home and school cooperation sound ridiculous to mainstream school people, is it any wonder that John Holt's ideas, particularly that contemporary education is antithetical to learning, appear "beyond the fringe" to them? Fortunately, some educators and many parents have found that Holt's ideas about learning could easily be put into practice, and the positive results have been reinforced by a growing number of people considering homeschooling since Holt's death in 1985.[14]

Building on the ideas of Paul Goodman and Ivan Illich, John Holt went far beyond delaying school or formal academics and maintained that school may not always be the best place for children. He sought to help create places other than school for children to live and learn throughout their youth. Holt wrote about and testified before state legislatures that schools would be much better off cooperating with homeschoolers rather than trying to shut them down, if only for schools to see what other possibilities for learning exist.

> [The homeschooling movement is] in effect, though certainly not by design, a laboratory for the intensive and long-range study of children's learning and of the ways in which friendly and concerned adults can help them. It is a research project done at no cost, of a kind for which neither the public schools nor the government could afford to pay.[15]

In his work at *Growing Without Schooling* from 1977 to 1985 Holt provided examples of how people can use community resources to learn and find work worth doing without traditional credentials, as well as earn school credentials with cooperative school districts without causing major disruptions to school operations. Today, several school districts are listed in *Growing Without Schooling*'s cooperative school district directory; there are other school officials who don't want to be listed, but who do cooperate with homeschoolers in their districts. Sometimes this cooperation is as minimal as letting a child take one class per semester. Other times it can be as much as granting a child a local high-school diploma, or having the school provide access to tutors and materials on mutually agreed-upon terms. David Guterson, in *Family Matters*, describes at length how some cooperative school districts operate.[16]

Homeschoolers can use classes, traditional teaching methods, even textbooks and purchased curricula, to learn what they desire to know, but they do so on their own terms. They have determined what, when, why, how, and from whom they want to learn, and are therefore in an entirely different relationship with their schooling than students who are in class simply because of their age. Many things can make schoolish arrangements for learning desirable, and certainly interesting teachers will attract willing students no matter where or how they teach. For most people, it is the idea that children must be socialized by compulsory schooling rather than family and other institutions, that prevents them from accepting homeschooling as an alternative. They picture home-schooled children as being socially inept since they only socialize with their parents and siblings; however this is far from true. Research on this topic has consistently shown homeschooled children to be well socialized.[17]

The vast majority of homeschoolers seek out or create social opportunities for their children to be with other children and adults besides their immediate family. Some homeschooling parents create clubs around certain interests their children may have, such as science, rocketry, magic, or theater, and conduct weekly meetings at their homes or in local libraries. Some share their expertise in exchange for money, barter, or no payment at all. A single mother we know charges families a modest fee for tutoring children in math at her home. Another mother offers a free literature class in her home twice a week to ten homeschoolers. Both mothers are former schoolteachers, by the way! My wife, who is not a school teacher or a private investigator, ran a "detective club" for a year in our house, engaging eight homeschoolers and one public-school child of various ages in activities that fostered their interests in science, logical reasoning, and reading. This year a father we know who makes his living as an illustrator is teaching an art course once a week in the evening at his apartment, as a way to share his love of art with his boys and their friends. Ordinary people, using their own resources, can be highly effective teachers when they share their own interests with children who wish to learn from them.

Some homeschoolers create resource centers to be used by large numbers of homeschoolers, often forming alliances with local libraries for space and materials. In London, England, Leslie Barson created "the otherwise club" in her home as a place for children to work together on projects of their own choosing. As the club and her children got older and bigger, Barson wanted to reclaim her home. So she found a local community center that let her group meet two days a week for 2,000 pounds a year. Barson charges a membership fee of one hundred pounds per family, and has been able to gain charitable status for the group.[18]

Other homeschoolers find and publicize courses and offerings at local museums, historic sites, community centers, and gymnasiums. In Boston, Harvard University's Peabody Museum and the Boston Museum of Science advertise courses for homeschoolers. Technological advances now allow Internet courses for learning everything from jazz improvisation to secondary-school courses leading to diplomas. There are also video and audiotape lectures by experts in all kinds of fields that can be borrowed from libraries, or from homeschoolers who share the cost and the materials.

Most homeschooling, and certainly the formation and continuation of these clubs and groups, is performed by people not certified by schools as teachers, nor are their activities considered to be mandatory or graded. The participants get what they put into each activity, and should they decide not to learn in these settings, there is no external failing grade or other penalty for them. They can come back to these places and learn what they need when they are ready for it, or they can choose, or create, other situations for themselves to learn what they wish to learn. These parents and children are not therefore recreating compulsory public school in their communities, nor are they creating alternative schools; they are creating alternatives to school.

I hasten to add that some children need alternatives to home as well. Clearly not every family is motivated to work with their children the way the homeschoolers I describe here are. However, the only place besides home for most children is school, a situation we have created with our compulsory education laws, and often school is not a good place for these children either. When neither home nor school is a safe, productive spot for children and teens to be, the sorts of third places that I describe above can be expanded to accommodate them. I doubt we will soon get people to change compulsory education laws in America, but there is wriggle-room in these laws, as homeschooling and many out-of-school programs sanctioned by various school departments demonstrate. By expanding these exceptions to allow children and teenagers to engage in or observe real work—manual labor, professional office work, volunteer work—we will help them learn what is needed to do work well by watching or apprenticing with adults who share their interests and work. They also learn how to interact with others to get jobs done, and how to leave work they don't enjoy and find work they want to try. These are skills that are not only not taught in school, but actually atrophied in most schools. In school one typically works in silence, in competition for grades, and is penalized for sharing information, and one cannot change courses when it is apparent that one does not have the capacity or interest to continue with a particular course in school and would like to try something different.

Not all things are apparently educational, but that does not mean they are not important learning experiences for children. To me and many homeschoolers, play is a child's work. Children typically use fantasy play, in particular, not to escape from the real world, but to get into it. When they pretend to be doctors, fire-fighters, police, and soldiers, they are using their imaginations to explore these roles. My own children often played school when they were younger! People benefit from periods of play throughout their lives, and some people are able to find or create adult work that often grows out of their childhood play. School is all too often opposed to children's play, a trend that is increasing as schools march to the drums of testing and standardization. The *London Times* published an article recently about research done by Dr. Jacqui Cousins, an advisor to the United Nations on early education, that shows four-year-olds in nursery schools feel upset and anxious about expectations for them to succeed at school from a very early age. Some spoke seriously about "'not getting a job if I don't work hard.'...One girl said that she had to work hard and not play so she could 'get ready to pass my Key Stage One tests' (the tests given to five- to seven-year-olds)."[19]

Further, allowing children and teens to have safe, private, quiet spots where they can read, pray, meditate, or think away from the barrage of mass media that floods into our homes, schools, and communities is just as important as putting children into group situations for play or class. Homeschoolers have noted the importance of allowing their children time to do nothing, periods of apparent inactivity where dreams, aspirations, and personal issues are worked on. In school, these periods are called "daydreaming" and students are penalized for withdrawing into such a state. One homeschooler writes, "If my boys attended public school, it would be impossible to afford them large blocks of time to go deeply into any activity. We have learned that even doing nothing is important. Doing nothing allows the time needed to assimilate or put meaning to what they have learned during busier moments."[20]

## How Schooling Hinders Learning

Of course, most educators are aghast at such suggestions. Children are like trains to them; they must pull into certain stations at certain times or else they must be repaired. More national curricula, higher standards, more and tougher tests, longer school days, and more money for schools are the remedies educationists propose to work on children to make them effective students. I propose that adults and our social institutions, including public schools, can work with children rather than on them. Using children's various interests and abilities, as well as parents and adults who work outside of schools, we can create all sorts of places for children to be when they don't fit, for whatever reason, into school.

This does not have to be for every family. Families that wish to use school as they always have would be free to do so. However, by also providing opportunities for children and adults who wish to learn in other settings, we can create a true learning society, one that allows people to have second chances, or as many chances as they need, to learn what they need to learn when they want to learn it. Further, having places for children to be besides school will allow teachers more time and energy to work with the students that remain in their classes.

Compulsory school is sometimes referred to as a necessary evil since there appears to be no other place or method for children to learn and grow in modern society. Since World War Two we have, through law and custom, increasingly made school the center of our children's lives, turning school into their entire world and fueling their belief that if they fail in school they will fail in later life. The past thirty years have seen a marked increase in the drugging of children in our schools to make them more compliant to compulsory schooling—Ritalin, Prozac, and Lithium are commonly dispensed to children of all ages in America in order to help them cope with the social and academic life of school. Further, the increase in violence at schools, recently demonstrated in Littleton, Colorado, where fifteen students were killed and many others wounded by two fellow students, is a vivid reminder that not all children are content with the social life of school or with the type of future school prepares them for. Educators and politicians often cite video games, the availability of guns, and poor parenting as the reason these acts of violence take place, and they fund programs to address these issues. However, these short-sighted fixes completely overlook the perpetrator's choice of targets and clearly stated reasons—their hatred of school and its social castes—and thus obscure the real issue that needs to be addressed: How do we help children learn and grow when they are not doing so in school? I am not proposing that these children be homeschooled, but that we look at homeschooling for ideas of other places for children to be besides school.

Educators spend much time and energy developing interdisciplinary studies and motivational techniques that, at best, can only be extrinsic motivators for all students, reducing learning to a race for grades and privilege for the vast majority who are simply going through the paces of schooling. What homeschooling taps into is the intrinsic motivation of children to learn, using the innate abilities that enable children to learn to speak, walk, and reason from their infancy until they enter school. Schools can do this, but all too often, as noted above, the economics of running a conventional school prevents any meaningful connection be-tween a student's desire to learn and the school's mandate to teach. Gunther Schuller, former head of the New England Conservatory of Music, quit high school when he was younger, and commented, "I have the feeling I would not have been a very good music student in, for example, the rigid programs which allow for almost no electives, which some of our schools demand."[21]

A homeschooler writes about her thirteen-year-old son and how his interdisciplinary curricula developed to provide a contrast between school-mandated studies versus self-motivated studies:

> [Steve] had developed a strong interest in freshwater fish. Aside from actually going fishing, which is his very favorite thing to do, he managed to read every available book in the library, including five volumes of a fish encyclopedia. He worked out a deal with a friend who is a graduate student in fisheries, to supply him with worms and perch fillets for his specimens. In return, Steve received a large, fully equipped aquarium, in which to keep his own specimens. A highlight of the year was when he went to seine a local river (drag the river with huge nets to bring up small fish to study) with the curator of the University Life Science Museum. Next week, he starts an appren-ticeship with the ranger at a nearby lake (who happens to be one of the most knowledgeable naturalists around). He will be learning, among other things, how to manage a camping and fishing facility. This interest in fish led into many other areas, as a real interest always does: climate, pond and stream ecology, life cycles of insects, tc. My older children continually reinforce my belief that when a child has an interest in something, [he or she has] a real need to plunge much deeper into the subject than a normal school curriculum ever allows.[22]

Perhaps one of the reasons we are witnessing the decay of support for public education, at least in America, is that now that so many of us have passed through the educational process, we, as adults, are realizing how empty and disconnected from real life the rituals of education are—and some of us are having a hard time forcing our children to go through the exact same process. The purpose of compulsory education for our children is commonly stated as being to fit the pupils, morally and intellectually, for the duties of citizenship. To achieve this end, our schools implement a curriculum that is designed to turn all children into good citizens.[23] Of course, the treatment is dubious and the results are haphazard, as the never-ending parade of school reforms throughout the past 150 years testify. Yet it appears that education is changing the definition of citizenship with very little debate. John Holt observed:

> Thomas Jefferson felt that education was needed to help become and be what he called citizens. By citizens he did not mean what most of us mean when we call ourselves taxpayers or consumers. A citizen was not someone who worried about how to fit into society. He was a maker and shaper of society. He held the highest office in the Republic; public servants were his servants, not his bosses and rulers.[24]

We are consuming education at a more rapid rate than at any time since we started counting degrees,[25] and families are going further and further into debt to fund education for children. But no matter what type of education one consumes, there is no guarantee that one has actually retained and understood all the education received, despite tests passed and degrees earned. For instance, a recent film shows an interviewer asking young adults who just graduated from Harvard if they could explain why the seasons change on earth. No one could do so satisfactorily. A 1993 Gallup poll noted that one in seven adults couldn't identify the USA on an unmarked map; one in four couldn't find the Pacific Ocean. In 1996 it was reported that only 6% of Americans know the name of the chief Justice of the United States; 46% didn't know the name of former House Speaker Newt Gingrich.[26] The assumption that people become good citizens, or well-rounded individuals, simply by passing through a professionalized school system is a false assumption.

Jacques Ellul, forty-three years ago, had it right in his book *The Technological Society*. He wrote that education no longer has a humanist end or any value in itself; it has only one goal—to create technicians.[27] We are in the midst of a change in the relationship between society and school, one in which the idea of "good citizen" now merely means an employed person who has been certified by the schools as competent. However, there is no evidence at all that shows even a modest connection between school performance and later job performance. Many adults hold higher education degrees, yet perform jobs that are completely unrelated to those degrees. In 1971 various studies of the links between employment and school credentials, plus original research on the subject, were analyzed by Professor Ivar Berg, and he found no rational reason for employers to demand advanced degrees of their employees.[28] A more recent study concluded that the vast majority of skills taught in school are not transferable to the real world. "Growing evidence...points to the possibility that very little can be transported directly from school to out-of-school use."[29]

In an article entitled, "Trends in American Education," two professors write, "Despite our best efforts, there is ample evidence that success in school is not a reliable predictor of high attainment in later life. . . Somehow we are going to have to learn how to tie learning activities to both student characteristics and concerns and the broader tasks of life which they face outside and beyond the classroom."[30]

Rather than try to create learning centers where people of all ages can gain skills and socialize in a variety of settings throughout their lives, conventional educators are determined to redouble their efforts because, as these professors note, they see "no real substitute for organised learning outside our formally constituted schools." But there are existing substitutes for organized learning outside of formally constituted schools, and they are desirable and possible to achieve.

## Notes

1. *Newsweek*, October 8, 1998.

2. *Growing Without Schooling: A Record of Grassroots Movement*. Cambridge, MA: Holt Associates, 1999, p. 25-30.

3. John MacKnight, *The Careless Society: Community and Its Counterfeits*. New York: Basic Books, NY, 1996, pp. 39-40.

4. Aaron Falbel, "Beyond GWS: Growing Without Education," *Growing Without Schooling* #130, September/October 1999, p. 29.

5. See Cafi Cohen, *And What About College: How Homeschooling Leads to Admissions to the Best Colleges and Universities*. Cambridge, MA: Holt Associates, 2000.

6. Chris Sims, "Learning To Live Her Beliefs" *GWS* #116, May/June 1997, p. 11.

7. Alan Thomas, *Educating Children at Home*. New York: Continuum Publishing, 1999; quoted in *GWS* #130, September/October 1999, p. 27.

8. Neil Postman, *The Disappearance of Childhood*. New York: Delacorte, 1982, pp. 45-46.

9. Thomas Armstrong, *The Myth of the A.D.D. Child*. New York: Dutton, 1995, pp. 156-159.

10. These examples and more are in *An A In Life: Famous Homeschoolers*, by Mac and Nancy Plent. Farmingdale, NJ: Unschoolers Network, 1999.

11. Roland Meighan, *The Next Learning System: And Why Home-Schoolers Are Trailblazers*. Nottingham, UK: Educational Heretics Press, 1997, pp. 7-8.

12. CBS Script of a radio broadcast with Raymond Moore, "What's New In Learning," September 15, 1974.

13. Raymond Moore, *Adventist Education at the Crossroads*. Mountain View, CA: Pacific Press Publishing Association, 1976, p. 136-137.

14. For Holt's ideas about learning, read any of his eleven books. In particular, *How Children Learn* (New York: HarperCollins) and *Learning All the Time* (HarperCollins).

15. John Holt, "Schools and Homeschoolers: A Fruitful Partnership." *Phi Delta Kappan*. February 1983.

16. David Guterson, *Family Matters: Why Homeschooling Makes Sense*. Harcourt Brace Jovanovich, 1992, pp. 182-204.

17. See M. M. Delahooke, "Home Educated Children's Social/Emotional Adjustment and Academic Achievement: A Comparative Study." Doctoral dissertation, California School of Professional Psychology, Los Angeles, 1986. Dissertation Abstracts International, 47 475A; M. Mayberry, J. G. Knowles, B. Ray, and S. Marlow, *Home Schooling: Parents As Educators*. Thousand Oaks, CA: Corwin Press Inc., 1995; L. Montgomery, "The Effect of Home Schooling on the Leadership Skills of Home Schooled Students," *Home School Researcher*, Vol. 5 (1), 1989, pp. 1-10; L. E. Shyers, "A Comparison of Social Adjustment Between Home-Schooled and Traditionally Schooled Students." Doctoral dissertation, University of Florida, 1992; J. W. Taylor, "Self-Concept in Home-Schooling Children." Doctoral dissertation, Andrews University, Berrien Springs, MI, 1986.

18. Leslie Barson, "The Otherwise

Club" in *GWS* #120 January/February 1998, p. 6.

19. "Life Is Too Hard, Say Children Aged Four," *The London Times*, 6/16/99, p. 12.

20. Toby Rhue, in *Freedom Challenge: African American Homeschoolers*, Eugene, OR: Lowry House, 1996, p. 172. See also "On Doing Nothing" in *GWS* #117, July/August 1998.

21. "Self-Taught Musicians" in *GWS* #37, January/February 1984, p. 25.

22. "How Interests Develop" in *GWS* #53, September/October 1986, p. 3.

23. The academic standards for the elementary years of schooling are spelled out by the state of Massachusetts in General Laws c. 71 #s 1, 2, and 3 (1984 ed.): "Such schools shall be taught by teachers of competent ability and good morals, and shall give instruction and training in orthography, reading, writing, the English language and grammar, geography, drawing, music, the history and constitution of the United State, the duties of citizenship, health education, physical education and good behavior...In all public elementary and high schools American history and civics, including the Constitution of the United States, the Declaration of Independence, and the Bill of Rights, and in all public schools the Constitution of the Commonwealth and local history and government, shall be taught as required subjects for the purpose of promoting civic service and a greater knowledge thereof, and of fitting the pupils, morally and intellectually, for the duties of citizenship...requires physical education for all public school students."

24. John Holt, unpublished manuscript, "Notes From Talks To Students," 11/23/71.

25. Douglas L. Adkins, *The Great American Degree Machine: An Economic Analysis of the Human Resource Output of Higher Education*, Berkeley, CA: Carnegie Commission on Higher Education, 1975. See also Ivar Berg, *Education and Jobs: The Great Training Robbery*, Boston: Beacon, 1972, pp. 178-179.

26. Daniel Schorr, "Americans Lose On Name That Official," *Christian Science Monitor*, February 2, 1996, p. 18.

27. *The Technological Society*, p. 348.

28. *Education and Jobs: The Great Training Robbery*.

29. Lauren Resnick, "Learning: In School and Out," *Educational Researcher*, Dec. 1987, p. 16.

30. Donald Barnes and Alexandria Rekkas, "Trends In American Education," *Educational Practice and Theory*, Vol. 17, No. 2, 1995, p. 21.

# About the Author

*Pat Farenga has worked at Holt Associates/Growing Without Schooling magazine for nineteen years, and has been president since 1985. He and his wife homeschool three girls. He is an author and expert on homeschooling, speaking at conferences and on national and local radio and TV shows. His recent book is* The Beginner's Guide to Homeschooling *(Holt Associates, 2000).*

# Work, Community, and the Development of Moral Character

*by Dayle Bethel*

WORK, I PROPOSE to show, serves as a key mechanism in the human growth and learning process. Authentic work—that is, work that is attuned to the nature of the unique individual one is—is essential for the development of moral character and social consciousness. In this essay, I will draw particularly from the pioneering work of David Norton, a colleague with whom I spent many hours in close fellowship and stimulating intellectual adventuring over a period of nearly two decades.[1] Our discussions developed out of a mutual concern and recognition that in the societies in which we lived and worked (Japan in my case, the United States in his), a low state of public and private morals and an accompanying lack of integrity in social life have become increasingly evident in recent years. Some social critics had begun to speak of a "crisis of moral character" in these societies. In Japan, for example, scarcely a week goes by without some new revelation of bribery, favoritism, insider trading and theft, or collusion among government and business leaders at the highest levels. But not only at the highest levels. Graft, political payoffs, and personal gain at public expense permeate Japanese society at every level. A current case that was recently exposed involved a group of doctors and hospital administrators who were found to have hoarded vast sums of money by falsifying hospital records and collecting health insurance payments for empty beds. And Americans certainly cannot claim that their country is any better or any different in this respect.

## Ethics in Modern Life

This situation, according to Norton, is due to the fact that integrity rarely occurs as a personal characteristic in either country, and this lack of integrity is a result of the pervasive influence of modern ethics. A direct consequence of a lack of integrity in a society is the kind of rampant corruption and moral decay we are now witnessing. Norton notes in his writings that modern ethics discards the virtue of integrity as being inconsequential in human affairs. Since integrity and the other moral virtues that integrity produces constitute the core of a truly human life, their absence in a society has far-reaching consequences.

We can begin to grasp the extent of the influence of modern ethics in industrial societies by contrasting it with pre-modern or classical ethics. The basic principles of classical ethics can be found in the ancient cultures of both the East and the West. Modern ethics, on the other hand, is an outgrowth of the scientific-industrial revolution that began in the West some four hundred years ago. The domination of Japanese culture by modern ethics is due in part to Japan's choice of the American model of industrial development during the early decades of this century, and its reinforcement following defeat in World War II. Modern ethics can be best understood as a revolution in human thought that occurred in Europe during the 16th and 17th centuries. The roots of modern ethics can be found in the *realpolitic* of Niccolo Machievelli and Thomas Hobbes and in the classical liberalism of John Locke.[2]

The contrast I want to emphasize can be considered under the headings of "ethics of rules" and "ethics of character." Modern ethics is an ethics of rules, whereas classical ethics is an ethics of character. These two modes of ethical theorizing lead to greatly different types of personality structure, as well as greatly different types of personal and social behavior (and, it should be noted, greatly different types of institutional structures). Rules ethics and character ethics start from very different primary questions. For modern moral philosophy the primary question is, "What is the right thing to do in particular situations?" and it is answered by finding the rule that applies to the given situation and acting in accordance with it. The source of human behavior is understood, in this instance, as being external to the person. One's behavior is determined by calling upon rules formulated by others than oneself.

By contrast, classical morality begins with the question, "What is a good life for a human being?" This leads directly to the problem of the development of moral character, because any adequate description of a good human life will necessarily include attributes that are not evident in persons in the beginnings of their lives, but are developmental outcomes. The attributes on which classical ethics focuses are the moral virtues, and it will here suffice to refer to Plato's famous four—wisdom, courage, temperance, and justice—to recognize that none of them can be expected of children, but only of persons in later life, and only in the later life of persons in whom the requisite moral development occurs.

## Principles of Character Ethics

Classical or character ethics rests on two presuppositions. One is that there is something innate in every human being that guides that person's life, something that is unique to that individual. In classical Greek philosophy, this "something" was called "daimon"; in Roman culture it was referred to as "genius," and the American Renaissance thinker, Ralph Waldo Emerson, used the same term. Norton, a founding member of the contemporary character ethics movement in philosophy, used the terms "natural talents" and "personal excellences" to signify this innate something that resides within and guides each individual's life. Tsunesaburo Makiguchi, a Japanese educator, described this innate "something" as an inborn capacity in every human being to create value. These innate potential personal excellences (genius) are "potential" in that they await progressive actualization over time. Until they are actualized, they are simply possibilities.

It is through discovering and actualizing these few, interrelated possibilities that are uniquely one's own that one finds life's meaning and purpose. As this occurs, there wells up from within the individual the motivation to actualize them even when actualization requires sacrifices and involves great effort and pain. Conversely, in those situations in which an individual attempts to actualize possibilities that are not one's own, this internal motivating power is lacking and must be supplied from sources external to the individual.

It is through the discovering and actualizing of one's own unique potential that a person finds true happiness and life satisfaction, a deep-down happiness that can come to a person in no other way. At the same time, the full actualization of any person's potential manifests objective worth in the world, which can be enjoyed and utilized by others who need and can appreciate it. Thus, the split between self-interest and other interest to which modern ethics gives rise has no basis here.

Strong objection to this position has come from "environmentalism," the doctrine spawned within the past century by rigorously empirical psychology and sociology, which until very recently was widely accepted, at least in Western societies, as "common sense." According to the environmentalist view, "personality" in any differentiated sense is the product of cultural factors, coming into being in the growing person's progressive interiorization of cultural contents—likes, aversions, norms, beliefs—which are prevalent in the life of one's culture and family. The primary objection to this view, Norton asserts, is that it ascribes to personhood a radical duality that is both theoretically unintelligible and practically unworkable.

A second presupposition of character ethics is the unique, irreplaceable potential worth of every human being. That is, each individual human being's worth is equal to that of every other individual's. This presupposition is in contrast with the conventional belief that "genius," or "natural talents," are haphazardly distributed. (Geniuses, in modern thinking, are those lucky two or three percent of a population who are endowed with "greatness.") But, according to character ethics, in their root meaning as potential personal excellences, "natural talents" are universally distributed but haphazardly recognized and, consequently, haphazardly cultivated.

## Work, Community, and Character Formation

In essence, then, to be a person is to be an innate potential excellence requiring actualization, and responsibility for such actualization is the foundation of moral life. The reason that work is regarded as an unpleasant necessity in modern societies is that persons, by innate disposition, differ greatly from one another with regard to the work that is theirs to do. For each person, there are many kinds of good, useful, productive work that are nevertheless intrinsically unrewarding. On the other hand, there are a few (usually interrelated) kinds of work that will be experienced as intrinsically rewarding, such that the individual will identify with them and on his or her own initiative invest the best of his or her self in them.

But currently—as for several centuries—no attempt is made to match persons to their meaningful work (or in education, to assist them toward the self-knowledge that such matching requires). In consequence, persons who by accident or good fortune find their meaningful work are extremely few, and the vast majority, having no experience to the contrary, endorses the prevailing view that work is an unpleasant necessity.

Within the context of the classical philosophical traditions of both the East and the West, then, with contemporary character ethics as their modern and more fully developed expression, nothing is more important for those who would nurture children than, first, assisting children in discovering and recognizing their unique potential excellences or natural talents, and, second, supporting children in the developmental task of actualizing those potential excellences. Such guidance should be the primary contribution to the child's growth by both the family and the school. And in a good society, this initial contribution to the child's welfare will be supplemented by systematic efforts to aid individuals in their search for intrinsically rewarding work.

Meaningful work during the growth years is essential for the development in individuals of moral character. But moral character, and its offspring social consciousness, can evolve in human personalities only in a nurturing environment. It is here that the crucial role of community comes into sharp focus. The pivotal role of the local community in human learning and character formation was the theme of a remarkable book— *Jinsei Chirigaku*, or *A Geography of Human Life*—published in Japan in 1903.[3] The author, Tsunesaburo Makiguchi, a Japanese teacher, held that direct, intimate contact with nature and with caring persons, within the context of a local community environment, was an indispensable element in the development of moral character in children and young people. The local community, he maintained, contains everything necessary for effective learning:

> If we think seriously about it, we can see that every aspect of this universe can be observed in this small area of our homeland. And because our homeland is the place where we live, where we walk, where we see and hear and gain impressions, it is possible for us to observe all these things directly. Thus, it is possible for us to explain the general nature of complex phenomena anywhere in the world through use of examples which we can find in abundance even in the most remote village or hamlet. (Volume 1, pp. 38-39)

> Let me stress my basic position again; every aspect of the entire universe can be found in the small, limited area of our home community. But we have to be sensitive to these untold riches all around us and we must learn how to be effective observers. (Volume 1, p.42)

Makiguchi was driven by his insights into this reality of human existence. He sensed that the social, economic, and political conditions developing in the Japan of his day threatened the existence of local communities and the natural world. He feared for his society and its people, especially its children, if Japan were to lose the intimate, interdependent connections between people, their communities, and the land. The underlying cause of this situation, he believed, was the importation into Japan of the Western system of compulsory education, which isolated children in school rooms during the learning years of childhood. He became so preoccupied with this concern, he wrote on one occasion that he could not think of anything else.

This conviction of the indispensability of community and rootedness in human experience is shared by growing numbers of people today. David Orr, a contemporary educator, points to the difference between an inhabitant and a resident to emphasize the significance and supreme importance of the principle of rootedness in human life.[4] "An inhabitant," Orr writes, "is rooted in a place, in a community, whereas a resident is a rootless occupant. An inhabitant and a particular habitat cannot be separated without doing violence to both." The global environmental crisis, he believes, has been created by the "virtual disappearance of inhabitants rooted in communities and contemporary society's mass producing of residents to take their place. This is because the inhabitant and a place mutually shape each other. The resident, on the other hand, shaped by forces beyond himself, becomes that moral non-entity we know as a 'consumer,' supplied by invisible resource networks which damage his and others' places."

John Gatto, winner of New York City's Teacher of the Year Award in 1991, expresses similar convictions. "One thing I know," he writes, "is that eventually you have to come to be a part of a place, part of its hills and streets and waters and people—or you will live a very, very sorry life as an exile forever." And of communities, he writes that "an important difference between communities and institutions is that communities have natural limits, they stop growing or they die."[5]

The loss in our modern civilization of community and the experience of rootedness in a particular habitat has had far-reaching consequences for human beings and their societies. Contemporary life, according to one perceptive critique of our present civilization, is characterized by increasing entropy, economic and technological chaos, ecological disaster, and ultimately, psychic dismemberment and disintegration.[6] One has only to read of the horror described in accounts of such incidents as the Columbine High School massacre to realize how accurate Morris Berman's depiction of modern culture is.

According to Berman, we have created a "disenchanted" world, "a world of mass administration and blatant violence, a world in which persons are alienated from each other, from nature, and from themselves, a world populated by human shells with a 'sickness in their souls.' The recovery of community is central to any hope for a peaceful world order. As M. Scott Peck has written: 'In and through community lies the salvation of the world.'"[7]

## Community Based Learning

Translated into practical terms, these principles governing human growth and learning and the roles of work and community in learning can be summarized, for the purposes of this essay, in the following manner:

1. The earth is perceived as a unity and all phenomena on the earth, including human beings, are perceived as interconnected and interdependent.

2. Education is organized in terms of a specific place, a "community" or a "region," that is, a localized environment, which the student can experience directly.

3. The curriculum consists of the interconnected phenomena making up the natural and social systems within that local environment. Books

and other second-hand materials can be used in support of the direct, personal experiencing of natural phenomena by the learner, but not in place of direct experience.

4. Direct-experience learning implies and requires that learning take place in the midst of the phenomena, natural and social, which constitute the environment, that is, the community that the child can experience directly at each stage of development. Classrooms and buildings serve as resource centers and for some kinds of skills development and as gathering places for planning, reflecting on the things observed and studied in their natural setting, comparing perceptions and understandings of phenomena with fellow learners and with books and other second-hand material.

5. Learning is never imposed, but grows out of each learner's own curiosity, questions, and explorations, stemming from personal interests and motivation. In other words, learning must be a process of elicitation, of drawing out the unique potential within each student, and not, as in most of today's schools, inculcation or putting in of information that someone else has decided is necessary.

6. Responsibility for guiding children and young people in this community-based learning interaction is shared by parents, learning counselors, mentors, resource specialists, older students, and other adults in their varied community roles and specialties.

It is not possible within the framework of this chapter to consider all of the implications of such a perception and approach to teaching and learning, but let me note just two imperatives.

First, in the traditional perception, a child's education is perceived to begin when he or she enters elementary school or, perhaps, kindergarten, and to be the responsibility of teachers and educational administrators. In the alternative perception, the child's education begins at birth and is his or her responsibility, guided and nurtured by parents or other adult guardians.[8] The child's learning, as he or she grows older and becomes aware of the larger world beyond the family, will essentially be an extension and expansion of the discovery and exploratory studies and activities he or she has been engaged in under the general guidance of his or her parents.[9]

There will be two differences: First, exploratory activities will expand to include the larger immediate community in which the child lives, later the region of which his or her local community is a part and, in time, the child's learning interests and activities, his or her "community," will become planetary, providing the early stages of learning have been well grounded.

Another difference is that other persons will now begin sharing with the child's parents the responsibility of guiding his or her learning. Some of these other persons may be associated with a community resource center, where there will be mentors, librarians, counselors, and others who can help the child, still in close coordination with his or her parents, to develop a program of learning, exploration, and community participation. The child's program will develop naturally out of what he or she and others have learned about his or her interests and inner potential.

The second imperative is that included in such a guided program of direct learning, there will be opportunity for each child to engage in some type of meaningful work in an apprenticeship or part-time work experience with a cooperating business in the community, an artist, a professional person, the community government, on a farm, etc. This is a crucial element. The opportunity to participate in the life of his or her community through sharing in its productive work will do two things for a child. First, it will enable the child to feel and be an important, functioning part of the natural world and understand its interrelationships. Second, it will give him or her opportunity to gain further understanding of and confidence in his or her inner self.

The nature of a child's work experiences will change as the child grows older. At first, it will consist of sharing in the necessary work of the family. Wise parents will have permitted the child to begin helping with real jobs when he or she was very small—setting the table, cleaning, taking out the trash, baking cookies, etc.[10] The child will have grown up understanding that everyone in the family community shares in doing the work necessary to the family's welfare and survival. Work experience in the larger community will build on and extend this earlier introduction to work and sharing of responsibility. In cases in which the early experience is lacking or inadequate, the community mentor's role—and the opportunity to make a crucial difference in a young child's life—increases in significance.

Every person who would seek to improve education—whether teacher, parent, or some other creative person—must do so in concrete situations, with whatever combination of constraints and assets the situation affords, but guided by sound principles of teaching and learning. The extent to which existing educational structures permit one to apply sound principles is a part of the situation that every change agent must deal with. But perhaps the time has come at last, as the flaws and dehumanizing dimensions of our centuries-old scientific-industrial culture become increasingly apparent, when inadequate educational structures can be changed or transcended and all who bear educational responsibility will be freed to apply principles of teaching and learning that are compatible with the growth and actualization needs of learners. This can be our hope as we enter a new century and a new millennium.

## *Notes*

1. A second source of the ideas and insights of this chapter is the writings of Tsunesaburo Makiguchi. His monumental work, *Jinsei Chirigaku* (A Geography of Human Life), published in 1903, together with later writings provide an outline for a holistic, community-based approach to education that is just beginning to be recognized in Japan.

2. "Education for Moral Integrity," in *Compulsory Schooling and Human Learning.* Dayle Bethel, (ed.), San Franisco: Caddo Gap Press, 1994, p.4. See also Norton's *Personal Destinies.* Princeton, NJ: Princeton University Press, 1976.

3. Makiguchi, *Jinsei Chirigaku, op. cit.*

4. *New Directions in Education,* Ron Miller, ed., Holistic Education Press, 1991, p. 91.

5. *Skole,* 1992, Vol. 9, No. 2, p. i.

6. Morris Berman, *The Reenchantment of the World.* Cornell University Press, 1981, p. 15.

7. *The Different Drum: Community Making and Peace,* New York: Simon & Schuster, 1987.

8. Obviously, this implies the need for more effective education for parents. However, the realization that many parents are not presently adequately prepared to fulfill this role does not justify disregard of the principle involved.

9. Invariably, this kind of statement is met with the observation that today's parents are just too busy to spend this kind of time with a child. I have found that an effective answer is that every family has to solve its own problems, but parents who love their child will take enough time to get intimately acquainted with that child. They may enlist the help of grandparents, older brothers or sisters, or perhaps close neighbors, under their guidance. Even good baby sitters or understanding nursery school teachers can help parents carry out their responsibility to their child. The main thing is that the child have parents (or parent substitutes) who understand and accept their responsibility for the child's learning through integration into its two worlds of nature and of people. This parental responsibility extends from infancy through adolescence.

10. This does not happen in many families, and the reason it doesn't is easy to understand. Soon after a child begins to walk and communicate, she is deeply motivated to model the behavior of the adults around her who are important to her. She wants to help. She wants to do the things those adults do. She wants to be recognized as an important member of her social world. Here is where so many parents fail. When a child wants to help set the table, pour the milk, or whatever, how natural—and routine—it is for a busy, tired, impatient mother to respond: "You can't do that, you'll break it." Or "No, you are too little, go into the other room and play." "No, this is for big people." How many of these precious, once-in-a-lifetime opportunities are missed! This is the beginning of miseducation.

# About the Author

Dayle Bethel is dean of The International University's Asia-Pacific Centers in Kyoto and Honolulu. His special interest is in the role of education in the formation of persons and societies, and he has been an active participant in movements for holistic educational alternatives both in Japan and in the United States. He can be contacted via e-mail at dbethel@aloha.net

# Carrying on Despite
# the Violent Twentieth Century
## A Tenacious History of People's Education

*by Chris Spicer*

THERE IS A STORY from Middle-Eastern tradition about the Hodja, a clever and wise spiritual leader. When the people have assembled for their weekly worship in the mosque, the Hodja asks from his pulpit, "True believers, tell me please if what I am about to say to you, you know already." Thrown off by his question, the people reply that there is no way they could know of the wisdom of the great Hodja. So he leaves them, saying that it would be of no use to talk about things unknown to them or to him. The gathered followers are larger in number the next week, and the Hodja again puts forth his question. This time, the people respond: "Oh yes, of course we know what you are about to say to us." But the Hodja again departs, saying it would be a waste of everyone's time to speak of things everyone knows already. A week later, when the mosque overflows with curious seekers, the people are ready for the Hodja's question. Half of them stand, confessing ignorance to knowing what the Hodja might say. Then the other half stand, claiming to know exactly what he will say. The Hodja nods solemnly and speaks. "Now I know how I can help you. The half who knows what I am going to say will now tell the other half exactly what that is. For this you have my blessing."

The essence of people's education? Is it, boiled down, so basic? We anciently-inspired (from time-honored cultural wisdom), but reactively motivated (against twentieth century institutional oppressions) "progressive" learners/educators speak of the heart, of freedom, of nurturing creativity, of listening to and learning from the earth and its nature, and of reconfiguring the role of "student" and "teacher" in the learning

endeavor. Are these represented in this metaphor for the learning potential, waiting to be tapped from our collective human experience, knowledge, and relationships? Can such complexity be represented in a such a
basic idea of people's coming together to share what they know, to learn
from each other, and (we hope) to act on that exchange by incorporating
the resulting insights and knowledge into their daily lives?

My quick answer is yes—and no. The critical elements of people's
education may be lurking in the Hodja's community. But to suggest that
real learning will in fact happen in such an unstructured setting would be
wrong, if only because it doesn't guarantee a democratic process
(including an accounting of majority/minority power), nor a clarified
agenda and reflection. Yet at the core of the Hodja's message is a fundamental philosophy: We have in us, collectively, much knowledge and
experience, and given the freedom to name our needs and goals, we have
the drive and passion to pursue them.

In this chapter I discuss the concept of people's education, particularly
through one set of roots originating in nineteenth-century Denmark, but
also through an exploration of a twentieth-century melding of experiences—including the Danish—in North America, which I would suggest
needs a new framing and recognition.

## People's Education: The Ideas of N. F. S. Grundtvig

The term "people's education" is one translation of the Danish *folkeo-
plysning* or the Swedish *folkbildning*, terms originating in the religious
and social movements of the nineteenth century, and much inspired
by—among others—Danish philosopher, poet, educator, and clergyman
N.F.S. Grundtvig. It describes the pedagogical ideas of a broad category of
non-formal (as opposed to the mainstream, credential-based) learning
organizations that grow from the grassroots and include such models as
evening schools, folk high schools (*folkehøjskoler*) and day folk high
schools, study circles, participatory research projects, and community-
based centers (particularly those serving "marginalized" learners, though
also some serving mainstream people in such places as public libraries).
"People's education" is a term that also is translated in other historical
and cultural contexts as "folk education," "folk development education,"
and of great importance to the North-American context, the Latin-
American-inspired "popular education," as exemplified by the work of
Brazilian educator Paulo Freire.

N.F.S. Grundtvig was a bishop, educator, philosopher, writer, poet,
and hymn writer—most certainly having one of the most profound im-
pacts on Denmark and its people. He lived in the early nineteenth
century—an extraordinary time, one in which Denmark lived a relatively
non-violent response to the violent period of Europe's industrial revolution. The seeds of Denmark's transition from monarchy to democracy—
and thus an opening for the ideas of Grundtvig—can be highlighted

briefly by two significant events. First was a number of late eighteenth-century socio/political transformations, including the elimination of both the slave trade and censorship of the press, and most significantly by a set of land reforms that transferred significant power to the rural peasantry.[1]

Second was the devastating loss of Denmark's Norwegian territory to Sweden, which came about from the 1814 treaties ending the Napoleonic Wars. While the emerging democratic movement experienced a major setback from this social and economic disaster, it perhaps also framed the uniqueness of Denmark's path to national rebirth and social enlightenment. It was to this devastation of hope and prosperity, and to the German aggression later in the century, that Grundtvig provided a different way out: "What we have lost externally, we must regain internally."

It is always a serious challenge to attempt a brief description of the foundations of Grundtvig's thinking. My clearest understandings have come from the folk high-school teacher and administrator Frederik Christensen, who describes Grundtvig's pedagogical genius as "the indirect method: First you must learn to love life, then you can reform the world. Nearly all other pedagogical philosophies stress the opposite: First you must reform the world, then you can love."[2] The essence of this indirect method was rooted in two beliefs Grundtvig held about being human and learning: 1) "The spiritual life which people are meant to live includes a claim to freedom, since 'freedom is the element of the spirit,'" and 2) "Every individual is born into a specific society and thus inherits particular traditions, history, and language. To be a human being is to accept oneself as part of a certain people with a particular cultural identity and to take pride in it."[3]

Building on these fundamentals, I highlight three elements of Grundtvig's ideas about our human learning needs to set the stage for a discussion about the practical application of these ideas, the folk high school. These include his beliefs about our human identity—individual, cultural, and democratic.[4]

*Individual Identity and Meaning.* Grundtvig understood personal growth as a process of understanding identity to include communal, cultural, and political pieces. Two aspects of the individual are significant. The first is that the individual is only whole as a part of a community of other individuals. Danish scholar Knud Bugge describes it this way: "Grundtvig thought individual freedom could be destructive because if you take it to its extreme, then it means that the individual should have the right to clamp down on other people, suppress them, and use them as materials for his own gains."[5]

The second point is that the individual, as a common person, is the source of knowledge and meaning. Scholar Steven Borish describes Grundtvig's belief that the real source of enlightenment is to be found lying latent in the common people and not in "those he contemptuously referred to as 'the learned ones.'"[6] To Grundtvig, education was for the purpose of responding to the need and struggle of the common people's lives, to help probe identity and address needs of the community, whether it be to nurture young people into community leadership instead of leaving for "greener pastures" or to address the spiritual life of the community.

*Cultural Identity.* For Grundtvig, the individual is connected to a time and place. That is, to a particular historical, cultural, and social/political context. As a "fortress" against external (primarily German) aggression, the folk high school was a place to immerse oneself in Nordic myths, language, and tradition. Yet Grundtvig was also concerned about people as members of a global community, requiring us to cross borders of race, class, nationality, culture, and a myriad of community differences. In his smaller nineteenth-century world, he envisioned a Nordic university that brought people together across the different Scandinavian cultures. A twentieth-century application can be found at the International People's College, which brings together students from all over the globe.

*Democratic Identity.* Two ideas are central to Grundtvig's thinking about democracy:

1. Since the source of enlightenment is to be found in the common people, then so is the key to full participation and empowerment in the life of the community.

2. The role of the individual in strengthening democracy is as an active citizen who understands his or her history, and through dialogue, engages in celebration, resistance, and problem-solving to effect democratic social change.

These principles of humanness and learning suggest particular responses that begin with getting to know each other better in an experimental school or community whose primary focus is on building a larger culture of democracy that values differences, promotes dialogue, and shares power. Ultimately, it is about building a civil society that allows and nurtures its citizens to reach beyond their struggles for material survival. Here is where the folk high school comes to flower.

## The Folk High Schools

Grundtvig's greatest legacy—the *folkehøjskole* (folk high school) was from the beginning a school for young adults—in their late teens or twenties. Since the first school was founded (not by Grundtvig) in 1844, it has been an evolving structure that has always struggled to balance the need for organization and institutionalization with the necessity of individual and small group freedom. In sum, it can be captured by the following:

1. Purpose: To enliven and enlighten the individual as an integral part of the community; To transform our communities to be more democratic, just, and sustainable.

2. Pedagogy: Learning experiences must honor:
- A full range of expression, of heart, mind, and body;
- A partnership between students and teachers in a dialogue of free and critical inquiry;
- The community experience (history, mythology, etc.), including analysis that probes its history in light of its current needs;
- A democratic experience, especially valuing the "common person."

3. The knowledge and skills: "cultural competence" (experience with people different by class, ethnic identity, gender, etc.); critical thinking and communication skills to support analysis and problem-solving.

4. Organizational structures that support the pedagogy. Particularly important are decision-making and evaluation processes that empower participants to name their needs, direct their progress, and measure their collective success.

In practice, the folk high school has two defining characteristics:

1. A residential school. The oft-used image of students washing dishes together, talking after meals and into the weary—or wild—hours of the evening describes an environment where personal barriers are lowered much more quickly and completely than in partial day-to-day interactions. The resulting trust and openness would create the learning conditions for significant personal empowerment and transformation. But residential learning is more than connecting with one's fellow students. It is a demonstration of the very nature of learning.

2. The free pedagogy.   Here are such ideas as "the living word," Grundtvig's answer to the deadening effect of dependency on books that, as documentation of the past, would provide few inherent bridges to students' lives. By breathing new life into students, by connecting the past to current events and circumstances, a teacher stands a much better chance of making ideas and history available and relevant to the student. Also central to a folk high school class is a shifting of control of direction from the "expert" teacher to the collective knowledge of the students, as coached and supported by the teacher. Students and teachers become co-learners, and the student team collectively drives the agenda and the measure of success in reaching that agenda. Thus, externally motivating measures like examinations and grades have as little relevance as qualifications for embarking in folk high school study in the first place.

## Toward an Understanding of People's Education in North America

Our North-American efforts to understand and make use of Grundtvig's ideas are met with a consistent caution from Danish educators and learners. The folk high school is not for export. That experience is rooted deeply in Danish history and culture, and is not necessarily a model to be replicated. Paulo Freire addresses the same concern: "It is impossible to export pedagogical practices without reinventing them. Please tell your fellow American educators not to import me. Ask them to re-create and rewrite my ideas."[7]

In fact, our North-American history is rich with largely unrecognized traditions of people's education. To illustrate, I briefly consider the ideas of three educational experiences—indigenous education as described by Tewa Indian educator Gregory Cajete, women's "public homeplaces" as identified by Mary Belenky and colleagues, and popular education as practiced by Myles Horton and his colleagues at the Highlander Folk School. Cajete tells us, "In reality, all education is rooted in or has evolved from an Indigenous past."[8] If so, then the basic principles he describes ought to identify something universal that appears in experiences over time and cultures. In fact, this is the basis of my argument for this concept of a North-American people's education. The experiences highlighted here suggest some powerful and universal truths. While a stronger case needs to be made by examining the differences among these traditions, my purpose is to begin the conversation by pointing to the common ground.

*Indigenous education.* For Cajete, learning is a whole, experiential process rooted in everyday life, "Education for life's sake. Education is, at its essence, learning about life through participation and relationship in community, including not only people, but plants, animals, and the whole of Nature."[9] It is a value-laden process using experience, storytelling, ritual and ceremony, dreaming, tutoring, and artistic creation. At its heart, indigenous education is a spiritual endeavor, and "it is no accident that learning and teaching unfolded in the context of spirituality in practically every aspect of traditional American Indian education."[10] The path toward such learning is firmly centered in both the community of the people, and more comprehensively, the community of Nature. Cajete describes two "triad" foundations of tribal education. One is a set of "winter" or inward elements for the learning about our inner selves—the mythic, visionary, and artistic. The other is a set of "summer" or outward elements—the affective, communal, and environmental foundations. These foundations form a context for all teaching and learning. As Cajete writes, "Nature and all it contains formed the parameters of the school," but also, "The life of the community and its individuals are the primary focus of tribal education...The community is a primary context for learning to be 'a human, one of the People.'"[11]

With such educational foundations, it becomes clear why learning is both holistic and experiential, of daily life, and based in the spoken word. Storytelling is a central tool. Cajete writes, "Storytelling related the ever-evolving group life processes and the introductory understanding of its members as part of a unique people."[12] Of course, storytelling is central not only for the content of the story, but for the skills of listening, memory, imagination, and communication that it helps one to practice. The final point to be emphasized here is the highly contextual nature of indigenous education. "Native Americans taught what needed to be taught in the context they thought it should be taught and at the most opportune time."[13] Education is not a process wedged into a particular time and place.

*Myles Horton and the Highlander Folk School.* Myles Horton co-founded the Highlander Folk School in 1932, shortly after returning from a tour of folk high-schools in Denmark. Having searched for several years to find alternative educational models for the communities in his native Eastern Tennessee, he also instinctively knew that there was no formula,

but rather a set of principles. The job was to get started without being overly concerned about how the program would take shape. His idea-forming years included contact and inspiration from such 1920s progressive educational thinkers as Reinhold Niebuhr (Union Theological Seminary), Eduard Lindeman ("father of adult education") and John Dewey.

Horton was a political activist from the start. First off, he knew from experience that there was no such thing as neutrality. Secondly, from his religious background, "I wanted to work on the side of society that didn't live by owning. If you're going to have a democracy, that's the kind of people you build it on."[14] Highlander became a school where community leaders examined and developed strategies for confronting labor issues, racism during the civil-rights movement, and in recent decades environmental and economic justice issues.

From these fundamentals, Horton's evolving analysis of society became the basis upon which to implement a compatible approach to learning. At the heart of this were concepts of freedom and power that demanded that learners be in charge of their learning. At the heart of learning at Highlander were two principles: 1) the content of the study was determined by the students, and 2) the process would incorporate drama, song-writing and singing, and dialogue to enable new learning experiences, interests, and needs. As experienced, adult community members, the students demanded an easy exchange with a receptive teacher and enabled an ownership of the process, where role of teacher and student often were switched about.

Other important principles of Horton's educational thinking, according to adult educator Peter Jarvis, were 1) the importance of a learning group to enable individuals to develop meaning from experience, and to provide the context for future learning and action, and 2) the central role of action: it provides not only the experience from which to learn, but one of the goals of education. Constantly at play during a Horton workshop, as

Jarvis summarizes, are crucial operating principles including "a clear goal, shared experience, respect for individual and collective experience, trust in the learner, action, and empowerment of the learner."[15]

*Public Homeplaces.* Based on the ground-breaking work identifying "women's ways of knowing,"[16] Mary Belenky and her colleagues (Lynne Bond and Jacqueline Weinstock) have used their developmental framework to document the work of four organizations serving isolated and excluded women's groups—which they call public homeplaces. Public homeplaces are community-based, non-formal women's groups that often begin with specific community projects, but live on to support other organizing and learning activities. They "are places where people support each other's development and where everyone is expected to participate in developing the homeplace. Using the homeplace as a model, the members go on working to make the whole society more inclusive, nurturing, and responsive to the developmental needs of all people—but most especially of those who have been excluded and silenced."[17] They add, "Leaders of public homeplaces...are intensely interested in the development of each individual, or the group as a whole, and of a more democratic society."[18] In fact, many of these communities are born from generations of oral traditions that are rooted in African American and other cultures that have been part of the multicultural roots of North America.

As part of their study, the researchers looked for common philosophies and practices in these community organizations, and describe them as "the philosophy and practice of developmental leadership." I list three of them:[19]

• The central role of *dialogue*. Homeplaces encourage a crucial balance of speaking and listening, using approaches that nurture voice through open-ended questions.

• *Praxis*—the importance of action linked to dialogue. Whether engaging in theater or other art projects, community events or services, the actualizing of ideas and the chance to reflect on the results is central to learning.

• Public homeplaces are characterized by *feelings of home and family*. In describing their experience, leaders and participants use maternal metaphors that emphasize nurturing, cooperation, equality, and "raising up" (vs. their experience of men's "ruling over").

Belenky writes, "Leaders of public homeplaces...work to articulate the goals that people in the group have in common...They also look for the strengths in the people's culture as a building foundation for the whole community...Then they look for ways to mirror what they have seen, giving people a chance to take a new look at themselves and see strengths that have not been well recognized or articulated."[20] Importantly, homeplace participants build connections beyond their local arena. Building a global perspective beyond and connecting to the local is not only essential to the empowerment process, but to a broader understanding both of human needs and ways to meet those needs.

*Paulo Freire.* A discussion of North-American people's education would not be complete without at least a brief mention of the work of Paulo Freire. Freire's work developed during the politically progressive era of the mid-twentieth century in a Catholic-dominated, multi-cultural Brazil. Freire was concerned about the disenfranchised, illiterate poor, and like Grundtvig, passionately believed that learning begins with the people's community experience. Yet according to Jarvis, Freire "recognizes that both the dominated and the dominant are in their different ways imprisoned within the structures of society and that both need to be liberated."[21]

A central Freire concept is "conscientization," the process of analyzing and understanding one's cultural reality. His more methodological "problematizing" (or problem-posing education) is a way of seeking "generative themes" that illustrate the reality of everyday life through a process of "codification" of words into visual images. Key to the process of learning for Freire is dialogue and its implications for shifting the roles of teacher and learner. He writes, "Through dialogue, the teacher-of-the-students and the students-of-the-teacher cease to exist and a new term emerges: teacher-student with student-teachers. The teacher is no longer merely the-one-who-teaches, but one who is himself taught in dialogue with students, who in turn while being taught also teaches. They become jointly responsible for a process in which all grow."[22]

Without space for a fuller immersion into Freire's ideas, it is nonetheless important to note the contrast between Grundtvig's "indirect method" with Freire's more direct call for social analysis and change through the process of conscientization. In more specific terms, the "indirect" Grundtvigian emphasis on enlivening the learner to understand one's social identity, and to be involved in strengthening that social life can be a strong complement to the Freirian concern about critical analysis and the importance of the fight to change. Both are essential pieces toward the goals of human liberation, democratic community building, and environmental sustainability—goals that are at the center of each—and to a pedagogy of North-American people's education. In fact, there is an easy resonance between the ideas of each educator and the ideas that conclude this chapter.

## Conclusion

Throughout the educational traditions identified in this brief review, some common themes continually emerge. I suggest these five basic principles to frame a pedagogy of North-American people's education:

• The purpose of learning is enlivenment (love) and to empower communities to solve life's problems and its injustices—learning for life, for freedom, understanding and love.

- Knowledge is based in the life experience of a people.
- A democratic educational setting—a community-based approach that supports the growth of relationship building, analysis, action. and reflection.
   * Centrality of dialogue
   * Centrality of the group of learners
   * Sharing the role of teacher and learner
- Holistic learning—our ways of learning tap a variety of ways of knowing: cognitive, emotional, spiritual, and physical.
- Praxis/experience—learning is an experiential cycle that links action and reflection to create knowledge and change.

Such principles reflect the learning ideas of many more traditions of non-Western, non-formal education, at the heart of which is a reflection of basic human identity—our spirit, our freedom, and our individual roles in a greater community of a local and global people and of the natural world. That the practices of our North-American mainstream institutions of formal education have chosen to ignore a persistent, wise set of voices of educators throughout the nineteenth and twentieth centuries—of wisdom of the ages—is partly a statement about the depth of our challenge to transform ourselves and our world. But that these persistent voices continue to practice and emerge anew is a powerful statement about their vitality and their truths.

## *Organizations*

Institute for People's Education and Action, 107 Vernon Street, Northampton, MA 01060, USA, phone: 413-585-8755, e-mail: cspicer@k12s.phast.umass.edu, URL: http://www.peopleseducation.org

Folk and People's Education Association of America, c/o Merry Ring, Women's Center, Lakeland Community College, 7700 Clocktower Drive, Kirkland, OH 44094, USA, phone: 440-975-4706, e-mail: mring@lakeland.cc.oh.us

Center for Grundtvig Studies, Aarhus Universitet, Hovedbygningen, Ndr. Ringgade, 8000 Aarhus C., Denmark, phone: 45-89-42-22-84, fax: 45-86-13-04-90

Grundtvig Studies Center, Grandview College, 1200 Grandview Avenue, Des Moines, IA 50316, USA, phone Rudolf Jensen: 515-263-2951, URL: http://www.gvc.edu

Aspen Educational Research Center, P.O. Box 336, Woody Creek, CO 81656, USA, phone: 970-923-4646, e-mail: stranah@csn.net

BorderLinks, 710 E. Speedway Boulevard, Tucson, AZ 85719, USA, phone: 520-628-8263, e-mail: Borderlinks@igc.apc.org, URL: www.igc.apc.org/borderlinks

Catalyst Center, 720 Bathurst Street, Suite 500, Toronto, Ontario, Canada, M5S 2R4, phone: 416-516-9546, e-mail: catalyst-centre@web.net, URL: www.web.net/~ccentre

Highlander Research and Education Center, 1925 Highlander Way, New Market, TN 37820, USA, phone: 423-9933-3443, e-mail: hrec@igc.apc.org

Institute for Human Rights and Responsibilities, P.O. Box 416, Gelena, OH 43021-0297, USA, phone: 614-965-5118, e-mail: Djehnsen@infinet.com

National Congress of Neighborhood Women, 21 Park Place, Brooklyn, NY 11217, USA, phone: 718-783-2298.

Pedagogy and Theater of the Oppressed, P.O. Box 31623, Omaha, NE 68131-0623, USA, phone: 402-554-2422.

# Notes

1. S. Borish, S., *The Land of the Living: The Danish Folk High Schools and Denmark's Non-Violent Path to Modernization*. Grass Valley, CA: Blue Dolphin Pub., 1991.

2. F. Christensen, "To Be a Folk High School Teacher," in *The Folk High School 1970-1990: Development and Conditions*. Ebbe Lundgaard, Ed. Copenhagen: Foreningen for folkehøjskoler (The Association of Folkhighschools), 1991, p. 82.

3. C. Foucault-Mohammed, "The Danish Folk High School: Key to the Success of Democracy," *Labor Education*, No. 75 - 1989/2. Geneva: International Labour Office, 1989, p. 30.

4. C. Spicer, "Learning from the Danes: Charting New Waters," in C. Warren (ed.), *Democracy is Born in Conversations: Recreating Grundtvig for Lifelong Learners Around the World*. Nyack, NY: Circumstantial Productions & Folk Education Association of America, 1998.

5. C. Warren (ed.), *Democracy is Born in Conversations: Recreating Grundtvig for Lifelong Learners Around the World*. Nyack, NY: Circumstantial Productions & Folk Education Association of America, 1998, p. 48.

6. Borish, p. 170.

7. P. Freire, *Teachers As Cultural Workers: Letters to Those Who Dare Teach*. (D. Macedo, D. Koike, and A. Oliveira, translators). Boulder, CO: Westview Press, 1998, p. xi.

8. G. Cajete, *Look to the Mountain: An Ecology of Indigenous Education*. Skyland, NC: Kivaki Press, 1994, p.186.

9. *Ibid.*, p.26.

10. *Ibid.*, p. 42.

11. *Ibid.*, p.41.

12. G. Cajete, *Igniting the Sparkle: An Indigenous Science Education Model*. Skyland, NC: Kivaki Press, 1999, p.56.

13. *Ibid.*, p.53.

14. P. Jarvis, *Twentieth Century Thinkers in Adult Education*. NY, London: Croon Helm, Ltd., 1987, p. 250.

15. *Ibid.*, pp. 262-3.

16. M. Belenky, B. M. Clinchy, N. R. Goldberger, and J. M. Tarule, *Women's Ways of Knowing: The Development of Self, Voice, and Mind*. New York: BasicBooks, Inc., 1986.

17. M. Belenky, L. A. Bond, and J. S. Weinstock, *A Tradition That Has No Name: Nurturing the Development of People, Families, and Communities*. New York: Basic Books (HarperCollins), 1997, p. 13.

18. *Ibid.*, p. 14.

19. *Ibid.*, pp. 258-275.

20. *Ibid.*, p. 14.

21. Jarvis, p. 270.

22. P. Freire, *Pedagogy of the Oppressed*. New York: Continuum Publishing, 1989, p. 67.

# About the Author

Chris Spicer is director of the Institute for People's Education and Action, which offers intensive courses and book and video sales and is a program of the Folk and People's Education Association of America (FPEAA), a network of individuals and organizations throughout North America. He acted as director of FPEAA for more than ten years.

# Education Can Lead the Way to a Sustainable Society

*by Wendy Priesnitz*

MUCH OF THE DEVELOPED WORLD is facing an economic, social, and political crisis. The financial and emotional gaps between the rich and the poor are growing. Child poverty and the abuse of women and children are at epidemic proportions. Indigenous people are still fighting for their basic rights. At the same time, our social safety nets are being stretched and torn. Logging companies are ravaging the last of our old-growth forests. Tobacco companies are cynically trying to buy their way out of responsibility for their deadly product. The ozone hole is growing, our garbage dumps are overflowing, our nuclear power plants are leaking, and toxic chemicals have been found in mother's milk.

We are experiencing the results of a global economic restructuring based on the premise that the world is no longer made up of cities or even countries, but a single world order dominated by transnational corporations and mass consumerism. Governments seem incapable of responding. Worse than that, their agendas appear to be set by corporations and financial institutions. Our political parties—including the so-called progressive and populist ones—are no longer attached to community life. They have become the creations of pollsters and media advisors, or are paralyzed by lack of vision or preoccupation with money. We have evolved a type of "democracy" in which the elite have centralized power for their own benefit.

## The Roots of the Problem

This situation has crept up on us, and it is only recently that most people have begun to notice. In order to understand the roots of this complicated problem, I have begun to examine our institutions and how they work. One of the main problems with institutions is their use (and abuse) of power. We learn early in our lives that power usually flows from the top down, often as a consequence of physical domination: big kids over little kids, teachers and principals over students, strong men over physically weaker women, big countries over smaller ones. Those of us who dislike the consequences of this distribution of power usually work outside formal channels of society and arrangements of power to protest, resist, and sometimes overturn decisions made by the "powers that be." We learn that democracy involves citizens influencing public policy, rather than authoring it. We learn that the object of political debate is one of persuasion, in the same way that children learn to wheedle and pout and throw tantrums in order to get their way. Because we are never able to take the initiative, we resort to criticizing and complaining. Our negative experiences with power lead us, in our organizations, to fear and condemn power. We confuse misuse of power with the positive power to lead and to propose alternatives. Many of us have never even experienced the kind of collective power that can be used to build alternative institutions. We have been told one too many times to sit in our seats and listen, and to put up our hands when we have to go to the bathroom.

## Goring the Sacred Cow

If we are going to improve the lives of our communities, we must recreate our institutions and rethink how we relate to them. And if we look critically at how we educate ourselves, we'll find an institution that long ago ceased to serve our needs. Unfortunately, the public education system is sacrosanct among most progressive people. In the past, a strong, publicly funded school system contributed to a democratic, egalitarian, socially just society. However, schools, as they are currently constructed, do just the opposite. They create institutionalized values, perpetuate social hierarchies, disempower us, and encourage a destructive level of consumerism and consumption. To confuse compulsory schooling with equal educational opportunity is like confusing organized religion with spirituality. One does not necessarily lead to the other. Schooling confuses teaching with learning, grade advancement with education, a diploma with competence, and fluency with the ability to say something new. Of course, the process of changing such an emotionally charged institution is a highly politicized one, as author Ivan Illich realized almost three decades ago when he wrote his book *Deschooling Society*. The process challenges not just our beliefs about education and learning, but a lot of vested interests—like how corporations make profits and who manages the affairs of our communities. And that is precisely why we must make major changes. Those who care about social equality and democracy must examine how the institution of schooling creates and reinforces our current unequal, non-democratic, consumer-based society.

Let's face it: The majority of the problems facing society today—pollution, unethical politicians, poverty, unsafe cars...the list goes on—have been created or overseen by the best traditional college graduates. Whether these problems were created by design or accident, we cannot fix them by continuing the status quo. We need to create a society that chooses action over consumption, favors relating to others over developing new weapons, and encourages conservation over production. And this just won't happen unless we de-institutionalize learning. Here's why. Beginning in kindergarten, young people are treated as unneeded and legally minor. They are obliged to attend an often unfriendly—sometimes threatening—place, which robs them of their basic human rights. They are taught about human rights and government in social studies class, but they're not allowed to experience—let alone practice—these vital components of good citizenship.

School is a substitute for everyday life, and childhood a rehearsal for personhood. It replaces real experiences with pseudo experiences. It dismisses the value of children's own experiences, thoughts, and opinions, substituting the opinions of textbook authors who often have different worldviews than the students. At the end of the school assembly line, students with little authentic knowledge are bumped out into the adult world like so many sausages—and expected to suddenly make mature decisions. Fortunately for their sanity (but unfortunately for the state of the earth), the parameters of their decision-making have been defined by their school experience and mostly involve choosing whether to buy Coke or Pepsi.

And that's not surprising. The chief function of state-run public education is not to empower citizens to make responsible decisions about the future of the earth or the harmonious cohabitation of the people on it. It was created to groom workers for the factories of the Industrial Revolution. And if those factories are to make a profit, somebody has to buy the stuff they make. The educational system is the perfect mechanism for ensuring a culture of consumers. For this reason, we should not expect politicians and their corporate masters to look eagerly toward changing the educational status quo. On the contrary, schools and corporations are quickly merging. A good example is the principal of a school in the American South who recently suspended a young boy because he dared to wear a Pepsi T-shirt during an event sponsored by Coke. This corporate agenda is being pursued to all corners of the developing world. The majority of people who don't go to school—but want to—are motivated by a desire to emulate the North-American way of life. In virtually every country, the amount of material consumption by college graduates sets the standards for everyone else. The trouble is, of course, the planet won't survive if the developing world ends up replicating North America's levels of consumption.

## The Cult of Experts

Our society worships a cult of experts, which promotes the belief that education is the result of treatment by an institution called a school, just like the cult of medicine teaches that wellness is the result of treatment by another broken institution—the hospital. In fact, learning does not need manipulation by others. Real learning is a result of experimentation, making mistakes, correcting mistakes, creating hypotheses, and proving them.

## Delivering "Received Ideas"

As author and schooling critic John Taylor Gatto explains, after we fall into the habit of having other people do things for us, we lose the power to think for ourselves. Maybe that's why so few of us challenge the premises of nursing homes, television, day-care centers, schools, and the global economy. These things are received ideas, not the result of individuals' thinking about what would make their own lives—and those of their families and communities—better on a day-to-day basis. School measures a student's mastery of a prefabricated curriculum on a standardized scale. When we submit to others' standards to measure our own growth, we put ourselves and others into assigned slots. When everything fits so nicely together, there's no need to look for an underlying agenda.

Aside from these covert agendas, schools don't accomplish their stated goals very well. Experiments conducted thirty years ago in Puerto Rico showed that students were more effective at introducing their peers to the world of science than their teachers. After having received 12,000 hours or more of teaching, many people can't read well enough to function in their daily lives. Many high-school graduates have no skills to make a living or even any skills with which to talk to each other. Of course, education is more than just skill development. Unfortunately, schools also aren't very effective in delivering what may be called a liberal education. In fact, most of the desirable things we learn in life—an understanding of our heritage, how to love and to play, to think, to work independently, to listen to music, to appreciate poetry or Shakespeare, to facilitate a meeting—are seldom learned in school. We learn these things by living our lives and, in most cases, in spite of attending school. The ability to interact well with others—to be well socialized—is one of the recognized goals of our school system. Ironically, most homeschoolers will tell you that the main reason they want to avoid school is the competition, aggression, bullying, and violence that occur there.

## So What is the Solution?

The solution to this crisis of learning is to de-professionalize the educational environment and put learning back into the hands of the learner. This will not be easy. Deschooling ourselves is as difficult as renouncing limitless consumption. But here are some ways to begin.

• We can rid ourselves of the idea that learning can be produced in us—and that we can produce it in others. We can abolish all curriculum that's not created by the learner. We can get rid of textbooks, lesson plans, testing, grading, report cards, course requirements, homework assignments, schedules, and attendance regulations.

• This will allow us to treat young people in ways that demonstrate our trust in their desire and ability to learn. We will then be able to create a learning environment—which includes role-modeling, safety and respect, access to requested resources, consolation when things go wrong, and celebration when things go right. Then we can get out of the way and not meddle in the process unless we're invited.

• There is no reason to judge people's employability (or anything except their ability to write tests and essays) by their degrees. So if you're hiring someone, learn about their abilities, personality, and character, rather than their university degrees. Of course, to really embrace this idea, we'll all have to stop flaunting our own university degrees!

• Another step is to de-expertize teaching. Many people in a variety of different roles and occupations have much to offer children—as role models and as learning facilitators. So why should teachers and schools have a monopoly on helping people learn things? Sharing skills can be done informally, or there is an increasing number of more formal mechanisms, like skills exchanges and Natural Life's Mentor Apprentice Exchange.

• We also need to place more value on the knowledge and experience accumulated by our senior citizens. We need to find ways to help people of different generations teach and learn from each other.

• On the same theme, we can work together in our communities to create a learning society. We need to tell our politicians to fund museums, theatres—and yes, even school buildings—so they can afford to provide spaces for people of all ages to explore, interact, and learn on their own initiative. Institutions should exist to be used, rather than to produce something. If they're effective, people will use them willingly.

• One of the most challenging changes we need to make is in our attitudes towards childhood. In addition to trusting children to learn, we need to respect and advocate young people's right to make their own decisions (within parameters that address their physical and emotional safety, of course) and their ability to live democratically and co-operatively if given the opportunity.

• Lastly, we need to like children and to want them around all day. This means trusting them with access to the tools of our trades and allowing them to participate in—and learn from—the life of their communities.

No, these are not simple solutions. But we have a choice. We can continue to pour increasing amounts of money into a system that is delivering proportionately declining returns—and creating a generation of angry, frustrated people who aren't much interested in democracy. Or we can put money into creating appropriate opportunities and infrastructures to help people learn in ways that do not require huge amounts of real estate and bureaucracy, ways that do not make people abdicate the responsibility for their own growth, ways that allow children and young people to participate fully in the lives of their communities—and get a good education at the same time.

## About the Author

*Wendy Priesnitz is a Canadian deschooling pioneer. She and her husband helped their two daughters (now twenty-six and twenty-eight) learn at home when it was almost unheard of in Canada. In 1979 she founded the Canadian Alliance of Home Schoolers, and continues to share her experience and long-term perspective through workshops, speeches, articles and books, and consulting to individuals and governments. Among the nine books she has authored is* School Free—The Home Schooling Guide *(The Alternate Press, 1987), which is a Canadian best-seller. A follow-up book about deschooling society, entitled* Challenging Assumptions in Education, *has just been published. As owner of Life Media, a twenty-four-year-old publishing company, Wendy edits* Natural Life, *a news magazine focusing on personal and grassroots efforts leading to economic, political, and social change, In 1996 she was elected leader of the Green Party of Canada. She is also an award-winning journalist, writes a weekly newspaper column, and is listed in* Who's Who in Canada. *Information is available at URL: http://www.life.ca*

# Possibilities in an Autodidactic Future

*by Charles D. Hayes*

IMAGINE WHAT WOULD HAPPEN if we as a nation were to spend a third of our current education budget for the simple but direct purpose of enabling anyone who wanted to learn anything to do so—anytime, anyplace, without qualification. To be an autodidact is to behave as if such a system were already in place. The means are there, if you really thirst for knowledge. You can learn anything when you begin to think of an education not as something you get, but as something you take. This is a very simple sounding premise, but it flies in the face of traditional education. Furthermore, you don't have to pay a fortune to acquire learning unless that's the way you prefer to do it. From the multiplication tables to quantum mechanics, if your desire to learn is strong enough, you can find a way to quench your thirst for knowledge. Einstein didn't come up with the theory of relativity in a classroom.

Compulsory schooling, the purpose of which is to outlaw ignorance, seems instead to have certified it on a grand scale. The anti-intellectual attitudes of millions of so-called educated people serve as living proof. More to be pitied than those who have fallen through the "educational" cracks are those who have been intellectually lobotomized in the name of learning. Marking time in lives of stultifying mediocrity, with no strong interests in much of anything, they put up with jobs they hate and pretend to enjoy the mindless entertainment they pursue to compensate. Holding elitist status in material possessions, and having far more wealth than eighty percent of the human beings on this planet, such people nevertheless complain about how poorly the world treats them. On nearing the end of their lives, those who have viewed their existence as barely tolerable drudgery begin to panic at the realization that they have never learned to truly think for themselves or felt the exhilaration of intellectual engagement. Would that all human beings could experience throughout their lives the plain, ordinary wonder of existence that comes through active curiosity.

Entertainment today is a cheap substitute for the thrill of intellectual pursuit. Just a few metaphorical feet above popular culture lies a jet stream of ideas shaped by the geniuses of our species: a legacy of ideas by philosophers, great literature by authors expressing the essence of the human condition and an historical record of how their actions squared with their theories. This is anything but an ivory tower. The great book advocates Robert Hutchins and Mortimer Adler called it the Great Conversation and it is accessible to all who seek it. If you are poor and lack fine clothing, you still can try on elegant garments in a department store. Similarly, if you can't afford a nice car, you still can sit in one at a dealer's showroom. But no matter what your situation, if you have a thirst for knowledge, you can enter the great conversation of humankind. You can try on the ideas of the greatest thinkers who have ever lived, take them home, and keep them with you forever.

It is foolish to assume that economically and politically marginalized individuals can and will en-masse develop a thirst for knowledge without some kind of liberation. Brazilian educator Paulo Freire argues that "freedom is acquired by conquest, not by gift." In *Pedagogy of the Oppressed*, Freire tells us, "One of the gravest obstacles to the achievement of liberation is that oppressive reality absorbs those within it and thereby acts to submerge human beings' consciousness." Thus participation in the great conversation becomes a critical condition for obtaining the kind of political power that leads to deep understanding and liberation. A thirst for knowledge is, in part, a product of a radicalized awareness of one's being in the world. Expanded awareness is an integral component of self-direction and is an antidote to both indoctrination and intellectual and economic poverty.

Self-directed learning is often characterized as being anti-cooperative, and yet a group of people with an insatiable curiosity and burning desire to know are as eager to cooperate as anyone you will find. Enthusiasm for learning is contagious. Still, it is a mistake to think of learning and the knowledge it provides as a possession. Learning is effectively a position or, better yet, a positioning device. The learning we achieve as individuals serves as an invisible university in which our understanding of the world grows and envelops new territory, accommodating new ideas and tolerance for people and cultures that see the world differently than we do. This acquired knowledge doesn't rid us of the anxiety and despair that are part and parcel of the human condition, but it places us in a much better posture to cope with it.

Near the limit of our understanding is a wall, or an abyss, if you will, that shields us from our greatest fears and prejudices. With increased knowledge and understanding we expand the distance between the wall and ourselves. They give us room to breathe, room for toleration. We are less threatened by those we don't understand. Simply stated, we have room not to hate. Thus, a liberal education enhances the social sphere, even if the connection is not so readily observable. In spite of all of the distress brought about by the velocity of the changing times we are living in, the sheer diversity and profundity of differing viewpoints offer the most hope for achieving a more critical consciousness among individuals and throughout society. This is true because, for the first time in history, the social creation of reality is happening in plain sight, and everyone who is willing to look can see it.

To be a participant in the great conversation is not the same as using knowledge as canned goods for a particular purpose—to justify your own status or position or that of your clan. Partaking in the great conversation is a setting aside of absolutes while you search. By nature the great conversation is unsettled business supporting the notion that life is a journey and not a destination. Historian Daniel Boorstin puts this in perspective when he says, "It is not skeptics or explorers, but fanatics and ideologues who menace decency and progress. No agnostic ever burned anyone at the stake or tortured a pagan, a heretic, or an unbeliever."

In the lives of human beings, ideas matter. To be knowledgeable of many great ideas is to increase the size of one's perceptional horizon. It creates a stage big enough to live a meaningful life. It doesn't mean that you can't find precise answers to specific questions, or that you can't find the particular knowledge you seek. It means simply that the conversation, by definition, never is over. Ideas that seem to have suffered the death-blow of a knock-down argument have a way of resurfacing with new relevance. The philosopher Immanuel Kant is buried often, but he still lives.

Wealth and resources aside, no culture, country, or community has a privileged lock on reality. None can say with absolute confidence that this is the path the rest must take. None can say that theirs is the economic system, religion, worldview, or philosophy that humankind must accept without discourse. Indeed, it is because of the nature of socially constructed reality that awareness and dialog, whether real or imagined, are so important. For it is only through increased understanding and awareness of the fabric of social reality that we are able to determine the temper and mettle of injustice. Through such inquiry we come to realize the wisdom of Paulo Freire's insight that only power that is sustained through the comprehension of those who are themselves oppressed has the substance for genuine liberation. All other attempts invite what Freire calls false generosity.

Does anyone doubt that slavery never would have been overthrown if the argument had not been about anything more than improving conditions for slaves? Or that slave masters never would have been moved sufficiently by dissonance to change the system had not the slaves understood the injustice first?

An autodidactic philosophy has a better chance to create a community dedicated to lifelong learning because, by nature, it keeps the conversation going without spoon-fed dogma and canned polemics. An educational process overly dependent on the consumption of predigested content quashes critical consciousness.

A society with an autodidactic educational philosophy is the final requisite for a mature, viable democracy. Indeed, a society of individuals who take it upon themselves to see to their own intellectual development sets the very foundation for democracy through the actions of those citizens' everyday lives. It is a dynamic community because it is made up of people who are living their lives as if they are really interested in them. Without such involvement, we are doomed to live lives void of authenticity—lives the French philosopher Jean Paul Sartre would have said demonstrate bad faith.

We seem to have a tendency to hate and despise those who question our version of truth and who threaten to burst our perceptional bubble of reality. This dissonance, however, is the very stuff that drives the conversation. Removed though we might be from the great ideas of the humanities, each of us in our own individual lives has a storehouse of real life experience to compare with the grand theories about the world. When you contrast your experience with theory, then you have something to add to the conversation. People who can't sustain an argument about community without withdrawing into factions of us against them do not in fact have a community. Make no mistake; knowledge does not make one person better than another. Knowledge does not make me better than you; it is capable only of making me a better me. Moreover, the only hope we have as individuals that others will share our worldview rests in our willingness to live and thus teach *by example* such that we leave as evidence that our way is worthy of emulation. Autodidactism itself guarantees nothing but greater participation in one's own education and openness to a sense of reality uncontaminated by dogma.

The digital world we expect the third millennium to produce is itself not a panacea for the frailties of human culture, and yet it offers unparalleled mechanisms not only for keeping the great conversation going, but also for making it richer in dimension and diversity than ever before in the history of humankind. Throughout the world, barriers to information are breaking down as privilege gives way to access. More and more the responsibility for learning resides with the learner. Imagine what kind of a learning community we might achieve if we could find both public and private support for creating the learning-environment equivalent of a system that assumed the role of Socrates while each of us took the part of a Plato. This is not at all a far-fetched idea. It is one that will increasingly arise, if we simply behave autodidactically.

As a community, we face a challenge on two fronts: the first is to awaken those who were put to sleep in an attempt to educate them, and the second is to reach those who have been ignored altogether. We must use persuasion instead of force, discourse instead of instruction, and a sense of enthusiasm and adventure over reproach. As learning communities, we must connect the library both metaphorically and practically in an interactive fashion to bring those who seek knowledge together with those who have wisdom and the enthusiasm to inspire. As communities we must make a compelling, visible case for literacy in all segments of the population. Being literate should be seen as so desirable that to be illiterate and not to seek help is unthinkable. Our case will become legitimate and believable largely through our demonstrated willingness to make available the resources every person needs for learning: anything, anytime, anywhere and at any pace without stigma.

Most of us who are adults today, even those of us who are strong proponents of self-education, grew up with the predominant psychology that an education is something you get. For us, an education as something you *take* is an expectation that we can clearly pass on to our children and grandchildren. And we can support efforts to promote learning communities whose thrust is supportive of educational autonomy. An autodidactic future is one where the same autonomy that enables individuals to develop their own interests also predisposes them to continue and participate in the great conversation of our time. The possibilities of such a society are breathtaking.

# About the Author

Charles D. Hayes is a life-long learning advocate, a self-taught philosopher, and an author and publisher. At seventeen he dropped out of high school to join the US Marines. After four years of duty he became a police officer in Dallas, Texas, and later moved to Alaska, where he has worked for more than twenty years in the oil industry. In 1987 Hayes founded Autodidactic Press, committed to life-long learning as the lifeblood of democracy and the key to living life to its fullest.

At the start of the year 2000, his book Beyond the American Dream: Lifelong Learning and the Search for Meaning in a Postmodern World was selected by the American Library Association's CHOICE Magazine as one of the most outstanding academic books of the previous year. His other books include Training Yourself: The 21st Century Credential, Proving You're Qualified: Strategies for Competent People Without College Degrees, and Self-University: The Price of Tuition is Desire. Your Degree is a Better Life. Promoting the idea that education should not be thought of as something you get, but as something you take, Hayes' work has been featured in USA Today, in the UTNE Reader, and on National Public Radio's Talk of the Nation. His web site—www.autodidactic.com—provides resources for self-directed learners, from advice about credentials to philosophy about the value life-long learning brings to everyday living.

# Learning Communities, Teaching Communities

by James N. Rose

THE EARLIEST YEARS are when self-esteem becomes established, when sensations of competence versus inadequacy are encountered and recognized, and personal behavior choices are formed and guided. Wanting to learn, being enthusiastic to learn, desiring the opportunities to apply what is learned—all through life—begins with the foundations laid down in the first years—during every moment of them.

The inborn skills and abilities to learn are nurtured and honed in every environment and situation, not just the formal one labeled "school." What later environments—where specialized knowledge is highlighted and available—are good at is enhanced by the experiences, priorities, and modes of learning skills available only in preceding situations. The greatest "learning" is in no unimportant way instilled and nurtured during the outset of life. From those experiences of passage come the personal knowledge—established in our first days and years of life—that *we* contribute to our own learning and competence, which ever after leads to our impacting the world as much as it affects us.

## Learning as a Tradition of Life

"Creating learning communities" isn't so much a new idea in the schema of human experiences as it is the recognition that that's what we have been doing all along, and are now striving to do better. Every life embodies wisdom. Every life embodies a competence. Every life has a "voice" with the potential to contribute something creative to the whole of humanity even as everyone creates his or her local life. The questions come then, How can society organize itself to ensure that every voice—no matter how young—is sought, honored, and valued? Can we balance "social efficiency" with respect for the carefully considered thought? And can we value style and design as much as we do pragmatic outcomes?

One of the most important things about life is having a sense of place in the world. We humans have an extended capacity to learn and share learning, to relate to the world and our companions in truly amazing ways. This ability comes from our being thriving, adapting organisms, part of the universe's process of evolution. In the broad view of things, we might even say that evolution is a kind of living "organism" more than some observed "process." Life in its full richness is a "learning creature"—and we are conscious members within and of that expansive life.

The "creature" called Life does more than adapt. It learns, and through its learning *transforms* its parts into new ones, perpetually changing itself in the process of exploring and responding to the world's fullness and deep meanings. And humans reflect, in very direct ways, that extraordinary ability to mold and transform. We are born neither fully realized nor mentally restricted. It is as we grow individually and together that we adapt through learning, transforming ourselves and our world in the process.

## All and One: Learning and Teaching

The foundation of my views on education comes from an idea called the "integrity paradigm"[1]. This view of the world says that the essential *dynamics of learning* are present even at the most basic levels of existence, and therefore learning is an ever-present part of every moment of every day of every life. Then, just as evolution requires a world of energy, information, and encounters to explore and fulfill all *its* potential, so each human thrives on what she and he experiences. Every complex organization, entity, and organism exists reliant on communication—"else-knowledge" that becomes internal and, therefore, "self-knowledge." The knowledge may be different, the architectures unequal, but the relationships are the same. Individually and as groups we are ever and always learners. From the moment we begin and all through our lives. Learning is our essential act of existence—the essential act of being human. *Learning and applied learning are the very essences of life, all life, all throughout life.*

## A Learning World, a Learning Community of People

What does this mean for us exactly? It means that to become competent learning communities we need to become *teaching communities*.

Every member, every person, must be an "educator," available at a moment's notice to share knowledge, wisdom, skills, and perceptions with those in need. So the responsibility falls on each of us—whether fully matured or not, whether "formally" trained as educators or not—to "teach." This requires that we come to appreciate teaching as something every person does for everyone else, and then ultimately what every person accomplishes for themselves: self-directed learning.

Self-directed learning is an important part of the learning sequence: transmission, transaction, transformation, self-direction, as Ron Miller refers to it (see "Philosophies of Learning Communities" in this book). Human beings are extremely intricate, involved with our environments and with each other. We are social creatures who communicate and form societies, commercial groups, belief communities, and so on. We are artistic creators who continuously add new dimensions to our ever-involved lives. Human networking is so complete that learned "personal knowledge" is often almost immediately available as "collective knowledge." The responsibilities for learning and for teaching therefore are sublimely meshed together. And wonderfully, it is not beyond any of us to be both educator and learner, teacher and student.

## How to Do It

There are none more needy, more hungry or ready to learn, than our infants and our children. Their hunger—our hunger—is the open mind and body, ready to encounter and accept all information and experiences offered. Learning takes place where the body and the mind are—within the family and community environments, where "home" is an idea. It includes the world we ourselves learned about and grew into, our shelter, our families, as well as the contributions we made in transforming our first worlds into something new and enriched.

The place where each newborn's adventure of life begins may be similar to what existed years or only moments before, but it is also different, special and unique. It is constantly being changed by the community and the child in wondrously subtle, creative ways. What was old and as constant as the hills is available to be learned anew. What is malleable and current and local is available to be learned too. And importantly, the skills and confidence to be a creative member of the human family are there, to be nurtured and promoted.

Learning and styles of learning begin with the very first breath. Each new life, in that instant, begins to build a relationship with the world. And we need to diligently be there for the building process. At that point, learning is strictly somatic—visceral, simple, physical—but the lessons remain for a lifetime. Sentience lives here, deep and thriving, gathering, absorbing, and evaluating. Learning what it can rely on and what it can't. What it can control, and what it can't.

It is here that the mind begins being part of a dance that never ends, the flow of signals and sensations, breath and air, touch and pressure, sensations that are pleasant, soothing, rough, uncomfortable, cool, warm, loud, mellow. Signals, skills, and sensations are the stock in trade of the alert minds of infants and youngsters, as they/we establish learning techniques to absorb, appreciate, and value what will affect our selves, our world, and our self-in-world. And who are better guides for these fresh and deserving minds than us, the people who have gone before, learned what it took, remembered what we ourselves required, and are here to make their journeys smoother because of the knowledge and skills we gained. Especially using the key of human life: intricate, exquisite "language."

The linguistics expert Benjamin Whorf portrayed language as a kind of relativity. [2] Experiences become memes—recurring mind patterns. Memes then join with sounds and bodily gestures which, as markers and signals, become "experienced" as events themselves, on a level equal with the phenomena they track and trace, represent and refer to. The instant a word or thought, sensation or memory flashes into your voiced mind, you are not only the thought's creator; you are also its first experiencer.

What seems static or patiently quiet inside of us is really a world constantly being created, invented, made new again with each thought, experience, and stream of impressions. It is ideas and thoughts testing the responsiveness of the world to *us*, and us to *it*, all the time and all at the same time. As this is true for adults, it's just as true for our young ones.

## Now to Do It

The first educators in a child's life typically include its mother, father, or other nurturer. These people have to appreciate the abilities already there in this new and special person. An infant brings "needs" into the world, but more importantly it brings skills. It will accommodate to feeding routines, to sleeping schedules, to good and bad sensations, to being warmly held and snuggled, to being free to flail and touch, smell, sense, explore, where the hunger for nurturing *experiences* is just as strong as the hunger for *sustenance.*

An infant is experiencing, learning, acquiring, reacting, acclimating, testing, seeing, prompting, and communicating—all of this accomplished at every moment. Sensations are coordinated with sensations, infused with and evaluated for meaning. A baby takes everything in, from the most complex environment to the simplicity of upturned cheeks—smiles. Children learn earlier than we traditionally gave them credit for. Through interacting with our children even at the earliest stages we are laying the foundations for them for future life encounters, for life-long learning and expectations, long before they are introduced to their first formal classroom. So we must empower adults to see themselves as very real "educators." And the task becomes providing a framework to guide competence in that work as excellent educators and nurturers of learning.

## Realizing What You Already Know

The first thing you must realize as a parent or a caregiver is that "reporting" is not the gauge of learning in infants, the way we depend on it for older learners. Unfortunately, we are so used to the formal presence of testing and evaluation processes that we assume the reverse situation. We assume that if there is *no* testing mechanism present, then *no* learning is taking place. Nothing could be further from the truth.

A child is taking in and permanently remembering all its encounters. If any "testing" is going on, it is the child who is accomplishing it *internally*, and we can only wait for later results. Seeing a child apply its learning to the perfection of motions, of coos and sounds that, practiced, become language, and to repetitive play-backs of the sensations of its own body, which become coordinations and successes, provides confirmation that learning went on. For early learning situations, "perfection" should be appreciated loosely and simply, as being adequate to secure the concept or skill and repeat it in a purposeful way. In the child's world, "close enough" is "good enough." Fine-tuning is left for later.

To be a good educator you have to know all this and applaud, encourage, and give positive feedback to every accomplishment, even the smallest. Because to the youngest of minds and bodies, nothing is insignificant. Everything either means something or has the potential to mean something. What works is good, and even what doesn't is stored for comparison later against other things and situations. Time is a free-running stream of experiences and *all things* are considered.

There is a process that toddlers typically go through that shows this. Often youngsters trip and fall. A younger child might react in ways that can be interpreted, "Unexpected event—Oh, I should cry and be upset!" But for toddlers, something more wonderful happens that gives us an insight about learning. In the instant after the fall, when the body is self-sensing itself for true injuries, there is a pause before committing to tears or complaint. If the child realizes that he or she is not seriously injured, or if the child is encouraged by an older companion to *perceive* itself as unhurt, sometimes this phenomenon occurs: the child will re-enact the fall several times. The child isn't trying to injure itself. What's happening is that the child is studying the event in a more controlled way, being aware of it ahead of time, and re-staging body sensations, conditions, where and how it was moving or where things were in its path. It is going back and accounting for future use the factors it wasn't aware of in the heat of the first event. Besides learning and fixing these factors in memory, this acting out also encourages and reassures the child that the shocking situation was survived successfully.

This acting out usually doesn't last too long, maybe a minute or so. Just long enough to figure out what happened and to make a mental note, to either prevent it or cope with it again. Then the child usually runs off to play where she or he meant to in the first place, with maybe a quick word or hug of sympathy requested from you. Importantly, moments like these are windows into the personal and social psyche of learning. When they happen in our presence, we are involved participants, supporters of young evaluation skills and opinions.

When a child throws a spoon full of food across the room, it's not thinking about "mess." It just wants to try to "throw" and to "make things happen." It's the adult world that has chosen which "throws" are preferred (ball outside the house versus spoon full of food inside) and which "things to happen" are acceptable or allowable. Even-handed encouragement about our behavior preferences (and the consequences of making a "mess") are the way to react. In wisdom and awareness, it's ourselves we have to constrain as much as the infant. The child can learn about throwing, messes, fun, anger, and responsibility for actions all at the same time, depending on the calmness and substance of our *educational* reactions.

Situations and events aren't always crisp and singular. Many how's, what's and why's are involved. What *we* focus on may not be where the child's learning or attention is concentrated. So don't be surprised if children learn more than you intend, or surpass your expectations, sometimes in areas you didn't even realize you were "teaching." Human hunger for learning is more powerful and active than imagined. It can be a lot to keep up with. Just stay with it and do your best.

## Focusing Your Teaching Skills

Just as every day is an opportunity to learn something or teach something yourself, so is every moment of a child's life. It ought to be done in proportion though. You never know when a "teaching moment" will occur, so you have to be ready all the time. But neither should you push too hard to see learning accomplished. Incorporating ideas and skills requires time, and we who aren't inside the brain of the learner have to give her or him the freedom to encounter and the important time to digest what is being learned. What the child is consistently exposed to will make up part of its life-space and thought repertoire, whether reported or repeated to you or not.

Think of the ground or floor. It "talks" to children all the time, and children "talk back." This is true for all of us, actually. We respond by learning muscle control and body comfort and useful positions to act out ambulating skills—balancing, maneuvering, stopping, going, falling, rising, and so on. We learn as children and then continue through the whole of our lives to "converse" with the floor and the gravity field we live in. It's a "conversation" that never stops.

We are always involved with that pervasive, ongoing "conversation" and we quickly become premiere accomplishers of upright walking. Can you imagine the levels of competence we can achieve in attitudes, thinking, reasoning, reading, recognition, joy, communication, and so on, when exposure to *those* things are as consistent and reinforced and encouraged in regular ways from the earliest moments of being? The achievements can be extraordinary. These are things that every parent and caregiver ought to be aware of.

Constant exposure is the key. Building complex associations, verbalizing textures, colors, uses, situations, feelings, sensations, and attitudes gives a voice, a word, a place in the world for everything the child is coming to know. These connections-building-on-connections become the heart of the learning process we use throughout our lives. Context and diverse associations are what make things meaningful, and become what we make value judgements on as we mature. They become more intricate and subtle—almost intuitive—as we get older and more skilled at taking things in. But it is a process we have with us from the very beginning, waiting only to be encouraged and helped along.

The key is helping infants, toddlers, and all growing minds to use all their newly developing skills, as they are acquired and practiced, so that the learners can identify their environment and world for themselves. We need to continually share our associations and hopes. Children will learn what we offer. The more consistent the offerings, the better the chances for being retained and used later on. Beyond that, children's own self-reliance and honed abilities become the invaluable foundation for continual self-education.

## Confident Enablers Are Successful *"Personal Skills"* Conveyers

We need to be *enablers* of our young. The most upsetting thing in life is to feel dis-empowered. And what more upsetting situation can there be than if you can't communicate all that you have inside you? Why else do you imagine the "terrible twos" got that reputation? It's the time in most children's lives when they have all this internal "knowing" bubbling about inside them and few words or communication skills to make that internal world known, their desires and needs understood.

In perspective, the early ways of learning are often the best—practical, tactile, transcendent, and real. And the best adult learning comes when we re-open ourselves to those early ways. Value and trust, skills and confidence, meaning and pertinence. They aren't just cognitive; they are visceral. They are valuable in every encounter, every situation, and every role we experience and engage in. Not just momentarily, not just in local applications, but plurally, together. The integrity of society is as important as the integrity of each member. The integrity of the whole *is* the integrity of its members. Success, as the Integrity Paradigm states[1], and E.O. Wilson has pointed out using the notion of "consilience"—relies on balancing all integrities, as best as possible, all at the same time.[3] Integrity and competence—separately and together.

We have—all of us—to become educators of our young. Especially, we have to be early educators of our youngest and most promising potential.

The issue isn't what to teach, but *that* we teach, continually instilling a simultaneous love of learning, a love of what's learned, and love of the teaching process, accomplished through the sensations of success and connecting with meaning.

Parents and educators should be committed to the happiness and competence of all children—as individuals and as members of our communities—where each child deserves the opportunity for living a fulfilling, safe life, as part of a supportive society of an ever-unfolding learning adventure of our created, creative universe.

For more information contact the Ceptual Institute, 1271 Bronco Circle, Minden, NV 89423 USA, e-mail: intengrity@ceptualinstitute.com, URL: www.ceptualinstitute.com

## Notes

1. James N. Rose, "Concept Rhymes," Ceptual Institute, Internet: http://www.ceptualinstitute.com/nuc/nuc_com012.htm, 1998; James N. Rose, "Understanding the Integral Universe," Ceptual Institute, Internet: http://www.ceptualinstitute.com/uiu_plus/UIU-complete11-99.htm, 1992.

2. Benjamin Lee Whorf, *Language, Thought and Reality* (ed. John B. Carroll) Cambridge: MIT Press, 1956.

3. Edward O. Wilson, "Consilience: the Unity of Knowledge," New York: Alfred Knopf, 1998.

# Future Learning Environments

*by Don Glines*

THE EDUCATION STRUCTURES that currently exist world-wide—those commonly referred to as "schooling"—are almost impossible to justify for the present; they are certainly not appropriate for the decades ahead. In fact, they have not been defensible for the *majority* of citizens for the past one hundred years. Evidence supporting these conclusions abounds. Report cards offer one stark illustration, for 30% of the grades given in typical districts are D and F, 40% are C, while 30% are A and B—or similar assessments at the primary level. Thus, 70% of the students are at best average, mediocre, unsatisfactory, or failing. Many high-performing youth are bored. Such results are now unacceptable. New lifelong learning systems are essential. The crucial concept for accomplishing this priority is "Imagineering"—imagining, inventing, and implementing. People in communities must imagine what could and should be, invent designs to achieve their dreams, and implement the plans to foster much more successful environments. Significantly different non-traditional visions are required if learning, not schooling, is to flourish.

In meeting this challenge, creative change processes are required to overcome years of neglect. More important than any method is the embracing of an open-ended, individualized, person-centered philosophy that reflects total dissatisfaction with most present forms and outcomes of public education. Beyond the belief, such a commitment should lead to bold actions that unleash the potential for breaking the existing lockstep, discontinuous, iron-cast, undemocratic requirement patterns.

Article 10 of the *Declaration of the Responsibilities of the Present Generations Toward Future Generations,* adopted by the 29th General Conference of UNESCO (The United Nations Educational, Scientific, and Cultural Organization) in 1997, states: "Education is an important instrument for the development of human persons and societies. It should foster peace, justice, understanding, tolerance, equality, and health for the benefit of present and future generations."[1] These lofty goals cannot be accomplished at their desired levels under the old competitive, repetitious, cognitive-focused, group-paced, 20th century formats that dominate nations. Such systems continue to widen the gap between those who master the demands successfully and those who do not adapt well to the conventional rituals—whether North American, Asian, European, or other models.

The arrival of the new century provides the opportunity for educators to philosophically state, "If schools are to be significantly better, they must be significantly different." Most futurists would add, "It is time to do the impossible; the possible is no longer working." Major industries spend ten to fifteen percent of their budgets on research and development (R&D), while smaller companies allot five to ten percent. Education spends only one-fourth of one percent on R&D. Most of what is claimed in that category is only for questionable "standardized test" assessments. It is no wonder that schooling—not learning—yet dominates. There are limited opportunities for true innovation and experimentation. The few improved approaches that are developed, usually through university-led studies, are not widely adopted. The often significant research from the past, showing, for example, the advantages of nongraded schools, is rarely used. Tradition prevails!

There are numerous possible societal futures, but only a few of them are most preferable. If there are to be preferable futures for coming generations, the macroproblem—the combination of multiple global dilemmas—must be addressed and resolved.[2] Each topic, such as natural resources, pollution, nuclear weapons, poverty, and crime, can no longer be isolated by one-at-a-time solutions, for sustainable existence requires interdependence.

Education, as one of the multiple categories, must do more than independently promote technology, economic competition, and basic literacy. Increases in achievement test scores have not made a significant difference in the quality of young people's learning experience. As illustration, suicide rates have remained high in many Asian school cultures where students perform well. The age 11 examinations given in most European countries, which divide students into classical, vocational, or technical programs, have resulted in an educational have and have-not separation. The comprehensive school concept in North America has maintained an assembly-line mentality without individual deviation. It has maximized the outcome potentials for at best fifteen percent of the learners. As again evidenced by the marks they receive on report cards, the other eighty-five percent are either ahead of or behind what is being "taught" in a given class, or are interested in entirely different activities. They are not truly excited about most group-paced learning.

Unfortunately, the preparation of teachers and administrators globally, the established bureaucracies designed to maintain traditional patterns, and the changing swings of political pendulums have blinded potential visions of what should or could be, and have limited reform efforts to rearranging the now too-familiar deck chairs on the *Titanic*. The problem may best be illustrated by the famous American comic strip, *Peanuts*, by Charles Schulz. Lucy, a friend of Charlie Brown, acting as a psychiatrist, asks Charlie a most profound question: "Charlie Brown, on the cruise ship of life, which way is your deck chair facing?" Charlie ponders, and then replies, "I don't know; I've never been able to get one open." School people, like Charlie, have been unable to open their educational deck chairs.

In another philosophical discussion with Charlie, his friend Linus says, "I guess it's wrong always to be worrying about tomorrow. Maybe we should only worry about today." Charlie Brown replies, "No, that's giving up; I'm still hoping that yesterday will get better." The majority of the current politicians involved with education policy, and educators mired in the bureaucracy of survival, still hope that somehow "yesterday will get better." More creative futurists, concerned with tomorrow, must begin to apply mounting pressure for change in their communities, for conventional schools as they exist cannot improve, other than to slightly raise test scores. The traditional group-paced classroom of twenty-five to thirty students is akin to a doctor giving flu shots to the first thirty patients examined, regardless of their individual illnesses or injuries.

For future generations, finally opening the educational deck chairs is a global priority. The "how" does require a focus on *Imagineering*. Futurists of all walks of life are now required to help communities with envisioning. Education today is not learning; it is politics. Governments and local school controls have chorused the whims of those who sing loudly for "accountability" or other trendy, popular voter tunes that will keep them in power. It is time to help the majority unlearn what has been, and then help them learn what needs to unfold. Futurists believe that educators and community leaders must be *disoriented* before they can be *oriented*. They must "unlearn" how schooling has been conducted during the past century before they can "learn" how to envision the possibilities for the future.

Ironically, over the previous ten decades, there have been several exciting, creative renewal efforts, but all remained the exception in the public education system. These successful, temporary programs were not able to permanently overcome tradition on a large scale, as illustrated by the innovative 1907-1937 Gary, Indiana program.[3] This was a model work-study-play philosophy and platoon scheduling total community (children and adults) school system, open fifty weeks a year, twelve hours a day, seven days a week, at the same cost and with better student retention than comparable Indiana districts. When the superintendent passed away, World War II arrived, and Gary demographics changed, this exciting, successful innovation died too.

Startling, disturbing, yet delightful is the fact that the available *reliable research overwhelmingly supports moving away from the "regular" practices* toward easy-to-implement, already-studied, non-traditional methods.[4] Though not "futuristic," these starting points are a foundation for what could be, and include nongraded environments (versus grade-level schooling), individualized instruction (rather than group-paced assignments), personalized curriculum (versus mandated curricula for everyone), continuous progress (versus limited or unattainable expectations), self-directed evaluation (not letter or number "report cards"), twelve-month opportunities (rather than restricted calendars), affective and psychomotor domain focus (as opposed to cognitive concentration only), all-day caring, food, and clothing needs for youth in poverty (as opposed to limited social services), and personalized rehabilitation plans for discipline cases through person centers (as opposed to blanket suspension and expulsion practices).

To achieve these visions, communities should turn to creative educators; there are a few. Persons preparing to be future leaders should take "classes" in envisioning as more important than budget and management training. Creativity is a talent to be cultivated.[5] This may be easier to state than accomplish, but unless the current lockstep educator training programs are abandoned, there will be little hope. Not all educators can be visionaries, but those who are natural leaders can lead followers. Pioneering communities should focus on hiring the leaders and teachers who can help disorient and then orient the populace out of the existing forms of *schooling* into potential *learning* systems for future generations.

Imagining is not enough; Imagineering truly is required. One illustration from the 1960s provides the documentation that *Inventing* and *Implementing* must combine with *Imagining* to equal Imagineering—to dream, to create, to accomplish. The United States government provided extensive funds for a project titled *Designing Education For the Future.*[6] Eight Rocky Mountain States (Colorado, Utah, Wyoming, Arizona, Nevada, New Mexico, Idaho, and Montana) received money to design and create new and/or improved learning systems for the region. The project staff enlisted many of the brightest education minds of the times; involved almost all the eight-state school board members and government officials; catered to the local school trustees of major cities; produced five-book volumes on what to change, why, and how; and conducted numerous major regional conferences focused on what could be and the processes needed to achieve new directions. Almost forty years later, nothing has changed in the schools of those eight states (except to add computers). Education in that region is still as traditional and rigid and "copycat" as it was before the project. A carefully planned, documented, financed proposal to create change was ultimately rejected by "experts" and others who lacked vision and creativity; they maintained their python grip on convention.

To overcome continuing repetition of such disappointments in education, communities can reflect upon a variety of successful improvement models. One is the creation of industry-style R&D centers. The space program, as illustration, has its volunteer astronauts, constantly improving spacecraft, preparation and launch sites, and mission support personnel. This coordinated design has transformed the knowledge of the universe and energy, and has improved communications, air travel, and weather projections.

Research and development centers of a critical-mass proportion can provide local systems, states, and nations the opportunity to support educational astronauts who are willing to explore new horizons. Though the space industry received a special budget—such would be desirable for creating new learning systems, as well as rockets meant to reach the moon—the fact is that the leading education communities can achieve significantly different, and potentially better, learning environments on their existing budgets. They can use school-within-school plans, magnet schools, cluster school choices of diversified learning options, community learning centers, laboratory school concepts, schools-without-walls, and prototype alternative experimental designs.

Rigid state and national mandates usually can be waived through permissive statutes when sound proposals are submitted. Such R&D centers should be staffed with creative, inventive, imaginative, take-a-risk, envision-the-alternative-futures personnel. They would enlist a cross-section of pioneering volunteer students. Families willing to assist in the development of new learning approaches would enroll their children and participate in the ongoing designs evolving from continuous Imagineering. The process involves implementing well-researched successful practices; testing experimental but potential additional methods; providing alternate means for evaluation; and offering parents, students, teachers, and administrators immediately available optional programs and learning climates.

Research and development futures-focused visions can be both dream and reality, as was almost the case around 1970 in the state of Minnesota, where plans were drawn for the Minnesota Experimental City (MXC), a joint government and private capital venture. The MXC was to be the most *experimental*—not model—city in the world. It was designed for 250,000 people of all ages, and was to be constructed on 60,000 acres of basically virgin northern Minnesota land. Only 10,000 acres were to be cemented, with the other 50,000 available for open preserve, wildlife, agriculture, play, and recreation. It was to be partially covered with one of the Buckminster Fuller geodesic dome configurations; featured were waterless toilets throughout the city. No automobiles were to be allowed (they were to be parked outside in an area reached by an automated highway), being replaced by an extensive people mover system throughout the city boundaries. The central "core" of the MXC was to contain common services and facilities. People were to live in satellite cluster villages to conserve energy and create shared outdoor commons. Everyone was to have access to all the latest available technological equipment.

The exciting phase for education was that the city was to be constructed with no schools or universities. More learning was projected caringly, humanely, inexpensively, and efficiently for more people than ever before. Everyone was to be a learner; everyone was to be a teacher. Learners and facilitators were to be connected in person, but initially often through the LORIN system (a computer-based resource network). The city was to serve as a lifelong learning laboratory.

As outlined by Ronald Barnes, MXC director for educational planning, the system was based upon almost reverse principles when contrasted with conventional systems.[7] In the MXC, learning was to be conceived of as life itself; it was never to stop. Learning was to occur everywhere, for people could learn on their own. Everyone was important regardless of how much he or she knew. Learning was to be a life-long process tailored to individuals. People could make their own decisions regarding what and how to learn, and could form positive social networks on their own without schooling.

Although there were to be no "school buildings," the system did involve places for people to come together and share. Facilities such as homes, businesses, and public places were to be used. Beginning Life Centers were to offer a creative environment for very young children. Stimulus Centers were to offer films, tapes, sounds, smells. Gaming Centers were to allow for the study of complex realities in a simple fashion. Project Centers were to provide persons with opportunities to work on experiential outcomes. Learner Banks would store tools, equipment, and non-print and print materials. Family Life Centers were to encourage the family to learn together and to communicate openly. Learners would use these sites whenever they needed or desired, not because they were required, especially on a daily scheduled basis. The learning and every other system in the MXC were to remain experimental, fluid, and open to change.

To help with the transition toward potential learning futures, the Wilson Campus School at Minnesota State University, Mankato, piloted many of the MXC concepts.[8] This well-documented and, at the time, most innovative, open, flexible, year-round public learning system in America proved conclusively that there are better non-traditional approaches than those currently in use for enhancing the growth of spirit, mind, and body for many youth and adult populations. Initially, Wilson made sixty-nine deviations from the conventional school patterns. These involved non-grading, individualizing, personalizing, eliminating requirements and compulsory attendance, creating an infant-through-college and senior-citizen age mix under one roof—including evenings as a community center—introducing teaming and suites rather than classrooms, incorporating self-evaluation, stressing self-direction and responsibility, considering everyone both a learner and a facilitator, focusing on urgent studies and global dilemmas, volunteering and tutoring where needed, spotlighting the affective as the priority domain, employing caring self-selected advisors and facilitators, encouraging community service, and instituting year-round continuous learning.

Wilson proved that the education proposals for the MXC were viable—that students of all achievement levels and economic backgrounds could improve toward their potential, and that new learning systems were possible. The program was achieved through creative Imagineering. The staff imagined what they wanted, invented ways to create reality, and implemented their dreams. Though a beautiful environment for people, documented by ten years of student success, Wilson fell prey to a political process. In a tight budget year, the legislature closed all university laboratory schools to provide "new" college buildings without additional construction. Monumental efforts were made to keep Wilson open, but to no avail. As consolation, the legislature did recommend that each major district should have its own laboratory program to continue educational research and development in Minnesota. Unfortunately, they did not mandate a plan or establish a consortium of volunteers. In the era of conservatism that followed, and without visionary leadership, the required Imagineering never reached fruition. Thus ended one of the most noble education experiments of the 20th century.

Learning will not be better worldwide if it remains as a practice of schooling. The publications *Education Now* and the *Education Heretics Press* currently best document this conclusion.[9] In envisioning the decades ahead, leaders must focus not only on the creative design of what, but on how communities might implement the new concepts (perhaps through the astronaut-style R&D centers), and most of all, how educators might disorient communities so that they understand what is currently wrong, and thus become receptive to helping envision, create, and maintain the impossible!

Imagination is crucial. Imagine being on a trip to see the MXC, the most experimental city in the world. What would be seen from a distance? Would the city have tall buildings? Would it be underground? Would the central core be covered with a climate-controlled dome? What would one see upon arriving in the city? What would the MXC justice, health, employment, transportation, recycling, housing, and communication systems reflect? What would be the format for the most experimental learning plan in the world? The wonderful statement of Roald Dahl regarding dreams and realities in *Charlie and the Chocolate Factory* speaks very well to the specific possibilities articulated in each of these questions: "We make realities out of dreams and dreams out of realities. We are the dreamers of the dreams."[10]

Artists paint pictures with drawings. Authors paint pictures with words. Educators now must paint creative processes and programs with visions of "Pure Imagineering." Education can be changed if communities will 1) educate the constituents on the need for new societal and educational paradigms; 2) begin a process of disorienting away from the old school structure while orienting toward the new; 3) develop a philosophical base for education that is person-centered, not group-paced and aged-based; 4) establish R&D learning centers with volunteer participants; 5) Imagineer what is desired—invent how to do it—and then implement the imagined prototype; and 6) hire inventor leaders and staff.

Creative change processes can evolve in most communities if imagination is released and supported during the efforts to both transition into and transform global learning systems. In this regard, Jonathan Swift spoke for all futurists, including educational futurists, when he stated in *Gulliver's Travels,* "I have seen what others can only dream; I know these descriptions are true...for I have been there."[11] If the aerospace industry has the technology and intelligence to place humans on Mars in the next twenty years, then certainly in a two-decade span educators can learn how to eliminate the 7th grade. This is the worst year for most students, for such a "grade level" is impossible to support. Youth in the "7th grade" are spread from grade 3 to grade 13 on achievement tests. Physiologically, they are spread a minimum of six years. Only fifteen percent of the "7th graders" actually conform to the imaginary norm.

Reflecting upon the proposed Minnesota Experimental City, the 7th grade was abandoned, along with all other "grade levels" and buildings called "schools." For three years, the state legislature supported the creation of the MXC to explore new dimensions for urban living. However, surprise election results again changed history. The conservatives, the leaders of whom had supported the MXC project, lost control of the house, senate, and office of the Governor. They were replaced by Democrats who then let the final approval process die without a vote, only one year before the planned ground breaking ceremony. The conservatives had encouraged the process, for they were determined to continue to promote quality cities in Minnesota.

It is time for politicians to set aside partisanship when societal futures are at stake. Among similar views of many, in *Turning the Century,* the late futurist Robert Theobald clearly outlines the need for and process of bringing community leaders together to rethink the coming decades and the interdependence of all global systems.[12] In transitioning education, it is essential to seek futures-oriented, creative people who will not maintain for everyone the existing structures of schooling. Instead they will envision the possibilities, design new proposals as exemplified by the MXC, and constantly self-renew to ensure continuous improvement. Through Imagineering, significantly different and better learning systems truly can evolve for the benefit of both present and future generations.

# Additional Readings

Lester Brown, *State of the World.* New York: W.W. Norton, 1999.

Jerome Glenn and Theodore Gordon (ed.s), *1998 State of the Future.* New York: American Council for the United Nations University, 1998.

Don Glines, *Educational Futures Trilogy.* P.O. Box 711386, San Diego, CA: National Association for Year-Round Education, 1995.

Don Glines, *Year-Round Education: Traditions and Innovations.* San Diego, CA: National Association for Year-Round Education, 2000.

Don Glines and David Mussatti, *Year-Round Education: Paths to Resources.* San Diego, CA: National Association for Year-Round Education, 2000.

Clive Harber (ed.), *Voices for Democracy:*

*A North-South Dialogue on Education for Sustainable Democracy.* 113 Arundel, Bramcote Hills, Nottingham, UK: Educational Heretics Press, 1998.

Willis Harman, *Global Mind Change: The Promise of the 21st Century,* 2nd ed. San Francisco: Berrett-Koehler, 1998.

Roland Meighan, *The Next Learning System.* Nottingham, UK: Educational Heretics Press, 1997.

Ron Miller, *New Directions in Education.* Brandon, VT: Holistic Education Press, 1991.

James Moffett, *The Universal Schoolhouse.* San Francisco: Jossey-Bass, 1994.

Schoolboys of Barbiana. *Letter to a Teacher.* New York: Random House, 1970.

William Van Til, *My Way of Looking At It.* San Francisco: Caddo Gap Press, 1996.

# Notes

1. *Future Generations*, 24, 1998, pp. 16-17.
2. *The Futurist*, October 1977, pp. 274-278.
3. Don Glines and William Wirt, *The Great Lockout in America's Citizenship Plants: Past as Future.* P.O. Box 711386, San Diego, CA: National Association for Year-Round Education, 1995.
4. Wayne Jennings, "Startling, Disturbing Research on School Effectiveness," *Phi Delta Kappan*, March 1977, pp. 568-572.
5. Michael Michalko, *Cracking Creativity: The Secrets of Creative Genius.* Berkeley, CA: Ten Speed Press, 1998.
6. Designing Education for The Future Project, 1362 Lincoln Street, Denver, CO. 1965-67.
7. Ronald Barnes, Transitions Inc.

639 Pueblo Lane, Prescott, AZ. 1972.
8. Kathleen Long, "Teacher Reflections on Individual School Restructuring." Ph.D. Diss, University of Oregon Library, Eugene, OR 1992; Don Glines, *Creating Educational Futures: Continuous Mankato Wilson Alternatives.* San Diego, CA: National Association for Year-Round Education, 1995.
9. Education Now / Educational Heretics Press. 113 Arundel Drive, Bramcote Hills, Nottingham, England.
10. Roald Dahl, *Charlie and the Chocolate Factory.* New York: Penguin Books, 1994.
11. Jonathan Swift, *Gulliver's Travels.* New York: Pocket Books, 1996.
12. Robert Theobold, *Turning the Century.* Indianapolis: Knowledge Systems Press, 1992.

# About the Author

*Don Glines is the director of the Educational Futures Projects in Sacramento, California. He has combined a concern for global futures with the need to replace current schooling rituals by creating entirely new learning systems based upon existing and new research, common sense, and visions of the future. His three volumes, the Educational Futures Trilogy, document the need for and methods of transitioning education for coming generations. He may be contacted at P.O. Box 2977, Sacramento, CA 95812, (phone) 916-393-8701.*

# Community Design in the Year 2012

*by Patrick Walkinshaw*

HELLO, MY NAME IS Noble and I have been asked to share with you a glimpse of my world. At the turn of the century our region faced a critical decision as to how to create communities to best honor human and cultural development. Today, twelve years after the millennium, we have begun to see the results of our hard work and creativity. I trust that the following will provide you with the insight you are looking for.

To begin, a little introduction of who I am and where I live. I am an apprentice with our local Planners' Guild. I live with my family, which consists of my biological parents, another young person who is ten years old, her parents, and my "grandfather," who is a long-time friend of my parents. We live in a community of 7,500 people in the Finger Lakes Bioregion on the North American continent.

I understand that you are interested in community design—how to create a community that works for all members and is in harmony with the natural world. Let me start by outlining the principles we used to guide our planning process twelve short years ago.

308

1. Every individual is born with a unique purpose and an appropriate life situation to achieve that purpose.

2. Each individual can be trusted to know what is best for him or herself and to clearly articulate his or her truth.

3. Social systems and physical design should both maximize an individual's ability to discover his or her path and encourage cooperative and harmonious group work.

4. We are a part of natural systems in mind and body. The health of those systems has a direct correlation to our own health.

5. Appropriate design harmonizes with the subtle energy flows of the earth and its inhabitants.

6. We humans are social creatures and gravitate towards each other. We also need our individual space.

7. Form flows from function. As we evolve as a species, so will the forms we create.

8. Honesty, responsibility, and awareness are attributes we value and model.

Once we agreed on these truths, we critically examined our social systems and infrastructure and found some glaring inconsistencies. The most obvious place where we weren't honoring our principles was in our treatment of young people. We realized that forcing young people into age-segregated, competition-focused educational systems severely limited their ability to find their unique truths, dramatically narrowing each person's potential. We acknowledged that adults were treating the young with a certain condescension and lack of respect. It became obvious that age discrimination was the basis for placing children in oppressive systems. How had this happened? How had we allowed ourselves to continue to discriminate against people based on age, while actively fighting discrimination against all other groups?

The emphasis in our culture on the material world, the worship of the false gods of wealth, fame, and fortune, together with a general lack of spiritual awareness set the stage for many adults to feel threatened by the questioning minds and free spirits of the young. The answer to their fear was to control and mold the young to fit into adult society.

As we delved deeper into these emotions, we realized that to effect change in our systems we needed first to shift our belief patterns and acknowledge the divine within all of us. Clearly, this was no easy task and took many years of a serious community commitment. The transformation, however, had begun.

Once we began to liberate our energy from the constraints of fear, new options for our young organically appeared. Creativity flowed as if a dam had burst. No longer did adults create and provide youth services and institutions as if the young were helpless and mindless. Instead, young people became co-creators of systems that truly acknowledged and honored the worthiness of all people.

We came to realize that effective youth development begins even before conception. We redefined sexuality as a healthy and sacred expression between people engaged in loving relationship. We encouraged people who were interested in having children to consciously choose the appropriate time to conceive and to invoke the child's spirit while love-making, effectively focusing the energy of the couple and creating a fertile environment for the new being. Ritualization of conception prepares the parents and supporting community for the changes to come.

Simultaneously, we radically decentralized our health-care system, placing traditional and alternative medical practitioners throughout our neighborhoods at nodes of activity to encourage direct interaction with the population they serve. Pre-natal counseling is now integrated with the family's overall continuing healthcare. To properly honor the magic and mystery of the birth process, we created special birth settings throughout the community staffed by midwives and made accessible to the whole family. We shied away from routine medical interventions in labor and delivery in order to foster birthing as a natural, healthy process, rather than as a condition to be managed or healed.

I should mention here the importance of ritual in our community. Birthing is just one of the natural cycles we choose to acknowledge and celebrate. Rituals are our way of honoring individual paths, embracing community, and centering our lives around natural reference points. Each ceremony is initiated by the family or neighborhood in their religious or spiritual tradition of choice. A sample of typical ceremonies include: conception ritual, welcome baby to the world, rite of passage from adolescence into adulthood, appreciation circles marking traditional birthdays, passage into the role of elder, and funerals. We celebrate the cycles of nature as well, in full-moon ceremonies and seasonal celebrations like solstice, equinox, and harvest. At any given time during the year one can enter a neighborhood and experience the song and dance of community ritual. By reclaiming ritual as a central part of our lives, we gained a reverence for life and enhanced our connection as a community.

Again, we went back to the basics of effective child-rearing that have passed the test of time in many of our cultures around the world. Every mother is supported to nurse. Work and community environments were modified so that babies can be carried in arms throughout the day. Touching, holding, and intimacy are basic needs for babies (and all of us), so we stopped questioning whether too much love and attention would spoil a child, and committed ourselves to providing our children with an environment full of physical and emotional closeness.

We also realized that placing the entire burden of child-rearing on the biological parents made little sense, often leading to the parents' feeling overwhelmed and frustrated and the baby's being deprived of attention. So we expanded our definition of family care-givers to include children, elders, and other non-related adults. Presently children receive care primarily from the elders, who have the time and the life wisdom to offer the attention children need. I cannot stress enough how vital elders have been to fostering stability in a child's life and in the passing down of customs and values. No longer must children rely on peer groups or young parents to answer their questions about the world. As an added benefit, biological parents have more time to follow their own creative endeavors without losing the pleasure of watching their children grow up.

To support these new family structures we needed new building forms, and we found that clustered housing best met our needs for community and family. We infilled existing city blocks with dwellings of various sizes and shapes, depending on intended use. The area at the center of the blocks has become common land, accessible to all by a network of paths. We found that many streets could be either ripped up and planted or turned into "slow streets" for resident traffic only. Within the city, the network of slow streets and paths creates safe passage for pedestrians, bicyclists, roller-bladers, etc. Distinct neighborhoods consisting of a few hundred people have formed, each with an organizational body to oversee the common spaces and zoning practices. These neighborhoods have distinct subcultures with unique values, habits, and beliefs. Each neighborhood has clearly defined boundaries, is open to anyone who wishes to live there, and provides a way for people to truly belong to a social group of their choosing. Young people raised in our neighborhoods experience an important grounding in the beliefs of their birth families, and at the same time are exposed to many other ways of living.

We have eliminated rental properties in the traditional sense so that no one profits from another's basic need for housing. Every family and individual has autonomy over their home whether or not they have actual financial ownership. All money paid for living in the house or toward improvements builds equity for the occupants. This way, we ensure that people are invested in the properties and neighborhoods they inhabit.

The homes themselves are built to suit the situation of the individual or family. Households for one person are simple structures usually containing one large room with many alcoves; households for couples balance personal and shared space; households for a small family balance a couple's realm with the children's realm; and teenagers often have their own cottage-like space connected to the main house with a separate entrance for greater privacy. Senior housing radiates into the community from a central health-care facility, so elders are integrated in the community while having any health-care needs met. In all homes, as well as in work areas and community gathering spaces, close attention is paid to creating common spaces where people naturally tend to gather for socializing and shared meals. Common areas are adjacent to the corridors of the buildings so one can view the space and the people inside without disturbing them if one chooses not to stop and chat. Outdoor public squares are designed in much the same way, providing an important social function.

Now I would like to share with you what the community looks like from the perspective of a young person, beginning with my home. As a young child I had my own space, and my play area was a swath extending from my room through the common areas to the outdoors. My toys and clothes were easily accessible to me on low, open shelves, and I had many nooks and hideaways for privacy. Once outside I had access to large expanses of common land unbroken by traffic, connecting about fifty households, which gave me many potential playmates. The common land has free-form organic "playgrounds" with nets, crates, ramps, boxes, barrels, trees, ropes, water, etc., where my friends and I could create and re-create playgrounds of our own. There are also numerous .places for individual and team sports, as well as public access to wild areas, farm-land, and greenways that extend from the country into the heart of the city. Youth activities are visible to passers-by and nearby dwellings, serving as an invitation for others to participate and providing a measure of safety.

In every neighborhood at least one home is identified as a gathering place for children. Large, rambling houses with sizable yards that are accessible by bike and pedestrian paths are chosen, and permanent adult residents make the home accessible twenty-four hours a day, seven days a week. It also functions as a place for communal eating and socializing, so there is always a bustle of activity. Young people of any age can visit at their leisure for a few minutes or even overnight, if they desire a change of pace from their family life. Each household in the neighborhood con-tributes to the cost of running the home, and the resident youth worker can focus on building relationships and community.

We have special learning systems used by young people and adults alike. A network of learning centers has replaced the outdated institu-tions of elementary, secondary, and university schooling present in your society. Learning has been recovered as an exciting, life-long process, and, combined with each individual's creativity, forms the "glue" that binds our community. Learning centers are open to all ages and everyone is encour-aged to both teach and learn. Learning facilitators are available for support, but many children find that they prefer exploring the world with other children or through less formal relationships with adults. Centers usually have several rooms with a wide range of possible activities. Some centers focus on particular subjects such as art or mechanics. Classes are formed and reformed depending on interest. A database of apprentice-ships and resource people is accessible so that learners can link with community members, businesses, and guilds doing work of interest. All forms of intelligence and modes of learning are nurtured and given room for expression. Much of the time energy is directed toward community service and the creation of new systems that continue our movement toward becoming a sustainable society.

We teenagers have gathering spaces of our own that we manage and direct. Teens gain independence and opportunities to learn business, group decision-making, and conflict-resolution skills. The gathering spaces serve as "hang-out" spots as well as places for creative expression through the visual or performance arts. Starting twelve years ago, these teen centers were where young people and supportive adults organized to address the oppression of the young and began to reevaluate the princi-ples and values of our communities. From the beginning, youth activism has provided vital energy toward the changes we as a community have instituted.

Play areas, learning centers, and teen centers are interconnected with all community activities, including the working world. Whether on a farm, in a computer-programming firm, or at a local tailor shop, young people are invited to observe, ask questions, and participate. Work is organized by career guilds that oversee a variety of essential community services such as health, planning, agriculture, transportation, etc. Each guild has a specific training and apprentice program open to anyone drawn to that particular work. Guilds offer basic living stipends to all members and are supported by local taxes.

Our communities now embrace a bioregional perspective, one that recognizes the unique natural habitats and landforms of a region. We continue to work towards meeting the basic needs of our communities while maintaining the health of our ecosystems. We have found the most effective and responsive businesses to this perspective are those locally owned and cooperatively operated. Our transition away from a global economy was aided by the use of local currencies that recycled money within our community. While trade with other bioregions still occurs, it has become less necessary.

Unlike in your current communities, our young people have a voice in all community affairs. There is no minimum requisite voting age, and we have eliminated age-based laws—a logical outcome of our acknowledgment of the inherent worth of each individual. Rather than discriminate based on age, we have focused on measuring ability. For example, to obtain a driver's license, a detailed training and evaluation process is required regardless of age. Obviously, we have no compulsory schooling and we have eliminated age limits on employment, since free choice is honored for all ages. Young people are no longer considered the "property" of their parents, and any alleged abuse or violation of personal boundaries is presented for neighborhood conflict resolution, where young people and adults have equal voice. We truly believe "it takes a village to raise a child," and continue to redesign systems to reflect our principles.

As you can imagine, the forms and design elements I have described were the result of years of process and construction, still ongoing today. Our transformation was initiated by refining the community decision-making process and inspired by such literary works as *A Pattern Language*, by Christopher Alexander et al, Malidoma Somé's *Ritual*, and Starhawk's *The Fifth Sacred Thing*. Once we acknowledged the principles on which to rebuild our communities, we gave decision-making back to the people who were most immediately impacted. Individuals are now empowered to set up their lives as they choose, families decide how to set up their living places, neighborhoods make decisions related to general zoning and common space use, communities of between 5,000 and 10,000 people make decisions on issues related to the areas between neighborhoods, the Bioregional Council deals with matters of the bioregion as a whole, the World Council deals with planetary issues. Our system encourages creativity to flow on an individual level and allows people to have a real voice in their communities. We are continuing to see new forms emerge as we experiment and reevaluate our changing way of life. I am proud to say that we have an empowered populace that actively delights in living, learning, and experiencing the world with others.

## About the Author

Patrick Walkinshaw is an artist, activist, and visionary living in the Finger Lakes Bioregion of Upstate New York with his wife Kristen and his new son Noble.

# Rewiring a Community's Brain for the 21st Century

### Aligning the Cosmic Dance

*by Rick Smyre*

THERE ARE UNSEEN CONNECTIONS growing in our local communities as a result of constant change. The fast pace of these connections creates complex cultural and historical processes that call into question traditional underlying assumptions of how we learn, educate, govern, economically develop, lead, and especially how we think. Look around. Tectonic plates of cultural change are in evidence everywhere. In all sectors of society, there are apparent contradictions at work. Business gurus tell us to "think globally, act locally." Concepts of education differ, emphasizing both updated, traditional public-school approaches and new market approaches. "Small is beautiful" coexists with the age of the huge. And everywhere there are increased connections in an increasingly fast-paced, interdependent, and complex world.

But just as soon as new connections are made, others are broken. Knowledge is quickly obsolete. Management students in the '60s were taught to build models that represented the future. Today, students are taught to develop probable scenarios in order to respond to different situations as they occur. In the '60s the concept of accurate prediction was a central principle of strategic planning. Now computer models look for patterns instead of specific outcomes.

It is as if new organizational and community brains are emerging, connecting diverse people and ideas without prediction, offering innovations that build on the backs of past thinkers, yet shifting in basic concept as we move to a totally different type of society—one increasingly mobile, interconnected, and constantly integrating the old with the new.

As society becomes more fluid and changing, underlying concepts of how society works also change. There is transformation, moving beyond the type of change that improves what has existed for years, i.e., reform.

Traditions break apart as larger and more complex systems emerge from the integrations of existing values and structures. Many of the assumptions that have undergirded our industrial society for two hundred years are crumbling. This chapter will attempt to establish a framework for understanding how new concepts of learning will be needed to help identify, develop, and apply a few of these new assumptions.

As a result of our present societal stresses, a twenty-first century futures context seems to be evolving—as if a new community brain were developing, connecting diverse people, new ideas, and fundamentally different concepts, methods, and techniques.

Few local leaders have recognized that communities are in the early stages of a dramatic transformation. Most leaders who have begun to see change as important have continued to use a traditional filter to understand it. First identified by Alvin Toffler in the book *Future Shock* in 1972, the idea of an increased pace of change as a cultural phenomenon seeped into the consciousness of communities over the next thirty years, as if a new neurotransmitter suddenly increased the connections of an expanding brain. By the early 1990s, the idea of a "learning community" was introduced by Peter Senge in *The Fifth Discipline*. Over the last decade, it has become apparent that the dynamic of constant change and the transformation of society require a different approach to learning in several ways. Without the structure of the learning experience adapting to the evolution of a futures context, communities will continue to utilize obsolete ideas within the context of inappropriate structures.

Traditional learning focuses on content. An underlying assumption has been that appropriate knowledge is already known and must be transferred from one generation to another. As new knowledge is gained, it is added to the old. Accountability and testing reinforce the idea of standard knowledge. Tradition focuses on the one best answer. True/false and multiple-choice testing have been the mainstay of evaluating whether learning has occurred.

## Learning in a Society of Constant Change

But as the pace of change increases in society, knowledge explodes, more people are born, telecommunications expand, and connections increase exponentially. A society of interdependence replaces a society of independence. New patterns emerge from new connections. There is a richness of outcomes as the cosmic dance of reality unfolds.

In a society that is changing and evolving, standard answers are not appropriate. For example, someone who studies civil engineering in college will need to understand that 25-30% of the knowledge learned by the time of graduation will be obsolete. Thus, the concept of content must change from absolute information to core competence. The learner must become a dynamist, comfortable with new information and challenging old knowledge. Learning in the future will be generative, not static. For this to occur, any learner will need two additional skills—the ability to ask appropriate questions and the ability to connect apparently disparate ideas within a futures context. The connection of these skills will lead to continuous innovation.

Recently I was asked to design a new approach to learning that would allow students in various parts of the world to take advantage of our Community-of-the-Future concept of transformational learning. I attempted to create a research and development project that would test my ability to frame a new type of experience leading to real, individual "transformation" of thinking on the part of those with whom I would be working over the Internet. Realizing that time was limited and that my initial two test students were motivated, I designed a radically different approach of interaction. I titled the project "reciprocal learning" to reflect the fact that I would be learning to facilitate a new approach to systemic thinking within a futures context (transformational learning), and at the same time the students were hopefully benefiting from my guidance.

Here's how it worked. I identified a list of books, web sites, and articles appropriate in various ways for an "overview of community transformation." Ordinarily, I would have suggested specific readings. This time, however, I reversed the process. Instead of asking questions to find out if the students had understood the readings, I asked different types of questions that would help guide the students in their own self-organized learning processes. For example, "What will need to occur for communities to rethink and restructure their local institutions if one assumes that the very assumptions of how we lead, how governance occurs, how we do economic development, and how learning occurs, will be transformed due to an increasingly fast-paced, interconnected, and complex society?"

I wanted each of the students to struggle to think about what factors, issues, concepts, and actions would need to be considered. I wanted each of them consciously and subconsciously to take control of their own learning—and did they ever! Each student achieved more than I expected with the most optimistic scenario. The most interesting outcome, and the center of my learning experience, was that each student developed a different path to understanding the concept of COTF's Community Transformation.

As a result of my experience, I quickly conceived the first principle of reciprocal "transformational" learning: *The role of a teacher is trans-*

*formed to that of a coach.* The second principle of reciprocal learning flows from the first: *There are many paths to success and the coach cannot predict the outcomes of learning.* From this experience I found that motivated students can quickly increase their learning through self-organization as they integrate new information, form questions, and make innovative, disparate connections. I also found that this type of learning does not occur unless all three factors are involved simultaneously. I now have a better understanding of the great potential of reciprocal learning, and I now know that chaos/complexity theory can be applied to education and be successful.

Diana lives in California, and has a strong advanced educational background with a broad range of knowledge. She is not a typical student. However, I have often found that the more content knowledge one has, the less open to new ideas one may be. I wanted to see if Diana would be open to new ideas, and to see if I could take advantage of her background of knowledge in a positive way. When I framed the learning experience for Diana and for Michael, a student in Japan, my objective was to help them come to an understanding of the new COTF concepts of community transformation. Would it be possible to shift the thinking of well-educated students from old ways of looking at things? Would it be possible to add totally new knowledge in such a way that the students would understand COTF's twenty-first century approach to community transformation?

After I gave the list of resources and questions to Diana and Michael, I told them to get back to me when necessary—but that I didn't want them to do so until they needed my guidance. Within twelve days, I heard from Michael and began an intermittent dialogue. However, it was two months before I heard from Diana.

When I heard from her, it took me by complete surprise. Not only had she begun to understand our concepts, she had mastered the underlying assumptions. As far as I was concerned, she had met the objective of the course.

> Sorry to keep you waiting so long. I have read most of the Creating Learning Communities book which has been a great introduction to alternative education philosophies and projects (I will deal with these articles in another message).
>
> However, to address the issues you raised [regarding concepts that help construct a framework for reorganizing the learning experience, ideas on learning, and examples of reforming vs. transforming concepts, and underlying assumptions from Creating Learning Communities contrasted with Hunter's article (in Pathways to Sustainability), and comparison of Hunter and Ellis on their perspective of "context"], I found it was helpful to get a better grounding in the COTF/futures terminology and concepts, so I have been reading your articles.[1]
>
> These readings have helped me address some of the areas in a general way. I hope this initial venture into the field combined with a more long-term focus, i.e., the issues you raised which I will keep in mind as I proceed, will be my own parallel processes, and that after

additional reading, I will see things a little more clearly. In the meantime, I propose to:

1) Read more from the COTF website, specifically follow links on the "Principles" page;

2) Go back and read more in Pathways to Sustainability (I have read several chapters already, but reading the last chapter stimulated me to want to read more);

3) Find out about The Natural Step (from Sweden) and The Ecological Footprint (Wackernagel and Rees);

4) Attend a community planning and development public hearing at which community residents will express their opinions on the General Plan and an Environmental Impact Report;

5) Read the booklet about the Blackburg Electronic Village (which I sent away for).

Thanks for any comments you might have on how I am proceeding and my seven points below. At this stage, I am still finding my way around the terms and concepts and will be adding to my understanding of them as I read more, but I feel like I now have a better grasp of them, thanks to your articles. I will keep plowing ahead with the proposed next steps listed above and any others you might suggest.

Sincerely, Diana

1. Futures Context. "The Gretsky Factor and Community Transformation" article [Cook, Kerley, and Smyre, 1997] gave me a good sense of what thinking in a "futures context" means. The concept of a futures orientation is illustrated well in the descriptive metaphor of the hockey puck, which symbolizes the increasingly fast-paced changes of life today. The ability to anticipate where the hockey puck will go and respond quickly is a great way to depict the capacity to anticipate future trends and find innovative approaches to deal with them. Two important issues raised in "Lament of a Local Leader"[Smyre, 1999] which illuminate the idea of leadership as well as the necessity for a "futures context" are that experience is not an adequate basis for making decisions because the future contexts of problems do not exist in the realm of past experiences, and in addition to anticipating future trends, understanding the "interactive impact" of those trends on issues is also essential.

2. Models of Education. "Beyond the Deck Chairs" [Smyre, 1998] and "Altering the Cosmic Dance" [Smyre, 1999] also clearly lay out the differences between the current model of education (standardized content, one best answer, the teacher as expert, passive student) and a transformational learning model (generative, fostering questions, context based, learning style tailored to the individual, welcoming diversity of ideas, processes, and people, encouraging feedback and making connections between complex ideas, seeing issues in the context of a futures orientation, use of technology, cooperative learning groups). The role of process leaders (facilitators of transformation) is to help people examine underlying assumptions related to learning, governing, economic development, etc., and help them develop a shared vision of a desirable future for their community.

3. Transformational Learning and Community Transformation. "The Gretsky Factor and Community Transformation" article also helped me understand more clearly the common theme in many of the articles, which is the relationship between concepts of learning and

community transformation, that a new approach to learning is necessary for communities to prepare for the impact of future trends and an environment of continuous change.

4. Strategic Planning/Strategic Framing. A point that intrigued me in "Beyond the Deck Chairs" and "Webs of Intricacy" [Smyre, 1998] is the contrast between "strategic planning," and "strategic framing." The difference seems to be that strategic planning is a slow process that assumes a degree of control and predictability and is unsuitable for dealing with the fast-paced changes occurring in society today and in the future. It is useful, however, to tackle issues that require short-term solutions. On the other hand, the idea of strategic framing allows for a rapid and flexible response to issues as they arise by building capacities for dealing with complex issues ("Transformation in Action" [Kruth and Smyre, 1999, the last chapter in the book Pathways to Sustainability]). This approach is made possible by "webs of intricacy," small groups of people throughout the community who develop familiarity with certain issues and come up with innovative solutions that can be tested out. This illustrates "parallel processes," which help bring about transformation.

5. The Concept of Individualism and the Common Good. "Webs of Intricacy" explores the origins of the idea of individualism and recommends a reexamination of its underlying assumptions. "Transformation in Action" points out that one of these assumptions is the idea of "enlightened self interest," which claims that society benefits by the motivation of individuals desire for economic gain. In a time of increasing population density, instant communications, and a deteriorating environment, the isolationist view of the independent individual, who stands on his own and takes whatever he can get from the natural environment or from other people, can no longer be supported. A call is made for a shift to a more "mature" individualism that values interdependence. The idea of the "common good" grows out of this perspective of the individual (a central concept in social psychology is that man is a social animal who develops in the context of interaction with others). This kind of person will welcome collaboration with others to solve community problems ("Beyond the Deck Chairs"). A community made up of these kinds of individuals will be more concerned about the shared community environment and will work with others to raise the quality of life in the community.

6. Concept of Leadership. "The Lament of a Local Leader" emphasizes the goal of developing a new concept of leadership and understandings to enable leaders to facilitate consensus on shared visions of their community's future. An important aspect of leadership is the ability to develop capacities in others, as opposed to the common idea of a strong leader who takes over and directs the activity of followers.

7. Reforming vs. Transforming. "The Lament of a Local Leader" defined the difference between "reforming" and "transforming." Reforming old ideas and structures is appropriate in times of slow-paced change, but when change becomes fast-paced, transformation is necessary. Transformation is brought about through experimentation and development of new approaches based on new assumptions. It also occurs at different rates in different areas of activity. "Transformation in Action" adds that "reforming" is trying to facilitate change by being more efficient, while "transforming" involves reevaluating the underlying assumptions "in all relationships and larger systems."

I decided to restructure the concept of evaluation. Since Diana and Michael had used different approaches and read different resources to come to a basic understanding of community transformation, I decided to determine their ability to change roles and become facilitators. I asked them to become community coaches and think about three questions they would ask and two concepts they would consider the most important if they were helping to nurture (coach) local citizens in community transformation.

I didn't hear from Michael for ten days. When I did, the first key concept he had identified was "the importance of creating an environment where people themselves see a need to change." Once I saw this, I knew that Michael, too, had more than good content, he had come to understanding. The experiment was a great success, and I will begin to evolve the concept with others with less motivation and with different educational backgrounds.

As a result of this experience, I have come to the conclusion that the ability to evaluate a new system of learning in a dynamic society will require the ability to rethink how testing occurs. Core competencies will continue to require traditional testing methods, but new concepts of evaluating how to connect knowledge holistically will be required. Learning to evaluate the idea of asking the right questions will become a new field of study. Finally, the field of "generative connections" will evolve as a way to evaluate creativity within a futures context.

## Rewiring the Community

> It is as if the Milky Way entered upon some cosmic dance. Swiftly the brain becomes an enchanted loom where millions of flashing shuttles weave a dissolving pattern, always a meaningful pattern, though never an abiding one; a shifting harmony of subpatterns.
> —Sir Charles Sherrington, Experimental Physiologist

As the pace of change in society continues to escalate, the patterns of community transformation will begin to resemble the patterns of brain behavior with many new connections made as others disconnect forming a shifting harmony of subpatterns.

For local leadership to create new institutions of dynamic structure capable of vitality and coherence in a constantly changing society, it will be important for them to go beyond the linear thinking of traditional education. They will need to develop the ability to make connections among diverse and apparently non-related factors in order to insure continuous innovation.

One of the ways this can be done is to introduce leaders to the study of the brain and how it works in simple ways. Such an approach, when combined with other techniques, will insure that local leaders begin to understand the importance of forming new connections—connections of people, connections of ideas, connections of small and large networks, etc. This will lead to the creation of an environment for generative learning based on brain-like, adaptive concepts. The focus on traditional need for certainty gives way to an understanding and comfort with the apparent chaos of ambiguity. The ability to discern new underlying assumptions and patterns will become a prized skill in the future.

> Rather than allow learning and evolution, rigid technocratic standards freeze the status quo, preventing experiments that might produce new and improved ways. A dynamic system, whether a single organization or an entire civilization, requires rules. But those rules must be compatible with knowledge, with learning and with surprise. Finding those rules is the greatest challenge a dynamic civilization confronts.
> —*The Future and Its Enemies*, Virginia Postrel

## The Principles of Transformational Learning

Those who still search for certainty have little tolerance for society's complexity. In a society of increasing connections and complexity, the old concept of specific and standardized rules to be used for all occasions will need to be replaced with the idea of general principles, capable of adaptation and tailored to any specific environment.

The following principles will be key elements of transformational learning and undergird any local community approach to adapting its citizens and institutions to the challenges of the twenty-first century:

• Emphasize individualized learning, yet employ mechanisms appropriate to all learning styles. As the society becomes more complex, interconnected and moving at a faster pace, it will be a challenge to devise methods to ensure that *learning offers a balance of core competency content and individualized knowledge that allows any individual to evolve in his or her own appropriate way.* The very mindset of educators will need to be released from today's stifling standardized curricula.

• Shift the idea of teacher to learning leader. Leadership in general will move from top-down direction, prediction, and control of outcomes, to the natural idea of facilitating and motivating diverse people in methods of adapting to changing circumstances. This will impact the professional teacher and educator in several ways: 1) The concept of teacher helping to fill the glass of knowledge with predetermined information *will shift to the guide or coach concept,* 2) The methodology of lecture will be minimized as the key approach to learning for only those 8% who are auditory learners. More and more the use of questions and indirect concepts of facilitative learning will be used

• Establish a futures framework within which issues are considered. The idea of a shifting context of information will become the new environment of learning. All people will need to become adept at adaptation.

Life-long learning has come to the forefront of interest. A futures context requires that the idea of a "mindset" be discarded and replaced with the concept of "mindflex." All learners will need to become comfortable with rethinking, reorganizing, and redesigning. *Understanding the impact of trends of the future on all issues will be a necessity to develop appropriate plans. Those who are able to understand the changes in context brought about by the transformation of change will be capable of vitality in a dynamic society.* As Bill Gates tells his teams of software writers, "Cannibalize your products within eighteen months...if you don't do it, someone else will."

• Be open to new ideas of any kind. Filter those that do not resonate with an understanding of a new reality. One of the greatest obstacles to learning within a constantly changing society is the need for certainty. The idea of certainty of outcomes will be replaced with the idea of continuity of principles. Multiple outcomes will be appropriate for the diversity of life that continues to evolve in a web of innovative connections. Certainty of values will be the glue that holds communities together. It will be important for all education and learning to search for, emphasize, and bring to consensus a family of values that will ensure the vitality of a dynamic society. Many of those values we hold dear today, such as leader/follower, will shift to new ideas. *The value of and/both will replace the idea of either/or as we learn there are many ways to do things and many answers to the same question.* Einstein, when told by a student at Princeton that he was giving the same exam that had been given the last semester, offered the reply, "Yes, but the answers have changed."

• Establish experiments and receive feedback. *The biological concept of feedback will become a cornerstone idea for learning as we continuously are faced with new challenges and an evolving context of circumstance.* The traditional focus of strategic planning assumes the ability to predict outcomes and control processes. Neither is possible in a constantly changing world. What is expected to evolve *is a concept of parallel processes,* where strategic planning is used for short-term needs where all factors and outcomes are defined and seen as appropriate (think about any manufacturing process), and a process of planning that gives emphasis to the building of capacities for longer-term transformation and adaptation. In the former process, those involved will need to sees things commonly— thus, one large group can focus on standardized answers. In the latter process, there will need to be experiments of different approaches to see what works and what doesn't—thus requiring small groups of interested people who want to take the risks of creating the new.

• Protect the competition and integration of ideas. In an interdependent world, competition does not have to be arbitrarily created. The old saying, "Throw the ideas on the wall and let's see what sticks," has an element of truth in an evolving age of interdependency. *The idea of multiple connections in a system of factors will become a cornerstone idea of learning as we develop new and appropriate ways of thinking and acting.* The scientific method focused on the competition of ideas, and the competition of those who debated truth. This will still be an important idea for those involved in the arena of natural sciences where objectivity of concept and design is assured by the independence of input. However, the age of quantum mechanics reflects parts of reality where the concepts of independence and linear thinking do not apply. No longer is total predictability possible.

• Focus on collaboration among diverse people and ideas and allow them to combine in different ways. Look for the value in what is said or written in order to connect it to one's own experience. In so doing, the quantum nature of one's own reality continuously emerges, and constantly redefines the learning experience. *The result of one phase of learning is the mechanism of the next—but always at a higher level of consciousness.* One's assumptions are tested by the sense of meaning that ensues. Recently I was asked to go to Scotland to work with the Scottish Council Foundation, the nation's leading think-tank. We attended the introduction of what is called the "Scottish scenarios," looking ahead to a vision for Scotland. One of the excellent concepts that was introduced as a key part of developing an appropriate vision for Scotland was the idea of collaboration. As the presentations ensued, it became obvious that the idea of what collaboration would require was not seen in an interdependent way. For example, the point was never made that for connections of diverse people to occur, all people involved in a societal process of collaboration on issues of community importance would have to change their traditional approach of debate, to one of finding value in what any other person says. For this to happen, one has to change one's approach to listening. No longer will one listen to find fault—this leads to debate. In the future for true collaboration to occur, one will listen to affirm the other person and find some value in what is being said, without accepting all comments as truth. Thus, when adding this idea of dialogue within a futures context, a concept of "generative dialogue" will emerge.

• Focus on the use of the Internet, multimedia and telecommunications. New tools of communication open up totally new vistas of learning. Not only does the Internet give any individual the ability to find any information in the world instantaneously (greatly minimizing the value of the concept of teacher as content provider), it also allows the ability to introduce new concepts and methods of learning (such as computer simulations). *As we move to a society of continuous innovation, electronic means of learning will be integrated with face-to-face dialogue of generative discussion.* In addition, telecommunications will allow individualized information gathering at the same time that it provides a platform for real-time group discussion.

• Develop a new system of evaluation to judge the systemic integration of core competencies, the ability to ask appropriate questions, and the ability to connect disparate ideas in continuous innovation. *As knowledge explodes, the ability to know will lessen in importance and the ability to connect knowledge with innovation and creativity within a futures context will increase in importance.*

• Utilize the technologies of the day to ensure real-time curriculum. Textbooks are often obsolete as soon as they are published. The risk of including new theories and ideas can be met with resistance from many sources, including educators, who are supposed to be open to new ideas. The future will open new ways to provide information. Modules of knowledge will come in many forms—articles, web sites, teleconferences, and, yes, sections of books (but usually not textbooks). *The role of the learning coach will adapt to the use of new curriculum as part of a continuous, evolving, dynamic system of learning concepts.*

• Build webs of learners throughout an organization and community. Understand that the subpatterns of change will demand a new concept of individual learner—one who relishes the interplay of learning for oneself and learning for others simultaneously. The ideas of "learning webs" will be added to Peter Senge's popularization of the idea of "learning communities." *Although many people have accepted the idea of learning communities, few have realized that the traditional concept of standardized learning will prevent a true "learning community" to evolve in effective ways.* As organisms and organizations become larger and more complex, their existence and integrity can only be maintained if small units continuously form and are held together with new mechanisms that emerge as a result of a new environment. This is true of the development of DNA and cells, physical ecological systems, and even communities. *Until educational and community citizens and leaders begin to understand the concepts of complexity, parallel processes, and non-linear systemic change, it will be difficult for any community to become a learning community.*

## Webs of Learning in a Community

Web themes (under many names) are already bubbling in society at large. Similar rules apply up and down the line. Three big insights—learning, collaboration, and intricacy—give more substance to the kinds of changes we need.

> The way to create a sustainable civilization is...to figure out how to cultivate intricacy. We already have some clues. Intricacy is encouraged by education, empowerment, infrastructure, mutual support, liberation, and love. It grows best when fertilized and organized in circles with human faces and common-cause. It grows best when spurred by binding ideals like liberty, equality, justice, compassion, and when serving a higher design. It requires lots of lessons about how to encourage collaboration, creativity, and distributed concern.
> —Sally Goerner, *After the Clockwork Universe*

My friend Sally combines authentic humility, a towering intellect, and a sense of historical meaning. Within the wisdom of her insights is one mechanism of twenty-first century learning—*the need for intricacy.* Intricacy refers to the order that arises from interweaving. I will add another key parameter for tomorrow's learning framework—*a need for intimacy.*

One of the most important attributes of understanding how to evolve a twenty-first century learning environment in any community is to connect structure, content, process, capacity building, and emergent meaning in a simultaneous dance of movement. In a society of dynamic change, the structure of learning found in the creation, distribution, and testing of knowledge is transformed into small and dynamic webs (networks of diverse people, organizations, and ideas), object-oriented curricula (smaller modules of information), interdependent questions (the interplay of learners and learning coaches), multiple learning styles and media, and learning leaders (coaches and facilitators instead of providers of information only).

The very nature of the learning experience changes as the needs of society expand. With more choices come more connections. More connections bring tension to standard answers. The explosion of knowledge exposes the inability of a teacher to "know." *Quickness of needs demands quickness of response; complexity of issues requires interaction of talents in intimacy and intricacy.* The need to tell others is superseded by the need to ask. If knowing is asking and knowledge is generative, what is the role of learning? It is transformed from knowledge acquisition (competencies of knowing) only to a system of creative thinking within a futures context. *The very nature of learning becomes the creative interaction of diverse people, ideas, and technology to ensure that innovations of thinking are applied to test the assumptions and values that undergird our constantly changing society.* The present emphasis of education to build skills for employability will soon be balanced with the art of thinking about why, *as the issue of meaning for life again takes center stage.*

My silent generation was taught to gain knowledge by listening so that others would listen when *my* experience earned *me* the right to tell them what to. The baby boomers carried the idea of individualism to levels never intended by those who were our libertarian forefathers. The early leaders of individual independence understood the importance of the concept of community. We now watch as cutthroat competition and narrowed truths (confusing the idea of "what I interpret to be truth" with truth itself) cause increasing social dysfunction. In his book *The Crisis of Capitalism*, George Soros warns of the disconnection of our economic, social, and political sectors, reminding us of Adam Smith's admonition in *Theory of Moral Sentiments* (1759) that any economic pursuit separated from a context of ethics and community morality would ultimately slide the society into a wasteland of greed and corruption.

> In societies where individuals enjoy more freedom of choice than at any other time in history, people resent all the more the few remaining ligatures that bind them. The danger for such societies is that people suddenly find themselves socially isolated, free to associate with everyone but unable to make the moral commitments that will connect them to other people in true communities.
> —*The Great Disruption*, Francis Fukuyama

The X'ers and the Net Generation yearn for a sense of real intimacy lost in their parents search for individualism. When Toffler (1972) identified acceleration in the pace of society, he warned of the strain in community where learning is defined only in individualistic terms. Fukuyama and Putnam have now brought forth the principle of social connectedness and laid it in our laps. Is it knowledge we have been given, or a call for learning—or both?

*Learning can be a process where people help each other to be successful, not just economically, but as moral and ethical people as well.* Interactive learning can help us lose the insecurity of finding our place in the world, and give us the potential to be a part of networks of many people who are creating a new and vital culture for the future of our children and grandchildren.

Alexis de Toqueville was greatly intrigued by the internal contradiction of America's sense of community and yet strong demand for individuality. One of his most important observations is as valid today as it was in 1832: "Don't think that Americans' emphasis on accumulating wealth is for it's own sake...it is a search for identity."

An emphasis on a new concept of interactive and transformational learning to build a new 21st century culture could bring diverse people into a new environment where meaning comes from using new methods, concepts, ideas, and techniques to build a society capable of integrating the needs of individuals and the needs of community. *What better way to provide individual and community meaning than by creating a new concept of intimacy brought about by the connections of learning.*

## The New Concomitance

*The world of either/or is being left behind.* As connections increase, increased concomitance occurs. Things that appeared once separate are now seen as linked in association. And so learning is transformed by increased interactions. A traditional, linear learning framework assumes that there is *one* reason for the dysfunction. As leaders, we ask the question (usually a policy question), what is *the* cause of social dysfunction in our communities? *The very nature of how we frame the question—based on how traditional education has taught us to think—often precludes our ability to resolve issues.* There are many factors interacting simultaneously to impact the issue of social dysfunction—poverty, lack of personal initiative, learning disabilities, governmental policies, breakup of the family unit, etc.

In other words, there is no standard answer to any changing situation. Each situation, though fundamentally the same at first glance, always has different factors at work that make it unique. It gets more complex when there is constant interaction. The very nature of our growing interdependency influences content and context at the same time. Consider social and learning situations, where many interactions occur all the time.

For example, many of us were taught that individual meaning came from individual achievement and recognition. Yet some young people seem to be saying there is no meaning without family, and others look to spiritual reasons for meaning. In the past, we would have asked the question, "Who is right?" That is the right question if the underlying theories of learning are supported by the assumption that all things (to include reasons for meaning) exist independently of each other, and that one factor is in control.

*However, in an interdependent world, questions need to be phrased differently, i.e.,* "What value can be found in what you say, or in the interplay of all factors that interact to create meaning for this particular situation?" This is not to say that all statements are true, all opinions are valid, all values appropriate, or that there is truth in all aspects of what we do. This approach does reflect the need for new questions that look for ways to "connect" appropriate ideas and actions, whether designing a new product, analyzing a complex situation, or building a new foundation for a set of ideas to explain meaning in a constantly changing world.

And so we come to the idea of concomitance. Concomitance is "connection and interaction without being separate." Why is there a need for citizens to have an understanding of concomitance in the 21st century? *Because we live in an interdependent world, and interaction with each other in daily life changes not only who we are, but the situation in which we find ourselves.* Thus, as we create the content of life through out actions, we are also changing the context—and a never-ending dance of new realities emerges, usually with increased complexity (consider the impact of the Internet on all of our lives).

Apply this idea to the concept of learning. When I was a school-board chairman for a county in North Carolina in 1980, I remember talking to a speaker from Chicago who had come to our community to work with teachers and administrators on the idea of learning styles. It was a new concept for most of us. She proposed (backed up with several years of research) that there were four learning styles, not just an auditory (lecturing) one. In fact, she suggested that only 8% of all people learn through the mechanism of lecturing. I learn content best if I write down what I want to remember, like 4% of the population. However, I connect disparate facts, factors, ideas and situations for innovation easily. I began to understand that as we discover more content of information, and begin to apply it in order to change our actions, we are impacting the context of the situation.

As a result of the new input about learning styles, those teachers interested changed some of the context (that over which they had control) in their teaching and in their own learning experiences. Later, some of them discovered new methods that they tested and that were concomitant (connected and not separate) with past experience, changing the context of the learning experience for themselves and some of their students.

*We are moving to a new age involving many players in an interaction of learning experiences, where the content and context are constantly changing and ultimately seen as inseparable,* yet always moving in a new cosmic dance of concomitance. The emphasis on "content only" will shift to one of an interplay of content and context. Outcomes will loop in a feedback mechanism to actually change the original context.

As we change our filters of learning, we will see a new world of changing hues, patterns, constant interactions, and parallel processes. We will be forced to ask different questions. We will look for new connections. Old facts will crumble as we change the context, and the new facts that emerge will interact to change the context of the original situation and how we see the world. *We are now in a quantum society where multiple questions lead to multiple answers.*

## A Starting Point

If transformational learning evokes a new vocabulary—webs of intricacy and intimacy, content as context, integrated and parallel processes, capacities for transformation, concomitant meaning—how does a community begin the journey, and where will it end? What actions can be taken so that any local community is able to prepare itself for the challenges of an interdependent society, whose underlying assumptions will emerge only as we learn to think differently?

I have a friend who is president of a chamber of commerce in a medium-sized community in Texas. He finds himself in the middle of a transition of power in the community from a benevolent dictator who got things done to a time of broadened involvement but slower action. And, as usual, the cry, "Where is our community leadership?" has erupted. His dilemma is how to build simultaneous bridges among people, ideas, cultural gaps, and differing historical perceptions—all at the same time.

As we talked, I led by asking questions, and giving opinions when asked directly—but mainly I listened. Eventually the chamber president offered his opinion: *"I guess we need to build relationships and have people learn to think differently if we are going to get anything done."* From there, we evolved to the idea of thinking about the need for a futures context to allow diverse people to get past their preconceived notions. And we talked about the need to have only those interested and open to new ideas as a starting group for dialogue. He thought, and then ventured that he probably could find six or seven people in his community leadership who would fit those criteria. And that's where we will start—a dialogue among six or seven people who are willing to listen, be open to new ideas, and see the importance of thinking about the future in new ways.

## Rethinking Structure

Peter Senge points out the need to change mindsets when establishing a learning community. I believe we have to develop "mindflex," using my wife's good term. If there is continuous change in our future, moving from one mindset to another will not be enough. When Tom Peters used the phase "thriving on chaos," he focused on a quality (capacity) that would be important to the future of learning.

*To be open to new ideas, one must thrive on the idea of transformation.* One must continuously search for patterns where none seem to exist. One must be able to see the whole at the same time that small "webs of intricacy" form in connection, to allow new complex patterns to emerge. Just as one is taught to see the "big picture" and "what's in front of you" at the same time when learning to drive, we must be able to step back to see how to form dynamic structures as we link small networks of people and institutions.

When moving from a world of large hierarchies and standard answers to one of complex webs and multiple answers, our ideas of structure must be rethought. We must relearn how to learn, and rethink how dynamic yet stable structures can occur—and biology becomes our guide.

> "The new biology contains a tremendous heresy. The main way life has become more complex is through cooperation! Organisms band together for mutual benefit. Cooperative groups survive better than individuals. Over time some cooperatives become so tightly coupled that they become an inseparable whole, a new "unity" as biologists call it. This incredible integration turns out to be the basis of the stepladder of life. Thus, specialists working together have an evolutionary edge over an organism which tries to do life all alone. The way to create dynamic strength, therefore, is to follow a new theme— specialize and integrate."
>
> —Sally Goerner, *Beyond the Clockwork World*

For a community to learn to think about itself in new ways and integrate "new specialties into an integrated whole," *it must first find a way to build the capacity to learn about new ideas.* A community also must have leadership who can appreciate the need to talk about new ideas as well as "doing something." It must begin to utilize the idea of parallel processes. While many people work on issues, some people will need to think about new ideas. Any community must relearn how to learn.

And so the concept of "webs of intricacy" arises. When any large system reaches a point of instability, it breaks apart. When any educational system gets too big, it loses it ability to learn. New business studies show that about 200 people are optimum for interaction in manufacturing units. Facilitation has shown that ten to twelve people is optimum. When eighty people need to talk, what occurs? Four groups of twenty people are formed and then reconnected at the end of any process.

If a chamber executive has only six or seven people who are open and interested in talking about new ideas, if 200 people is an optimum size for a manufacturing plant, if ten to twelve people is optimum for a dialogue group, maybe nature is telling us something. For true transformation to occur, we need to build webs of small groups who are interested in generative dialogue to understand what is happening and why. When initially forming new learning experiences for people to think about the future, build small networks of interested people—"webs of intricacy." Let any action to be taken come from the dialogue of those involved. Don't preset the outcome and control the process. Why start small? Because only those interested will take the time and listen to each other and to new ideas. In addition, any major effort to transform ideas and actions at the front end of any process will cause traditionalists to feel threatened because their filter of understanding will be different from ideas that are transformative. What is needed is a system of multiple processes that allows all people to join in appropriate ways to think about the future. While many structures and concepts need transforming, there are traditional ideas that can be updated and become a part of any overall transformative system. The search for spiritual meaning by individuals from throughout the world in an age of constant change is one example of how basic traditional concepts can be updated and integrated into appropriate new learning experiences (for example, John Polkinhorne, a particle physicist and Anglican Bishop in England, is working to bridge the gap between science and religion).

Over time, as communities build small networks of learning in different places, for different reasons, with different people, under different conditions, new ideas slowly will begin to filter into the thinking and activities of many organizations. New approaches will begin to occur. New ideas will begin to be accepted.

With the use of parallel processes, small groups of interested people will be able to work on new ideas within the frameworks of pilot efforts, while traditionalists will still be able to continue business as usual—but begin to have dialogue from time to time about new approaches. *Those interested in relearning for a different future will learn directly. Those that initially don't see the need to rethink their traditional assumptions will be able indirectly to learn over time, often without even realizing it.*

## Rethinking Content

Traditional learning has always been focused on providing content, or so it seemed. Students answered true/false tests and gave the one best answer—and then those same students entered business and found out the meaning of the term "art of the possible." Any worker in an organization of any size understands the difference between providing the best answer and providing one that those in authority will accept. Only the very brave and very comfortable challenge this age-old "reality."

When one idea predominates any part of the society, content is constant. We learned that scarcity of land, labor, and capital were the basic principles of economics (now the idea of increasing returns is a new rule of the new economy); we learned that lecturing was the way to teach (and now we have four learning styles and many more methods); and we learned that elected officials had all the power (now look at the use of referenda, or the way the Internet brought 60,000 people to protest the World Trade Organization meeting in Seattle).

In a relatively static world standards were easy to develop and apply. But standard answers no longer work in a changing world. So how do we look at the future? How can we prepare a community to think differently, if traditionally all of the citizens have been trained in one way of thinking? Remember, in a constantly changing world, there will always be an interplay between context and content.

Several years ago, one of my Pennsylvania associates, Lewis Jaffe, coined the phrase, *"They don't know that they don't know."* I think back twenty years and remember when I didn't know about learning styles, or non-linear thinking, or the use of the Internet. They all existed in primitive forms (compared to today), but I didn't know they existed—and I didn't know that I didn't know. Today each of these things is a basic tool of our Communities of the Future work. In fact, we have established a concept called "local twenty-first century thinks-tanks" to help interested local citizens learn about future trends. On purpose, we don't jump to action; we spend time dialoguing about trends and how a futures context can be developed.

## A Futures Context

Those of us involved in the nationally evolving Communities of the Future network have begun to focus on the need to evolve a futures context in local communities. We have concluded that a key obstacle to preparing local communities for the twenty-first century is the need to have citizen leaders comfortable with the transformational changes occurring in the society.

There are two key issues. *One, to become familiar with future trends and their interactive impact. Two, to rethink underlying assumptions that support the cherished beliefs of how we educate and learn, how we lead, how we do economic development, how we govern, even how we think.* Without removing these obstacles to transformational change, few people will be able to develop a twenty-first century filter based on the way society is organizing itself.

All communities can take two important actions to begin the process of evolving a twenty-first century learning environment, leading to the creation of a futures context for each local area: 1) Establish networks of local twenty-first century think-tanks for fifteen to twenty-five people at the time. 2) Focus on the introduction of trends that will impact local communities, to include:

• By the year 2004, it is expected that 70% of all houses will have computers.
• By 2008, speech recognition will be available for all computers.
• By 2013, 30-35% of all diseases will be treated using genetic therapy

in combination with telemedicine.

• By 2015, only 4-8% of jobs will be provided by direct manufacturing.

• By the year 2018, it is expected that over 50% of all goods and services will be bought over the Internet.

These and other trends can be introduced into the dialogue to help citizens understand that their ways of doing things need to change. *As an example, if business trends evolve as expected, local economic developers need to begin to build "capacities for the digital economy" right away.*

A second action that local community colleges can take is to establish "futures institutes" to help develop a base of interest in the future within the faculty and student body, as well as in the community. It is interesting that in a time of immense change, few administrators have recognized that their graduates will not be effectively prepared unless the concept of identifying trends of the future is integrated into the curricula. Although it is often difficult to distinguish between fads, trends, and outright foolishness, unless local communities begin to learn to think within the framework the future, there is little chance that actions taken will be connected to a context of what is coming, instead of what has already occurred. *The trick for communities will be to learn how to integrate appropriate values that give people real meaning, develop effective processes of decision-making, and build capacities for transformation—all at the same time.*

## Rethinking Process

Traditional community processes have been predominately exclusive. The opportunity to lead was earned over time and the knowledge of the past was passed on to the "up-and-coming" leadership as the years passed. All that was necessary was to combine traditional knowledge with experience, and one could lead. The processes of decision-making were relatively simple and usually top-down. In most small communities, a few made decisions for the many.

In the future, the emerging complexity of society and the real-time information available due to improved technologies ensures that more and more people will have the opportunity to be involved with decisions that affect their lives. A great challenge is to evolve a civic environment that encourages people to participate. Leaders will be faced with the contradiction that as many people drop out, others will want to have more control over issues that impact their lives.

> As we approach the twenty-first century, America is turning into an electronic republic, a democratic system that is vastly increasing the people's day to day influence on the decisions of state.
> —Larry Grossman, *Electronic Republic*

As the electronic infrastructure increases in use, more and more people will expect to give their opinions, not as input, but as a part of the decision. One learning experience that will be needed will be to evolve methods of direct electronic involvement. A second will be to have a family of processes integrated in parallel to allow different sizes and types of groups opportunities to impact their communities for the common good.

## Framing a Learning Community

The idea of integrated and parallel processes is based on the new theories of chaos and complexity. Over the last twenty years, the idea of community-based strategic planning processes, called visioning or futuring processes, were developed to involve more people in setting the agenda and making decisions for any local community. *The strength of this process is that it quickly develops specific ideas, and task forces are established to implement any concept developed by the overall group.* It is appropriate to have action taken within a reasonable period of time.

The limitation of this approach is that it requires everyone to agree on an action and does not allow transformational ideas to evolve. Another limitation is that such a process is usually presented as representing the entire community, when usually less that 1% of the citizens have been involved. With lessening levels of trust in local communities, it is increasingly difficult to "sell" an idea to citizens, as often expressed by local elected officials.

In the future, local elected officials will be faced with the challenge of building a shared vision within a constantly changing society. "Selling an idea" will soon lose much of its appeal as a concept, as more leaders understand the need to integrate many citizen ideas in newly structured processes of decision-making.

It is suggested that any "learning community" will need to establish parallel processes, where strategic planning is done in parallel to community research and development process projects. Usually small groups of interested people will work together to develop an innovative idea based on the trends of the future. Any idea is designed to be tested in the community.

No matter whether immediately successful or not, learning occurs. The results are fed back to the group and others in the community, and the next adaptation will include new ideas based on the experience of the first or second implementation of the new concept.

*Any community will need to rethink its learning process.* Old ideas of failure will need to be recast as a part of learning. Some of the situations in my life that would have been considered failures using traditional methods of assessment became the greatest learning.

Therefore, leaders will need to help develop environments where people are not afraid to fail, but encouraged to risk and try in new ways and in new contexts.

## Rethinking Capacity

Experience has always been the capacity builder for any community. Apprenticeship programs have been used for years to prepare the next generation. It was their personalized learning experience, because what had worked in the past would work in the future. Such a concept by itself is not appropriate for an increasingly complex, always changing society. In a world of constant innovation, new knowledge will always have to be linked and applied in new ways to that which exists.

*The idea of traditional capacity-building will shift in a "learning community" to one of "building capacities for transformation."* Any community will need to rethink how to introduce new concepts and test them, always providing feedback for what works and what doesn't.

## Suggested Community Actions

There are many ways to build capacities for transformation. Let's define what is meant by the concept of "capacities for transformation." The Center for Communities of the Future defines five such capacities:

- Evolving a futures context.
- Developing process leaders who are able to help network and integrate innovative ideas, people, and organizations within a futures context.
- Creating and expanding an electronic infrastructure.
- Developing an environment of the common good for the 21st century where the old idea of "self-interest, rightly understood" is transformed in an interdependent society to that of "helping each other succeed."
- Helping citizens develop twenty-first century skills such as the ability to access the Internet, facilitating small groups, and understanding how to network diverse people.

*A "learning community" will begin to realize the importance of establishing full-time master capacity builders to work with people and organizations to help them build capacities for transformation.* For example, a "community capacity builder" on the staff of any city could be responsible for such needs as preparing citizens for electronic town meetings or working with the chamber of commerce to develop process leaders.

## Rethinking Meaning

Several recent studies are telling. One reflects the fact that many aging baby boomers wish they had spent more time with relationship building and not professional achievement. *Another recent poll found that 43% of those polled thought values was the most important issue for the 2000 election.*

More and more. the idea of meaning for life slips into the dialogue of people in local communities. Seldom has this idea had more power than when cast against the tragedy of Columbine. What does it say for a society whose traditional economic indicators are out the roof, yet many of its youth are in poverty and groups of children see suicide as a reasonable act? *Ecclesiastes notes, "Where there is no vision, the people perish." A 2000 update would add "where there is no vision and meaning..."*

Several commentators have recently observed that the lack of balance of values disconnects the society. The fact that optimization of any factor in a system destroys the system is appropriate for today's society. *If meaning cannot be found in individual materialism by itself, there is a need for any learning society and community to evolve a concept of "concomitant meaning" that integrates a balance of values into a dynamic context providing vitality and a sense of purpose as we enter the 21st century.*

## Taking the First Step

Start slowly. Develop small, yet diverse "generative dialogue" groups to begin a discussion of what they think will give meaning in the twenty-first century. Call each a "twenty-first century values conversation." Include many young adults. Coach facilitators in the art of generative dialogue. Introduce articles and excerpts from periodicals and books to help evolve the conversation within a futures context. Utilize many of the following ideas in the context of the dialogue:

- Relationship building
- Concepts of spirituality
- Helping each other succeed
- How to create openness
- Needs of a family
- Thinking systemically
- Building a futures context
- Networking for capacity building
- The twenty-first century individual in an interdependent society

The idea of values is an important one. For too long we have taken for granted what is of value for us as individuals and families and communities, and have come up wanting. "I gave you everything..." "But not yourself, Daddy."

## Conclusion

We are at a historical divide without the ability to use tools from the past to guide us. Seldom in history have men and women had a chance to impact the future of civilization in such potentially positive or disastrous ways.

*At the heart of our challenge is the need to change who we are at the same time that we change our institutions and communities.* An even greater challenge is the need to recognize that we must transform our society, not reform it by making old ways more efficient.

The future of learning is at stake. It is both a goal and a mechanism. If we don't work to change how we see the learning experience, we will just rearrange the deck chairs on the *Titanic*. If we don't build capacities of transformational learning in our communities, we will not be able to make the new learning experiences extensive enough to build a critical mass for our society. *Of most importance, we must forget the concept of failure.* Without a new concept of learning, there will be no success. Radical individualism must be viewed as insecurity and cast away. We must learn a form of collaboration that will require both the strength of a more mature individuality and the capacity for deepened and authentic relationships within an interdependent world. It is our destiny to be given the opportunity to develop a concept of learning that brings people together all over the world in a cosmic dance of meaning.

## For Further Reading

Francis Fukuyama, *The Great Disruption*. The Free Press, 1999.

Sally Goerner, *Beyond the Clockwork World*. 1999

Lawrence Grossman, *The Electronic Republic*. New York: Penguin Books, 1995.

Virginia Postrel, *The Future and Its Enemies*. The Free Press, 1999

Richard Restak, MD, *The Brain*. Bantam Books, 1985.

Sir Charles Sherrington, quoted in Restak, *The Brain*.

Andrew Cohill, Ph.D., and Joseph Kruth (ed.s) *Pathways to Sustainability*.

## About the Author

Rick Smyre is the President of the Center for Communities of the Future and a nationally recognized futurist whose focus is in the area of "building capacities for transformation" for local communities. He has published several articles, including "Beyond the Deck Chairs" in the summer '98 Futures Quarterly Journal of the World Future Society. Contact Rick Smyre at RLSmyre@aol.com

*Part Five*

# INFORMATION
# AND
# CONTACTS

# Directory of Resources

THIS IS BY NO MEANS a comprehensive listing, but it suggests what sorts of models, organizations and publications already exist. These are some of the pioneers exploring new ways of teaching, learning, and building community. They show what is possible. We hope their stories will inspire many others to follow.

## Existing Community-Based and Other Alternative Learning Centers (in zip-code order)

### Pathfinder Center

P.O. Box 804, Amherst, MA 01004 USA / 256 North Pleasant Street, Amherst, MA 01002 USA
Contact: Ken Danford or Joshua Hornick
Phone: 413-253-9412 / E-mail: plc@valinet.com or ken@pathfindercenter.org
URL: http://www.pathfindercenter.org
Pathfinder provides services for families and activities for teens that make teen homeschooling practical and successful for any family. See Joshua Hornick's essay, "Pathfinder Center," in this book for more information.

### Living Routes—Ecovillage Educational Consortium

72 Baker Road, Shutesbury, MA 01072-9703 USA
Contact: Daniel Greenberg, program director
Phone: 888-515-7333 or 413-259-0025 / Fax: 413-259-1255 / E-mail: routes@ecovillage.org
URL: http://www.gaia.org/LivingRoutes
The mission of Living Routes is to develop and support a diverse, yet coordinated set of ecovillage-based educational programs that empower participants to

help build a sustainable future. At its core is a growing set of semester and summer programs that provide deep and direct experiences with the concepts, skills, and tools of sustainable living. In these programs, students create their own "learning communities" within "living communities" as they help design and build ecological structures, learn effective methods of decision-making and conflict resolution, research sustainable strategies, support each other's personal and spiritual growth, and work to enhance the health of wider communities and ecosystems.

An integral part of Living Routes' vision is to develop a network of research, development, and demonstration sites focusing on sustainable technologies, land use strategies, and social patterns. Research projects integrated into Living Routes programs that compare these systems within participating communities and campuses will provide premier educational opportunities for students and interns, vital input for ecovillage development, and excellent venues in which to make these learnings available to the broader public. Living Routes will work closely with the Global Ecovillage Network and a consortium of ecovillages, academic institutions, and other organizations to create an international "communiversity" that is global in scope, yet bioregional in focus. Programs are now being developed at the Findhorn Foundation, Crystal Waters, Green Kibbutzim, and North American ecovillages.

## NetSchool of Maine

145 Maine Street, Brunswick, ME 04011 USA
Contact: Frank J. Heller, MPA, founder/proprietor
Phone: 207-729-6090
URL: http://www.netschoolofmaine.com

NetSchool of Maine is an Internet-based, instructional and home-education alternative and supplement for parents and learners of all ages. It is a large, well-maintained storehouse of information and resources on distance learning and education. It is partially maintained by advertisers and parents/students who use its consulting services, and partially by its parent, Global Village Learning of Brunswick, ME. Technical details, success stories, how-to manuals, distance-learning scholarships, technology trends, and other extremely useful and hard-to-obtain information is on this site. With its growing list of tutors and mentors, NetSchool is well positioned to apply as a distance-learning based charter school for Maine.

## Pine Tree Folk School

RR 2, Box 7162, Carmel, ME 04419-9651 USA
Contact: Jan Falk
Phone: 207-848-2433 / Fax: 603-825-0341 / E-mail: jgfalk@mint.net
URL: http://www.mint.net/folkschool

Pine Tree Folk School is a non-profit organization founded by Maine activists who are committed to providing education for social change. We bring to our work many years of experience in economic empowerment, labor, peace, and women's issues, as well as skills in group facilitation and adult learning.

Pine Tree Folk School supports people of Maine's efforts to take collective action to shape their own destiny.

Our latest project is the "Computer Help Network," which uses popular education principles to help grassroots organizations work together to learn how to make better use of information technology.

# Liberty School—A Democratic Learning Community

P.O. Box 857, Blue Hill, ME 04614-0857 USA
Contact: Arnold Greenberg, director
Phone: 207-374-2886 / E-mail: LIBSCHOOL@Netscape.net or grnbrg@downeast.net
URL: http://ellsworth.org/liberty/

Liberty School offers students in grades 9-12 a diverse and innovative educational program that merges challenging and creative academic studies with artistic work and other educational opportunities.

It is vital for everyone affiliated with the school—students, parents, and faculty—to feel that Liberty School is their school, and each individual is an important member of the school community. Students serve on the Community Council in charge of managing the school, are represented on the Board of Directors, and are involved in all aspects of running the school with faculty and parents. They play a large part in determining their own education rather than being forced to pursue a predetermined curriculum. They have significant choices available for gaining meaningful knowledge and experiences ranging from a variety of courses offered by faculty to independent projects to travel and foreign study opportunities. We hope to develop responsible individuals who can use their knowledge to pursue more knowledge and become fulfilled, self-aware, and alert to the surrounding world.

Liberty School is an independent school, approved by the Maine Department of Education to receive tuition from towns that do not have their own high schools. Liberty School is in the process of beginning a 13th year called Homesteading and Community. This program will be a one-year experience in growing and preserving food, building solar shelters, living cooperatively and learning to live a more home-centered existence in the twenty-first century.

# The Community School

Box 555, Camden, ME 04843 USA
Contact: Emanuel Pariser, co-director
Phone: 207-763-3498 or 207-236-3000 / Fax: 207-236-2505 / E-mail: emanuel@cschool.acadia.net
URL: http://www.thecommunityschool.org

See Emanuel Pariser's essay, "The Community School: Developing the Approach of 'Relational Education,'" in this book for more information.

# The Free School

8 Elm Street, Abany, NY 12202 USA
Contact: Chris Mercogliano
Phone: 518-434-3072 / E-mail: albanyfreeschool@yahoo.com
URL: http://www.empireone.net/~freeschool

See Mary Leue's essay, "Which Way: Top-Down or Bottom-Up? The Story of the Albany Free School," in this book for more information.

# The Teen Community Center Project

312 East Seneca Street, Ithaca, NY 14850-4312 USA
Contact: Patrick Walkinshaw
Phone: 607-273-1888

The Teen Community Center Project is an independent non-profit that is dedicated to providing a safe gathering space for teens to self-define and be empowered to take responsibility for their lives. This teen-run and -directed effort supports individual learning and creative expression as well as provides a place for local teens to belong to a supportive community of peers and adult allies.

# Upattinas School and Resource Center

429 Greenridge Road, Glenmoore, PA 19343-8931 USA
Contact: Sandra (Sandy) M. Hurst, director
Phone: 610-458-5138 / Fax: 610-458-8688 / E-mail: upatinas@chesco.com
URL: http://www.chesco.com/upattinas

A family cooperative, democratic learning center for K-12 that offers full- and part-time day programs and full home-education support, including enrollment and graduation. PA Private Academic School License and approval to grant Form I-20 for immigration. Open, relaxed, joyful learning environment where everyone participates in decision-making, both about their own learning and the policies of the center. Certified teachers, community aides, families as hosts to foreign students. Extensive travel and camping program.

# Meeting Ground

605 Mountain Gap Drive, Huntsville, AL 35803-1629 USA
Contact: Lisa Bugg
Phone: 256-882-0208 / E-mail: KaeKaeB@aol.com

Meeting Ground is a small group of people connecting and creating community in the Northern Alabama area. Our first line of connection has been through homeschooling, but we are slowly growing beyond that single networking strand. Searching for deeper meaning within our family lives and ourselves has brought us many joys and many hurdles to cross. Our focus is on learning, both for children and for families. We share resources, ideas, and time. We are slowly putting together a list of tutors, mentors, and opportunities in the community for learners of all kinds.

# The Home Education Resource Center of Central Ohio

3589 East Main Street, Columbus, OH 43213 USA
Contact: Belinda Augustus
Phone: 614-237-0004

About seven people form the core group of homeschoolers that have gotten this resource center going. Our main idea was to provide a way for homeschoolers to have access to books and materials, especially those that it would be too expensive for families to purchase individually. We wanted to have available the kinds of materials that a family might just use once or occasionally—expensive items like microscopes and skeletons.

Many organizations have materials, equipment, and curricula that they are giving out for free to schools, but they aren't as receptive to giving them to a homeschooling family because they would rather know that the materials are being used by a larger group. As a resource center, we can assure donors that their materials will be used by a large group of children. Most of the materials in our library have been donated from corporations and foundations. The Ohio Department of Natural Resources has materials they're willing to just hand out to groups. Other materials have come from families who used something once and no longer need it. Another way we get materials for the library is through families' participation in book clubs like Scholastic and Carnival. Finally, we are able to get free samples from vendors because we offer to keep their catalogs available with the sample. In the future, we may decide to purchase items and then rent them out at a very low-cost—say $5 a use—until they are paid for. Before opening the Resource Center, we had been running a homeschool library with books and materials out of my house, but it was outgrowing my home and was difficult to keep organized. We thought it would be wonderful to have this lending library available in a more accessible space. The other reason for starting the Resource Center was to have a place that could house support-group meetings, classes, and workshops. Libraries and recreation centers have been supportive and many homeschoolers' meetings have been held in those places, but they are often a low priority for these institutions. The library might easily bump the homeschoolers' monthly meeting for something else.

We wanted a regular space just providing support for homeschoolers. All the resources are right there, including homeschooling magazines, legal information, and the chance to tap into a network of others. Homeschoolers who return their children to school generally do so within two years, and it's likely that this is because they have not tapped into a community. We wanted to make that easier.

Finding a space was of course the big challenge. At first we thought of rehabbing an old building, but that would have been a great deal of work. Finally we found an old school building that is rented out to various groups—a preschool, church groups, etc. When we were figuring out how to support the center financially, we decided that active members—people who regularly attend classes and workshops—would pay $10 a month. Those just coming to support-group meetings or using the reading room are not charged. Members outside the immediate area pay $30 a year for borrowing privileges from the library, and if they want to take a class or workshop, they just donate a couple of dollars at that time. Our rent is $550 a month including utilities, so we knew that we would need fifty-five families paying the active member rate to make this work. I looked at how many families were actively using the library when it was at my house and decided it was likely we would find enough people. We're going into it with close to forty families signed up, and since I'm getting about one call a day right now, I feel confident that as the school year begins and the word spreads, we will find the remaining families we need.

The space we have is one large room, a former office, with partitions so that one end is the library, another has chairs and a carpet for the babies to crawl on, and the other area is a large open space for classes and workshops. We have regular weekly Spanish class scheduled, as well as a photography project and a geography club that will prepare for the National Geography Bee. We are fortunate to have two talented science instructors among our parents who will give hands-on workshops. It's wonderful to have workshops that are parent-led. One of the ideas that has been the cornerstone of this resource center is that each of us possesses some talent and if we had an opportunity to share it, we can tap into those talents. There are so many wonderful programs that the community will bring to the schools, and now that we have an organized center, they are delighted to bring those programs to us as well. Families, of course, take as few or as many workshops as they want. As for the library, our rules for borrowing are that families can borrow materials as long as they like, until a second family requests that material. At that time, the first family has two weeks to return the item. Running the library from my home, I found that the system worked well. (From *Growing Without Schooling*, #131, Nov./Dec., 1999, pp. 20-21.)

# The Rainbow Dragons

35 Vermont Avenue, Youngstown, OH 44512-1122 USA
Contact: Deborah Harding
Phone: 330-782-8982 / E-mail: musik1@earthlink.net

We are homeschoolers related to a 4-H group. We have kids in grades 1 through 11. Some of the things we have implemented this year are a borrowing library of resources including textbooks, a newsletter that the kids write, a newsletter for the parents, field trips, and study groups. The study groups are age specific. For example, we take a different country every month and find web pages for the kids to read. We put up multiple-choice questions on a quiz page for reinforcement. Then we might find someone from that country to come and speak to the kids. For example, for Japan we have a speaker, the kids get together to do some origami and calligraphy projects, and the last night of the project we all make a Japanese meal and eat it on the floor with bathrobes (for kimonos) on. These projects really involve the kids.

# Heart 'n' Home School

3104 Creek Ridge Drive, NewAlbany, IN 47150-9512 USA
Contact: Angela Zimmerman
E-mail: sweetland1@juno.com or angelaz@mindspring.com

We number about one hundred fifty families (about four hundred school-age children), and are in our eighth year as a group. We have been able to do many things as a group, including some regularly meeting co-ops teaching various topics, a cross-country running team, Hebrew and Spanish language classes, partnerships for tutoring, as well as science fairs, drama camp, art classes/fairs, Keepers and Contenders for the Faith groups, field trips, etc. These are things we provide for the children. We also provide support for mothers through monthly meetings where we hire professionals to teach us on various topics of education or we share our curriculum on a given topic in smaller discussion groups. We provide a monthly newsletter and "one-list" to the group as well.

# Reach Homeschool Group

2525 Patrick Henry Street, Auburn Hills, MI 48326-2326 USA
Contact: April Morris
E-mail: 2morris@oakland.edu

We are an inclusive homeschool group open to anyone homeschooling for any reason with any method. All we ask is that respect is shown for each individual's reasons and methods. We meet monthly at the local public library for a general meeting and have monthly field trips. We meet weekly for classes.

This is our first year, so we are still "learning as we go!" We meet on Wednesday afternoon and alternate each week with science or art. And meeting each week are two German classes and two French classes. We have divided the classes loosely by grade (not always an easy task with homeschoolers), approximately K-3 and 4-8. A typical day is: 1:30-2:30 the K-3 kids meet for art. During this time the older kids will play outside on the playground or inside with games (depending on the weather). At 2:30 we switch for the older kids to do art. At 3:00 the younger kids will have a half-hour language class, and at 3:30 the older kids have their language class.

All classes are taught by homeschool moms who were teachers or have some other professional background in the area taught. Fees were decided on by each teacher and handled individually with each teacher. This will change next year, though we have not ironed that out yet. Some teachers just charge for materials; others also charge a small fee for their time. We meet at a local church that is allowing us to use their facility free of charge (we have no formal affiliation with the church, as we are an inclusive group). At this time all problems are handled through me as the contact person.

## St. Paul Open School

90 Western Avenue South, St. Paul, MN 55102 USA
Contact: Jennifer Diederich
Phone: (651) 293-8670

We are a K through 12th grade community encouraging individual growth and self-directed learning from each other and the world around us. We believe that balancing independence and community responsibility is vital to learning and that takes place in the context of the entire community. See Robert Skenes' essay, "Experimenting with Futuristic Systems of Learning: A 'Snapshot' of The St. Paul Open School," in this book for more information.

## Turning the Wheel Productions

1123 Country Road 83, Boulder, CO 80302-8767 USA
Contact: Rex Lanigan
Phone: 303-449-5720 / E-mail: ttwheel@aol.com or lanigan@bigwave.ca
URL: http://www.turningthewheeel.com

Turning the Wheel Productions is an intergenerational dance/theatre company committed to the collaborative creation and performance of works of art that are rooted in and restorative for the communities in which they perform and teach. Founded in Boulder, Colorado, in 1989, Turning the Wheel has taken on the challenge of making art accessible to people of all ages, experiences, and cultural and socioeconomic backgrounds, while building systems that support healthy community. They have developed a model for using creative expression and performance as a way of addressing community problems and issues in cities across the country.

## Family Playce

3590 Peralta Boulevard, Fremont, CA 94536-3738 USA
Contact: Marcia Williams
Phone: 510-818-9864 / E-mail: edfamhere@aol.com

Family Playce is dedicated to providing a respectable and creative learning environment in which family can flourish, allowing originality, independence, and self-expression for each individual, and incorporating with respect the curiosity of children and wisdom of adults in a diverse program of imagination and discovery.

Family Playce serves as a community center for homeschooling families and offers programs ranging from providing learning experiences for children during the day and after-school art or theatre programs for children, to programs such as authors speaking, floral design, and forums for the general public.

A small core group sets the atmosphere. There is no paid help, but a lot of volunteers enable Family Playce to stay afloat. The core group brings in others—all the center can handle currently—by word-of-mouth advertising. On a typical weekend the center had a small Fall Festival. Children had worked for several weeks on game booths, plays, and activities.

The center has been in its current location only since September, 1999. It has a resource lounge with a sofa and books and magazines on parenting, education, and homeschooling. The house is set up in multi-purpose areas that can be used for various activities. The kitchen is used for art or science. Another room is set aside for the toddlers, but there is as much time spent in that room by ten-year-olds as by three-year-olds! A large percentage of the boys between the ages of ten and thirteen were called "hyper" by the schools. Their parents were told, "Your child cannot come to school unless he is on Ritalin (or other drugs)." The center encourages children to be themselves, and allows them to express themselves within learning experiences of their own choosing. Drugs are not used.

Children love this learning center. They never want to leave when it's time to go. The participating families feel that the current schooling system makes alternative learning centers necessary—not only for learning, but also to assure family rights, community solidarity, and the moral/value condition of our society.

# South Street Centre

P.O. Box 227, Boulder Creek, CA 95006-0227 USA
Contact: Betsy Herbert or Estelle Fein
Phone: 831-228-2540 / E-mail: southst@cruzio.com

South Street Centre was founded in 1987 to provide a form of learning opportunity that recognizes all stages of a person's growth. It honors and supports parents in their roles as caregivers and mentors of their children by providing counseling, guidance, resources, materials, and inspiration for parents and children to design their own forms of self-learning. South Street Centre is housed in a rented home with cozy corners for the family sharing that is key to the center's program. Afternoon teas for parents provide information and assure parents' involvement in their children's learning process. The facilities are open to meetings and discussion of the full range of community issues and any other topics on the minds of the homeschooling and other families who are members.

## South Street Centre PlayTime Program
### by Betsy Herbert

PlayTime is one of four weekly programs at South Street Centre, which is housed in a turn-of-the-century home in downtown Boulder Creek in the Santa Cruz Mountains. We have been serving homeschooling families for the past dozen years with activities that bridge the gap between home and community. Some of our programs are contracted by our local school district. I, Betsy Herbert, am a co-founder, the administrator, and one of the educational facilitators of the Centre.

Every Wednesday morning eight families come to South Street to spend a couple of hours focussing on the needs of their two- to four-year-olds, with some

older and younger siblings in tow as well. We call this program PlayTime. One of the purposes of PlayTime is to dispel the myth that homeschooling begins when the child is five. Homeschooling is an educational lifestyle that begins at birth, or before.

On cold or rainy mornings we gather indoors, nursing mothers occupying the couches and rocking chair, and clusters of parents and children sitting on the rugs, setting up Brio trains, building with blocks, arranging dinosaurs, playing board games. There is a distinct period of greeting and "settling in," choosing places, playmates, and activities. All of the adults are paying attention to the play, watching it develop, initiating dialogue, and listening to conversation.

When a level of concentration and peacefulness is established, parents begin to share with each other the ups and downs of their everyday lives, offering one another support for the arduous task of family-making. All the details are aired and shared, all the while making sure that babes, toddlers, and children are safely engaged. I, as facilitator, oversee this scene, joining in the various interactions, offering occasional guidance.

About halfway through our time together, two or three parents head for the kitchen to put together our potluck lunch. I usually prepare a grain and some cooked greens. Homemade breads, cheeses, tofu, yoghurt and fruits, vegetables, soups, and desserts complete the menu. This is arranged, buffet style, on the big kitchen table. Each child and adult has a bowl, and we walk around the table and fill it. We eat at a large low table in the playroom. In good weather, we picnic in the garden.

For many of us, this meal is a highlight of our week. It is gratifying to prepare foods that are fully appreciated. Babies and children often get their first taste of a new food at the South Street table. We use the occasion to share stories of favorite foods and mealtime rituals, and to trade recipes.

After lunch, the children play some more, and the quality of their play is fueled by the contentment that comes from our meal. Parents clear the table, wash the dishes and complete their morning's visit. Some make arrangements for the children to play at each other's homes during the coming week.

We end with a story, some puppetry or dancing, and our song, "Goodbye South Street," which includes a verse for each individual child. Everyone leaves PlayTime nourished and nurtured.

### About the Author

*Betsy Herbert has been active in education and the arts for several decades: at Goddard College, in alternative schools in New York City and Philadelphia, in rural Vermont and New Mexico, and in the homeschooling community of Santa Cruz County, CA. South Street Centre was founded in 1987 and has served to bridge the gap between the grassroots homeschooling community and school-district supported homeschool programs.*

---

## Bayside Children's College

1025 Center Street, Santa Cruz, CA 95060 USA
Contact: Karen Funk, director
Phone: 831-454-0370 / E-mail: karen@baysidechildrenscollege.com
URL: http://baysidechildrenscollege.com

See Karen Funk's essay, "Bayside Children's College," in this book for more information.

## Linkup—Parent Designed and Monitored Program for Homeschooling Families

Eastham Community Center, 1404 Seventh Street, Oregon City, OR 97045
Contact: Larry Didway (503-650-5491, didwayl@orecity.k12.or.us) or Becky Taylor (503-657-2407, taylorbe@orecity.k12.or.us)
Phone: 503-657-2434 / Fax: 503-657-2536

Linkup is a tax-supported public program for homeschooled students grades K-12. Linkup's mission is to assist homeschooling families by offering educational opportunities including math, science, communications skills, and access to the tools of technology in a safe, professional, "family friendly" environment. Linkup opened in 1996. The program, beginning with fewer than one hundred students, currently serves nearly five hundred students.

Linkup enables homeschooled students to access Oregon City School District as part-time students under the direction of their parents, and develops customized programs to enhance homeschooling educational opportunities. Linkup teaches technology as a tool to help students in their acquisition of the skills, information, and processes needed in math, science, and communication. Parent participation is required at varying levels in all classes.

The Linkup Manager and Parent Advisory Team (PAT) are responsible for the direction and staffing of the program. The PAT is made up of homeschooling parents whose children attend Linkup. Parents are selected to serve rotating two-year terms.

Three basic programs are offered. The Parent-Partnered program works with parents to design a combined program of home and classroom instruction in academic content areas of language arts, math, science, or second language, for grades 6 and up. The Home Teaching Mentor Program pairs experienced home-based instructors with K-6 students and parents to help provide an individualized education program for each student. Time is divided between basic skills and integrated unit studies. Attendance and district testing are required. The Elective Program offers a selection of classes in a variety of subject areas.

## The Teacher-Family Space

2705 East Burnside Street, #108, Portland, OR 97214-1767 USA
Contact: Robin Linsley
Phone: 503-233-0151 / Fax: 503-233-0185 / E-mail: atspace@teleport.com
URL: http://www.teleport.com/~atspace

Non-profit. "The place for adults who raise, teach and interact with children and young adults." Funding is from fees or grants. Sample programs: scholarship tutoring—grant money provides free tutoring, teens as tutors Summer program—teenaged volunteers lead language enrichment activities for young children, teens work for pizza—younger children attend free, family learning picnics—a free program for children to five years old where children and their caregivers join the staff for a "learn-through-play" experience at a park or other neighborhood location (meets twice weekly), and parent/teacher workshops, such as Guides for Loving Discipline; Supporting Children in Grief, and How to Help Your Child Learn to Read.

## Oregon Unschooling Chautauqua

5125 SW Macadam Avenue, #200, Portland, OR 97202 USA

The Chautauqua is a September "kick-off" event for about twenty-five unschooling families. The Chautauqua takes over a Campfire Camp at the Oregon coast, an exquisite and private environment for discovery, exploration, growth, and natural beauty. During the five-day temporary community, families work and play together, share meals, activities, and rustic cabins. Families bring favorite games, crafts, and activities to share. Exploring activities, ideas, forest, and beach occupies all. Relaxing, visiting, and loafing are very popular. Oregon Chautauqua is a non-profit organization. Expenses are paid by fees.

## Home School Village

243 Fifth Street, Silverton, Oregon 97381-1828 USA
Contact: Ronald Johnson, founder
URL: http://www.home-school-village.com

It is the mission of Home School Village to be a place for children and adults, in school or out of school, homeschooled or unschooled, to freely share ideas, experiences, and knowledge (practical or impractical, possible or impossible), and communicate with like-minded people concerned with the wonder of learning. By communicating with other people and sharing, thinking about, and accepting ideas and experiences on Home School Village, we believe people can be inspired to direct their own learning. We encourage kids and teens to participate in Home School Village. Home School Village is like a piece of clay that is constantly being molded and created by its members.

## HomeSource

P.O. Box 40884, 1600 Taney Street, Eugene, OR 97404-0163 USA
Contact: Paula Williams, facilitator
Phone: 541-689-9959 / Fax: 541-689-1051 / E-mail: paulaw@betheltech.com
URL: http://www.betheltech.com

A program serving six hundred to seven hundred K-12 pupils with a one-to-five teacher-to-student ratio and contracts with off-campus community resources for other activities, including tennis, horseback riding, symphony, etc. They offer computer technology, with twenty computers on site, hands-on math manipulatives classes, etc. Some students take classes at HomeSource and also are enrolled in another public-school program. Apparently there is some sharing of funds between districts in that case. See their web page for all their many offerings.

# North Star School and Homeschool Resource Center

1880 Lawrence Avenue, Pt. Orchard, WA 98366 USA
Phone: 360-876-7706
See Marcie O'Brien's essay, "North Star School and Homeschool Resource Center," in this book for more information.

# Puget Sound Community School

Seattle, WA (a nomadic school in the process of changing our mailing address)
E-mail: pscs@pscs.org
URL: http://www.pscs.org
The mission of the Puget Sound Community School is to honor the uniqueness of students by trusting their natural abilities, respecting them as individuals, and providing them with educational opportunities in which equal status is given to all pursuits. We invite the participation of all people regardless of race, gender, ability, or sexual orientation. PSCS is dedicated to being a leading example of community-involved education.

# Mentor Apprentice Exchange

RR 1, St. George, Ontario, NOE 1NO Canada
URL: http://www.life.ca/max/index.html
Twenty-seven-year-old Heidi Priesnitz has always sought out teachers and mentors. As a young, unschooled learner, she found numerous people in her family and community willing and able to share knowledge with her. At nineteen she formalized the process by starting the Mentor Apprentice Exchange (MAX), a directory and newsletter dedicated to fostering informal mentorships and apprenticeships.

MAX has since evolved into a section on the *Natural Life* newsmagazine's Internet website that lists contact information for apprenticeship opportunities in a variety of fields, and for individuals of all ages who are seeking apprentice positions. (*Natural Life* is published by Heidi's parents.) There is also a great deal of useful information designed to help prospective mentors and apprentices make the most of the situations they create.

Heidi describes the learning process this way: "Two people work together—one person who wants to gain specific skills or knowledge, and another person who is experienced in those particular areas. The apprentice offers hands-on assistance in exchange for the mentor's skills and wisdom. This barter can take place in any field of activity, between two people of any ages. Apprenticing yourself to someone who has the skills you want to gain is an inexpensive and exciting way of learning. By placing listings in MAX, you can introduce yourself to mentors in a variety of fields. You will also be able to read through the list of apprenticeships available in such areas as organic gardening, felt-making, publishing, horse training, woodworking, beekeeping, canoeing, drum-making, metal sculpting, and solar design. Through apprenticeships, you can find work that you enjoy, or gain the tools you need to establish a business of your own. If you're looking for real-life, hands-on learning situations, try an apprenticeship!" She adds, "This holistic approach to apprenticeships allows for greater integration of business, education, and community."

## Windsor House Alternative School

440 Hendry Avenue North, Vancouver, BC V7L 4C5 Canada
Contact: Helen Hughes, director
E-mail: hhughes@idmail.com

Windsor House is a parent-participation, democratic, academically non-coercive school with about one hundred and fifty students ages five to eighteen and ten staff people. Students are not made to go to classes, nor are they stigmatized for non-attendance. The school is situated in a '60s-style elementary school on a lot with trees, a playground, a field, and a blacktop area. There are tennis courts in the adjoining park. The school is publicly funded by the School District #44, North Vancouver, BC, Canada. A weekly Resolutions Meeting makes all of the rules of the school (except rules set out by our school district concerning safety). Each person in the community gets one vote. Students may ask for classes and activities, and efforts are made to provide what the students have requested. Parents as well as staff offer classes and activities that they enjoy doing themselves. The main focus of the school is for people to run their own lives and be engaged in undertakings of their own choice.

## The Travelling Folk High School

Stegøvej 2, DK-5400 Bogense, Denmark
Phone: 6481-3205 / Fax: 6481-3143 (from the US dial 011-45-the number) / E-mail: drh@post3.tele.dk
URL: http://www.drhjboghense.dki3.com

In 1850 Grundtvig conceived the idea of the "folk school." He wanted to create education for the ordinary folk, the common people. His manifesto was "enliven and enlighten." He wanted young people to get together to enliven one another's lives in the daily tasks of living, and to enrich their communities. His ideas were socially and politically incorrect for the times. It was feared that ordinary people would be empowered and emboldened to upset the status quo. Nearly a century later the first folk school was established by Christian Kold. There are now over a hundred folk schools in Denmark and The Danish Folk School Movement has spread worldwide.

Tvind Folk School was one of these offspring. In the 1970s young people gathered at Tvind and accepted the challenge of building the largest windmill in the world, surpassing the one then being built by NASA in the USA. Studying aerodynamics, material science, engineering, and physics, they completed the task and the windmill generated more electricity than could be used by the surrounding area.

The Travelling Folk High School at Bogense has adopted this same philosophy of education with African Development as the theme. For six months students study social sciences, development, anthropology, fund-raising, and hands-on appropriate technology in Bogense, Denmark. They then take their skills and knowledge in teams to Namibia, Angola, or Malawi, where they work with the people there, helping them solve local problems with local resources and local skills. Then they return for two months to Denmark for further exchange and discussion.

## Schumacher College—An International Centre for Ecological Studies

The Old Postern, Dartington, Totnes, Devon TQ9 6EA UK
Contact: Hilary Nicholson, administrator
Phone: 0-180-386-5934 / Fax: 0-180-386-6899 (from the US delete the first 0 and
dial 011-44-the number) / Email: schumcoll@gn.apc.org
URL: http://www.gn.apc.org/schumachercollege/

Schumacher College was founded in 1991 upon the convictions that the
worldview that has dominated Western civilization has serious limitations, and that
a new vision is needed for human society and its relationship to the earth. The
College offers rigorous inquiry to uncover the roots of the prevailing worldview. It
explores ecological approaches that value holistic rather than reductionist perspectives and spiritual rather than consumerist values. It also offers a learning experience that is consistent with an holistic philosophy. A unified residential education
offering physical work, meditation, aesthetic experience, and intellectual inquiry
creates a sense of the wholeness of life. At the College, people find refreshment,
and often new direction. People aged from twenty to over eighty come to the College
from all over the world to explore issues of sustainability, diversity, equity, and
wholeness; to interweave meditation, reflection, shared work, study, field trips, and
community life; and to take an acive part in the self-organizing processes that
enhance individual and group learning.

## Wandsworth Home Education

SW London, UK
Contact: Shan Jayran
E-mail: kids@hogonline.co.uk
URL: http://www.hogonline.co.uk

Wandsworth Home Education is a new home-education meeting on Tuesdays.
We have a good venue—a large hall, outdoor grassed play area, kitchen, etc., for £15
for two to three hours. To cover this cost we need six families at £2.50 attending
every time. This was not reliable at first, so we made the meetings fortnightly to
encourage people to make them a priority (so far, so good). The meeting has within
three months naturally structured itself. Parents bring food and share lunch, also
sharing support on their home-education experiences, updating news of events,
welcoming anyone new. Although such groups overtly aim to serve children's social
needs, it's clear that an adult "staff room" function is just as important.

The children tend to group in three clusters. "Littlies" stay close to us adults and
tumble excitedly on the mats. "Middles" actively range wide outdoors with a ranger
theme and some play fighting. "Olders" (ten to fourteen years old) tend to move
uncertainly between the kids outside and the adult talk. Occasionally we provide an
activity (painting a huge picture, storytelling) but mainly the children create their own
objectives. Perhaps the most striking item through hours of vigorous exchange is the
almost complete lack among home-education kids of accidents, whining, or conflict
needing adult intervention.

Finally, we have also noticed how the children have an acute instinct for closure.
Without any signal from us adults, about half an hour before the end, the age-
clusters converge and some kind of large group game emerges. The littlies are
absorbed without harm or condescension while middles and olders perform hair-
raising agility feats. We are waiting to see what the children will teach us next.

# The Open University, UK

Walton Hall, Milton Keynes, MK7 6AA UK
Phone: 0-190-827-4066 / Fax: 0-190-865-3744 (from the US delete the first 0 and dial 011-44-the number) / E-mail: ces-gen@open.ac.uk
URL: http://www.open.ac.uk/frames.html
   The Open University (OU) is Britain's largest university. Since its establishment by Royal Charter in 1969, it has opened the door to higher education for more than two million people. Open University courses are designed for students studying at home, in their own time, anywhere in the UK, Ireland, Europe, and around the world, and courses are open to all regardless of educational qualifications. See Ray Ison's essay, "Supported Open Learning and the Emergence of Learning Communities: The Case of the Open University UK," in this book for more information.

# The International University Asia Pacific

Japan Center: 4-1 Kaibara-cho, Shugakuin, Sakyo-ku, Kyoto 606-8043 Japan
Contact: Motoshi Suzuki
Phone: 075-722-2373 (from the US delete the first 0 and dial 011-81-the number) / E-mail: motoshi@mbox.kyoto-inet.or.jp
Honolulu Center: 1441 Victoria Street, #402, Honolulu, HI 96822 USA
Contact: Dayle Bethel
Phone: 808-523-2906 / E-mail: dbethel@aloha.net
   See Motoshi Suzuki's essay, "The International University, Japan: A 25-year Experiment in Restructuring University Education," in this book for more information.

# Haven

E-mail: humans@haven.net
URL: http://www.haven.net
   Haven is an online community offering a different kind of learning. We nurture learning that trusts in paying attention to our deepest interests and follows those interests wherever they may lead. Our central interests are ecstatic, real-world paths to life-long learning, the creation of right livelihood and sustainable businesses, the practice of deep ecology, and the profound interconnection of these broad topics. We invite you to discover what draws you in here. See Claudia L'Amoreaux's essay, "Haven, A Collaborative Lifelong Cyber-Learning Community," in this book for more information.

---

## Iroquois Learning
### by candace, an Iroquois Shaman

very interesting opportunities [for new learning systems] are emerging. do realize, however, that native americans have "apprenticeships" that often last for most of a person's life, and that we do not believe one comes into true maturity and capability until after age 40. until then, even with all the mentoring and apprenticeships we provide, we are still guiding and testing and trying and coaching our young—and we do not commonly believe they are yet prepared.

for us, life is a school. the apprenticeships and nurturing of gifts is constant, and young [people] are often removed from their biological families and live with those elders who have similar gifts. they often spend more of their lives with these elders, working for them, then later with them, than they spend with their "families." the young [adult] under age 40, or even after if unproven in wisdom and judgment, does not have equal power to decide or act on what effects others, although if they choose to act as though they do, no one will stop them. the mentor/elder, may first try to insist, then if that doesn't work, will back away and not be involved any longer with the younger member until that person realizes the insufficiency of his or her preparation to date and comes back willing to learn. the most difficult and extreme case of this training is of course, what i was trained in—shamanism—or spiritual responsibility. —by Candace Cole-McCrean e-mail: snowy@worldpath.net

# Organizations and Networks (listed alphabetically)

## Alliance for Parental Involvement in Education (AllPIE)

P.O. Box 59, East Chatham, NY 12060-0059 USA
Contact: Katharine Houk, director
Phone: 518-392-6900 / E-mail: allpie@taconic.net

### AllPIE's Tenth Year: Millennium Musings
#### by Katharine Houk

The Alliance for Parental Involvement in Education (AllPIE), conceived in 1989 and born in 1990, is approaching its tenth anniversary. Created and run by parents, this non-profit group offers parents support and information about education, especially alternative educational options. It serves many people involved in home education, but also helps people start new educational alternatives such as small schools and learning centers, and it provides information on parent involvement to people working for change in public schools. AllPIE publishes newsletters and booklets, sponsors workshops and conferences, offers phone consultation and support, acts as an informational clearinghouse, maintains a mail-order lending library, and publishes a resources catalog containing helpful books, as well as tapes of sessions from past AllPIE conferences and back issues of AllPIE's newsletters. This work is done by parent volunteers. It is funded by donations, memberships, publication sales, and income from workshops and conerences.

As I look back over these past ten years I can see the unique position that AllPIE has held within the education community in the state of New York and within this country. When Seth Rockmuller and I were first inspired to start AllPIE, we were homeschooling parents who were committed to the homeschooling way of life and learning. Yet, because we had dealt with public, private, and alternative schools as parents and as professionals, we knew that starting an organization exlusively for homeschoolers was not the direction we wanted to take. We realized that the world of education is enormously diverse, and that there is tremendous power in the learning that takes place when people, face-to-face, share their educational experiences, resources, knowledge, and beliefs. AllPIE's overarching vision attempts to embrace all parents concerned about their children's education.

In many ways this path based on inclusivity has been a difficult and lonely path to take. Often Seth and I felt trapped between a rock and a hard place. In the beginning (and even to this day) there were homeschoolers who distrusted AllPIE because it included parents and children, teachers and officials, who were not committed to homeschooling, but who had chosen or were forging other educational options. On the other side, there were those involved in public and private education who were suspicious of a group that so enthusiastically welcomed homeschoolers, especially in the early days when homeschooling was not as socially acceptable as it is today.

Homeschoolers found (and find) it necessary to create safe spaces, groups for homeschoolers only, and indeed such groups and places continue to be essential. Because we believe this is so, we have worked, whenever the opportunity has arisen and to the extent that our energy (and AllPIE's charitable organization status, which restricts lobbying) would allow, to help homeschooling groups form, grow, and thrive. But AllPIE's vision has always been wider. We drew inspiration for this inclusivity from John Holt, who was involved in the early 1980s, not just in supporting homeschoolers, but in finding ways that the basic ideas involved in homeschooling could influence and shape educational philosophy and practices wherever education takes place. Such shaping requires interaction.

In one way, our early intent then was bold and subversive. We put home education right up on AllPIE's letterhead with public and private schools, because we firmly believe it is a valid and extremely valuable educational alternative. With high hopes and faith in people and the processes of growth and change, we sent news of the fledgling AllPIE organization not just to homeschooling groups, but to the U.S. Department of Education, private and alternative school organizations, and as many places as we could find where people were thinking about and concerned with education. Part of our mission was to make homeschooling more acceptable and better understood. Indeed, individuals and groups that reach out in non-threatening ways to explain to the broader educational community what homeschooling is about have helped homeschooling to achieve the acceptance that it has increasingly enjoyed.

AllPIE's conferences, while largely attended by homeschooling families, always include sessions of interest to families with children in public and private school as well. Of particular interest to me have been the hybrids that have resulted from this inclusivity—those groups, learning centers, and small schools that have resulted from the cross-fertilization of ideas (and sometimes sparks!) generated by diverse people sharing ideas and bumping together (literally! We always start conference weekends with a dance because touch and eye contact are important modes of communication). These alternatives represent the beginnings of the grassroots, community-based reform of education.

Another way that AllPIE's inclusivity and wider focus have created difficulties is that money is scarce, and grantmakers tend to seek one-issue groups with narrowly defined projects and agendas to recieve their funding. Families who are home-schooling are often on tight budgets, and it makes a certain amount of sense that they put their hard-earned dollars toward homeschooling support groups, rather than to organizations with wider and more far-reaching goals. So although AllPIE has a database of over 15,000, only a small fraction contribute financially to the running of the organization. Yet, somehow, AllPIE pays its bills, continues to offer resources and support, and holds to its vision.

With high hopes and faith in people and the processes of growth and change, Seth and I look forward to AllPIE's *next* ten years. And we invite you to participate with us in this endeavor!

# Alternative Education Resource Organization (AERO)

417 Roslyn Road, Roslyn Heights, NY 11577-2620 USA
Phone: 800-769-4171
URL: http://www.edrev.org

The major clearinghouse for information, contacts, and consulting on alternative schools of diverse types, community learning centers, home education, and international alternatives. Produces a nationally distributed radio talk show, an informative newsletter called *The Education Revolution*, numerous videos, and a comprehensive directory of alternative schools and learning resources.

# American Homeschool Association

P.O. Box 1083, Tonasket WA 98855-1083 USA
Contact: Mark and Helen Hegener, founders
Phone: 800-236-3278 / E-mail: AHA@home-ed-magazine.com

The American Homeschool Association (AHA), founded in 1995, is a not-for-profit networking and services organization for homeschooling families, sponsored in part by the publishers of *Home Education Magazine*. The purpose of the AHA is to broaden the knowledge and understanding of homeschooling, and to support the educational decisions made by individuals and families. The AHA reaches these goals by facilitating networking and communications between homeschoolers, and by increasing awareness of the helpful organizations and businesses seeking to support homeschooling families. The AHA offers a free quarterly online newsletter, a free networking e-mail list, and a helpful website with state laws, resource listings, and links to other helpful sites. We constantly work to make the AHA a valuable source of information, encouragement, and support for homeschooling families.

# The Center for Communities of the Future

Box 3508, Gastonia, NC 28054-0020 USA
Contact: Rick Smyre, president
Phone: 704-864-9196 / E-mail: rlsmyre@aol.com
URL: http://www.bev.net/cotf/

Communities of the Future (COTF) is a network of people and organizations throughout the US and in other countries who are committed to helping local communities prepare for a continuously changing and increasingly complex society by building "capacities for transformation." The Center for COTF is an unique, evolving virtual center that focuses on developing capacities for Transformational Learning, the Digital Economy, and Knowledge Democracy. The capacities for transformation such as process leadership development, building a futures context, and electronic infrastructure are introduced into the thinking and activities of local communities. See Rick Smyre's essay, "Rewiring a Community's Brain for the 21st Century: Aligning the Cosmic Dance," in this book for more information.

---

## The Future of Learning
### by Rick Smyre

As a futurist, I know better than to predict the future or to try to control what happens. So let's look ahead and guess, based on some knowledge, intuition, and common sense.

When educational historians of 2100 look back to the dawn of this millennium, they will be struck by the magnitude of qualitative change that occurred between 1975 and 2025. Within this fifty-year period, the very concept of what learning means will have been totally transformed.

The simultaneous impact of electronic communication, interconnections of ideas, people, and organizations, and constant innovation in all sectors of society, marks a watershed in the very nature of thinking. This transformation in thinking is not only the result, but also the cause of change. No longer will the simplistic notion of cause-and-effect be enough to understand reality. The speed of making and breaking connections as a part of constant innovation builds a natural reciprocity into all reality. Twenty-first century learning will emerge from the transformation from a static world to one based on continuous change—and any change will be both a cause and an effect at the same time.

The dawn of the 21$^{st}$ century marks the dawn of the need to think systemically—in wholes, not parts. Seeing connections will become a twenty-first century skill.

This will lead to a new way to think about how to evaluate any learning process. Traditionally learners were tested on their knowledge...the ability to remember content. In the future, evaluation will focus not only on content, but also on how to ask appropriate questions and how to connect disparate ideas. Content of knowledge will still be important, but only in relation to how one piece of knowledge can be connected to some other piece—the basis of constant innovation. This will be true whether the arena of thinking is related to the skills of business, the understanding of ecological sustainability, or the way people in a community work together to help each other be successful.

The future of learning will center on the ability to ask appropriate questions and the ability to connect disparate ideas. The more content knowledge one learns, the more subtle and deeper questions that can be asked, and the more appropriate and integrated any system will become.

Therefore, we are leaving the world of either/or and single answers, and moving to an age of and/both and interactive systems. As our society becomes faster, more interconnected, and increasingly complex, old ways of educating will no longer be enough. We will need to understand and use new concepts like "reciprocal learning." If you say you have never heard of this idea, then you have just touched the future. We will need to rethink and retool all our institutions, which will require rethinking how we think and learn. Welcome to the new millennium!

# Center for Interim Programs

195 Nassau Street, Suite 15, Princeton, NJ 08542-7004 USA
Phone: 609-683-4300/Fax: 609-683-4309/E-mail: HollyBull@interimprograms.com
Founded in 1980, with offices in Massachusetts, New Jersey, and California, Interim is a service that enables people to pursue structured alternatives to formal education or work by matching clients' interests with over 2,800 internships, volunteer positions, and apprenticeships worldwide, to create "time off" that can give new direction, sharpen hazy career goals, rejuvenate those on the verge of burnout, and give a much needed break between high school and college. Since 1980 we have tailored creative time off for over 3,000 young people between the ages of fifteen and seventy.

## Ceptual Institute

1271 Bronco Circle, Minden, NV 89423 USA
E-mail: integrity@ceptualinstitute.com
URL: http://www.ceptualinstitute.com
See James Rose's essay, "Learning Communities, Teaching Communities," in this book for more information.

## Civic Media Center

1021 West University Avenue, Gainesville, FL 32601 USA
Phone: 352-373-0010 / E-mail: cmc@gator.net
URL: http://www.gator.net/~cmc
If you have realized that the news you get in the mainstream press isn't really comprehensive or even truthful, and a lot of news and views are filtered out of the mainstream press outlets, libraries, and thus, public debate, then you've found a home. We are one of the few alternative libraries in the US. We carry books, journals, 'zines, videotapes, audiotapes, and newspapers by independent, non-corporate press on a wide variety of subjects, and we host many educational, cultural, social, and musical events and groups. See James Schmidt's essay, "How to Maintain an Alternative Library: The Civic Media Center Six Years On," in this book for more information.

## EarthNet Institute

1904 Frisco Road, Cabool, MO 65689-9859 USA
E-mail: wolford@eni.edu
URL: http://www.eni.edu
EarthNet Institute (ENI) is an educational institution dedicated to sharing information globally. It is organized as a worldwide membership association, comprised of charitable, altruistic individuals and organizations networked for meaningful action against major world problems such as starvation, homelessness, ignorance, poverty, disease, mental illness, terrorism, war, slavery, domestic abuse, animal and human rights violations, and environmental devastation.
EarthNet provides education programs, extension services, field research, liaison and networking activities, and community-based programs in diverse places where intervention is often most useful. Membership is open to all that bring gifts and/or talents for the use of the underserved. Please enroll or initiate membership at our website.

## Educational Futures Projects

P.O. Box 2977, Sacramento, CA 95812 USA
Contact: Don Glines, director
Phone: 916-393-8701
See Don Glines' essay, "Future Learning Environments," in this book for more information.

## Enabling Education Network (EENET)

Center for Educational Needs, University of Manchester, Oxford Road, Manchester M13 9PL UK

Phone: 0-161 275 3510 (from the US delete the first 0 and dial 011-44-the number) / E-mail: eenet@man.ac.uk
URL: http://www.eenet.org.uk

EENET is an information-sharing network supporting and promoting the inclusion of marginalized groups in education worldwide. Its membership is open to individuals and organizations in all parts of the world, but it gives priority to the needs of countries in the south. Many EENET members are concerned for disabled children and marginalized people. EENET broadens the concept of education beyond the classroom to include community-based strategies and the encouragement of self-help groups.

## The Folk and People's Education Association of America

Women's Center, Lakeland Community College, 7700 Clocktower Drive, Kirkland, OH 44094 USA
Contact: Merry Ring
Phone: 440-975-4706 / E-mail: mring@lakeland.cc.oh.us

The Folk Education Association of America (FEAA) is a grass-roots association of North American folk schools, peoples' learning centers, community and academic institutions, resource organizations, and individuals. The common thread is involvement or interest in learning that affirms life and strives to build communities that are just, democratic, and environmentally sustainable. Inspired particularly by the Danish and broader Scandinavian "folk" education experience and by Latin American liberatory or popular education, the membership is connected to an international network of experimental, community-based, and participatory program leaders. See Chris Spicer's essay, "Carrying on Despite the Violent Twentieth Century: A Tenacious History of People's Education," in this book for more information.

## The Institute for People's Education and Action

c/o Chris Spicer, 107 Vernon Street, Northampton, MA 01060-2818 USA
Phone: 413-585-8755 / E-mail: cspicer@k12s.phast.umass.edu

Affiliated with the Folk Education Association, the Institute offers a program of intensive workshops in popular/folk education, participatory research, and community education, and sells related books and videos.

## International Healthy Cities Foundation

Public Health and Urban Planning, University of California at Berkeley, 410 Warren Hall, Berkeley, CA 94720-7360 USA
Contact: Leonard J. Duhl, MD, executive director
Phone: 510-642-1715/Fax: 510-643-6981/E-mail: len-duhl@socrates.berkeley.edu
URL: http://www.healthycities.org/ (or http://www.healthycities.org/ for website in multiple languages)

Healthy Cities is a worldwide program (7,500 communities), concerned with participation in a holistic and equitable way. It involves maximizing the assets of the people and community. Healthy Cities and Healthy Communities is a process to increase the competence of communities (its citizens, organizations, and institutions) in improving their quality of life and health. To do so requires all sectors to come around a "common table" and search for solutions that fit a "win-win" value system. Working on whatever is of concern, starting with easily achieved programs, they learn skills to deal with more and more complex issues.

Further information is at our website—click the tutorial button for a short description of the process that is now taking place in 7,500 communities worldwide. All are different. There is no central organizer, but communities help each other and share expediences. The Community Toolbox is another important resource at http://ctb.lsi.ukans.edu/

## The Leadership Project, Inc.

5905 Slater Road, Shawnee Mission, KS 66202-2839 USA
Contact: Kelly Patrick Gerling, Ph.D.
Phone: 913-248-1010 / Fax: 913-248-1002 / E-mail: lproject@aol.com

The Leadership Project is a research think-tank and consulting firm founded by Kelly Patrick Gerling, Ph.D. By studying the thinking and behavior of leaders who fulfill healthy values, Gerling and The Leadership Project are forming an approach to leadership development that works from the inside out, helping leaders fulfill important values in their organizations. The current version of their research on leadership and values is a process called Values-Based Leadership, which is being applied in corporations, non-profit organizations, school districts, and government agencies.

## National Coalition of Alternative Community Schools (NCACS)

1266 Rosewood, #1, Ann Arbor, MI 48104-6205 USA
Phone: 734-668-9171
URL: http://www.ncacs.org/

NCACS is a non-profit network of schools, groups, and individuals committed to participant control whereby students, parents, and staff create and implement their own learning programs. NCACS sponsors a directory and other publications, conferences, exchanges, accreditation, and alternative teacher education.

## National Community Education Association

3929 Old Lee Highway, #91A, Fairfax, VA 22042 USA
Phone: 703-359-8973
URL: http://www.ncea.com

Supports schools (mainly public schools) and community leaders to provide expanded learning opportunities in response to individual and community needs. After school and extended day programs, social services, alternative schools, and life-long learning approaches are among the models promoted. Supports principles of local control and self-determination. Publishes books and other materials.

## National 4-H Center—Innovation for Community and Youth Development

7100 Connecticut Avenue, Chevy Chase, MD 20815-4999 USA
Contact: Mark Tirpak
Phone: 800-368-7462 / E-mail: tirpak@fourhcouncil.edu
URL: http://www.fourhcouncil.edu

It is clear that youths need opportunities to make meaningful contributions to their communities and their own lives. Collaboration between youths and adults starts at the board level of the 4-H Innovation Center. Involving youths as full partners in decision-making is a hallmark of their operations down to the community level. Emphasizing the transformational power of youth has developed from the long history of 4-H service to young people. 4-H was born in the early 1900s in response to young people's need for better agricultural education. Progressive educators began extending nature study, agricultural, and technological education in families with programs that enabled youths and adults to learn together. Many communities organized 4-H clubs, with parents serving as volunteer leaders and cooperative extension agents providing educational material. Today the community-club model still engages young people, ages nine to fifteen in "learning by doing."

While continuing to serve youth in rural areas, 4-H also works with diverse groups of youth in a variety of urban and suburban locales. In 1998 the 4-H council created the Innovation Center for Community and Youth Development. The core aim of the Center is to propel innovations and build a national movement to involve youths as full partners with adults in meeting community needs. Among the highlights of the activities are the following:

At The Table—a program that aims at building a national movement for youth in government—a world where young people are invited to the table as full partners wherever decisions are being made that affect them.

Bridging the Gap—a project to improve youth development in isolated communities by helping youths and adults to identify local cultural, historical, geological, and organizational assets, and then using that knowledge to promote community development.

The 4-H Innovation Center hosts an e-mail discussion group that you can join at www.fourhcouncil.edu/cyd/innovate.htm

## National Home Education Network

E-mail: info@nhen.org
URL: http://www.nhen.org/

The National Home Education Network (NHEN) exists to encourage and facilitate the vital grassroots work of state and local homeschooling groups and individuals by providing information, fostering networking, and promoting public relations on a national level. NHEN supports the freedom of all individual families to choose home education and to direct such education. The organization was formed to encourage the distribution of accurate information from a variety of viewpoints, rather than to promote one particular philosophy over another. It is a forum for all homeschoolers who wish to openly and freely exchange information.

## Road Scholars

7 Florence Road, Harrington Park, NJ 07640-1702 USA
Contact: Leslie Van Gelder, director
Phone: 201-768-8961

Founded in 1998 by educators who believe that people learn best through experience, Road Scholars, Inc. provides one- and three-week-long courses for college-age and adult participants. Curriculum is made to come alive. Ellis Island, Eastside Tenements, the Lewis and Clark expedition, and other real-life experience are coupled with academic study. Courses in literature, history, urban studies, sociology, ecology, and economics are included in the curricula. Classrooms may be around campfires, on city street corners, or under a canopy of old-growth trees, and may include local experts or storytellers as well as the faculty and students in the group. To build solidarity and give a sense of belonging to each member the courses are limited to fifteen participants each.

## School of Living

432 Leaman Road, Chochranville, PA 19330-1618 USA
Phone: 610-593-6988

Founded in 1934 by Ralph Borsodi and incorporated in 1954 by Mildred Loomis, the School of Living is dedicated to learning, teaching, and practicing principles of living that are self-empowering. It has a general aim of establishing decentralized, ecologically sound, self-governed, and humane communities. It administers a regional Community Land Trust, publishes a quarterly journal for members, *Green Revolution*, sponsors workshops and designs courses in permaculture, fosters alternative education resources, and has begun a Building WithOut Banks loan fund.

## The Simplicity Circles Project

711 North 60th Street, Seattle, WA 98103-5605 USA
Phone: 206-782-5105 / E-mail: cecile@simplicitycircles.com
URL: http://www.simplicitycircles.com

A simplicity circle is a participatory, small-group form of personal and social transformation, in the tradition of the Swedish study circle and the Danish folk school, that helps people lead lives of high satisfaction and low environmental impact. Simplicity can be viewed as "the examined life," a search for ways to live in harmony with the self, with others, and with the planet. It is an attempt to restore balance to our own lives and to nature. The Circle of Simplicity includes a step-by-step outline of how to conduct a simplicity circle—no need for training, no need to join anything. Coordinator Cecile Andrews is a community educator and the author of *The Circle of Simplicity: Return to the Good Life*, published by HarperCollins, 1997. The Simplicity Circles Project is part of Seeds of Simplicity, a national membership organization of Cornell University's Center for Religion, Ethics and Social Policy. For more information call toll free: 1-877-UNSTUFF, E-mail seed@seedsofsimplicity.org or go to www.seedsofsimplicity.org

## Study Circle Resource Center (SCRC)

P.O. Box 203, Pomfret, CT 06258-0203 USA
Phone: 860-928-2616 / E-mail: scrc@neca.com

Over the last nine years, study circles have taken hold in dozens of communities across the country, belying the pundits who decry the inadequacy of political participation by America's average citizens. These communities have found in the study-circle model a way of bringing together a broad cross-section of everyday people, across customary political and social dividing lines, to deliberate on complex and controversial public issues that affect their lives, and to take action on those issues. Through the commitment and creativity of local organizers, the study circle has become an innovative structure for deliberative democracy. Nationally, study circles have been widely acknowledged as a practice that effectively addresses such issues as race relations, education reform, crime and violence, growth and development, and criminal justice.

A study circle is a small, diverse group, usually eight to twelve participants, that meets regularly over a period of weeks or months to address a critical public issue in a democratic and collaborative way. It sets its own ground rules for a respectful, productive discussion, is led by a facilitator who is impartial and who helps manage the deliberation process, but is not an "expert" or "teacher" in the traditional sense. It looks at an issue from many points of view; does not require consensus, but uncovers areas of agreement and common concern. It progresses from a session on personal experience of the issue to sessions providing multiple viewpoints to a session that looks at strategies for action.

Community-wide study circle programs are organized by a broad-based coalition of community organizations working to make sure that people from all sectors of the community are included. They involve many study circles happening at the same time across a community, provide a basis for problem-solving, lead to action at many levels, and create new personal relationships and community networks.

By participating in study circles, citizens gain "ownership" of the issues, discover a connection between personal experiences and public policies, and gain a deeper understanding of their own and others' perspectives and concerns. They discover common ground and a greater desire and ability to work collaboratively to solve local problems—as individuals, as members of small groups, and as members of large organizations in the community. Community-wide study circle programs foster new connections among community members that lead to new levels of community action. They also create new connections between citizens and government, both at an institutional level and among parents and teachers, community members and social-service providers, residents and police officers. More than a hundred communities are in various stages of planning and organizing community-wide programs.

SCRC was established in 1989 to promote the use of study circles on critical social and political issues. It is a project of the Topsfield Foundation, a private, non-profit, non-partisan foundation whose mission is to advance deliberative democracy and improve the quality of public life in the United States. SCRC staff members offer their services to community leaders, free of charge, at every stage of creating a community-wide study circle program. They give advice on all the steps in the organizing process, help to develop strong coalitions within communities, advise on material development, and write letters of support for funding proposals. SCRC can also provide up to five hundred free study-circle guides for these large-scale programs. Occasionally, an SCRC staff member can visit a community to participate in organizing meetings and conduct facilitator trainings.

# Syntony Quest

Contact: Alexander Laszlo or Kathia Laszlo, co-founders
Phone / Fax: 415-346-1547 / E-mail: info@syntonyquest.org
URL: http://www.SyntonyQuest.org

Syntony Quest is an evolutionary learning organization dedicated to helping those who wish to learn how to cope with change and uncertainty in ways that foster community and sustainability. It responds to these challenges by tapping the creative potential of individuals and groups and facilitating the emergence of evolutionary learning community through conversation, design, and action.

Syntony is a purposeful creative aligning and tuning with the evolutionary flows of which we are a part. It involves a conscious "listening" to the rhythms of changes and an intentional learning of how to play our own melodies in ways that harmonize with the larger evolutionary piece. Syntony is the process of finding and creating meaning and evolutionary opportunity, both individually and collectively. The Syntony Quest engages those who seek to journey toward a sustainable and evolutionary society in partnership with the earth.

Our purpose is to catalyze learning processes that empower individuals and groups to develop the competencies necessary for the co-creation of sustainable and evolutionary futures.

Our activities include:
- Design of evolutionary learning communities
- Community development projects
- Provision of learning resources
- Action-research on new educational models
- Workshops and seminars on systems thinking and its application to social and environmental concerns

Syntony Quest is a 501(c)(3) tax-exempt public benefit organizaiton.

# Publications (Periodicals and Alternative Presses)

## Autodidactic Press

P.O. Box 872749, Wasilla, AK 99687-2749 USA
Contact: Charles D. Hayes, publisher/author
Phone: 907-376-2932
URL: http://www.autodidactic.com

A small press and website dedicated to the proposition that life-long learning is the lifeblood of democracy and a key to living life to its fullest. We advocate the philosophy that an education should be thought of not as something you get, but as something you take. Our website offers self-education with the resources aim of inspiring adults to create and carry out a life-long learning philosophy. *Self-University Newsletter* is free online for those who wish to teach and encourage the value of self-education. In each issue of the newsletter, author Charles Hayes features contemporary books in the context of life-long learning. The website offers a Self-University Campus page as an avenue to other learning resources and is constantly updated.

### Autodidactic Resources
### by Charles D. Hayes

In many ways directories and resource lists contradict an autodidactic philoso-phy of education. By nature, the self-taught will be inclined to identify resources for themselves, and the purest of autodidacts might even resent the suggestion that a list should be consulted at all. Still, there are occasions when those who've internalized an insatiable interest in reaching greater understanding will thrill at the discovery of a particular resource and regard it as a priceless treasure. The essential problem of satisfying people with acutely developed, eclectic interests is that the uniqueness that they bring to their investigations is so wide and vast that any attempt at list-making is inevitably too limited in scope.

Each book the autodidactic individual reads leads to others. One footnote leads to a score of resources. One question leads to countless more, and when their interest is strong enough, such individuals perceive that no barrier can exist to keep them from finding the answers that elude them. They will spare no effort in locating experts if necessary. It's not that self-directed individuals disregard lists because they are lists; rather, their drive for information is usually specific enough to eliminate the possibility that a list someone else prepared is inclusive enough.

Arranging resources so that the self-taught will find them is a bit like going on a photo safari in Africa. If you expect to take pictures of wild animals, you must go into their territory to chance viewing them in action. When you position yourself to snap pictures of elephants, you're likely to miss opportunities for photos of giraffes. With autodidacts, the more strongly motivated your quarry, the more exactly your materials must be positioned to get their attention.

All of this is not to discourage those who aim to help autodidacts in their quest for knowledge, but to illustrate the thought and care that must go into such efforts to make them worthwhile. The information on these pages provides a fertile beginning.

# Down to Earth Books

P.O. Box 163, Goshen, MA 01032-0163 USA
URL: http://www.crocker.com/~maryl/index.html

Publisher and online bookstore specializing in education, psychology, spirituality, poetry, and other topics. Titles include back issues of *SKOLE: The Journal of Alternative Education* (published between 1985 and 1999) and the four-volume *Challenging the Giant: The Best of SKOLE*. Website features reviews and articles.

# Dropout!

1114 21st Street, Sacramento, CA 95814-4208 USA
E-mail: dropout@emrl.com

Drop Out is a youth collective with the goals of informing the public about the alternatives to traditional methods of schooling, and to be a support system for those who are considering something different for their education. The mission of Drop Out is to promote honesty and diversity in education; to be a resource and support for the community, especially those whose educational needs have not been met by the school system; to maintain a physical space where people can be validated and empowered to affect change; and to be a voice against compulsory schooling and for youth liberation. The tools we use to carry out this mission include our radical resource library, the resource center, the events we put on, and the *Drop Out* 'zine. We fund these projects exclusively through donations and fundraisers.

*Drop Out* began as a 'zine by Pam Davis as a personal project with people who were interested in submitting articles and helping her out. The first issue came out in March of 1995 and was a combination of reprints, articles by Pam, and other original content. By issue five *Drop Out* evolved into a collective, and has been operating for two years. The way the 'zine is put together has evolved somewhat in the last few years. Once the collective decides to start production on the next 'zine, a date is set for the first meeting. During 'zine meetings people interested in working on *Drop Out* come together to read the various submissions, choose articles to go into the 'zine, get publications to review, decide who is going to write what, choose ads and graphics, and lay out the 'zine. There is no one editor since this is a collective process, so everyone working on the 'zine is an editor. 'Zine meetings are announced via calling everyone on our phone list, and distributing flyers around town. 'Zine meetings are typically weekly or bi-weekly.

The *Drop Out* 'zine is a sixteen-page tabloid-style newspaper, and we print 6,000 copies. They are mailed to subscribers, contacts for distribution, 'zine trades, and free to prisoners. We distribute the 'zine at events, infoshops (radical libraries, and places like Drop Out), local businesses, by travelers or bands coming through town, and by collective members or friends of Drop Out. With all these forms of distribution, *Drop Out* reaches people throughout the United States and Canada, with some making their way outside North America. The 'zine is how Drop Out began and is a big part of what keeps it alive because of the volunteers and money it brings in.

The office (or resource center) is the physical space where most of the work related to Drop Out takes place. It's where most things like our meetings and discussions occur. Our office also contains information and resources such as pamphlets, an alternative education library, the 'zine library, and our big general lending library with books along with video and audiotapes on various topics. It's really nice and convenient to have so much in one space. We also have a bulletin board where we post information about local events, and other pertinent information people might find of interest.

As a resource center, we are open Monday to Wednesday from 3 to 6 PM, a time chosen so kids can come by after school. We are also open by appointment. Office shifts are filled by volunteers. During their shifts, volunteers typically keeps the office in order, attend to daily office work such as mail, and assist people who drop by. For our decision making, we have monthly general meetings to discuss our current situation with money, the 'zine, and other stuff pertinent to Drop Out and its collective members. At certain times, we also form committees to deal with projects that require more time. Work gets divided among us all

We keep the ebb and flow of money and volunteers fairly consistent by promoting Drop Out in a variety of ways. Besides the 'zine, there are three main ways we get the word out about Drop Out and the things we believe in. These include tabling at events, speaking or holding discussions at events, and holding events of our own. But word-of-mouth is still a great form of promotion, and seems to be how we've gotten most of our volunteers now. Raising money has always been a big concern for us, and has required a significant amount of work. Generally, we make our money through various fundraisers such as shows and rummage sales. Those are the two main money-makers that we try to plan every so often. We also have made a little money through tabling at events. Drop Out owes a great deal financially to the generous people who send us money on a regular basis.

So that's Drop Out in a nutshell. We are approaching the five-year anniversary of the 'zine, and things are only getting better and better. As we venture into other avenues of media like television and radio, we hope that you can come join us too.

                              —by evan, the fungus kid, and corinna, from the Drop Out collective

# Educational Heretics Press

113 Arundel Drive, Bramcote Hills, Nottingham, England NG93FQ UK
URL: http://www.gn.apc.org/edheretics

Catalog features original books and monographs on diverse paths of learning and the ideas of innovative educators and homeschooling advocates. These publications are not widely known in the US but they contain many valuable insights. This organization also publishes a quarterly newsletter, *Education Now*.

# Encounter: Education for Meaning and Social Justice

P.O. Box 328, Brandon, VT 05733-0328 USA
Phone: 800-639-4122
URL: http://www.great-ideas.org

An independent quarterly journal that views education from a holistic perspective and focuses on its role in helping students develop a sense of personal meaning and social justice. Writings by scholars and practitioners explore the moral, spiritual, cultural, and ecological dimensions of education. Originally founded under the title *Holistic Education Review* in 1988, *Encounter* is the major forum for visionary, leading-edge thinking on teaching and learning.

# The Foundation for Educational Renewal

P.O. Box 328, Brandon, VT 05733 USA
Phone: 800-639-4122
URL: http://www.PathsofLearning.net

A nonprofit organization that publishes *Paths of Learning* magazine, sponsors the online Paths of Learning Resource Center (a database on alternative, holistic, and progressive options in education), and publishes books (including this one) on new ideas in education. The Foundation for Educational Renewal is nonsectarian, aiming to support a wide variety of educational approaches within a broadly defined democratic and holistic perspective.

# Growing Without Schooling (GWS)

2380 Massachusetts Avenue, Suite 104, Cambridge, MA 02140-1884 USA
Contact: Pat Farenga, director
Phone: 617-864-3100
URL: http://www.holtgws.com

Founded in 1977 by the late author and teacher John Holt, GWS is based on the idea that young people are good at learning and that learning happens everywhere. Our stories explore how people of all ages learn and grow and how others can best help them. GWS is an ongoing conversation among its readers, and it allows homeschoolers (and other interested people) to share experiences, thoughts, questions, and concerns. While there are often interviews with authors and teachers, no one is paid to write for GWS—the staff that publishes it is barely paid! Besides supporting homeschooling, GWS is a demonstration of Holt's belief that people can be trusted to learn what they need to learn to be good citizens. It is also an example of how a small number of people can affect larger social change simply by networking and meeting with one another. The annual directories of local homeschooling families, homeschooling groups in and out of the United States, friendly school districts, helpful professionals, grown-up homeschoolers, and more have made GWS a tool for social change and inspiration for many homeschoolers.

## Home Education Magazine

P.O. Box 1083, Tonasket, WA 98855-1083 USA
Phone: 800-236-3278 / E-mail: HEM-Info@home-ed-magazine.com
URL: http://www.home-ed-magazine.com

Published since 1993 by a second-generation homeschooling family, each bimonthly issue of *Home Education Magazine* includes outstanding.feature articles, interviews, news and updates, resource and book reviews, and several regular columnists writing on homeschooling fathers, working with younger children, high-school and college concerns, political action for homeschoolers, and many other topics. *Home Education Magazine* is widely recognized as the most balanced and informative magazine on homeschooling. Subscriptions to *Home Education Magazine* are $32.00 per year; $6.50 single issue postpaid.

## Paths of Learning: Options for Families and Communities

P.O. Box 328, Brandon, VT 05733-0328 USA
Phone: 800-639-4122
URL: http://www.PathsofLearning.net

*Paths of Learning* explores the diverse worlds of alternative education, from charter schools to homeschooling, including Montessori, Waldorf, democratic, progressive, and holistic approaches. Each quarterly issue features profiles of innovative learning environments, writings by young people, and interviews with provocative educators and critics like Herb Kohl, Alfie Kohn, Thomas Armstrong, and Grace Llewellyn. Articles explore topics such as educational freedom, child development, assessment and standardized testing, and much more. *Paths of Learning* is published by The Foundation for Educational Renewal (the publisher of this book) and is the successor to *SKOLE: The Journal of Alternative Education*, originally founded in 1985 and published for fourteen years by Mary Leue of the Albany Free School. At the Paths of Learning website, be sure to explore the Paths of Learning Resource Center, an online database containing summaries of hundreds of books, articles, research studies, and other materials on alternative/progressive forms of education.

## TRANET

P.O. Box 567, Rangely, ME 04970 USA
Phone: 202-864-2252 / E-mail: tranet@igc.apc.org
URL: http://www.nonviolence.org/tranet/

TRANET is a transnational network of organizations and individuals creating the new social paradigm. We recognize that our current paradigm has led us to a dead end. Environmental, economic, and social collapse threatens us in every aspect of modern culture. Old paradigms have led us away from cultures based on relationships among people and with nature. From the new Gaian worldview through the design of new social institutions to new technologies, techniques, and lifestyles, TRANET members help create, expose, and promote the new culture that we require for sustainable survival. TRANET's bi-monthly newsletter-directory is a compendium of abstracts from over 1000 publications, papers, projects, and people who are active in the Gaian Cultural Transition.

## Transitions Abroad

P.O. Box 1300, Amherst, MA 01004-1300 USA
Phone: 800-293-0373 / E-mail: trabroad@aol.com
URL: http://www.TransitionAbroad.com
    A bimonthly magazine with practical information and directories for living, learning, and laboring abroad. For over twenty years *Transitions Abroad* has helped independent-minded readers and self-learners immerse themselves in cultures and learning experiences. Live in an Israeli kibbutz, learn history on a tour to the Mediterranean, be a willing worker on an organic farm in New Zealand, teach English in China, do your graduate work in development studies in the Czech Republic, join other seniors in a semester in Greece, study Buddhism with the monks in Nepal, learn Spanish in the museums of Barcelona. This magazine will tell you how, where, and why you can teach yourself the wonders of the world.

## World Future Society

7910 Woodmont Avenue, Suite 450, Bethesda, MD 20814 USA
Contact: Susan Eckhard
Phone: 800-989-8274 / E-mail: info@wfs.org
URL: http://www.wfs.org
    The World Future Society is the professional association for futurists around the world. They publish *The Futurist Magazine* and *The Futures Research Quarterly*.

# A Couple of Recommended Books

## Transforming Schools into Community Learning Centers

by Steve R. Parson
1999, Eye on Education, 6 Depot Way West, Suite 106, Larchmont, NY 10538 USA
Phone: 914-833-0551
    *Transforming Schools into Community Learning Centers* demonstrates that the cooperative community life-long learning center (CCL-LLC) is truly an idea whose time has come, and is not confined to a subculture of homeschoolers. Steve Parson is a professor of educational leadership and policy studies who writes entirely about the transformation of *public schools* into more open-ended learning centers. He states at the start that piecemeal reform of public education is inadequate, and so he proposes "a new way of thinking about public schools" that substantially reflects many of the principles elaborated by alternative educators and homeschoolers here in this volume. He agrees that learning takes place throughout the community and should not be confined to school buildings, while he proposes to open these buildings, as resource centers, to the community as a whole (people of all ages) seven days a week, ten to twelve hours a day. He emphasizes local empowerment—shared decision-making at the grassroots level, including young people, instead of top-down management. He endorses cooperative, learner-centered styles of teach-

ing, even agreeing with the most radical "unschoolers" that "everyone is both teacher and learner." He involves families more in their children's learning, while also connecting young people to mentors in the community. He sees the community learning center as a collaborative public space where "citizens discover ways to work together to improve the quality of life for everyone in the community."

Still, there are interesting differences between Parson's vision of a publicly funded and accountable learning center, and the more grassroots (if not entrepreneurial) models presented in this volume. Public school learning centers retain the professional status of properly credentialed teachers and depend on the leadership of principals, as collaborative as this may be. Taxpayers, including individuals and businesses, are "stakeholders" in the learning programs they fund, and so have a say in their operation. More independent-minded alternative educators and homeschoolers will balk at these vestiges of the public school system, but Parson retains them because he believes that society owes *all* members of the community fair access to learning opportunities, and without public responsibility and accountability, it is not certain that independent (i.e., private) models will provide these opportunities. Given that Parson's model is so similar to the CCL-LLC concept in so many significant ways, this difference in perspective provides an opportunity for some fruitful dialogue about important questions of equity and inclusiveness. Alternative educators and "unschoolers" might indeed find ways to work with forward-thinking public school people to truly transform schools into community learning centers.

# The Home School Source Book (2<sup>nd</sup> edition)

by Donn Reed
Brook Farm Books, Bridgewater, ME 04735 USA
Phone: 877-375-4680
or, Box 101, Glassville NB 37L 4T4, Canada
Editor: jean@brookfarmbooks.com.
Phone: 877-375-4689.

The *Home School Source Book* goes well beyond the usual homeschool resource guide, providing self-learning resources for all ages, certainly including adult autodidacts. Half the book is commentary and essays about twenty-four years of homeschooling and the Reeds' experiences raising and learning with their four children (now grown and very independent). The other half is a catalog and directory of a vast wealth of materials they've found to be creative, challenging, and fun. There are no pre-packaged curricula, although you can read about places to get them. You can create your own ideal learning environment using these resources. You'll find most everything you need for a liberal arts education from pregnancy and birth through adulthood, such as copies of the American Constitution, models from the British Museum, books for adult reading (and education), kits, games, globes, and many books of children's and classical literature at $1 each. The bias of this book is toward a liberal arts education without a religious soapbox. You may not always agree with the author, but you'll always know where he stands, and he'll challenge you to think about issues. You'll find cartoons and some freebies (or almost free) too. The *Whole Earth Catalog* called this book, "A Whole Earth Catalog for homeschoolers." The *Sourcebook* ($20 US), and many of the resources mentioned in it, are available from Brook Farm Books.

# The Creating Learning Communities Online Resource Center and Network

*by Claudia L'Amoreaux*

T HE CREATING LEARNING Communities Online Resource Center is the web companion to the *Creating Learning Communities* book. The book's original chapters are presented in web-enhanced versions so people can delve more deeply into ideas presented. Authors are adding greater detail to their chapters through the use of hyperlinks, letting people choose particular topics they'd like to explore further. The chapters in Parts I and II present case studies of several Cooperative Community Lifelong Learning Centers (CCL-LLCs).

Part III offers different perspectives on learning, technology and the Internet. The chapters in Part IV explore the concepts and philosophies that are involved in the design of CCL-LLCs and present the necessary changes involved in the evolution of new learning systems. All the authors' emails are given, so visitors to the site can easily contact authors with whom they'd like to connect.

Mirroring Part V of the book, the resource section offers brief descriptions of community learning centers, and services and materials that support self-directed learning, with contact information and links to websites. We expect this will become a lively and rapidly growing part of the website—it's an online directory of working Community Learning Centers, Learning Communities and related organizations all over the world. We envision that eventually you'll be able to search these resources by location and/or type and probably a few other categories we haven't dreamed of yet.

We've added a section for additional chapters so the book can continually evolve, reflecting new developments in the community learning center movement and a broader perspective on models, philosophy and how-to strategies. A Coalition for Self-Learning welcomes contributions. As with the chapters in the *Creating Learning Communities* book, new contributions are submitted to A Coalition's members through the LearningCommunities listserv and then are posted on the listserv website where they can be downloaded by members for reading. Submitted chapters are then discussed and reviewed by the learning community members to determine if the subject matters fits with A Coalition's themes. If yes, the chapter will be added to the New Chapters section of the online book.

Visitors to the online resource center can participate in the Creating Learning Communities Network by joining the "LearningCommunities" discussion list. This is the heart of A Coalition for Self-Learning. The original Cooperative Community Lifelong Learning Centers list (CCL-LLCs) was started in February, '99. Helen Hegener, publisher of *Home Education Magazine* writes in the first post to the list, "I believe community learning centers are an important step in the ongoing evolution of education, and I also believe they could be a key bridge between the homeschooling community and other forms of public and private education. I'm looking forward to some thoughtful discussion on this list."

Bill Ellis, list facilitator and editor and publisher of the online journal *TRANET, A Chronicle of the Emerging Gaian Cultures*, writes (2/12/99): "Homeschooling, alternative education, and life-long learning have been one of the areas of TRANET interest for the last 20 years. I have had growing interest in the concept as an example of spontaneous self-organization. And as a model of how the future may be shaped not by the trends of today, but by 'flapping butterfly wings,' small unnoticed phenomena that break radically with the status quo...There is no time in the history of humankind that a radical transformation of society was needed, and was happening. I hope this listserv will lead the way."

The original discussion list has now branched into two lists— "LearningCommunities" and "CCL-LLCs." The "LearningCommunities" list hosts discussion about the future of society, with an emphasis on making the necessary transition from a human-centered to an ecocentric worldview, and from what author Riane Eisler calls a "dominator society" to a "partnership society." The members of A Coalition for Self-Learning call this new paradigm, Gaian, and put it forward as the basis for future life-long learning systems, grounded in evolutionary cultural change. The concepts and philosophy of creating learning communities are explored here in depth, as are the practical concerns and issues. Members exchange stories and experiences about creating model learning centers all over the world (from Denmark to Ukraine to New Zealand to Canada to Mexico and the U.S.). Autodidactics, charter schools, restorative justice, micro-credit, local currencies, and their respective roles in the new learning system are among the wide rane of topics explored on the list.

If the "LearningCommunities" list is the heart of A Coalition, the "CCL-LLCs" list is the nerve center. It's where the day-to-day and ongoing work of the learning community gets done. Here members design and evolve the website, plan events, and strategize for communicating the visions of A Coalition for Self Learning. Both lists are open to anyone. Discussions are archived and accessible through the online resource center.

Individuals and groups wanting to participate in or start learning centers in their communities will find working models for inspiration on the website and ongoing support on the discussion lists. As the online resource center grows, we plan to add photos, progress reports, and interviews, especially with young people involved in these learning centers. Hot discussion threads from the list will be featured as well. The online resource center also serves as A Coalition for Self Learning's media hub for coordinating efforts to let more people know about this powerful model for cultural transformation.

In the future A Coalition for Self Learning plans to host online conferences with individual authors and list members offering dialogues and workshops on specific topics. These and other related events will be announced on the listservs and on the website. Stay tuned! If there are particular topics you'd like to see covered, join the list and let us know your interests.

The Creating Learning Communities Online Resource Center was originally hosted by network member Ib Bang on his website in Denmark. As the project expanded beyond the original book, a small team of A Coalition for Self Learning registered the domain name LearningCommunities.org and created the current online resource center, hosted by ValleyNet, a Vermont non-profit web hosting service. Four Coalition members now share the role of webmaster. Both discussion lists are hosted on the eGroups ONElist website (originally separate discussion list-hosting websites, eGroups and ONElist merged in February 2000). You'll find the LearningCommunities list at http://www.onelist.com/group/LearningCommunities and the CCL-LLC list at http://www.onelist.com/group/CCL-LLCs

The Creating Learning Communities Online Resource Center and Network is difficult to predict—that's one of its most exciting features. Its future shape will be determined by some of you reading this book. We look forward to meeting you online at:

http://www.CreatingLearningCommunities.org

# Afterword

*by Kelly Patrick Gerling, Ph.D.*

Y OU HAVE READ some or all of this book. Where do you go? What do you do? Whether you are a parent, an educator in a traditional school, an educator in a non-traditional organization, a student, a writer, or another interested person, here are four suggestions:

- *Your own experience is your ally.*
- *Take action based on your own situation.*
- *This book can help.*
- *Networking will enhance your efforts.*

## Your Own Experience Is Your Ally

Think about your less-than-enthusiastic experiences of being educated. Perhaps there were periods of boredom, and incidents of pain (I recall many). Perhaps you watched the clock in the back of the classroom hoping it would magically speed up (I did). Perhaps you remember looking out the window, daydreaming about what you *really* wanted to do (I did that a lot! And a few times my daydreams were rudely interrupted by the loud sound of a book slamming on my desk).

Aside from such problematic experiences, you may have memories of enthusiastic learning at different times in your life. Recall what you did, explored, and learned of your own accord. Recall the fun of such learning. Remember what you learned because you wanted to learn it. (In my case, my dad took me fishing, gave me books to read, and invited me to watch dark skies for meteors and constellations. He asked questions and encouraged me to do the same. He told me the names of every tree we encoun-

376

tered—even the scientific Latin name. Overall, he encouraged me to explore my interests and he considered them to be important. He is the educator I remember most fondly.)

Your less-than-enthusiastic experiences of education and your enthusiastic experiences of learning *matter*. They help you determine what to prevent and what to advocate for students and their education.

## Take Action Based on Your Own Situation

Pay attention to *your* situation. It presents your opportunities for *what to do*. You can't do everything. *You can do what YOU can do.* If you are a parent, your children need your support and guidance. If you are an educator in a traditional school, you can be a source of innovation and change, getting and responding to feedback from students. If you are an educator in a non-traditional program of some sort, you can improve what is happening there. If you are a student, speak out, for you are a client of your educational organization. If you are a legislator, legislate innovatively. If you are an administrator, administrate to help. If you are a school board member, make significant proposals.

Whoever you are, you can help reduce or eliminate the experiences of boredom and incidents of pain in young people. And you can help young people experience opportunities for enthusiastic learning.

Helping people learn is natural. Human beings are pleasure seekers, tool makers, hunters, gatherers, and city builders; but above all, they are learners. Human beings *learn*. Think about whom you can help. Think about what you can teach. Do what *you* can do to make a difference.

## This Book Can Help

*Creating Learning Communities* represents a guide to the kinds of innovative, responsible action that will bring out the inner potential of young people.

Some of the ideas and assumptions in this book are borrowed from other fields and domains. Some emerge from anthropology. Some draw from biology and cosmology. Others hail from philosophy. You don't need to believe everything in the book to use it. Instead, you might consider this book to be like a smorgasbord.

*Creating Learning Communities* is a smorgasbord of ideas and options, methods and ideas. When you are walking through the line at a smorgasbord, you don't have to put everything on your plate. You may want to taste the unfamiliar, since it is available. You can sample the familiar and enjoy it. By the time you reach the end of the line, you've got a unique, tasty feast on your plate.

*Creating Learning Communities* helps you put together your own tasty educational feast, whether the plate is for you or someone else. If you have read the book once, consider it your first helping. Go back for seconds, focusing on what tasted the best or what you might have passed over the first time. Go back for thirds and more.

## Networking Will Enhance Your Efforts

Significant accomplishments happen in relationships with like-minded people. A great advantage of this book is that it represents an invitation to a relationship—a relationship with a community of educators, thinkers, and most of all innovators. The authors in *Creating Learning Communities* are available to you. In most cases, their contact information is listed in this book. Each person may be able to offer you help with your particular goals for improving the learning of young people.

I urge you to take advantage of the opportunity to contact this resourceful group of people. One or more may be able to assist you in doing what you can do in your quest to improve education. Call them. Write them. E-mail them. Join the discussion on the listserve that interests you the most.

The concept of creating learning communities instead of schools is just now emerging. No one knows whether learning communities will become a slight influence on mainstream society, a significant trend, or a full-blown movement. You and others like you will determine that. You *can* participate in creating learning communities. Use what this book offers to do what only *you* can do. Young people you know depend on it.

## About the Author

*Kelly Patrick Gerling, Ph.D. is a psychologist, writer, workshop leader, and consultant. He specializes in providing leadership development processes for corporations, agencies, and school districts. He co-authored the tape set (Nightingale-Conant) and book (William Morrow Inc.),* NLP: The New Technology of Achievement. *Kelly is also the author of* The New Fundamentals of NLP, *a tape set published by NLP Comprehensive in Lakewood, Colorado.*

For more information contact Kelly Patrick Gerling at The Leadership Project, 5905 Slater Road, Shawnee Mission, KS 66202-2839, USA, phone: 913-248-1010, fax: 913-248-1002, e-mail: kelgerling@aol.com

For photos and art, thanks to:

Dayle Bethel and Motoshi Suzuki, The International University
Nanda Currant, Theater of Restoration
Karen Funk and Beth Ellen Mae, Bayside Children's College
Betsy Herbert, South Street Centre
Joshua Hornick, Pathfinder Center
Sandy Hurst, Upattinas School and Resource Center
Claudia L'Amoreaux, Haven
Kathia C. Laszlo, Syntony Quest
Mary Leue and Chris Mercogliano, The Free School
Jerry Mintz, Alternative Education Resource Organization
Marcie O'Brien and Kara, North Star School
James Rose, Ceptual Institute
James Schmidt, The Civic Media Center
Chris Spicer, People's Institute for Education and Action


Original artwork by:

Demian Schroeder
Lucie McAllister

# Titles from
# The Foundation for Educational Renewal

# Other Books by Ron Miller, Ph.D.

All titles are available from
The Foundation for Educational Renewal
P.O. Box 328, Brandon, Vermont 05733 USA
800-639-4122
http://www.PathsOfLearning.net